RETHINKING THE STRUGGLE FOR PUERTO RICAN RIGHTS

Rethinking the Struggle for Puerto Rican Rights offers a reexamination of the history of Puerto Ricans' political and social activism in the United States in the second half of the 20th century. Authors Lorrin Thomas and Aldo Lauria Santiago survey the ways in which Puerto Ricans worked within the United States to create communities for themselves and their compatriots and defend their rights in times and places where dark-skinned or 'foreign' Americans often encountered exclusion and discrimination. Building on a survey of existing scholarship combined with extensive archival research, the authors argue that the energetic Puerto Rican rights movement which rose to prominence in the late 1960s was built on a foundation of civil rights activism beginning much earlier in the century. The text contextualizes Puerto Rican activism within the broader context of 20th-century civil rights movements, while emphasizing the characteristics and goals unique to the Puerto Rican experience. Lucid and insightful, *Rethinking the Struggle for Puerto Rican Rights* provides a much-needed introduction to a lesser-known but critically important social and political movement.

Lorrin Thomas is associate professor of History at Rutgers University – Camden.

Aldo A. Lauria Santiago is professor of Latino and Caribbean Studies and History at Rutgers University – New Brunswick.

American Social and Political Movements of the Twentieth Century

Series Editor: Heather Ann Thompson, University of Michigan

For a full list of titles in this series see: https://www.routledge.com/American-Social-and-Political-Movements-of-the-20th-Century/book-series/ASPM20C

Rethinking the Gay and Lesbian Movement
By Marc Stein

Rethinking American Women's Activism
By Annelise Orleck

Rethinking the Chicano Movement
By Marc Simon Rodriguez

Rethinking the Black Freedom Movement
By Yohuru Williams

Rethinking the American Labor Movement
By Elizabeth Faue

Rethinking the American Prison Movement
By Daniel Berger & Toussaint Losier

Rethinking the American Antinuclear Movement
By Paul Rubinson

Rethinking the Struggle for Puerto Rican Rights
Lorrin Thomas & Aldo A. Lauria Santiago

RETHINKING THE STRUGGLE FOR PUERTO RICAN RIGHTS

Lorrin Thomas & Aldo A. Lauria Santiago

Routledge
Taylor & Francis Group

NEW YORK AND LONDON

First published 2019
by Routledge
711 Third Avenue, New York, NY 10017

and by Routledge
2 Park Square, Milton Park, Abingdon, Oxon, OX14 4RN

Routledge is an imprint of the Taylor & Francis Group, an informa business

© 2019 Taylor & Francis

Library of Congress Cataloging-in-Publication Data
A catalog record for this book has been requested

ISBN: 978-1-138-05529-2 (hbk)
ISBN: 978-1-138-05530-8 (pbk)
ISBN: 978-1-315-16598-1 (ebk)

Typeset in Bembo
by Swales & Willis Ltd, Exeter, Devon, UK

CONTENTS

Series Editor's Introduction   vi
Acknowledgements   vii
Abbreviations   viii

Introduction: Rethinking the Struggle for Puerto
Rican Rights—An American History   1

1   Mass Migration and New Migrant Communities in
    the Postwar Decade, 1945–1955   7

2   "The Struggle for Puerto Rican Rights," 1955–1965   39

3   Mass Mobilizations for Social Justice, 1966–1973   75

4   Civil Rights in the Activist Decade, 1974–1980   123

5   Dispersion and Momentum since 1980   163

    Conclusion: Rethinking the Struggle for
    Puerto Rican Rights   194

Bibliography   202
Index   214

SERIES EDITOR'S INTRODUCTION

Welcome to the *American Social and Political Movements of the 20th Century* series at Routledge. This collection of works by top historians from around the nation and world introduces students to the myriad movements that came together in the United States during the 20th century to expand democracy, to reshape the political economy, and to increase social justice.

Each book in this series explores a particular movement's origins, its central goals, its leading as well as grassroots figures, its actions as well as ideas, and its most important accomplishments as well as serious missteps.

With this series of concise yet synthetic overviews and reassessments, students not only will gain a richer understanding of the many human rights and civil liberties that they take for granted today, but they will also newly appreciate how recent, how deeply contested, and thus how inherently fragile, are these same elements of American citizenship.

Heather Ann Thompson
University of Michigan

ACKNOWLEDGEMENTS

Lorrin Thomas and Aldo A. Lauria Santiago

The authors would like to thank series editor Heather Ann Thompson for the invitation to write this book. Our collaboration on this project inspired us to think in new ways about our individual and shared research projects over the past decade, and gave us the opportunity to engage deeply with recent interpretations by the growing numbers scholars writing about the history of Puerto Ricans in the U.S. In particular, we thank the participants of the Rutgers Workshop on the History of Puerto Ricans and Latinos in the U.S. for their contributions to our biennial conferences and to our many collective and individual discussions during these gatherings, which helped shape this book in crucial ways. Much of the recent work we cite here was published by these colleagues in the working group. We are grateful too for the creative, brave, and uncompromising work of an older generation of scholars who have helped shape and expand the fields of Puerto Rican and Latino Studies since the 1970s. Their pioneering scholarship has guided us on our own path in the field.

Dozens of librarians, archivists, and research assistants have helped over many years with the work on which this book is based, and we would like to thank them collectively for their assistance. Archivist Pedro Juan Hernández and the staff of the library and archive at the Center for Puerto Rican Studies have given invaluable support to nearly every historian writing about Puerto Ricans in the U.S. over the last several decades. Individually and as co-authors, we have benefitted tremendously from Pedro Juan's knowledge and his commitment to sustaining and expanding archival collections on Puerto Ricans in the U.S. We are also grateful to our colleague Ruth Glasser for her careful review of the manuscript and her thoughtful suggestions for revision. Finally, we thank the editors and staff at Routledge/Taylor and Francis for their assistance during every stage of the process, and Tasso Hartzog, who provided expert assistance as a copyeditor and proofreader.

ABBREVIATIONS

AFL-CIO	American Federation of Labor- Congress of Industrial Organizations
AGPR	Archivo General de Puerto Rico (General Archive of Puerto Rico)
CPRS	Center for Puerto Rican Studies
HSP	Historical Society of Pennsylvania
LGCC	La Guardia Community College
LMMF	Luis Muñoz Marín Foundation
NYCMA	New Yok City Municipal Archive
OGPRUS	Office of the Government of Puerto Rico in the United States
PRDL	Puerto Rico Department of Labor
RG	record group
RUSCUA	Rutgers University Special Collections and University Archives
SFSU	San Francisco State University
UBP	United Bronx Parents
USNARA	United States National Archive and Records Administration

INTRODUCTION

Rethinking the Struggle for Puerto Rican Rights—An American History

Rethinking the Struggle for Puerto Rican Rights examines the history of Puerto Ricans' political and social activism in the United States in the 20th century, tracing their efforts to live with dignity in a society structured around de facto divisions among its citizens. The book surveys the ways Puerto Ricans in the U.S. worked, through half a century and across many regions of the country, to create communities for themselves and their compatriots in times and places where dark-skinned or "foreign" Americans were often unwelcome, and where U.S. citizenship did not guarantee the protection of an individual's rights. Because it was hard in so many ways for marginalized people to build a stable life, and to take advantage of the opportunities the United States purported to offer, the central story of this book is one of struggle.

The book's title is borrowed from the writer and political activist Jesús Colón, who in the mid-1950s reflected on "the struggle for Puerto Rican rights" in an essay he wrote for a multi-ethnic audience of fellow leftists and Communist party members, seeking to convince them that the key to strengthening this growing population of New Yorkers was collaboration among "democratic forces." Colón lived and worked on the left of the political spectrum in his community, but he was no outlier. Indeed, he was very much a unifier, and his politics were more reformist than revolutionary. Rather than promoting political divisions or proselytizing his political ideology, Colón, like many of his leftist compatriots, devoted himself to building coalitions and approaching problems in an inclusive way.

The struggles for rights that Colón referred to—and those that emerged in the decades that followed—were episodic, not constant, and they varied over time, but were connected by certain consistent elements. We have structured this book around multiple stories of struggle, over many decades, emphasizing the heterogeneous origins and goals of those struggles but also focusing on what connects them across eras, even as the context in which Puerto Ricans fought to identify and claim their rights changed over time.

Puerto Ricans have lived in the United States since the 19th century, first in small and scattered groups of political exiles, labor migrants, or expatriate intellectuals who sought both refuge and work in the land of their prosperous and free neighbors to the north. By the early 20th century, after the U.S. took possession of Puerto Rico and turned it into an "unincorporated territory" of the United States following war with Spain in 1898, thousands of Puerto Rican migrants were drawn to the opportunities of the metropole. After a few early waves of contract workers were recruited to Hawaii (and some settled in San Francisco), Puerto Rican migrants began to build communities in New York City and then, after the Second World War, in a number of other cities and rural agricultural areas in the Northeast and Midwest.

In all of these settlements—large or small, rural or urban, permanent or transient—Puerto Ricans met challenges common to many foreign and impoverished newcomers, especially those marginalized further by a failure to qualify as "white" in the U.S. racial system. They also struggled with obstacles particular to their peculiar political status. Puerto Rican migrants who arrived after 1917 were natural-born citizens, but they were still often treated as *alien*, both unassimilable and dangerous. In a society that still sanctioned racial divisions, and maintained them through both symbolic and actual violence, Puerto Ricans' mixed-race heritage, for both migrants and the "second generation" born in the U.S., meant that they were excluded from the full privileges of white American citizenship.

"Citizenship of the second class" was a specter that island-based political leader Luis Muñoz Rivera had warned against in the early 20th century, as Puerto Rico's status under U.S. rule was still being debated. He was right, of course. For the last century, Puerto Ricans have grappled with unequal citizenship. Puerto Ricans who reside on the island hold the same legally defined citizenship as Americans living in the United States, but due to provisions of the Jones-Shaforth Act of 1917, island residents cannot vote in U.S. presidential elections, nor do they have voting representation in the U.S. Congress.[1] The subjects of this book, Puerto Ricans living in the United States, have confronted a less formalized version of second-class citizenship than their island compatriots, but on the whole it has been no less insidious. Puerto Ricans in the U.S. were not officially barred from voting, but many of them struggled nevertheless to achieve not just political representation, but the protections laid out in the Bill of Rights.

The idea for this book began with questions about how the era of mass social movements in the late 1960s and early 1970s shaped the experience of Puerto Ricans in the United States. Did a singular "Puerto Rican movement" emerge in the late 1960s, primarily inspired by and modeled after the African American rights movement of that era? Or would it be more accurate to describe this moment as merely the culmination of political engagement and the struggle for rights by Puerto Ricans in the U.S. over the course of several decades? Puerto Ricans by the late 1960s began organizing on a large scale to push for social, economic, and legal justice in their communities. The mobilization of radicalized Puerto Rican youth in the late 1960s and early 1970s resembled, in terms of both strategy and ideology, those of Black Power proponents, anti-war protesters, and Chicano activists; in terms of the basic challenge to the status quo, they also resembled gay rights activists and second-wave feminists. Many of the former participants in these events—some of them now scholars, journalists, and artists who have written about their participation in the social and political organizing in the 1960s and 1970s—described this moment of dramatic change as the *despertar boricua*, or "Puerto Rican awakening"—a movement for sure, no matter its temporal or ideological connections to the activism that preceded it.[2]

The stories and analysis we offer in this book show how a Puerto Rican movement emerged out of the zeitgeist of the 1960s—but we argue that it was built on a foundation constructed over several decades. Furthermore, while many characterizations of Puerto Rican political activism posit a singular Puerto Rican movement, limited to a short period between the late 1960s and early 1970s, we take a different view. Throughout this book, we argue that community-wide battles to secure the basic rights and dignities of citizenship began long before the student movements and surge in youth-dominated radicalism in the late 1960s. We present here a decades-long history of Puerto Ricans' struggles for rights, waged by evolving coalitions of workers and intellectuals, aspiring politicians and artists, students and educators, professionals and unemployed youth, all grounded in varied conceptions of what it meant to be Puerto Rican in the United States. The stories that comprise the narrative include as well the forces Puerto Ricans fought against: people and institutions who seemed determined to oppose the expansion of Puerto Rican communities, and obstructed their civil rights. We also pay close attention to Puerto Ricans' many allies in their struggles, especially liberals, leftists, and African Americans.

Given our insistence on the *longue durée* of the Puerto Rican struggle for rights in the U.S., we must address a question that sometimes bedevils scholars of other moments of social and political change: when do a series of coordinated and uncoordinated actions, generating new social patterns and awareness, come to be defined as a "movement"? There are no specific criteria, no litmus tests that historians use to define a social movement or to determine when it begins. Historians of the U.S. refer to the "antislavery movement" and the "Populist movement" of the 19th century; yet African Americans' push for civil rights as citizens, which began with the formation of networks of organizations and protesters after emancipation in the 1860s, is not generally referred to as a "movement" before the Birmingham bus boycott of 1955.

Another key part of the definition of a social movement rests on visibility and mass participation, although these are always relative measures. Did the emergence of militant, multi-racial Puerto Rican organizations like the Young Lords and El Comité provide sufficient evidence for branding this period as distinct from earlier decades, when organizations pushing for rights were less visible and less radical? We must also consider longevity, coherence, and range of impact. To what degree were non-participants affected by the ideas and actions of those who participated in the movement? To what degree did the ideas and arguments of the participants in the movement permeate the culture of Puerto Ricans or others more broadly? And how do we assess the specific participation of Puerto Ricans in larger movements that involved many other groups and ideologies?

There is no simple answer to the question of defining a singular Puerto Rican movement, or of when such a movement actually began. Disparate, politically heterogeneous groups of Puerto Ricans had struggled for rights in a coordinated, determined way for several decades before there was any mass participation or visibility beyond their immediate community. Then, with major shifts and political upheaval (antiwar protests, assassinations, riots) in American society in the late 1960s, thousands of mostly young activists were galvanized by the questions of racial justice and social equality that had become central to public debate. Even though the most visible mobilization of Puerto Rican activists may have centered around a radical politics that, like Black Power, was too far left to be broadly inclusive, Puerto Ricans as a group saw themselves represented and included in public debates in new, more positive—or at least more carefully considered— ways by the 1970s. Chicano and Asian American communities experienced similar shifts in the context of the mass mobilizations of the 1960s era.

Even as we acknowledge and carefully analyze these major changes in social and political dynamics, however, it is important to remember that Puerto Ricans had been sizing up, arguing about, and pushing to secure their rights as American citizens since even before they actually *became* American citizens in 1917. Rights—civil rights, political rights, labor rights, social rights—had been at the center of Puerto Ricans' lively debates since they became, first, U.S. nationals in 1900, then natural-born citizens in 1917. Our approach to this book about Puerto Ricans' struggles for rights across the 20th century reflects how Puerto Ricans themselves have talked about their experience as citizens in the United States, and it addresses the problem of breaking Puerto Ricans' activism out of the framework of a singular movement.

Another important part of the book's approach is its relatively broad geographic range. Because New York City was the primary Puerto Rican metropolis from the beginning of the first substantial migration from the island in the early 20th century, much of the published historical scholarship on Puerto Ricans in the U.S. (including our own) has focused on New York, with Chicago and Philadelphia a close second. Although significant numbers of Puerto Ricans soon began to settle in Newark, Camden, Hartford, Rochester, Cleveland, and other small cities as well as in rural areas of New Jersey, Connecticut, upstate New York, and Ohio, scholars are just beginning to write the histories of Puerto Ricans in these places.[3] We have relied on this growing body of work by other scholars in order to include examples in our narrative representing a broad geographic range. Because our goal is to provide an overview of Puerto Ricans' rights struggles over nearly half a century and in many parts of the country, we have been selective, and often could not include as much detail as we would have liked about smaller Puerto Rican settlements, especially those in rural areas. Throughout the book, we did our best to account for the heterogeneity of Puerto Rican communities in the U.S., especially in terms of variable racial and class identification.

Even as we highlight this heterogeneity, we trace the markedly consistent goals of Puerto Ricans in U.S. communities in the second half of the 20th century, no matter their economic status or educational achievement or racial identification, and regardless of whether they lived in barracks on a farm in rural Connecticut or in a Chicago row house or a Bronx tenement. Puerto Ricans, like all other Americans, wanted financial security, opportunities to improve their economic and social status, and recognition of and respect for their cultural traditions. These basic goals could not be achieved without equal access to employment and schooling, freedom from discrimination, and basic integration into American society.

"Civil rights" often serves as shorthand to describe these protections, although Puerto Ricans, like other marginalized groups who experienced enduring oppression in the U.S., learned that there is a limit to how much the legal affirmation of such rights can actually protect people in situations where their physical or economic security is threatened by individuals and institutions. The movements of the 1960s exposed to public scrutiny the historic problems of police brutality and discrimination in the workplace and in schools; and in the 1970s and 1980s, Puerto Rican activists—including lawyers and elected officials as well as grassroots leaders and community residents—mounted powerful campaigns to secure legal rights to bilingual education and bilingual ballots, and continued to fight for legislation on issues like political redistricting and funding for social programs that supported marginalized communities. New generations of activists continue with the same work.

Because the historical struggles for rights and fights for resources that we recount in this book often focus on concrete, daily life issues like job discrimination, precarious (or entirely blocked) access to decent housing and good schools, and other hazards of poverty, some of the broader implications of Puerto Ricans' social activism and political engagement may be at times obscured. Puerto Ricans' quest to secure civil rights over the last century has been about their own group's stability, but it has also been bound up with major issues facing the United States as a nation and affecting other groups in similar ways. In the 1930s and 1940s, Puerto Ricans fought for relief from economic depression, for labor rights, and against fascism; and, in the post-war decades, they battled the constraints of cold war politics, participated in racial justice campaigns and ongoing civil rights battles for equity, and battled the fallout of deindustrialization and urban crisis. Puerto Ricans' history in the U.S. reflects a commonality of challenges faced by any social group that has been marginalized and discriminated against in the United States. The subtitle of this introduction thus serves as a reminder that Puerto Ricans' struggle for rights is a shared story; it is, indeed, an American history.

Notes

1 Puerto Ricans on the island cannot vote in U.S. presidential elections because, according to the U.S. Constitution, only full-fledged states are given votes in the Electoral College. The Jones-Shaforth Act stipulated the election by popular vote of a single Resident Commissioner to represent Puerto Rico in the U.S. Congress. The Resident Commissioner can vote in committee but cannot vote on bills on the House floor.

2 See, for example, the contributors in Andrés Torres and José E. Velázquez, eds., *The Puerto Rican Movement: Voices from the Diaspora*. Philadelphia: Temple University Press, 1998.

3 Historical work on Puerto Ricans in the U.S. has developed substantially since the publication of the first book-length academic history on their experience, Virginia Sanchez Korrol's pioneering *From Colonia to Community: The History of Puerto Ricans in New York City, 1917–1948*. Westport, CT: Greenwood Press, 1983.

1

MASS MIGRATION AND NEW MIGRANT COMMUNITIES IN THE POSTWAR DECADE, 1945–1955

Introduction

The typical story of Puerto Ricans' settlement in the United States focuses on the "great migration" of islanders to the mainland following the Second World War and tends to represent New York City as the destination of nearly all new migrants. This version of the story is indeed accurate: between 1945 and 1960 at least half a million Puerto Ricans settled in the United States, the vast majority of them in New York City; a comparable number gave migration a try but soon returned to the island. By 1960, at least 150,000 children had been born to these postwar migrants. The postwar years did indeed constitute a new world for Puerto Ricans in the U.S.

Yet the actual history of the migration of Puerto Ricans to the United States in the 20th century has many dimensions not captured by this postwar statistical portrait. There were several thousand Puerto Ricans living in the U.S. even before the island became an "unincorporated territory" of the U.S. in 1898. Nearly all of those early migrants were either political exiles—participants, along with Cuban counterparts, in the ongoing 19th century struggle for independence from Spain—who lived in Tampa or New York City, or they were agricultural laborers fulfilling contracts on plantations in diverse states including Hawaii, Arizona, and the Carolinas. Puerto Ricans began arriving in the U.S. in substantial numbers (thousands per year) after the First World War, motivated by a combination of a postwar economic boom and their newly granted United States citizenship, which had been conferred by Congress as part of the 1917 Jones-Shaforth Act.

Although a few thousand Puerto Ricans settled in this era in smaller cities around the country—including San Francisco, Tampa, and Philadelphia, all of which had thriving shipping and other industries that employed large numbers of immigrants—New York City attracted the overwhelming majority. By 1940, about 62,000 island-born and about the same number of U.S.-born Puerto Ricans (an early "second generation") made their homes in a handful of neighborhoods in Manhattan and Brooklyn, joining communities of Spanish-speaking immigrants, from various countries, that had existed since the late 19th century.[1]

This relatively stable pattern of migration and settlement changed dramatically in the 1940s. Shortly after the U.S. entered the Second World War in 1941, island authorities pushed the newly created War Manpower Commission to recruit thousands of Puerto Rican contract workers for jobs in New York, Florida, Chicago, New Jersey, Pennsylvania, and Ohio.[2] After the war ended, the emigration that had steadily grown over the previous three decades quickly expanded to a deluge. The magnetic force of the booming postwar economy on the mainland, combined with the inability of Puerto Rico's underdeveloped economy to support a rapidly growing population—plus lowered transportation costs, expanded labor recruitment by private and government employers, and policy initiatives by the Puerto Rican Department of Labor—led the migration to spike dramatically. By 1947, the net number of migrants arriving on the mainland averaged about 2,000 per week. By 1950, 226,000 island-born Puerto Ricans were living in in the U.S., 187,000 of them (83%) in New York City.[3] A growing U.S.-born population of about 58,000 added to the demographic impact. The years of most intensive migration were 1949 to 1953, when about 250,000 Puerto Ricans settled in the U.S., overwhelmingly in New York City.

New York, with its enormous economy, varied industries, and well-established Spanish-speaking enclaves, was by 1950 home to as many Puerto Ricans as San Juan. During the decade after the war, Puerto Rican migrants were also settling in other cities in large numbers. By the mid-1950s, small but growing Puerto Rican communities emerged in a handful of larger cities including Newark, Jersey City, Buffalo, Chicago, Philadelphia, Hartford, and Miami; and the settlement of Puerto Ricans in urban areas was only the most visible dimension of the postwar migration. Along with the impact of policy initiatives by the Puerto Rican Department of Labor, demand for labor in agriculture as well as in industry in the U.S. produced a notable migration to rural areas too, especially in Michigan, upstate New York, Connecticut, New Jersey, and Massachusetts. Dozens of small Puerto Rican communities of a few hundred to a few thousand expanded in rural areas and small cities like Bridgeport, New Haven, Waterbury, and Hartford, Connecticut; Springfield, Framingham, and New Bedford, Massachusetts; Perth Amboy, Elizabeth, Passaic, and Camden, New Jersey; Rochester and Buffalo, New York; Bethlehem, Pennsylvania; Baltimore, Maryland; and Hialeah, Florida. In many of these places a dual dynamic of Puerto Rican workers migrating from the island or from New York City converged with Puerto Rican farmworkers relocating to industrial jobs after leaving their farm jobs. Within roughly a decade, the war-time and

TABLE 1.1 Population of Puerto Rican Descent, 1950

	U.S.	New York (State)	New York City	Pennsylvania	New Jersey	Connecticut
Born in Puerto Rico	226,110	191,305	187,420			
U.S.-born of Puerto Rican Descent	75,265	N/A	54,460			
Total	301,375		241,880	3,560	5,640	1,305

Credit: United States Bureau of the Census. *United States Census of Population: 1950—Special Reports. Puerto Ricans in Continental United States. Report Number: P-E No. 1A.* Washington, D.C.: U.S. Government Printing Office, 1953; United States Commission on Civil Rights. *Puerto Ricans in the Continental United States: An Uncertain Future: A Report.* Washington: U.S. Commission on Civil Rights, 1976.

post-war migration from Puerto Rico had formed a complex diaspora in the Eastern seaboard states and the Midwest.

No matter where they settled, the first challenge faced by nearly all postwar migrants was housing. Local housing markets, already failing to meet demand from returning veterans and their growing families, were strained by Puerto Rican migrants arriving by the thousands. Americans were already struggling to keep pace with social and economic changes in the postwar years, and many feared newcomers as competitors or outsiders. (With the closing off of most European and Asian immigration in the 1920s, fewer Americans in the Northeast and Midwest encountered foreign migrants by the 1940s.[4]) In this climate, Puerto Ricans frequently confronted landlords who refused to rent to them and neighbors who expressed open hostility. In New York and in some smaller cities, Puerto Ricans settled in existing African American and ethnic immigrant neighborhoods, in some areas gaining access to the low-quality housing vacated by more mobile white workers who moved to better neighborhoods or suburbs. Most Puerto Rican migrants wound up settling in expanding ghettoes where they had little choice but to rent expensive and dilapidated apartments.

Securing work was the other critical challenge. All over the U.S., soldiers returning from military service found jobs in booming manufacturing, construction, and service industries. In many cities, there were plentiful jobs for new migrants too, and many migrants arrived with low skill, low wage industrial jobs secured in advance by their relatives. A lucky few landed government jobs, which generally offered greater security than working in the private sector. Often, resistance and prejudice from co-workers created conflict for the new arrivals or put limits on their advancement. Many Puerto Rican migrants—especially those who were dark-skinned and perceived as "Negro" in the United States' binary racial system—also encountered racial discrimination in hiring and racial prejudice from coworkers and employers. Such experiences would motivate many

Puerto Ricans to participate in collective struggles for recognition by unions and employers in ensuing decades (earlier Puerto Rican migrants in New York City, though smaller in number, had also participated in the labor movement in the 1920s and 1930s).

Beyond the fraught arenas of work and housing, the other substantial challenges Puerto Ricans faced in their growing communities related to the needs of their children—schooling, recreation, summer jobs, and, increasingly during the 1950s, intervention in conflicts with police. Social service professionals often served as advocates and allies for new migrant families and helped them navigate both the educational and criminal justice systems. However, such advocates could only do so much to aid the newcomers. As Puerto Ricans in New York City's early migrant communities had learned in the 1920s and 1930s, political representation would provide the most important source of empowerment: the ability to advocate for themselves in matters of government policy and legislation. Even in New York, where Puerto Rican activist leaders had established relationships with the major political parties in the 1920s and 1930s, Puerto Ricans spent many years—in some cases decades—organizing through community service organizations and local councils before gaining any foothold in electoral politics. Achieving a political voice was a painfully slow process, which in many smaller cities was not even underway until well into the 1970s.

During the first years of the postwar migration, Puerto Rican populations outside New York City remained small enough to attract little attention from other residents. However, as their numbers expanded, and Puerto Ricans began to push to improve housing, work, and services, they often met increased resistance from the local governing elites and other ethnic groups within their working class communities. Like many other migrant populations, especially those that also encountered racial prejudice—Mexicans, Jamaicans, African Americans from the southern states—Puerto Ricans found that they were appreciated for their labor but not welcome as full members of receiving communities. In many cases, Puerto Ricans managed to achieve significant alliances with other beleaguered migrant groups in the postwar period, with whom they shared experiences of poor housing, low wages, lack of services, and rejection by established communities. This happened both in large cities like New York City, where housing and education became major issues for the community, and in small rural communities like those of eastern Michigan, where farm workers confronted grave violations of their labor contracts.[5]

No matter where they settled, and no matter what their relationships to unions, social services, political parties, or other migrant groups, life was hard for the 20 to 50 thousand Puerto Rican migrants who settled in the U.S. each year between 1943 and 1960.[6] Like most other immigrants to the U.S., Puerto Ricans struggled with the ongoing and pervasive problems of discrimination and economic uncertainty on top of daily hurdles—like cold weather and the difficulties of learning English—in order to provide better opportunities for their children.

Some migrants struggled more than others, and the difference in experience often had to do with race. In one typical representation of Puerto Ricans' poverty and prospects in the U.S. in the postwar period, a *New York Times* journalist contrasted the stories of two families that had recently settled in New York City from Puerto Rico. A man named Toño López, who migrated from the countryside with his wife and five children, seemed unconcerned that he had not yet found a job: "[W]e will make it work out. The children will be educated. That is good. Things will get better." López and his family were described as "white." In contrast, the Soler family, "negro" migrants from San Juan, seemed to face grimmer prospects. "They have seemingly moved from poverty to poverty," observed the journalist, suggesting they might soon need to rely on public assistance—thus reinforcing the hardening stereotype of the poor, dark-skinned migrants who would drain the resources of their new society. The reality, of course, was quite different.

Community Building: Community Life and Social Services

The greatest source of support for all new migrants was an existing network of compatriots, ideally including family members or close friends, who could help them navigate the multiple steps in adjusting to life in a new country. The many who came from rural areas also needed help in adjusting to life in a city. Even migrants who arrived in one of the cities with very small Puerto Rican populations in the early postwar years—Chicago, Philadelphia, and San Francisco—were able to rely on a foundation of community knowledge about finding jobs and housing and schools for their children. In this way they also quickly located the businesses run by Puerto Ricans or other Spanish-speakers (Chicago, for example, already had a large Mexican population by 1945), which could provide them with reminders of home—foodstuffs, musical recordings, and fashions—and a modicum of comfort.

Most Puerto Ricans who migrated to New York City in the postwar years settled in neighborhoods already populated by a second-generation middle class, hometown networks, and political, labor, and mutual aid societies that had been established one or two decades before by the earlier waves of migrants. New York City also offered better welfare benefits than most other cities, facilitated by an extensive social service network. Those experiencing housing troubles, an urgent financial shortfall, or other day-to-day problems could also turn to church-based support, or to one of the settlement houses that had operated in many city neighborhoods since the early 20th century. Navigating both city and federal bureaucracy was tricky, though, and many recent migrants were reluctant to try. The political networks established by Puerto Ricans and other leftists during the 1930s through the American Labor Party (ALP) and the Communist Party had helped many migrants with these problems.[7]

As the number of Puerto Ricans arriving in New York spiked after the Second World War, the gap between migrants' needs and accessible services grew. Leaders of community organizations pushed officials in New York City to acknowledge that a more formal structure of social services for migrants would be necessary. Mayor William O'Dwyer responded, somewhat slowly, by convening the Mayor's Advisory Committee on Puerto Rican Affairs (MACPRA) in 1949. The 46-member committee was charged with diagnosing the problems of the Puerto Rican community, which had almost tripled in five years, now reaching over 150,000, and with creating programs to fix those problems. Committee members were a mix of Puerto Rican professionals and community leaders and non-Puerto Rican social service and education officials.

There were a number of controversial exclusions from the list of appointees, and many left-leaning Puerto Rican community leaders charged O'Dwyer with an election-year ploy to win the support of centrist, postwar constituency despite having been supported by the ALP because of his pro-Roosevelt stance. However, the MACPRA did collaborate with a broad base of the city's Puerto Rican leadership, and managed to achieve some real gains for the community, including the recruitment and hiring of over 200 Puerto Rican social workers and the establishment of the bilingual teacher position in public schools, although the number of bilingual or Puerto Rican teachers remained small until the 1960s. The MACPRA was disbanded in 1955 by Mayor O'Dwyer's successor, Robert Wagner, who instead included Puerto Ricans in the City's new Commission on Intergroup Relations (COIR), which managed inter-ethnic and racial conflicts and complaints throughout the city.[8] Here Puerto Rican leaders were part of a larger, denser network of advocates including neighborhood-level commissions from which many alliances would be built. This move followed a trend in other cities in the early postwar years that reconceptualized the fight against prejudice as a collaborative process rather than one specific to certain groups.[9]

The more important reason for the dissolution of the MACPRA was that an initiative of Puerto Rico's Department of Labor was doing a much better job of monitoring and interceding in the problems of the new migrants. In 1948, island government officials, responding to reports of migrant leaders and complaints of migrants and their family members who remained on the island, created a well-funded employment and information office in New York known as the Migration Division.[10] Following an earlier agency called the Office of Employment and Identification, established in the early 1930s but closed in 1941, the new Migration Division continued to provide employment assistance and identification cards, since few Puerto Ricans had passports and many arrived without birth certificates. The new departments of the postwar Migration Division—which opened regional offices in Chicago in 1949, Camden in 1950, and Philadelphia, Cleveland, and handful of additional cities in 1955—included referral, lobbying, and research functions in education, community organization, social services, political participation and voter registration, cultural affairs, legal counseling, and the direct management of a farm labor program that brought tens of thousands of workers to U.S. farms. Staff developed and administered programs in all the departmental areas, and also served as intermediaries and advocates for migrants who required additional services from other local and state agencies. The Migration Division in New York remained the central office, and its staff was the largest. That office was staffed by around 30 employees in the 1950s and 160 by 1963, most in the New York office. The regional offices ranged from about five to 20 employees, depending on the size of the migrant population it served.[11]

The first director of the Migration Division, Manuel Cabranes, was a trained social worker who had migrated in 1931 to study at Fordham University and had then served as director of the Melrose House, a settlement house in the Bronx. During Cabranes's tenure, 1948 to 1950, the office remained small and focused most of its work on employment and managing political issues with the Mayor's office. But the continued increase in the migration, plus a crisis within the farm labor program and many other challenges, led to a restructuring in 1951 in which Clarence Senior was named national director. Senior was an American social scientist and former Socialist party leader who, from 1945 to 1947, served as the founding director of the Social Science Research Center at the University of Puerto Rico, where he led several studies on migration. Senior's expertise in this new area of research, and his role in the research for Columbia University sociologist C. Wright Mills' study of Puerto Rican migrants in 1947, made him the obvious candidate chosen by Governor Muñoz Marín to lead the Migration Division when it experienced growing pains.[12] Senior's political connections were also relevant to his position. As a long-time member of the Socialist party in the U.S., Senior was a firm advocate of labor rights and state support for housing and education initiatives. As national director of the Migration Division, Senior sought to use his political and academic connections to create opportunities for Puerto Ricans in these realms. He helped recruit Joseph Montserrat a young Puerto Rican activist and settlement house worker, who would direct the New York City office throughout the 1950s before becoming the national director in 1960.

In New York, Clarence Senior used his extensive contacts among leftists and union leaders to facilitate the hiring of Puerto Rican workers and organizing and incorporating them into unions. Most of these jobs were low skill and low wage jobs in industry and service work, but as the Migration Division's network and political sophistication expanded the office developed strategies to avoid problematic employers, corrupt unions, or non-union jobs altogether, and collaborated with the unions that started including growing numbers of Spanish-speaking workers among their ranks. The Migration Division also increased its attempts to find white collar and professional employment opportunities, although for the most part educated Puerto Rican migrants had their own networks and resources for finding the better jobs. Employment services were the most widely used and extensive of the Migration Division programs in all of its offices. For example, staff in the Chicago office, working with the Illinois State Employment Service, placed 5,358 Puerto Ricans in jobs in the Chicago area in 1953–54.[13] By the late 1950s, as it opened regional offices with ties to rural towns, the Migration Division had created a large farm worker program that brought 5,000 to 20,000 seasonal farm workers from the island to work on U.S. farms.

Although employment services were the focal point of the Migration Division, the agency also helped with conflicts or advice over housing and social services, and it provided information services in its weekly WADO (Spanish-language) radio show in New York City. Migrants usually shared apartments with relatives and friends upon arrival, and then had children and other relatives join them, adding to the overcrowding in the denser areas of Puerto Rican settlement. Affordability was the first hurdle, of course, but landlord exploitation and the low quality of housing stock available to Puerto Ricans were also perennial problems. The head of the New York State Commission on Housing, after returning from a United Nations-sponsored trip to investigate housing problems around the world in 1954, made headlines by asserting that Puerto Ricans in Harlem lived in conditions worse than any he had seen on his trip. This must have been exaggeration, since even migrants living five to a room in dilapidated tenements had access to clean (if only cold) water and reliable sewage removal; yet it certainly would have been accurate for the commissioner to say that Puerto Ricans in general lived in worse conditions than any other group of New Yorkers. The same was true for Puerto Ricans in Chicago and Philadelphia by the mid- to late-1950s, when migrant communities in both cities were growing rapidly. Migration Division officials in Chicago expressed worry about the development of "slums" of Spanish-speakers and urged Puerto Ricans not to settle in Mexican neighborhoods.[14]

Discriminatory practices by landlords were the other chief complaint of Puerto Ricans who sought help at Migration Division offices. In her study of the Puerto Rican migration to Philadelphia in this period, historian Carmen Whalen explains that "Puerto Ricans were blamed for deteriorating conditions in [their] low-income neighborhood[s]." Landlords used the familiar tools of racial exclusion to deny Puerto Ricans access to their properties and keep them out of their communities. In the Philadelphia neighborhoods where migrants first settled in the 1950s, notes Whalen, "For Rent" signs increasingly noted "whites only." According to historian Lilia Fernández, Puerto Ricans settling in some of Chicago's more heterogeneous neighborhoods in the 1950s "learned that being ambiguous about their ethnoracial origins worked to their advantage . . . When landlords mistook Puerto Ricans for Italians or Greeks, they did not correct them." Many Puerto Ricans, especially those of the second generation, also learned to assert their privileges as "white" and as English speakers.[15]

✳ Miranda (Mexican/Indian)

In New York City in the 1950s, some established migrants and second-Puerto Ricans (especially those perceived as white) slowly drifted ....
housing in neighborhoods beyond where migrants tended to settle first. Others entered the expanding public housing sector, which improved conditions for many—though at the cost of temporary displacement for thousands of other Puerto Ricans, since it was most often blocks of "ghetto" housing, inhabited by Puerto Ricans and African Americans, that were designated for razing and renewal with newly built housing projects. Another problem was access: during the first decades of building mass public housing projects in New York, working class whites were given preference over their African American and Puerto Rican neighbors. By the early 1960s, after applying significant pressure on city authorities over the slow pace of inclusion, about 18,000 Puerto Rican families had been placed in public housing complexes that provided clean, modern, low cost housing.[16]

For migrants who had children, the issue of access to decent schooling was a concern that followed closely behind the search for work and for decent housing. Puerto Ricans in New York had struggled with educational access and the problem of discrimination in schools since the 1920s and 1930s, and these were issues New York City officials were increasingly forced to acknowledge as the number of Puerto Rican schoolchildren grew exponentially in the postwar years. (Puerto Ricans in other cities would not begin to push for improvements in educating their children until the 1960s or 1970s, depending on the population size and level of community organization.) In the mid-1950s, the New York City Board of Education carried out a multi-year survey of Puerto Rican students, their schools, and their teachers in order to better assess how to educate the migrant children. Between 1954 and 1956, the Board of Education published a series of recommendations to help Puerto Rican children in schools, including the creation of additional language support, curricular changes, and the hiring of a number of "auxiliary" (usually bilingual) teachers, most of them Puerto Rican. It also organized training and travel by New York City teachers to Puerto Rico.[17]

New York's Migration Division office developed close ties to the city's Board of Education in this decade. Migration Division staff sought to improve the understanding of school officials, teachers, and other students with the struggles of migrant children; in fact, such training and collaboration had begun in 1947 through the University of Puerto Rico, even before the establishment of the Migration Division. Throughout the 1950s, the Migration Division's education department produced a variety of short films and pamphlets about Puerto Rican culture for distribution in schools. With these projects in particular, the staff built on the efforts of progressive educators in New York, who had worked to help Puerto Rican children's adjustment in city schools since the 1930s.[18]

Migration Division staff also collaborated with Puerto Rican community leaders working on educational issues. The Spanish-American Youth Bureau (SAYB) was perhaps the most important organization of this era that served the needs of migrant children specifically. It was founded in 1943 by Ruperto Ruiz, whose goal was to help Puerto Rican families to make the most of New York's educational opportunities. In addition to community advocacy and direct services to youth, the agency also collaborated with several professors of education from New York University to create what they called a "workshop-field study," a summer program that sent public school teachers to Puerto Rico to learn more about the culture of their Puerto Rican students.[19] Such initiatives, in turn, helped inspire similar programs outside of the Migration Division. For instance, the United Parents Association of the Board of Education organized "Goodwill workshops" in the early 1950s to facilitate the inclusion of Puerto Rican children and their families into neighborhood school communities.[20] The SAYB and the Migration Division sponsored regular conferences with social service providers, both public and private, during the late 1940s and early 1950s, and lobbied the city government to improve services and increase the hiring of Spanish-speaking staff to work with migrant children.

An even more far-reaching collaboration by the SAYB and the Migration Division, extending well beyond issues of education and youth, resulted in the establishment in 1952 of the Consejo de Organizaciones Hispano Americanas (alternatively known as the Council of Hispanic organizations, later renamed Council of Puerto Rican and Spanish American Organizations). Writer and community organizer Jesús Colón noted in the late 1950s that the Consejo was "regarded as the key Puerto Rican organization by all the mainstream organizations, by the trade union movement, by government and private agencies." The Consejo served as an umbrella for dozens of smaller Puerto Rican organizations, including hometown associations, business owners' associations, churches, sports clubs, labor groups, lodges, and local political clubs and committees adding up to about 10,000 members. Later, as the Migration Division began work with the emerging communities in other cities, regional equivalents were organized. The Consejo lasted through the 1960s, and its work bridged many of the New York Puerto Rican community's various efforts, including extensive participation in civil rights campaigns, voter registration, and labor movement struggles.[21]

The work of the Migration Division itself was extensive and very visible in the Puerto Rican communities they served, and from the start, these efforts were intended to complement, not replace, the work of other advocates in and on behalf of the community—much like the Migration Division's early collaboration with the Spanish-American Youth Bureau. Indeed, along with new advocacy organizations that emerged in Puerto Rican communities in a handful of cities in the 1950s, the Migration Division would play a supportive and creative role in Puerto Ricans' burgeoning struggles to secure social and civil rights in their new society.

The particular relationship between Migration Division offices and the surrounding community varied by city. In New York, Puerto Ricans had over three decades of experience in community-building and community organizing before the Migration Division office opened, whereas in many other cities, the Migration Division offices were established in the very early years of settlement, when only a very small Puerto Rican community had developed, which meant the staff also served as de facto community leaders and planners along with their regular programmatic and advocacy duties. To the extent that the Migration Division offices were, at their core, social service agencies run by Puerto Ricans and for Puerto Ricans, the closest analogue was the "hometown club" or mutual aid society, an organizational model developed in the late 19th century by earlier immigrant groups. Such local Puerto Rican organizations were generally not eclipsed by the work of the Migration Division, and instead, in cities where Migration Division offices opened, hometown clubs and mutual aid societies continued to add to the more formal services of the government-sponsored offices.

The Migration Division's collaborative role in the community was most evident in New York City, home to over a dozen hometown clubs by the late 1940s (several of which had been founded decades earlier). As the postwar migration spiked, labor organizer and political activist Gilberto Gerena Valentín sought to make this conventional model of community organization into something more powerful; as he explained it, he did not want to leave the tools of community empowerment entirely in the hands of a government agency. Gerena Valentín reported in his memoir that, by the mid-1950s, there were clubs in New York City representing "every one of the seventy-eight towns in Puerto Rico," and the same year he helped organize them into an umbrella organization, the Congreso de Pueblos, to which he was elected president. Gerena Valentín's vision for the organization was shaped in part by his longtime participation in the city's leftist labor politics—he even brought famed organizer Saul Alinsky to train Congreso activists—and by his connections to the growing Black civil rights movement.[22]

Much like the Migration Division, the Congreso clubs offered immediate social services to new migrants in need, helping with housing and employment and providing emergency funds for food and furniture. Congreso members frequently picked new migrants up at the airport, with blankets and coats in the winter. "If some family member lost his or her job," Gerena Valentín later wrote, "all they had to do was come to us and we would go to our job bank and help the person find work. If someone lost their apartment, our attorneys and the Housing Committee were there to help." In 1957, at the Congreso's second city-wide assembly, Gerena Valentín recalled 1,200 delegates in attendance. "With the founding of the Congreso," he wrote, "a new stage began in Puerto Ricans' struggle in New York City for their civil rights." [23]

Work and Economic Life: Labor Leadership and Labor Politics

Along with housing and schooling, the third—and often most important—in the trio of major struggles for Puerto Rican migrants was finding stable employment.

The Migration Division and some other service agencies were able to help Puerto Ricans navigate the world of work in their new urban settings and provided some guidance through the pitfalls of employer discrimination, racism, and worksite exploitation. But it was workers themselves who fought for empowerment within the labor unions that claimed to represent them.

Most second generation Puerto Ricans who grew up between the 1920s and 1940s in New York had achieved at least modest social mobility as adults, securing improvements in education, jobs, income, and living conditions in the midst of the post-World War II economic boom, often relying on the generous postwar GI benefits.[24] This generation and their migrant parents had participated in significant numbers in the leftist labor politics of the 1930s and 1940s through the militant industrial CIO unions, the Communist party, the American Labor Party, and the Socialist party. This world of radical and populist working class politics shaped many if not most of the Puerto Rican leaders that emerged in New York City before the postwar migration, and many of them helped create the possibility of greater economic security for their fellow Puerto Rican workers by the 1940s.

Puerto Rican migrants in the late 1940s and 1950s easily found low wage industrial and service jobs; this was especially true for women, who often secured work more quickly than men in the garment factories, sometimes even at higher wages than Puerto Rican men.[25] Men's employment patterns were more diverse and included jobs as operatives in a wide range of factories, maintenance work in residential buildings, or service work in hotels and restaurants. The two biggest determinants of how well Puerto Rican migrants fared in the search for jobs were their skill level (whether not they had training in a trade like plumbing or carpentry, for instance, or in the operating of machinery in a certain industry) and their ability to speak English. But even with the benefit of some education and experience in the labor market, most recent migrants first found work in factories that required few skills and paid low wages.

On the other hand, postwar Puerto Rican migrants in New York City benefitted directly or indirectly from the city's long history of militant labor organizing and its very high rate of union participation. The older generation of Puerto Rican workers helped provide their new migrant compatriots with access to important political alliances, organizational relationships, ideological arguments, and leadership. Indeed, according to Jesús Colón, a central figure in this world of politicized Puerto Rican workers, New York was "one of the most progressive cities in the country," a claim substantiated by the work of notable labor historians like Joshua Freeman.[26] Membership in a union provided rights to workplace seniority, to negotiated wage increases, and retirement and health benefits—although union membership could not protect either skilled or unskilled workers from many injustices in many aspects of the workplace. In fact, both union and employer practices often created obstacles to promotion and advancement to higher-paid workers in higher skill categories; Puerto

Rican migrants were especially vulnerable to these exclusions, as advancement to higher paid positions in the better workplaces required the collaboration of older, more skilled workers.

Another pervasive problem was the abuses committed by "independent" or "racketeer" unions, those that charged high initiation and membership fees and provided no benefits or representation for the workers. Clarence Senior, national director of the Migration Division, together with union leaders sympathetic to the struggles of Spanish-speaking workers, began a major campaign in 1953 to help protect vulnerable, low wage workers and those exploited by racketeer unions. Around the same time, migrants began training in the "labor schools" sponsored by the Association of Catholic Trade Unionists, and organized rebellions among their members against both industrial bosses and racketeer-controlled unions. This movement spurred leaders of the "legitimate" labor movement—unions affiliated with the recently merged American Federation of Labor–Congress of Industrial Organizations (AFL-CIO)—to collaborate with the assistance of the New York City mayor and other allies.[27]

The experience of Puerto Ricans in smaller cities varied significantly from those in New York City. Outside of New York, many workers migrated first as agricultural or cannery workers, with or without a contract and travel arrangements provided by the Migration Division; a large number of them later moved on to urban employment.[28] Most other cities did not have the active and extensively organized labor institutions open to Puerto Ricans and other Spanish-speaking workers, nor did they have the anti-discrimination practices common to unions in New York City and the history of anti-discrimination policies and agencies that state and city officials had created, which meant that industrial workers elsewhere were far more vulnerable to exploitation. (San Francisco was a significant exception to this pattern; historian Eduardo Contreras notes that before 1950, the CIO there established a "Minorities Committee" that urged action to "blast out" discrimination, including that which harmed Latino workers.[29]) And, because Puerto Rican migration flows to these smaller cities developed later than in New York City, postwar migrants outside New York also did not benefit from the support networks and leaders of pre-existing Puerto Rican communities, whose longtime or second-generation residents provided access to employment networks and tutelage within the unions.

Although seasonal rural laborers were far less visible or numerous than workers in factories, farm work was an important aspect of Puerto Ricans' experience in the U.S. in the mid-20th century. Starting in 1945, thousands of Puerto Rican workers per year migrated from the island to do seasonal work on farms on the eastern seaboard, from Maryland to Massachusetts. However, because of employer and contractor abuses, the Puerto Rican Department of Labor banned unlicensed farm labor contracting on the island in 1947 and began organizing its own contracts with associations of U.S. farmers. In this era—and extending into the 1980s—between 10,000 and 20,000 Puerto Rican farm laborers migrated seasonally with a government contract, while perhaps as many as 10,000 migrated on their own, most of them to harvest vegetables and fruits. These farm jobs, while representing only a small percentage of the total migrant flow between Puerto Rico and the U.S., were vitally important to rural Puerto Rican households, as most workers returned to the island annually and brought back modest savings to support their families during the idle months of the sugar cane growing cycle in Puerto Rico. Slowly, this seasonal flow of laborers formed small permanent communities in rural areas, although in many cases migrants soon moved into cities to find higher-paying work in factories.[30]

Members of this rural diaspora frequently experienced conflicts over labor conditions and basic rights. While working in the U.S., most of these migrants lived on farms or in central barracks provided by regional growers' associations, where conditions were generally poor. Many encountered uncomfortable or unsanitary barracks and insufficient or poor-quality food, as well as abusive treatment and other violations of their contracts. In Dover, New Jersey, for example, a farmworker interviewed by historian Olga Jiménez recalled that "there were many problems here . . . The police arrested the Puerto Rican men for any little thing; they arrested them for walking or for standing. If they were in groups of three or more, they were arrested." The national Migration Division office handled many of the disputes, investigating complaints that were often resolved with administrative measures or concessions from the farmers or regional agricultural associations that contracted the workers. Some of the most serious offenses spilled into the Spanish-language press in New York City or in Puerto Rico, and advocates included such examples in larger reform movements that sought to improve conditions of all migrant workers.[31]

Historian Eileen Findlay documented perhaps the worst crisis that reached such proportions early in the history of the farm labor program. In 1950, 5,000 farmworkers contracted by the Puerto Rican Department of Labor to work on sugar beet farms in eastern Michigan found their working conditions and treatment unacceptable, and they protested loudly. Governor Muñoz Marín received petitions from dozens of the workers, who threatened to leave their assigned farms to search for better opportunities in the Midwest if island officials failed to remedy their situation. Migrants' wives, partners, and family members, those who relied on the workers' remittances, also wrote scores of letters demanding that the island government find new positions for the men or return them to the island. They all expected Governor Muñoz Marín, known for his paternalist style, to fix the situation. The controversy, widely publicized in island newspapers and in New York City's Spanish-language press, motivated the Migration Division to develop a compliance and supervision infrastructure that would enable it to monitor farm worker conditions more carefully. The Migration Division also collaborated with a handful of Michigan social service institutions to manage the crisis. They established alliances with liberal leaders and organizations in Michigan, and with Tejano labor migrants (Mexican Americans from Texas) who worked alongside

Puerto Rican migrants and were able to testify to their contract violations. Some workers were placed in new jobs, while many migrated on their own to other towns and cities in the region, expanding the small diaspora of Puerto Rican workers in the Midwest.[32]

An early "experiment" in recruiting women migrant workers, between 1946 and 1948, had trained women in various aspects of domestic labor, although the program was terminated after workers in Chicago, New Jersey, and New York suburbs protested against unacceptable working conditions and quickly found other forms of employment.[33] The recruitment of men for industrial employment was far more successful. Initially, the Puerto Rican government extended a wartime program that had placed about 10,000 Puerto Rican men in industrial jobs in Chicago, Utah, Ohio, Pennsylvania, and New Jersey. This pattern continued for a few years after the war, when 2,000 young Puerto Ricans from the island were contracted (with the support of the CIO union) to work in the steel mills of Lorain and Youngstown, Ohio. In Lorain, the workers were monitored and supported carefully by the Puerto Rican Department of Labor and the Migration Division, which produced a report on the migrant labor program there in 1948. Wages were in line with pay on the union scale even though most were not active in the union at this point. In this period of the expanding postwar economy, the placement of island workers in Lorain encouraged others: "The Lorain project has been so successful that the management of the steel works at Gary, Indiana has sent scouts to observe . . . in the hope that Gary may import a group of Puerto Rican workers, perhaps about 500 men."[34]

Soon enough these workers were embroiled in local labor politics. In 1948, just after the Migration Division published its report on contract labor in the Midwest, the local CIO union went on strike. Puerto Rican workers' support for the strike made island officials nervous, and they paid a visit to workers in Lorain, urging them to avoid any links to communist groups that may have been involved in the strike. The anti-communist message was delivered by island leaders Ramos Antonini, president of the Puerto Rican House of Representatives, and by Tomás Méndez Mejía, leader of the island's largest labor union. Communist organizers' tactics of recruiting Puerto Ricans to participate in their anti–discrimination campaigns (though not necessarily to join the Communist party) may have been familiar to New York Puerto Ricans, but it was new for these migrant workers. An organizer for the leftist Puerto Rican Welfare League reminded the Lorain workers, "You are an American citizen. They can't push you around."[35]

The reception encountered by Puerto Rican contract workers in these various locations varied greatly. In many places, Puerto Rican migrants were initially perceived as a solution to labor scarcity, and they were celebrated by public officials, residents, and employers as a hard-working group that adapted quickly and took advantage of opportunities for advancement. In Chicago and Ohio, where Puerto Rican workers were compared somewhat favorably to Mexicans, it took some time for migrants to feel the impact of the prejudice, poor living conditions, and unsteady employment that comprised the status quo for other Latino workers. In New York City, Puerto Ricans before World War II had been able to tinker with their "Spanish," Hispanic, and "Latin" identities, and claims to American citizenship, in order to try to escape racial or nativist exclusion and create supportive communities via their efforts. But once these communities expanded in size, competition for jobs intensified conflicts with neighboring groups. While Puerto Rican workers' activism focused on the struggle to improve wages and conditions, they also developed community-centered and ethnic-based organizing as they made more general claims for equality.

Civil Rights and Leadership: Organizing against Discrimination

When Puerto Rican migrants began settling in New York City after the Second World War, at the rate of thousands per month, they were met with a tidal wave of prejudice and insult. They confronted a new level of hostility that earlier migrants from the island had not experienced, either in New York or in other places where Puerto Ricans established smaller enclaves in earlier decades, including Tampa, San Francisco, and Philadelphia. Puerto Ricans who migrated in smaller numbers and just a few years later to cities beyond New York—Hartford, Camden, Chicago—tended to struggle somewhat less with prejudice, at least initially. Puerto Rican newcomers who arrived en masse in New York City right after the war were seen as a "problem" almost immediately, maligned by city officials and elites as well as by working class residents of the neighborhoods where they settled, in Manhattan's East Harlem and Hell's Kitchen, in Brooklyn's Williamsburg and Red Hook. The United States had had no significant foreign migration since the start of the First World War, and during the interwar decades, European immigrant communities had culturally and politically coalesced into staunch defenders of monolithic "American" cultural values. That is, they had come to identify as "white," and were increasingly hostile towards an influx of new neighbors whom they could categorize as *not* white and definitely not American.

The dramatic rise in arrivals from Puerto Rico became fodder for the city's tabloid and right wing press early in 1947. Editors and reporters for the *New York World-Telegram*, the *New York Daily Mirror*, and the *New York Sun* saw an opportunity to stir up a panic about "the greatest mass migration in modern history—from poverty-stricken Puerto Rico to lush America," using dramatic images of destitute migrants streaming into already overcrowded neighborhoods and turning respectable tenements that housed white working class families into havens for racially ambiguous foreigners who seemed incapable of assimilating. Migrants were cast as mostly illiterate and largely unemployable, destined to rely on public assistance and to be duped and manipulated by Communists. The tabloids were not the only publications indulging in this postwar urban drama. The *New York Times* published its share of exaggerated headlines before it shifted its coverage—albeit in more moderate terms, like "Officials Worried by Influx of Migrant Puerto Ricans."[36]

The tally of new arrivals became a hotly debated issue, accompanied by worried projections about the crisis of welfare costs that the Puerto Ricans migration would produce. Some of the worst invective in this vein came from reporters Lee Mortimer and Jack Lait, whose 1948 bestseller *New York Confidential!* described "600,000 Puerto Ricans" (in fact there were only a third that many before 1950) as "a sullen, disappointed, disillusioned mass of people, alien to everything that spells New York." Mortimer and Lait, popular yellow journalists at the *New York Daily Mirror*, warned that Puerto Ricans were criminals who accounted for a supposedly massive crime wave (which was statistically impossible as described by Mortimer and Lait), that Puerto Rican youth were marijuana users and "natural cop haters," and that the whole bunch brought diseases and came for the welfare benefits.[37]

One actual fact that underlay the fiction-based attacks was the connection between Puerto Rican migrants and Vito Marcantonio, the radical congressman from East Harlem who was a member of the American Labor Party and a supporter of Puerto Rican independence. Marcantonio was often accused by conservative anti-communists of not only encouraging migrants to move to New York from Puerto Rico, but also paying for their transport and arranging for welfare payments as soon as they arrived in the city, thereby making migrants beholden to him as voters. One anonymous writer to Governor Muñoz Marín described this alleged scheme as the "red taint over the entire colony."[38]

Such invented stories added to the public outcry and inspired enthusiastic endorsement by politicians and city officials who had already rehearsed their racist rhetoric in denunciations of the city's Black ghettos. The anti-Puerto Rican press even had a few Puerto Rican apologists, like Diego Ramírez, who argued that the portrayal of poverty and disease among migrants was not intended to defame Puerto Ricans, but rather was a realistic representation of conditions on the island. Ramírez argued that

> anyone who lives in Harlem knows the sad conditions that exist there. Many Porto Ricans and other Latin Americans who live here live in such a way as to be a disgrace not only to themselves but to the whole Spanish people and the City of New York.[39]

The Puerto Rican community, especially the established members who were not recent migrants, were incensed over the attacks and mounted an ongoing campaign of protests that lasted through the early 1950s. During 1947 and 1948, community leaders organized regular picketing at the *World-Telegram* offices in Midtown, often with 1,000 to 1,500 participants. The Spanish-American Youth Bureau's president, Ruperto Ruiz, suggested that Puerto Ricans follow the lead of African Americans in terms of media relations: "much of the progress of the colored Continental people today," he said, was "due to the constant 'hammer-ing' of their press . . . [to] demand respect for them." The Puerto Rican media, he insisted, had to "learn their full lesson on how to serve fully their educational function as an agent of the community and of the Spanish-speaking people and culture." Although research by a sociology Ph.D. student in the early 1950s pre-sented some evidence that the African American, liberal, and left-leaning press were supportive of the migrants, the repeated complaints by Puerto Ricans show how systematically migrants were maligned by conservative and tabloid papers.[40]

The recently formed Migration Division joined other Puerto Rican com-munity leaders (many of them leftists) in defending Puerto Ricans' public image and encouraging them to assert their citizenship rights. Before the Migration Division was established, the island government had sponsored a major study led by the Bureau of Applied Social Research at Columbia University, a mas-sive survey-based project led by sociologist C. Wright Mills that also included Clarence Senior and other prominent researchers. The project sought to provide guidance for policy by studying the established and recent migrant community in New York as it experienced the massive postwar expansion. Puerto Rico's gov-ernor also intended to use the study to counter attacks on the character of Puerto Rican migrants and concerns about the economic and cultural impact of their migration. Mills and his collaborators concluded that most Puerto Ricans came to the U.S. to seek work, that most migrants saw their journey as worth the difficul-ties they experienced, and that they adjusted relatively well to the many problems they encountered. The researchers also argued that migrants needed support. It was the conclusions of this study, together with the urgings of the Spanish-American Youth Bureau leaders, that encouraged the Puerto Rican government to establish the Migration Division.[41]

Liberals and leftists, including leaders of many African American, Jewish, Catholic, and Protestant organizations, defended the rights of Puerto Ricans to migrate, to seek a better life in the U.S., and to make use of public services when-ever necessary. Progressive civic leaders and social service professionals argued that New Yorkers should accept and welcome these "newcomers," whose diffi-culties and differences would soon fade, just as they had for the earlier generation of Eastern and Southern European immigrants. Puerto Rican community lead-ers made the same case, asserting that Puerto Ricans' poor image in New York would improve if the public would recognize that they were "just like other immigrants"—an argument that was inaccurate to the degree that Puerto Ricans' mixed-race heritage made them very unlike European immigrants in the eyes of most Americans.[42] Puerto Ricans were also unlike other immigrants in terms of their status as citizens of the United States. And while Puerto Ricans' U.S. citi-zenship was widely misunderstood or unknown by the public and even by many officials in the U.S., some of those who did know about migrants' citizenship status feared its impact: because they were citizens, they could vote, claim social benefits, and they could not be deported, even if they committed a crime.

Defending the image of Puerto Rican migrants in the late 1940s and early 1950s was made more difficult by the charged political context of the Cold War. Many detractors warned that Puerto Rican migrants could be easily manipulated by Communists seeking new voters. Cold War anxieties also affected the broader political relationship between island and U.S. officials—especially as Puerto Rico's government sought to solidify its new commonwealth status in the early 1950s, in part by reassuring U.S. officials that the island was a reliable political ally. Island leaders thus tried to break the growing association between the Puerto Rican community and radical politicians in New York. This allegedly "red" group included East Harlem Congressman Vito Marcantonio, one of the most left-leaning representatives in Congress in the 20th century, along with other members of the American Labor Party (founded by former members of the Socialist party), all of whom embraced the Puerto Rican migrant community as exemplars of the political and economic failures of U.S. policy. Meanwhile, Puerto Rican officials, including the island's first elected native governor, Luis Muñoz Marín, and other high profile officials like San Juan's Mayor Felisa Rincón de Gautier, did their best to defend the image of migrants without critiquing the society that met their arrival with fear and hostility.[43]

Two high-profile attacks on the U.S. government by Puerto Rican nationalist migrants in the early 1950s amplified these Cold War fears. In early 1950, the Nationalist party in Puerto Rico had begun a protest campaign that included bombings and attempted takeovers of public buildings, an effort to halt the process of the island's transition from an "unincorporated territory" of the U.S. to a Commonwealth (an "Associated Free State" or *Estado Libre Asociado*). Supporters of independence derided this transition as "perfumed colonialism" in which Puerto Rico's continued colonial and territorial status was covered with a veneer of local political autonomy. They opposed the passage of Public Law 600, which gave Puerto Rican islanders the power to write their own constitution (with veto power retained by the U.S.) and the right to hold a binding referendum that asked Puerto Rican voters to support autonomous self-rule. It may seem paradoxical that the nationalists opposed a law that would grant a new form of autonomy to the island government; but they viewed Public Law 600 as a step toward a status change that would make Puerto Rico's ties to the United States stronger, locking it into a permanent colonial relationship.[44]

Then, in November of 1950, two nationalists who had been living in the U.S. for several years attempted to assassinate President Truman in Washington, D.C. The President was unharmed, and both would-be assassins were shot by Secret Service agents, one fatally.[45] Few Americans had a clear understanding of the nature of the United States' relationship with Puerto Rico, or of the contentious politics surrounding that relationship, but for the average reader of U.S. news, the assassination attempt made Puerto Ricans as a group appear volatile and dangerous. Officials in the New York and Chicago Migration Division offices condemned the attack, distancing themselves and the growing community of migrants they represented from the actions of what many considered to be nationalist "fanatics."[46]

Varied efforts to highlight Puerto Ricans as upright and worthy U.S. patriots emerged during these years, including some genuine expressions of inclusion and celebration of Puerto Rican military service and the island's new Commonwealth status. A 4th of July 1951 salute to the 65th Infantry men—members of the Army regiment based in Puerto Rico, which had sent close to 4,000 soldiers to fight in several European campaigns during the Second World War—included island and New York politicians and public officials and about 10,000 Puerto Ricans. In 1952, a similar event celebrated the U.S. armed forces fighting in Korea, with thousands of Puerto Ricans expected to participate, including "uniformed delegations of veterans from three Puerto Rican American legion posts—the Borinquén, Colonel Segarra, and the Puerto Rican post of this city." Renowned mezzo-soprano Flavia Acosta was slated to sing La Borinqueña, the island's national anthem.[47]

Other efforts to defend Puerto Ricans' patriotism were more organic to the community. In 1947, directly as a result of the right-wing press attacks, a group of professionals formed the "Puerto Rican Public Relations Committee," which came to include nearly 200 journalists, professors, and intellectuals, both island-educated and second generation. The group published a "Puerto Ricans in the news bulletin" and sought to improve the image of the Puerto Rican community through the use of public media "to counteract slanderous and unjust publicity about Puerto Ricans in the mainland by raising their prestige in the eyes of the English speaking public." The 1949 issue challenged news stories that emphasized Puerto Ricans on relief, deploying information about Puerto Rican soldiers including a marine guard chief at the Brooklyn Navy Yard, Jaime Sabater Pico. In another bulletin, the committee assailed the aggressive tactics of the right-wing press, whose attacks against Puerto Ricans tended to falsely describe residents of the ghetto as susceptible to the nefarious influence of radical groups. After Nationalist party militants attempted to assassinate President Truman in 1950, the committee sent him a telegram celebrating the fact that he was not hurt, noting also that "Puerto Ricans generally take pride in their intellectual tolerance of strongly differing ideas but at the same time condemn brute force as a means to an end."[48]

Another, more dramatic crisis erupted in March 1954. On the anniversary of the signing of the Jones-Shaforth Act and the extension of U.S. citizenship to Puerto Ricans (in 1917), four armed Puerto Rican nationalists entered the gallery of the United States Congress and opened fire, wounding five representatives. The Nationalist party in Puerto Rico, and its smaller but equally radical branch in the U.S., continued to be furious over the island's new Commonwealth status, which had been formalized in 1952—with the assertion by the popular governor, Muñoz Marín, that "the United States of America [now] ends every trace and vestige of the colonial system in Puerto Rico."[49] The day after the attack on Congress, a *New York Times* editorialist worried that Americans might seek retribution against "the friendly Puerto Rican people," and warned that "it would be a grave injustice today to indict Puerto Rico for the foul deed of a few demented citizens."[50] A press release from New York's Mayor Wagner reminded New Yorkers that:

> Our Puerto Rican citizens are good citizens. They are hardworking, God fearing citizens. They are citizens trying to find a better life for themselves and their families than they were able to in their native isle. It would be a particular tragedy if their efforts to attain that goal and to contribute to the building of New York, were to be prejudiced by the acts of a few madmen . . . but it cannot be, and should not be the crime of the Porto Rican community in New York.[51]

In spite of the fervent defense by migrants' many liberal allies, suspicion of Puerto Rican migrants in both Chicago and New York spiked in the aftermath of the shooting. Participants in the attacks came from these two cities and had been members of the local Nationalist party branches. Police in both cities made a few arrests of Puerto Ricans in the months following the shooting, inspiring protest by both cities' Spanish-speaking communities.[52]

In Philadelphia, the third U.S. city with a notable Puerto Rican population by 1954, there was no clear record of a backlash after the attack on Congress. The summer before, though, migrants who settled in the city's Spring Garden neighborhood had been caught up in a series of clashes with their primarily Irish American neighbors, a conflict that had inspired the first spate of anti-Puerto Rican press in the city. The spike in the Puerto Rican population in Philadelphia, an increase of 350% between 1950 and 1954, only amounted a about 5,000 new migrants, but it was enough to generate a hostile response from the migrants' closest neighbors, who—like many working class white Americans in this period—had come to value their "whiteness" and did not want that status threatened by an influx of non-white neighbors. After the clashes, the Philadelphia Commission on Human Relations (PCHR) conducted a study in Spring Garden and reported that "an unknown number of Spanish speaking American citizens of Puerto Rican ancestry had appeared almost overnight on an unknown number of city streets . . ." The PCHR hoped that the study would encourage the creation of programs to help with "the peaceful integration into the community of the new immigrants."[53]

At the same time that established Puerto Rican leaders in New York were defending the community against general prejudice and suspicion of sedition, a cohort of ambitious younger Puerto Ricans were beginning to set their own agendas for change. Antonia Pantoja, among a core group of this generation of young leaders, was an undergraduate at Hunter College in the early 1950s when she helped found the Hispanic Young Adult Association, a forum bringing energetic and ambitious young Puerto Ricans together to strengthen their community and its public image. Pantoja and her cohort originally modeled their organizing work after the "uplift" goals of groups like the National Association for the Advancement of Colored People (NAACP); they were inspired by African American and Jewish civil rights struggles and their leadership. Within a decade, one major result of the activist energy of these leaders was the remarkably successful organization Aspira, founded for the educational advancement and empowerment of Puerto Rican adolescents and young adults in 1961.[54]

In addition to the creation of institutions and organizations to solidify the social standing of the Puerto Rican community in New York, some leaders also began to emphasize the need for collaboration with African American leaders. In the early 1950s, the Spanish-American Youth Bureau organized a convention around the theme of "Negro-Puerto Rican Unity." Representatives of 66 organizations attended, including leaders of the NAACP and the Pan American Women's Association, the editors of *La Prensa* and *El Diario*, officials in the New York City departments of housing, education, and welfare, and Raymond Hilliard, Commissioner of Welfare and executive director of the Welfare Council of New York. Harris Present, who served as counsel for both the Spanish-American Youth Bureau and the Puerto Rican Employees Association, argued that "unified, the groups present a potential political factor which has not yet been realized." Recognizing the similar social and economic needs of African Americans and Puerto Ricans, he called for a joint organization that would be "open to all races and groups and work for the elimination of prejudice and discrimination."[55] This was a prescient acknowledgement that changing racial politics in the postwar U.S. required that Puerto Ricans navigate differently—and collaborate with their fellow "minority" leaders to solidify a constituency that could achieve political recognition.

Electoral Politics: Rights and Representation

In many respects, the postwar decade was an era of political opportunity for marginalized groups in the urban north. Unions had made a convincing case for the salience of labor rights despite the limitations imposed in the cold war era by the Taft-Hartley Act, which substantially limited the power of organized labor. Even those legal restrictions did little to stifle the growing demand for social rights affirmed by the New Deal, which, combined with the burgeoning movement for African American civil rights, inspired workers and racial minorities to seek political representation to secure the protection of their rights as American citizens. Puerto Ricans, though smaller in number than their African American neighbors (in New York City, Puerto Ricans comprised 3.5% of the population in 1950, compared to African Americans' 9.5%), saw that securing a political voice was the best protection against exclusion and discrimination.[56] The exploding Puerto Rican migrant population in New York in the 1950s made the goal of gaining recognition by political parties both more urgent and more possible.

Such efforts took a long time. In each of the cities where Puerto Rican migrants settled, there tended to be a lag of at least a couple of decades before any formal representation was achieved. This was true in New York, where a substantial Puerto Rican community had begun to develop after the First World War, and Puerto Rican New Yorkers first managed to elect a representative— Oscar García Rivera, a member of the New York State Assembly—in 1937. In fact, Puerto Ricans' experience breaking into New York electoral politics involved another nearly two-decade lag: after García Rivera, no other Puerto Ricans won elections for state or city offices until 1952, when attorney and Democrat Felipe Torres won a seat in the state assembly, representing the South Bronx.[57] In Chicago and Philadelphia, where the first sizable Puerto Rican communities outside of New York City formed in the decade after the Second World War, Puerto Ricans did not begin making their way into formal politics, either with appointed or elected officials, until the 1970s. In a few smaller Mid-Atlantic cities like Hartford, Camden, and Newark, Puerto Rican communities that began to form somewhat later in the 1950s reached a relatively high proportion of the population, around 15–20%, during the 1960s. This meant that community leaders and voters were able to command attention from politicians—and to support Puerto Rican candidates for public office—in the 1970s, after a shorter period of community expansion and development than in New York, Chicago, or Philadelphia. Because of the chronological framing of this chapter, and the later timeline of Puerto Ricans' entry into electoral politics in cities other than New York, this section focuses on New York City.

Building a Puerto Rican voting constituency was the first step in solidifying a place in the formal political arena. (Although Puerto Ricans had comprised a notable proportion of voters in a couple of New York City districts starting in the mid-1920s, this was not enough to draw consistent support from the major parties for Puerto Rican candidates.) By 1950, in the midst of the huge postwar migration, the political arithmetic was changing dramatically. With 40 to 50 thousand migrants arriving in New York City each year, their value as potential voters became obvious. In 1953, the *New York Post* ran a headline proclaiming "City Fathers Love Puerto Ricans at the Polls."[58] This assertion was more complicated than it seemed, however, in the new Cold War order. "City fathers" loved the prospect of winning the allegiance of 20 to 30 thousand new potential voters, presumably to either the Democratic or Republican parties, depending on which "city fathers" were consulted. Some Puerto Ricans—both new migrants and those who had been born in New York in earlier decades—did support mainstream political agendas "at the polls" in the 1950s. But the plurality, if not the majority, of politically vocal Puerto Rican voters had been pulled to the left during the pro-union, anti-fascist decade of the 1930s, and they continued throughout the 1940s and into the 1950s to support a left-of-center agenda that now included racial justice, police accountability, and fair housing.

Whereas Democrats had earned the majority of Puerto Rican votes during the 1920s and into the Depression years, by the late 1930s the American Labor Party (ALP) wielded more influence than the Democratic party in working class Puerto Rican communities in New York. The ALP, formed in 1937 as an alternative to the Socialist party, won the support of broad sectors of unionized workers, including many Puerto Ricans. After the Second World War, as the Cold War increased the conservatism of both domestic and international politics, Puerto Rican communities in New York constituted a solid voting bloc for the ALP. The ALP, in turn, gave Puerto Ricans unwavering support, maintaining offices with bilingual staff in several Puerto Rican neighborhoods and representing Puerto Ricans' interests in labor and housing disputes.

In East Harlem, still home to the largest concentration of Puerto Ricans in the 1950s, U.S. Congressional representative Vito Marcantonio affiliated with the ALP shortly after its founding and helped direct tens of thousands of Puerto Rican voters to the party. Marcantonio won overwhelming support among New York City Puerto Ricans, even those well beyond his district, by giving consistent attention to problems of daily life, like housing, as well as to bigger issues, like the status of Puerto Rico. A fierce advocate of Puerto Rican independence, Marcantonio held the allegiance of all but the most conservative Puerto Ricans during the roughly 15 years he represented his district.[59] He also encouraged community-based Puerto Rican leadership, and some Puerto Rican leaders capitalized on Marcantonio's influence and the experience they gained in working with him. Manuel Medina, Marcantonio's lieutenant and protégé, ran for city council on the ALP ticket in 1952 and nearly won in his district, which included East Harlem and the northern part of the Upper East Side. Medina had by that point become a well-known advocate of his community, someone who, like Marcantonio, was known to fight against any injustice brought to his attention by a community member. For instance, Medina convened a protest when a Puerto Rican mother, in the process of being evicted with her children, was physically assaulted by her landlord while police looked on. Medina also helped create the Harlem Council of Puerto Rican Affairs, which fought against incidents of police brutality and challenged discrimination in welfare, housing, and employment.[60]

His enthusiastic constituency notwithstanding, Marcantonio, along with other members of the left, came under fierce attack by a resurgent right during the Cold War. When Marcantonio ran for mayor of New York City on the ALP platform in 1949, he lost to the Democratic incumbent, William O'Dwyer, with about 12% of the vote (which was well behind their Republican/Fusion party rival, who got about 35% of the vote). Although O'Dwyer's victory turned out to be a landslide, the Democratic machine took Marcantonio's challenge seriously, mostly because they saw the potential political impact of the exploding Puerto Rican population. That year, the postwar migration from Puerto Rico to New York was approaching 50,000; Puerto Ricans were, according to the *New York Times*, the "fastest growing sector of the population." Democrats determined it was an important moment to try to secure the migrant vote.[61]

Luis Muñoz Marín, who in 1948 became the first elected governor of Puerto Rico, wrote an open letter to fellow liberal O'Dwyer a month before the New York mayoral election, detailing the threat posed by the candidacy of Marcantonio. "He is a follower of the Communist party line," Muñoz Marín warned. He also asserted—in error—that "(1) the overwhelming majority of Puerto Ricans are not followers of Mr. Marcantonio," and, correctly, "(2) that even among his followers a very large majority do not share his communistic political tendencies."[62] Muñoz Marín's letter and other such efforts represented not just a bold move on behalf of a political ally (O'Dwyer) to influence the outcome of a faraway election. It was also an effort to turn the tide of Puerto Rican voters away from the left and towards the mainstream liberal Democratic party, while also eliminating a political opponent (Marcantonio).[63]

Vito Marcantonio was also seen as problematic by Muñoz Marín and his allies because Marcantonio continued to support Puerto Rican independence. Muñoz Marín's political party, the Popular Democratic Party (PPD), had dropped independence from its platform in the 1940s; and Democrats in New York saw the persistence of Puerto Rican nationalism as a hindrance to their ability to harness the potential of this new voting bloc. Indeed, although the majority of Puerto Ricans repudiated the violence of radical nationalists, many politically active Puerto Ricans in New York remained critical of the United States' colonial relationship with the island, and it was one of the reasons so many Puerto Ricans gravitated to the ALP and Marcantonio as its charismatic representative. During and just after the war, both the Roosevelt and Truman administrations had said they would address Puerto Rico's "status problem" as part of the move to support democratic regimes and decolonization around the world, intimating that the resolution would be some form of independence.[64] The inauguration of the Puerto Rican Commonwealth in 1952 enraged members of the Nationalist party, of course, and also severely disappointed the migrant left, leaving many alienated anew from the political mainstream.

It was soon thereafter, as the media broadcast the optimism of "city fathers" about the growing migrant electorate, that the reputation of those Puerto Rican voters was gravely damaged by the nationalists' attack on Congress in 1954. To an American public that had little capacity to distinguish between communism and anti-colonialism, and that knew nothing about the ideological struggle over independence that originated with the U.S. takeover in 1898, the event simply seemed to affirm assumptions about Puerto Ricans' dangerous anti-American proclivities. Starting immediately after the attacks on Congress in spring 1954, the FBI and other law enforcement officials orchestrated a campaign against suspected Puerto Rican radicals. Within a week, almost 100 Puerto Ricans in the U.S. had been arrested, with the expectation that they would be charged under the provisions of the 1940 Smith Act, which made it a crime to engage in any activity seen as intended "to cause the overthrow or destruction" of the government. Before the end of the year, the FBI had arrested dozens of other suspects in New York and Chicago as well as in Puerto Rico, charging them with conspiracy to overthrow the government.[65]

Within two years, Congress passed a bill that doubled the penalties of Smith Act violations, imposing an automatic $20,000 fine and a 20-year prison sentence on anyone found guilty of such charges. In its reporting on this bill, the *New York Times* noted that "the proposed stiffening of penalties for seditious conspiracy is the outgrowth of the shooting in the House of Representatives in 1954 of five members by Puerto Rican nationalists." For tens of thousands of Puerto Rican migrants, the problem with this reactionary response to the 1954 shootings had little to do with either the Nationalist or Communist party; only a tiny minority of the Puerto Rican population in the U.S. were members of either party. The problem was, instead, the possibility that any critique of U.S. imperialism, or any affiliation with a leftist group presumed to be "red," could be interpreted as "seditious conspiracy."[66]

In this climate, McCarthy-era assumptions about radical foreigners could make life very hard for left-leaning working class migrants. For some, then, fear-driven conformity overwhelmed the many attractions of leftist politics. The popularity of the ALP dwindled in the early 1950s, and after Marcantonio's sudden death in August 1954, Puerto Ricans' support for ALP and other politically radical candidates became even more anemic and localized. Without their most powerful political champion, a shrinking proportion of Puerto Rican voters took the risk of supporting his radical party, even though the ALP continued to back numerous Puerto Rican candidates for local political office.[67]

Leftist stalwarts like Jesús Colón, Manuel Medina, and José Giboyeaux tried to keep the ALP alive by arguing for the continuing relevance of its platforms. Campaigning for city council seats in 1953, they urged their compatriots to "vote for . . . treatment as first class citizens."[68] Another Puerto Rican candidate, running in Brooklyn for a state assembly seat the year before, warned the many Puerto Rican voters in his district of the dangers of the status quo:

> We Puerto Rican people face bitter discrimination in our jobs, in housing and in our daily lives . . . We are a growing community. Our present Assemblyman . . . has ignored the desperate needs of the people of his district. It is time that we had someone from our own people to speak for us and to represent us in the government.[69]

These were the same kinds of issues the ALP had been emphasizing since the late 1930s; and although the experience of "bitter discrimination" during the decade of massive migration from Puerto Rico to New York had proven the need for such advocacy, the language of working class left was losing its power, and the political mainstream of the postwar era became increasingly intolerant of such messages.

Conclusion

While the pillars of Puerto Rican community activism in New York—older migrants who were members of the traditional left—lost ground in the postwar decade, a new cadre of leaders there was beginning to develop within the Puerto Rican community by the mid-1950s. Some were young professionals, many of them having completed post-graduate training in New York City in law, education, or social work; others came from the labor movement. Many were second-generation, born in New York to migrant parents, though some had emigrated as children or young adults and identified with both the established migrant community and the postwar newcomers. This leadership formed in an era of both familiar and intensifying challenges to the Puerto Rican community—stagnating wage labor and poverty, police abuse, persistent discrimination—when there seemed to be new possibilities for the collaboration of "minorities" in American society. During the 1930s, Puerto Ricans had made periodic alliances with African Americans and with some white ethnics too, but these were not enduring political relationships. Starting in the 1950s, though, Puerto Rican leaders, following their African American counterparts, began to view the challenges of political marginality as something that could be overcome through coordinated action.

For all Puerto Ricans in the U.S.—the quarter million who migrated during the postwar boom, the slightly smaller number who had arrived a decade or two before, and the 60,000 or so who had been born on the mainland—the postwar decade brought substantial opportunity as well as extreme challenges. Despite ugly media attacks that assailed the health, character, culture, and intelligence of new migrants, Puerto Ricans benefited, alongside all Americans, from a plethora of industrial jobs, and their household incomes rose. In the midst of ongoing struggles against discrimination in housing, schooling, and employment, Puerto Rican tenants, parents, and union members built alliances with other progressives—bolstered by the evolving support of the Migration Division—and worked toward agendas that supported Puerto Ricans' rights as Americans. Although racial prejudice and the pervasive conservatism of the Cold War muted their political voice in this era, Puerto Rican voters continued to back those who stood for equality, and Puerto Rican leaders (first in New York City, later in other cities) continued to run for public office in spite of long odds and consistent losses.

In the mid-1950s, writer and leftist community activist Jesús Colón wrote about the continuing problem of "the second-class status of the Puerto Rican minority in the U.S." in a pamphlet he wrote for the New York state Communist party organization, of which he was a member. A relatively small number of his compatriots were still members of the Communist party after 1950 (it had been much more popular among the working class before the Cold War), but Colón's message in that pamphlet was one he shared widely with his community in other writings and speeches. Rather than dwell on the burdens of racism or the oppressive legacies of colonialism, he exhorted his compatriots to find common ground and join together in "the struggle for Puerto Rican rights" in the United States. In the era that followed, many thousands of Puerto Ricans would heed that call.

Notes

1 United States Bureau of the Census. *United States Census of Population: 1950. Special Reports. Puerto Ricans in the Continental United States.* Washington, D.C.: U.S. Government Printing Office, 1953.

2 Several thousand of these wartime migrants had worked on the construction of military bases in Puerto Rico, an experience that gave them a taste of the industrial training, skilled work, and higher wages that migrants hoped to encounter on the mainland.

3 *Puerto Ricans in the Continental United States,* 23.

4 The legislation limiting immigration to the U.S. in the 1920s did not apply to the Western Hemisphere, so migrations from Latin America and the Caribbean were not restricted. Areas in the West and Southwest had attracted large numbers of Mexican labor migrants since the late 19th century, and this migrant flow increased substantially in the 1920s. Chicago was the only city east of the Mississippi that also experienced a significant rise in Mexican migration before the 1940s. In the same period, New York City drew most of its labor migrants from Puerto Rico, as well as a few other Caribbean islands.

5 Lauria Santiago, Aldo A. "A Better Life: Puerto Rican New York—A History of Class, Work, and Struggle, 1920–1970," manuscript; Thomas, Lorrin. *Puerto Rican Citizen: History and Political Identity in Twentieth-Century New York City.* Chicago: University of Chicago Press, 2010; Findlay, Eileen. *We Are Left without a Father Here: Masculinity, Domesticity, and Migration in Postwar Puerto Rico.* Durham: North Carolina Press, 2015.

6 Félix Cosme, "A Profile of Puerto Rico and Puerto Ricans Citizens on the Island and Puerto Rican Migration to New York City, Paper Presented before the Jewish Workmen's Circle," 14 Dec. 1964, OGPRUS-CPRS Box 3066 Folder 28.

7 Thomas, *Puerto Rican Citizen*; Lauria Santiago, "A Better Life."

8 Los puertorriqueños y demas hispanos ante las elecciones del proximo noviembre en la ciudad de Nueva York, no date, Jesús Colón Papers-CPRS Box 21 Folder 2. Lapp, Michael. "Managing Migration: The Migration Division of Puerto Rico and Puerto Ricans in New York City." Ph.D. Dissertation, Johns Hopkins University, 1991, 136. In 1950, Mayor O'Dwyer had been appointed Ambassador to Mexico, and his deputy Vincent Impellitieri became mayor for the remainder of O'Dwyer's term.

9 Allport, Gordon W. *The Nature of Prejudice: A Comprehensive and Penetrating Study of the Origin and Nature of Prejudice.* Garden City, NY: Doubleday, 1954. On San Francisco Mayor's Committee on Human Relations, see Eduardo Contreras, *Latinos in the Liberal City: Politics and Protest in San Francisco.* Philadelphia: University of Pennsylvania Press, forthcoming.

10 Ruperto Ruiz, Reply to Governor of Puerto Rico, Jesús T. Piñero's Denial of Certain Existing Facts about the Needs of Puerto Ricans in New York City, 21 Aug. 1947, Covello Papers-HSP Series VIII Box 73 Folder 8.

11 These lists of Migration Division departments and regional offices come from the *Guide to the Migration Division collection created by the Centro Library and Archive* (Centro, n.d.). "Oficina de Puerto Rico jamas deja indefenso al Boricua." *La Prensa,* 6 Jan. 1963. The office's budget increased to about $300,000 yearly in 1953, when the migration to New York was reaching its peak, paid by the island's government. Yearly report. Migration Division. 1952–53. OGPRUS.

12 "Cultural assimilation seminar," Fitzpatrick Papers-FU Box 31; "La renuncia de Cabranes." *El Imparcial,* Fondo Gobernadores-AGPR Clippings Box 2280.

13 Fernández, Lilia. *Brown in the Windy City: Mexicans and Puerto Ricans in Postwar Chicago.* Chicago: University of Chicago Press, 2012, 71.

14 *Ibid.*, 73.

15 Conclusions, Conference on Migration, San Juan, Puerto Rico, March 1–7, 1953, Covello Papers-HSP Series X Box 110 Folder 10.; Whalen, Carmen Teresa. *From Puerto Rico to Philadelphia: Puerto Rican Workers and Postwar Economies.* Philadelphia: Temple University Press, 2001, 190–3; Fernández, *Brown in the Windy City*, 79. By the mid-1950s, the Migration Division in Chicago was systematically aiding Puerto Rican families in their search for housing; in 1956–57, records showed that the office helped 600 heads of household to apply for apartments. Fernández, *Brown in the Windy City*, 103.

16 Talk by Charles Freuse, city administrator, at UPR on scale and challenges of running N.Y.C.; OGPRUS-CPRS Box 276 Folder 3218. By the end of 1964 about 17% of public housing units were occupied by Puerto Ricans and by 1968 about 114,000 Puerto Ricans lived in these projects. Joseph Montserrat to Frank Zorilla, 13 Nov. 1964, OGPRUS-CPRS Box 2948; Press Release, 1 Aug. 1968, OGPRUS-CPRS Box 3001.

17 New York, N.Y. Board of Education. *The Puerto Rican Study, 1953–1957: A Report on the Education and Adjustment of Puerto Rican Pupils in the Public Schools of the City of New York.* N.Y. Board of Education: New York, 1958; Morrison, Cayce. "The Puerto Rican Study—What It Is—Where It Is Going." *Journal of Educational Sociology* 28, no. 4 (Dec. 1954); Lopez, Madeleine E. "Investigating the Investigators: An Analysis of 'The Puerto Rican Study'." *Centro Journal* 19, no. 2 (fall 2007): 60–85; Dossick, Jesse J. "Fifth Workshop–Field Study in Puerto Rican: Education and Culture." *The Journal of Educational Sociology* 26, no. 4 (1952): 177–86.

18 They visited schools, trained teachers, offered dozens of lectures and paid to train N.Y.C. teachers on the island. Pedro Cebollero, decano, to señor Rector, 23 Nov. 1949, Colección Gobernador-AGPR Box 2280; Thomas, *Puerto Rican Citizen*, 203–8.

19 Thomas, *Puerto Rican Citizen*, 179.

20 United Parents Association, Understanding our New Neighbors: A Report of Goodwill Workshops, 1953–54, BCSP Papers Box 63 Folder 8.1.115.

21 Letter to Sternau, no author, 1953 OGPRUS-CPRS Box 2939 Folder 2; Jesús Colón, "The Growing Importance of the Puerto Rican Minority in New York City," n.d. [1958], Jesús Colón Papers-CPRS Box 10 Folder 9; Memo, Annie González to Carlos Cuevas, 24 July 1957, Council of Spanish American Organizations, OGPRUS-CPRS Box 2939 Folder 1. Pablo Rivera to Eulalio Torres, Council of Puerto Rican and Spanish-American Organizations of Greater New York, 13 July 1962, OGPRUS-CPRS Box 2847 Folder 15; Migration Division to Mayor's Committee on Exploitation, 28 Sept. 1961, OGPRUS-CPRS Box 2559; Rosas to Montserrat, Weekly Report, 18 July 1962, OGPRUS-CPRS Box 2555.

22 Gilberto Gerena Valentín, 11 Oct. 2002, Oral History Collection-CPRS tape 117.

23 *Ibid.*, 113–14. The usual membership fee was $3 per month. Gerena Valentín, Gilberto. *Gilberto Gerena Valentín: My Life as a Community Activist, Labor Organizer, and Progressive Politician in New York City.* New York: Center for Puerto Rican Studies, 2013, 108, 113–5.

24 The GI bill was the largest spending bill in the history of the U.S. See Freeman, Joshua Benjamin. *American Empire: The Rise of a Global Power, the Democratic Revolution at Home, 1945–2000.* New York: Penguin Books, 2013, digital, location 763–85.

25 The Commission on Human Relations report in 1954 said 72% of Puerto Rican women worked as operatives. Whalen, Carmen, *From Puerto Rico to Philadelphia: Puerto Rican Workers and Postwar Economies.* Philadelphia: Temple University Press, 2001, 151.

26 "The Growing Importance of the Puerto Rican Minority in New York City," n.d. [1958], Jesús Colón Papers-CPRS Box 10 Folder 1; Freeman, Joshua Benjamin. *Working-Class New York: Life and Labor since World War II.* New York: New Press, 2000.

27 Lauria Santiago, "A Better Life," Ch. 8.

28 Whalen, *From Puerto Rico to Philadelphia*, 151–4.

29 For more on the history of Puerto Ricans and other Latinos in labor unions in San Francisco between 1920 and 1980, see Contreras, *Latinos in the Liberal City*.

30 García Colón, Ismael. "Claiming Equality: Puerto Rican Farmworkers in Western New York." *Latino Studies* 6, no. 3 (2008): 269–89.

31 Jiménez de Wagenheim, Olga. "From Aguada to Dover: Puerto Ricans Rebuild Their World in Morris County, New Jersey, 1948 to 2000." In *The Puerto Rican Diaspora: Historical Perspectives*. 106–27: Philadelphia: Temple University Press, 2005, 117; Migration Division, Yearly and Weekly Reports. OGPRUS-CPRS.

32 Findlay, Eileen. *We Are Left without a Father Here*; Fernández, Delia. "Becoming Latino: Mexican and Puerto Rican Community Formation in Grand Rapids, Michigan, 1926–1964." *Michigan Historical Review* 39, no. 1 (2013): 71–100; Outline of discussion with Max Henderson. Confidencial. 2 August 1950. PRDL-AGPR Correspondencia de la Oficina de la Directora 1948–1950 Box A to C #163; Fernando to Petroamérica, 4 August 1950. PRDL-AGPR Correspondencia de la Oficina de la Directora 1948–1950 Box A to C #163.

33 Labor Department officials described the effort candidly as "frankly an experiment." PRDL-AGPR Correspondencia de la oficina de la Directora 1949–1950 Box 61–55 P to S, #165; Situación de los obreros Puertorriqueños contratados por Castle Barton and Assoc," Dec. 1946, Muñoz Marín Papers-FLMM, Sección IV, Serie 2 [Gobierno insular-Correspondencia general], Sub Serie—Cartapacio 9B 277; Rúa, Mérida M. *A Grounded Identidad: Making New Lives in Chicago's Puerto Rican Neighborhoods*. New York: Oxford University Press, 2012, Ch1; Fernández, *Brown in the Windy City*, Ch.1; "Maid Problem." *The New Republic*, 28 April 1947; Atención damas de Caguas y pueblos limítrofes, Flyer, PRDL-AGPR Correspondencia de la Directora 1949–1950 Box 61–55, P to S # 165; Petroamérica to Sierra Berdecia, 1 Nov. 1950. PRDL-AGPR Correspondencia de la Oficina de la Directora Box 61–55 A to C # 163.

34 Juan José Osuna, Educational Consultant to Manuel Cabranes, Director New York Office, 27 July 1948, OGPRUS-CPRS Box 2993 Folder 4; Visit to National Tube Co. Lorain OH, OGPRUS-CPRS Box 2993 Folder 4.

35 Rivera, Eugene. "La Colonia de Lorain." In Mary Hilaire Tavenner, ed., *Puerto Rico 2006: Memoirs of a Writer in Puerto Rico*. United States: Xlibris Corp., 2010.

36 "Puerto Rico to Harlem – At What Cost?" *New York World Telegram*, 1 May 1947; 22 Oct. 1947. "Relief Funds Being Spent without Proper Controls." *The New York Times*, 25 May 1947, 1.

37 Lait, J., and L. Mortimer. *New York: Confidential!* Chicago: Ziff Davis Publishing Company, 1948.

38 Communist Party, Puerto Rican Affairs Committee. *Handbook on Puerto Rican Work*. New York: Communist Party, Puerto Rican Affairs Committee, 1954; Meléndez, Edgardo. "Vito Marcantonio, Puerto Rican Migration, and the 1949 Mayoral Election in New York City." *Centro Journal* 22, no. 2 (fall 2010): 36; Puertorriqueño to Gobernador, 5 August 1948, Colección Gobernador-AGPR Box 454.

39 "A Letter to the Public," Dec. 1947. Luis Muñoz Marín papers-LMMF Section IV Series 8 Ultramar Sub-Serie 13.1 to 13.33 (NY correspondence).

40 Factual Report of the Cervantes Fraternal Society, Jesús Colón Papers-CPRS Box 18 Folder 8; Minuta de la reunion celebrada en la unidad Fraternal Hispana la noche de 28 de octubre de 1947, Jesús Colón Papers-CPRS Box 17 Folder 11; Subsidizing slums, no date, Jesús Colón Papers-CPRS Box 10 Folder 2; Spanish-American Youth Bureau, Comments and suggestions offered by Mr. Ruperto Ruiz, President of the Bureau, relative to the objectives for improvement of the Puerto Rican problems, proposed by Commissioner of Welfare of the City of New York for the Mayor's Committee on Puerto Rican Affairs [n.d. (1949?)], Covello Papers-HSP Series X Box 102 Folder 13; Goldsen, Rose K. "Puerto Rican Migration to New York City." Ph.D. Dissertation, Yale University, 1953; Muniz-Velasquez, Josefina. "Background of Puerto Rican Migration." Master's Thesis, Columbia University, 1949.

41 Mills, C. Wright. *The Puerto Rican Journey; New York's Newest Migrants*. New York: Publications of the Bureau of Applied Social Research, Columbia University, 1950; Meléndez Vélez, Edgardo. "'The Puerto Rican Journey' Revisited: Politics and the Study of Puerto Rican Migration." *Centro Journal* 17, no. 2 (fall 2005): 192–221. The research center hired a research assistant who 30 years later would become the first director of the Center for Puerto Rican Studies, Frank Bonilla. Interview with Frank Bonilla, Oral History Collection-CPRS.

42 "Confab to Strengthen Puerto Rican Unity; Same Bias Snags Both Groups." *New York Amsterdam News*, 13 Dec. 1952, 36.

43 Puerto Rican politicians campaigned in the growing Puerto Rican community against Marcantonio's run for mayor in 1949 and for his congressional seat in 1950. Meyer, Gerald. *Vito Marcantonio: Radical Politician, 1902–1954*. Albany: State University of New York Press, 1989; Meléndez, Edgardo. "Vito Marcantonio, Puerto Rican Migration, and the 1949 Mayoral Election in New York City." *Centro Journal* 22, no. 2 (fall 2010), 36.

44 See César Ayala and Rafael Bernabe. *Puerto Rico in the American Century: A History since 1898*. Chapel Hill: University of North Carolina Press, 2007.

45 The surviving assailant, Oscar Collazo, a resident of the Bronx, was sentenced to life in prison (though his sentence was commuted by President Jimmy Carter in 1979, after 29 years in jail).

46 "Denuncia la participación de los comunistas." *El Diario de Nueva York*, 31 Oct. 1950, 1; Fernández, *Brown in the Windy City*, 48.

47 Press Release of Committee, 2 July 1952; Papers of Mayor Impellitteri, NYCMA Box 85, Folder 987-9 (Roll 43).

48 Arizmendi, Elba. "The Structure and Functioning of Ten Voluntary Puerto Rican Groups Concerned with Better Social Adjustment and Welfare of Puerto Ricans in NYC." Master's Thesis, Columbia University, 1952, 8. *Puerto Ricans in the News*. Oct 1952, vol. 4 no 2. *Puerto Ricans in the News*. 1949. There were other similar middle-class efforts at defending the image of Puerto Ricans: Comité Professional para el Desarrollo Económico y Social de los Puertorriqueños. They seemed to run parallel to but had little contact with the labor- and left-led efforts with the same goals.

49 Quoted in James Dietz. *Economic History of Puerto Rico: Institutional Change and Capitalist Development*. Princeton, NJ: Princeton University Press, 1986, 238, from Juan Ángel Silén. *Historia de la nación puertorriqueña*. Río Piedras: Edil, 1973, 327.

50 "Madness in Washington." *The New York Times*, 2 March 1954, 24.

51 "Remarks by Mayor Wagner at Concert for Casita Maria, Hunter College Auditorium," 2 March 1954, Papers of Mayor Wagner, NYCMA Box 85 Folder 992.

52 Fernández, *Brown in the Windy City*, 87.

53 Whalen, *From Puerto Rico to Philadelphia*, 184. In a poll, less than half questioned knew Puerto Ricans were citizens: 61% said they should be excluded; 78% said that "Americans" did not willingly admit Puerto Ricans as neighbors.

54 Thomas, *Puerto Rican Citizen*, 209–14.

55 "Negro-Puerto Rican Unity Theme of Confab." *New York Amsterdam News*, 2 Feb. 1952, M3; "Sees Progress of Puerto Rican, Negroes in Unity." *New York Amsterdam News*, 23 Feb. 1952, 5; "Roosevelt Jr. hablara en la 5ta convención de las entidades hispanas." *El Diario de Nueva York*, 3 Feb. 1953. The following year the SAYB convention focused on the internal organization of the Puerto Rican community, with dozens of community, labor, human rights, and city leaders.

56 Community Council of Greater New York. United States Bureau of the Census. *Population of Puerto Rican Birth or Parentage*. New York, 1952.

57 "Guide to the Oscar García Rivera Papers," No date. Archives of the Puerto Rican Diaspora-CPRS; Wakefield, Dan. *Island in the City*. Boston: Houghton Mifflin, 1959, 265; "Felipe N. Torres, 96, Former Legislator and Retired Judge." *The New York Times*, 5 April 1994.

58 Puerto Ricans' sustained efforts to gain a political foothold in the city before the Second World War has been well documented; Thomas, *Puerto Rican Citizen*, 92–132; "City Fathers Love Puerto Ricans at the Polls." *New York Post*, 31 July 1953.

59 Marcantonio was first elected to Congress for East Harlem in 1934 and served with only one interruption from 1935 to 1949. In 1940 he ran for mayor on the ALP ticket and lost. A reelection campaign for Congress in 1954 also failed; he died later that year. See Gerald Meyer, *Vito Marcantonio: Radical Politician, 1902–1954.* Albany: SUNY Press, 1989.

60 "Great Meeting for Protest," flyer, 1950, American Labor Party Papers-RUSC Box 12; "Organize Harlem Council of Puerto Rican Affairs." *Daily Worker,* April 1952, clipping, Jesús Colón Papers-CPRS Box 36; Press release, 26 March 1952, American Labor Party Papers-RU Box 12.

61 "Puerto Ricans Get Campaign Warning." *The New York Times,* 17 Oct. 1949, 29.

62 *Ibid.* See also "Muñoz Marín's Foe Comes to Steer Puerto Rican Vote to Marcantonio." *The New York Times*, 27 Oct. 1949, 1; "Mayor Says Reds Rule City Relief, Aid Marcantonio." *The New York Times,* 1 Nov. 1949, 1. Marcantonio was sympathetic to Marxist ideology but was never a member of the Communist party.

63 Meléndez, Edgardo. "Vito Marcantonio, Puerto Rican Migration, and the 1949 Mayoral Election in New York City." *Centro Journal* 22, no. 2 (fall 2010): 198–234.

64 See Thomas, *Puerto Rican Citizen*, 139–41.

65 "91 Puerto Ricans Rounded Up Here." *The New York Times*, 9 March 1954, 1.

66 "F.B.I. Round-up Nets 10 Puerto Rican Reds." *The New York Times,* 21 Oct. 1954, 1; "12 Puerto Ricans Indicted in Plot." *The New York Times,* 30 Oct. 1954, 7; "Smith Act Is Stiffened." *The New York Times,* 14 July 1956, 6. Letter from Francisco Archilla to El Comite Puertorriqueño de Derechos Civiles en NY, 11 Feb. 1952, Jesús Colón Papers-CPRS Series VI Box 21 Folder 2.

67 For instance, on the candidacy of Emilio Carillo and Francisco Archilla in 1954, see "Candidates Battle for 14th AD Seat." *New York Amsterdam News*, 30 Jan. 1954.

68 ALP pamphlet, "Meet Two of Your Neighbors," 1953, Jesús Colón Papers-CPRS Series IV Box 14 Folder 1.

69 Luis Hernández, candidate for New York State Assembly, 14th Assembly District, Brooklyn, to "Dear Puerto Rican," Sept. 29, 1952, Jesús Colón Papers-CPRS Series IV Box 14 Folder 1. "Promete luchar por el derecho de los boricuas." *El Diario de Nueva York*, 5 Dec. 1955, 3.

2

"THE STRUGGLE FOR PUERTO RICAN RIGHTS," 1955–1965

Introduction

The Second World War created an extraordinary economic boom, producing new jobs, higher wages, and greater access to consumer goods for many in the United States. For Puerto Rican migrants, who had recently moved to the center of the global economy from the impoverished periphery, the boom's most important by-product was the chance to improve both the social status and the financial stability of the next generation. In New York City in the mid-1950s, Puerto Ricans expressed optimism that their families would be able to enjoy improved economic prospects, especially since it appeared that the worst of the anti-Puerto Rican discrimination of the earlier postwar years was waning.

Puerto Rican migrants in other cities also experienced the hopefulness of the era, particularly in Chicago, where employers often compared the new migrants favorably to the city's older Mexican migrant population. An expanding industrial economy also attracted growing numbers of Puerto Ricans to the many small and mid-sized cities of the Northeast and Mid-Atlantic, especially in New Jersey and Connecticut. Migration itself reflected these economic shifts—movement from the island had peaked during the manufacturing boom of the Korean War between 1950 and 1953, and then began to decline steadily (which by the early 1960s would produce a net return flow to the island). In spite of the leveling off of the migration numbers, the demographic results were still staggering: by 1960, 642,000 Puerto Ricans lived in New York, with another 250,000 spread around the rest of the U.S.[1]

The economic expansion lasted a long time, over two decades, despite short contractions. But for low-skill workers, particularly those whose economic vulnerability was compounded by other disadvantages—cultural foreignness, dark skin, inability to speak English—the new prosperity came with many caveats and evaporated sooner. By the early 1960s the plentiful industrial jobs that had attracted so many Puerto Rican migrants, and provided decent wages to many second-generation Puerto Ricans, began to disappear as factories closed, moved, or employed machines to replace human labor. Puerto Ricans in Chicago, New York, and other cities experienced the impact of this deindustrialization earlier than most groups (and later, in the 1970s, the damage from deindustrialization would hit Puerto Ricans hardest).

As the urban Northeast began turning into a rustbelt, city officials and policymakers had to contend with an expanding population of poor people— many of them former members of a stable working class whose incomes and job security were now steadily declining. During an era of liberal triumph defined by economic prosperity, the global dominance of U.S. capitalism, and the promises of expanding civil rights, urban poverty and the social unrest in urban ghettos became festering problems that highlighted liberals' ambivalence about state interventions to reduce the suffering of what many saw as unworthy minorities. The majority of Puerto Ricans in the U.S. lived in these declining urban areas in the 1960s. City officials tended to lump together the problems in their neighborhoods as an intractable system of "ghetto violence"—gang fights that led to physical confrontations with police or actual riots, complicated by increasing availability of illegal drugs and rapidly advancing urban blight— without acknowledging the degree to which abusive policing played a primary, instigating role.

During the early years of waning economic opportunity, Puerto Ricans were able to find some hope for security and mobility through labor union struggles, campaigns to expand educational opportunities, and the growth of anti-poverty programs. Activists argued that working class communities could be thriving centers if only they could have greater access to better wages and housing conditions. An experienced and multi-generational leadership built new organizations in this period, creating strong alliances with mainstream liberal as well as Black civil rights groups and building momentum toward mass mobilization of grass-roots support. At the same time, more marginalized and militant elements of communities fought back directly against repressive policing and urban renewal polices that produced improved public housing while destroying and displacing entire neighborhoods.

Electoral Politics: From Left to Liberal Alliances

In the mid-1950s long-time community activist and leftist Jesús Colón had written an internal report for the New York Communist party organization titled "The Growing Importance of the Puerto Rican Minority in New York City," which reflected on the status, achievements, and struggles of Puerto Rican communities in New York and in the U.S. in general. With prescient insight, Colón insisted that Puerto Rican efforts would require a fuller integration with what he saw as a politics of progressive alliance building:

> The struggle for Puerto Rican rights, for Puerto Rican representation cannot be only a task for the Puerto Rican people. While giving close attention to the development of these struggles in Puerto Rican areas, we must strive to make links with the labor movement and other democratic forces for the purpose of getting action by state, city, and political party officials.[2]

What shape these alliances would take—and their effectiveness in meeting the needs of the community—remained to be seen.

Between the mid-1950s and the mid-1960s, Puerto Ricans in New York City made important advances in electoral politics, first as voters with a growing demographic impact and then via a handful of successful candidates for city and state office. This happened in the context of a shift away from leftist politics, and was accomplished through the leadership of diverse groups of Puerto Ricans, including some members of the old Left but increasingly led by a growing young middle class within the community, a good part of whom had been born in New York City or grew up there. Even as politics leaned towards the center during the Cold War, almost any political aspirant of Puerto Rican descent felt the need to address the critical, everyday needs of so many in community and advocate for the rights to equality that so many were denied.

By 1955, the center of gravity of New York Puerto Rican communities' politics had shifted back to the Democratic party after nearly two decades of considerable support for progressive Republicans and the left-leaning American Labor Party (ALP). Although some of the community's prominent leftists continued to support the ALP, the combined impact of Marcantonio's death and the nationalist attack on Congress, both in 1954, drew many Puerto Ricans towards the Democratic party, which seemed like a stronger and more secure source of support during the charged years of the Cold War. During this decade, Puerto Ricans gained substantial visibility in both the major parties. When the liberal Republican Nelson Rockefeller campaigned for governor of New York in 1958, his first campaign-season meeting with his opponent, incumbent Democratic Governor Averell Harriman, took place at the tenth anniversary celebration of the establishment of the Puerto Rican Department of Labor's Migration Division offices in New York City. The front page of the *New York Times* featured a photograph of the two smiling candidates flanking Puerto Rico's Governor Muñoz Marín, and a lead paragraph asserting that the candidates "were brought together by the lure of the state's growing Puerto Rican population."[3]

Puerto Rican political leaders in the mid-1950s had a two-pronged strategy for achieving stronger representation, which involved the continued demand that elected officials respond to the community's needs—especially the perennial problems with employment, housing, and education—and also creating openings for Puerto Rican candidates. In 1952, Puerto Ricans in the Bronx managed to elect state assembly representative Felipe Torres, who ran on the Democratic ticket. Torres was only the second Puerto Rican to serve in the state assembly; Oscar García Rivera, the first Puerto Rican elected to any office in the United States, had served from 1938–40. The third was José Ramos López, a staunchly pro-union progressive who won a seat in the state assembly, representing East Harlem, in 1958. (Ramos López became a judge in the New York State Supreme Court in 1978.)[4]

Electoral victories would remain a rarity until the mid-1960s in New York, and the near-absence of Puerto Ricans in elected and appointed positions was a source of major frustration for all sectors in the community. But the consensus about pushing for representation was strong during the 1950s. In a letter to Mayor Wagner in 1956, the Puerto Rican National Merchants United, with 4,000 members, complained of the "inadequate political recognition" given to the Puerto Rican community in New York City:

> Our sons and daughters have served and are serving in the armed forces and have given their lives and blood in defense of our country. We are proud to say that there were more Puerto Rican casualties in Korea, proportionally, than from any other state.[5]

This sort of effort reflected Puerto Ricans' impatience with what had proved to be a slow process of incorporation. Facing continual pressure by Puerto Rican leaders, Mayor Wagner named Manuel Gómez a municipal magistrate in 1957. Gómez was the first Puerto Rican appointed official in New York City, and became known as the housing court magistrate most sympathetic to tenants.[6]

Despite many attempts, with candidates backed by many different parties and coalitions—Democrat, Republican, Liberal Party, ALP, independent, and even a short lived Spanish American Party—Puerto Ricans failed to win a seat on New York's city council until 1966. Lingering suspicion of their longtime leftism was part of what complicated Puerto Ricans' bids for political power up through the end of the 1950s—although when journalist José Lumen Román ran as an anti-communist to represent East Harlem on the city council in 1957, he also failed. In 1963, Gilbert Gerena Valentín and other representatives from the Congreso de los Pueblos met with Mayor Wagner to remind him that Puerto Ricans formed 12% of Manhattan's population and still had not a single representative on the city council. They also complained of constant problems with city agencies including the police (particularly their low intensity harassment of Puerto Rican clubs) and the schools (Puerto Ricans had the highest dropout rates in the city). The Congreso wanted support for a city council member, a Board of Education member, and meetings with various commissioners to discuss the community's complaints.[7]

During the 1950s, when the decline of the ALP, fears about the Smith Act, and a resurgent Democratic party made for a volatile period of political realignment in New York's Puerto Rican communities, the single most unifying issue among Puerto Rican leaders was voter registration. Leaders of the ALP, Democratic party, Communist party, and independents supported efforts by the Migration Division to carry out mass registration drives, united in their new push for successful Puerto Rican candidates and cross-ethnic alliances; Puerto Rican candidates could not win without registered Puerto Rican voters. At a 1956 citywide meeting of Puerto Rican community leaders, one of the top agenda items was the registration of Spanish-speaking voters. Some optimists in the group thought that, with the upcoming presidential election, 100,000 new Spanish-speaking voters could be registered in New York City. Joseph Montserratt, head of the Migration Division, acknowledged that in recent previous elections there were no more than 40,000 registered Puerto Rican voters, so this goal might be too ambitious. In the end, the very successful 1956 voter registration drive yielded about 50,000 new registrants, some of whom were non-Puerto Rican Latinos who lived in Puerto Rican communities.[8]

A common explanation for low voter registration in the early 1950s, both within and outside Puerto Rican communities, was that Puerto Rican voters were "apathetic." Jesús Colón and other left-leaning leaders argued that low voter registration among Puerto Ricans had little to do with "apathy" and a lot to do with the English-only literacy test for voting. A New York state election law passed in 1921 mandated that a literacy test be given to all potential voters who could not provide a diploma to prove that they had attended an elementary school in which English was the primary language of instruction; the target of this law was recent immigrants from eastern and southern Europe, an immigration stream that was soon blocked almost entirely by a series of laws passed during the 1920s. The English literacy test also excluded many new Puerto Rican voters, who had begun arriving in New York in large numbers just as the European immigration was shut down. Throughout the 1930s and 1940s, many Puerto Ricans reported that their Puerto Rican diplomas were rejected by officials at the polls, even though they were from schools where English was the primary instructional language.

In the late 1950s, Puerto Rican leaders began to systematically challenge the laws that prevented so many of their compatriots from voting. The first challenge to New York's literacy test for voting was mounted in 1958 by a Puerto Rican grocer, José Camacho, who had lived in the Bronx for 20 years but had been unable to register to vote because he was not literate in English. When a Bronx court denied Camacho's petition to take the literacy test in Spanish, his lawyer argued that Mr. Camacho was being denied a right of citizenship due to a "characteristic of his racial background"—meaning the state law violated the 14th and 15th Amendments of the Constitution, as well as the 1948 United Nations Universal Declaration on Human Rights. While the New York

Court of Appeals upheld the literacy law in 1959, with Republican support for the status quo, the case triggered an investigation by the U.S. Civil Rights Commission. Nevertheless, the law remained in place until outlawed by the 1965 Voting Rights Act. After a legal challenge by New York State that went to the Supreme Court in 1966, the Court upheld the explicit protection that the Voting Rights Act provided for Puerto Ricans. After 1965, Puerto Ricans (and other citizens) not literate in English could register to vote by showing evidence of having completed at least six years of schooling.[9]

Meanwhile, the presidential election of 1960, in which the young Democratic Senator John F. Kennedy ran against the Republican then-Vice President Richard Nixon, galvanized Puerto Rican leaders and voters to achieve unprecedented gains in voting registration and participation. The Migration Division headed a nationwide campaign, with organizing bases not just in New York but also in Philadelphia, Camden, Trenton, Boston, Miami, Cleveland, Detroit, Milwaukee, San Francisco, and Los Angeles—a geographic range that illustrates the remarkable spread of Puerto Rican communities by 1960. New York was not the only state that required voters to be literate in English; Connecticut, Massachusetts, and California all had similar laws, and all of them would be overturned in 1965 by the Voting Rights Act. Community volunteers worked alongside Migration Division staff and representatives from the Spanish-language media, local community groups, and political organizations—mostly Democratic but some Republican—to register voters. The outcome in New York was dramatic: over 250,000 Puerto Rican voters were registered by November, an estimated increase of about 150,000 registered voters. While this was not a high proportion of the voting-age population among Puerto Ricans, it was much higher than expected, given the historically low rates of registration resulting in part from the English-only voting law.[10]

The Republican party was also working hard for the first time, according to New York's Republican Puerto Rican campaign committee chair, to win Puerto Rican voters in the lead-up to the 1960 presidential election. With a popular Republican governor, New York State was not a guaranteed win for the Democratic party, and Puerto Ricans comprised a growing, young electoral force that could provide a swing vote. In addition to the Republican party's participation in voter registration drives, Rockefeller made two strategic appointments of Puerto Ricans after his election in 1958, an assistant Attorney General and assistant counsel to the state Division of Housing. Despite these efforts, the Republicans could do little to dampen the enthusiastic support of Puerto Ricans for the "Viva Kennedy" campaign in 1960. According to analysts of the "minority" vote in that election, Puerto Ricans voted overwhelmingly for Kennedy and helped bridge the 2.5 percentage points that gave the Democrats their victory in New York State.[11] Among those working on the Viva Kennedy campaign was a young Puerto Rican lawyer named Herman Badillo, who in 1970 would become the first Puerto Rican elected to the U.S. Congress.[12]

The 1960 election year marked a turning point for Puerto Rican voters and would-be candidates in local New York races, where the successful voter registration drive and the attention of both major parties during the campaign demonstrated the potential of Puerto Ricans' increasing political engagement. That year, Manhattan's East Harlem assembly district reelected Democrat José Ramos López to the state assembly, only the third Puerto Rican elected to state office. During the mayoral race the following year, when Puerto Rican voters supported Mayor Robert Wagner's reelection at rates higher than other Democrats in the city, the *New York Times* noted "In Harlem, Negroes and Puerto Ricans are beginning to demand a larger share of Democratic party control."[13]

Two years later, two more Puerto Rican Democratic candidates were elected to the state assembly: Carlos M. Ríos, representing East Harlem, and former state assembly representative Felipe Torres's son Frank Torres, representing the South Bronx. In 1962, Herman Badillo was appointed by Mayor Wagner as commissioner of the newly created Bureau of Relocation, to manage the impact of public housing and redevelopment in New York City. With this appointment, Badillo at age 33 became the youngest of the city commissioners at the time, and he was also the first Puerto Rican appointee at this level of government. The following year, longtime community leader and former head of the Spanish-American Youth Bureau, Ruperto Ruiz, became the first Republican Puerto Rican offered a high-level appointment, recommended by Governor Rockefeller to serve on the State Commission for Human Rights.[14] Powerful members of both political parties in New York were beginning to recognize the value of offering Puerto Ricans a larger share of political influence, partially driven by the visibility of the "Viva Kennedy" campaign that was strongly supported by Puerto Rican communities in the 1960 presidential election.[15]

The real watershed years for Puerto Ricans' gaining a foothold in New York politics came in the mid-1960s.[16] Although Gerena Valentín made a failed run for an at-large seat on the city council in 1965, on the heels of the Voting Rights Act that he worked to support, many other Puerto Ricans ran successful campaigns. Herman Badillo was elected Bronx borough president in 1965, a step that would move him first towards a seat in the United States Congress. Around the same time, Democratic representatives from East Harlem (José Ramos López, first elected in 1958), Brooklyn (Gilberto Ramírez, who would later, in the 1970s, become a state Supreme Court judge), and the Bronx (Robert García and Salvador Almeida) were elected (or, in the case of Ramírez, reelected) to represent their heavily Puerto Rican districts in the State Assembly, while Carlos M. Ríos was elected to an at-large city council seat.[17]

Aside from demonstrating an emerging force of a Puerto Rican electorate, these mid-1960s victories also showed that the Republican Party had not yet established an effective "Hispanic strategy" (a term that would be used by Republicans during Nixon's 1972 campaign) among Puerto Rican voters in New York. During the presidential race of the previous year, 1964, the Hispanic

Division of the Democratic National Committee reported that more than 85% of Puerto Ricans in the city said they planned to vote for Democrat Lyndon Johnson instead of his Republic rival, Barry Goldwater. The Republican Party had established its own Hispanic Division, and appointed a former member of San Juan Municipal Assembly, Luis Esteban Julia, to head up its efforts to attract more Hispanic voters in 1964. As both parties knew from previous election cycles, especially the 1960 presidential election, the impact of state- and local-level political relationships was key to shifting voters' allegiance—so some observers doubted the wisdom of Republicans' assigning an island-based politician to the task. Adding to Republicans' optimism about its Hispanic Division during the 1964 election was the fact that the Republican candidate for mayor in Philadelphia had won two majority-Puerto Rican districts in the previous year's campaign. To repay Philadelphia's Puerto Rican voters for their allegiance, the Republican party supported a Puerto Rican, Joseph Hernández, as a candidate for the Pennsylvania state legislature.[18]

Another mechanism by which Democrats and Republicans vied for the allegiance of Puerto Rican voters in the 1960s was through the redrawing of the lines that defined voting districts, a process known as redistricting. The drawing of districts frequently had a direct impact on the outcome of elections, since a high number of voters registered as either Republican or Democratic in a given district tended to produce predictable outcomes. The racial makeup of a district added another layer of predictability: because African Americans and Puerto Ricans overwhelmingly voted for Democrats, a district that included a plurality or majority of those voters would likely support Democratic candidates. Controlling the makeup of districts, in terms of party affiliation or racial identification, became a strategic tool of the major parties, especially during years of demographic change in many American cities.

In 1962, New York's Republican-dominated legislature imposed a redistricting plan for the state's Congressional districts that left intact the district that included all of Harlem and its heavily Democratic majority of African American and Puerto Rican voters. While this move was widely understood to be motivated by Republicans' desire to contain the impact of Black and Puerto Rican voters, to keep them from diluting and possibly disrupting the neighboring "silk stocking" Upper East Side district that reliably voted for Republicans, the reaction by Democrats was divided. A group of white Manhattan Democrats, supported by the county party organization, filed a lawsuit alleging racial discrimination in the redrawing of district lines, calling it unconstitutional; whether or not they cared about the alleged racial discrimination, the plaintiffs were certainly motivated by the goal of blocking Republicans' protection of a key district. On the other hand, Harlem Democrats opposed the lawsuit, saying that "virtually all Negro and Puerto Rican officeholders are elected from this district" and it should be left intact, according to the Republican plan. A group of Puerto Rican and African American Republicans from the Harlem district mounted a lawsuit to counter the original

Democratic suit, explaining that "Any attempt to reapportion the Negro-Puerto Rican vote through the four Congressional districts in New York County would result in the loss of the very representation that these groups now have."[19]

Puerto Rican candidates' increasing momentum in the early 1960s in New York City, together with the ongoing debates about voter registration and the impact of redistricting (magnified immeasurably by the campaigns for African American voting rights in the South in the early 1960s), showed how crucial electoral politics would be for Puerto Ricans' empowerment in that decade. Yet, as important as these efforts were and would continue to be, few of the political leaders in the Puerto Rican community could have predicted the degree to which activism beyond the formal political arena—the grassroots community organizations and storefront operations that were popping up all over ghetto neighborhoods by the mid-1960s—would shape the struggle for rights and define the activism that would surge through so many Puerto Rican communities by 1970.

Police Abuse and Community Response

Gains in participation in the formal political arena in the late 1950s and early 1960s certainly improved many Puerto Ricans' sense of optimism about their empowerment and recognition in New York City. On the flip side, the long-standing problem of police abuse in Puerto Rican neighborhoods seemed to be intensifying throughout the 1950s and into the next decade, threatening to undermine the social gains Puerto Ricans were making. Especially for Puerto Rican youth, the more visible members of the community who spent more time socializing in the street, the problematic relationship with police became a defining aspect of life in that era. While this tension would mark relations between youth and police in Puerto Rican communities in cities around the country by the 1960s, the complex dynamics of the relationship in New York City in the 1950s merits a detailed discussion.

Low intensity conflict with police and abuse by the police had been a constant in the poor neighborhoods of New York, in one form or another, since the 19th century. It was a particularly intractable problem in African American and Puerto Rican neighborhoods through the early decades of the 20th century. Early Puerto Rican migrants interviewed about their lives in New York noted problems with police as early as the 1920s. As one pre-war migrant, Félix Loperana, put it, "the police were the first who discriminated against us."[20] The desire to escape this tense atmosphere of police hostility, surveillance, and inter-ethnic tension was often the reason that Puerto Ricans cited as motivation to move "up" and out of the communities where they had first settled.

Every year notable cases of abuse against Puerto Ricans were highlighted in the press, and throughout the 1950s, about one case per year involved the killing of a Puerto Rican—almost always a young man—by police. These incidents set off increasingly vociferous protests at police precincts or City Hall and even complaints to Puerto Rico's governor Muñoz Marín. Initially, because of the relative lack of organization of the tens of thousands of recent migrants in New York, it was usually the networks of the old left that responded to these attacks, most often the American Labor Party, the Communist party, and even some of the more militant unions. Sometimes the NAACP included Puerto Ricans in its protests over police brutality—since this was a problem with which New York's Black residents had much experience to share.[21] Activist and writer Jesús Colón submitted to city officials a "Report on Police Brutality against the Negro and Puerto Rican People," in which he protested the tendency by police to stereotype thieves and drug addicts with "Latin or Negro" features. Even Mayor Impellitteri's Committee on Puerto Rican Affairs included police abuse in its February 1953 report, although it called only for the police department to monitor itself in cases of abuse.[22]

A few years into the 1950s, Puerto Rican leaders and community residents had developed familiar patterns of protest and legal challenges to police abuse. A particularly well-documented case in 1953 was that of Henry Rivera, a young Puerto Rican who charged that police detained and beat him at a Harlem subway station and then again at the station house, where he lost consciousness and was refused medical help. Rivera's family hired a lawyer, a member of Mayor Impellitteri's Committee on Puerto Rican Affairs, who demanded an investigation and pressed charges against the police.[23]

Lawsuits were often ineffective, though, since it was not uncommon for judges to express openly racist and nativist sentiments in decisions involving Puerto Rican defendants. For example, Judge Abner Surpless of the Brooklyn Felony court made comments like "it's just too bad these people are citizens of the United States"—after which a committee established by members of the ALP and other leftist organizations demanded the judge's ousting.[24] Puerto Rican defendants who were poor or spoke little English found it especially hard to navigate the criminal justice system. In an unpublished essay, Jesús Colón detailed the case of two youths who were arrested in 1955 for a rape in Central Park. They spent 159 days in prison before the flaws in their indictment were exposed in a series of articles by the *New York Post*. In an editorial about the controversy, the *Post* asserted that the judge in the case had shown "clear bias against the defendants. Among other things, he had observed from the bench—before the defense even had a chance to present its case—that they (the defendants) ought to be sent back to Puerto Rico."[25]

The election of Mayor Wagner in 1955 marked a change in police-community relations, as Wagner developed closer relations with Puerto Rican leaders, appointed more Puerto Rican officials, and made promises to pressure police to avoid abuses and violence. Police commissioners increased their recruiting of Puerto Rican and Spanish-speaking officers, while training others in basic Spanish with the expectation that better communication and cultural understanding could reduce conflicts in the streets.[26] For some analysts, while the Spanish language training held the promise of abuse-avoidance, it also served more general law enforcement goals in that it helped assure police their questions and instructions were understood. Small gestures could mean the difference between conflict and negotiation, and settlement houses began to train police in the East Harlem and West Side ghettos in Spanish, emphasizing contact with Puerto Rican youth in order to challenge police stereotypes and ameliorate distrust.[27]

These efforts, some more successful than others, at least responded to community pressures for redress, and the beginnings of public acknowledgement helped too. However, the longstanding tension in relations between police and youth in Puerto Rican neighborhoods in New York and other cities continued to fester. When New York Puerto Rican neighborhoods first expanded rapidly in the late 1940s and early 1950s, police sometimes played a protective role when existing neighborhood youth gangs preyed on recently arrived Puerto Ricans. The Black and Spanish-language newspapers, along with the Communist *Daily Worker*, were often the only papers that reported these confrontations that led to the beatings or arrests of young Puerto Ricans. On the other hand, even as they claimed an interest in protecting Puerto Rican youth from established gangs, police were known to rigidly enforce arbitrary rules of social order, including restricting the territory of ethnic and racial groups of youth to "their" neighborhoods. Police were quick to use physical force to disperse people congregating on stoops and street corners, and racial slurs were a standard of police vocabulary. Because youth spent more time than adults hanging out on the street, they were disproportionately subjected to these everyday abuses. On the other hand, not all youth and their parents saw relations with police as negative, and numerous memoirs of life in East Harlem represented the role of police as a kind of tough-love parenting, especially appreciated by parents themselves.[28]

Another mostly positive element of police presence in Puerto Rican communities related to their efforts at ending violence among turf-protecting youth gangs and encouraging gangs to transition to "straight" activities. These negotiations were the result of intense collaboration between police and social workers, settlement houses, parish priests, and other community activists during the mid- to late-1950s. Such intervention was partly inspired by an event in Brooklyn, when a delegation of Italian, Polish, Puerto Rican, and Jewish residents demanded police action against the Italian Comanches gang, who severely beat a young Puerto Rican man in Williamsburg and killed three Black youth in McCarren Park. An intervention strategy developed a few years later aimed to force the gangs into producing a truce after their respective turfs were locked down by police. This happened, for example, in August 1956 in the West Side, where a series of confrontations (some of them deadly) between Sportsmen, Dragons and Enchanters—all multi-ethnic gangs that included Puerto Rican, Jewish, and African American youth—led to interventions by a community coalition. Afterwards at least one of the gangs "went social," renouncing violence and creating a new culture focused on social events and community action. Not infrequently, though, Puerto Rican and other youth involved in gang fights simply ended up facing arrest and prison time, especially when conflicts resulted in major injuries or fatalities.[29]

The vilification of Puerto Rican youth and their gangs was popularized in *West Side Story*, the 1957 Broadway musical written as a love story but known just as much for its representation of gang conflict between the Puerto Rican "Sharks" and the white "Jets." The play resonated with audiences, especially in urban areas, in part because the problem of gangs and "juvenile delinquency" more generally had become a growing preoccupation during the 1950s, even beyond the neighborhoods they most affected. Across the country, the rate of juvenile court appearances by children aged ten to 17 had nearly doubled between 1948 and 1957. Despite evidence to the contrary, Puerto Rican youth (especially boys) were viewed by many, both inside and outside their communities, as susceptible to a life of crime.[30]

Even the Spanish language newspaper *El Diario* began to run stories about "juvenile gangsters" and their distraught parents in New York's Puerto Rican communities. An infamous crime in the late summer of 1959 involved a 17-year old Puerto Rican gang member named Salvador Agrón, who killed two "straight" boys in a West Side park, apparently for no reason, and came to be known as "the Capeman" because he was wearing a cape at the time of the murders. In the aftermath, amid the many recriminations against Puerto Ricans and their moral deficits, a judge in Brooklyn, Samuel Liebowitz, demanded that Mayor Wagner discourage Puerto Ricans from migrating to the city, arguing this would be the most effective step the city could take to turn back the tide of juvenile crime in the next decade. Demagogues like Liebowitz, feeding white New Yorkers' racist assumptions about urban social change, asserted that law enforcement—police and courts—needed elected officials to help solve the "youth problem."[31]

Not quite two weeks after the Capeman incident, a similarly dramatic murder case rocked the city of Chicago. Two Puerto Rican men, driving past a neighborhood tavern in a corner of Chicago's multiethnic Northwest Side, shot and killed an Italian American man standing on the sidewalk in front of the bar. The perpetrators did not know the victim; they claimed that they had set out that evening intending to merely to "shoot some windows out of some Dago joints," impelled by their resentment of frequent violence against Puerto Ricans by the neighborhood's older Italian American and Polish American residents. The murder of Guido Garro did not generate the same intensity of fear and anxiety that the Capeman murders produced, since it did not involve teenagers or gangs. However, the Chicago murder raised the same worrisome questions about violent responses to ethnic succession in the postwar city—and the same worries that members of the newer, poorer, darker ethnic group would prove to be more dangerous than their predecessors in these battleground working class neighborhoods.[32]

Even if the Garro murder did not become as infamous as the Capeman incident in New York, the Chicago story and its apparent morals were publicized across the U.S. by a *Saturday Evening Post* article, "Crime Without Reason," that appeared six months after the shooters were sentenced in 1960. Written by a journalist with a national reputation, John Martin, the article drew attention to the tensions that marked the Puerto Rican migration not just to Chicago but also to New York and Philadelphia. "History will relate whether the white people in Chicago and other American cities can reach an accommodation with today's newcomers, as they did with earlier immigrants who differed from todays in the color of their skin," wrote the author. Martin took the long view of the migration and its impact on urban social relations; and while highlighting the senselessness of the crime itself, he also pointed to the many-layered psychological impact of prejudice as one of the factors in the shooters' act: "Behind their crime lay a thousand injuries and insults to their people," he wrote.[33]

Sometimes the problems with law enforcement had to do with police inaction in the face of attacks on the rights of Puerto Ricans. In 1957 in Copiague, Long Island, a Puerto Rican family was forced to move after local whites threatened to burn down their house. The father of the family was a combat veteran of the Korean War living on a pension because of his injuries, and the police did nothing to help him and his family. Up through the early 1950s, public protests against the treatment of Puerto Ricans by police were mounted primarily by members of the left—for instance, a report by leaders of the Spanish Speaking section of the Communist party recorded about one killing by police each year, plus daily occurrence of beatings and dozens "who barely escaped with their lives." By the mid-1950s, though, violence against Puerto Ricans became an important issue debated in mainstream political circles including the Migration Division and Democratic party politicians.[34]

A major turning point was the 1957 killing of Bernabe Nuñez, a veteran from the Puerto Rico-based 65th Infantry Regiment. Nuñez was beaten to death at a bar in Brooklyn, reportedly for speaking Spanish in public. In response to this crime, Puerto Rican and Spanish-speaking leaders staged a massive rally in Central Park where thousands paid tribute to the service of Puerto Rican veterans. Organizer Tony Méndez, a Cuban American leader of the Hispanic community in the Democratic party, explained, "today we show the nation and New York that we . . . are good citizens who have shed our blood for this country in defense of the ideals of democracy." The mass for Bernabe at La Milagrosa church in Spanish Harlem drew a crowd of 7,000.[35]

The rate of police assaults improved by about 1960, but a few years later, in 1963, a surge in killings and beatings of Puerto Ricans by police led to a new round of protests. The city's Commission on Human Rights was prompted to pressure the police, especially after the killing of 18-year-old Francisco Rodríguez in February 1964 led to massive protests in East Harlem. Rodríguez, who was not a gang member (he had been named "boy of the year" by the local Boy's Club) was shot in the head by an off-duty officer when running from a knife fight. In a *New York Times* interview, community leader Gilberto Gerena Valentín, who at the time was a member of the city's Commission on Human Rights, accused the police of behaving "like they were running a plantation." The experience of Puerto Rican youth with the police mirrored that of African Americans, and a fatal shooting of a young Black man in Harlem the same year as Rodríguez's killing sparked a riot. "During the last year four killings of Puerto Ricans by the police under questionable circumstances have brought police-community relations in the Puerto Rican community to a low ebb," noted Migration Division officials in June 1964.[36]

One result of this turmoil was the creation of "Operation Friend," an effort in the mid-1960s to reduce tensions between police and the Puerto Rican community on Manhattan's West Side. One of the program's planners was Octavio Álvarez, a veteran of the Second World War, who had joined the police force in the 1950s. Operation Friend was successful at opening communication between police commanders and Puerto Rican community leaders and at producing more consistent communication with community members. Other innovations to reduce police bias included programs that sent officers on educational trips to the island, along with youth exchanges hosted by officers and organized by community leaders, Migration Division directors, and settlement house workers.[37] Despite these efforts, in East Harlem and in other Puerto Rican communities in New York, reports of beatings, arrests and killings continued, and so did the protests. The legalization of "no-knock" warrants and stop-and-frisk policies by a Republican State Assembly in 1965 created the potential for further problems.[38] Nothing would alter relations with the police as much as the wave of riots and demonstrations in majority Black and Puerto Rican neighborhoods later in the 1960s.[39]

Community Building: Community Action and Anti-poverty Organizations

In the mid-1950s, amid the urgent efforts by Puerto Rican and other Spanish-speaking leaders to improve the reputation of Puerto Ricans in New York during the era of mass migration from the island, an organization of the city's Spanish-speaking elite had instituted a "Hispanic Parade" in New York. The celebration of Hispanic culture was modeled after the parades and festivals the Irish and Italian communities had established in the city decades earlier. The goal of the event was to emphasize cultural cohesion and respectability. After the Hispanic Parade's second year, a faction of Puerto Rican community leaders, including Gilberto Gerena Valentín and other representatives of the Congreso de los Pueblos, accused the organizers of making the event "exclusionary" and "elitist." They demanded that the parade be renamed the Puerto Rican Parade in order to better reflect the majority identity of the city's Spanish speakers. They wanted the parade to empower Puerto Ricans to challenge the kind of treatment that the *Saturday Evening Post* journalist John Martin would later publicize as "a thousand injuries and insults," rather than serving as simply a distraction from those injuries and insults. The Puerto Rican Day Parade quickly became a major annual event that brought together tens of thousands of New York Puerto Ricans every June to celebrate a common heritage and traditions. Within a few years, the parade also become a model for similar celebrations of unity and pride in the growing Puerto Rican communities in Philadelphia, Chicago, Camden, and Hartford.

After the previous decade had ended with the drama of the Capeman murder and a wave of media hype about Puerto Ricans' dangerousness and criminality, a new generation of young Puerto Rican leaders in New York pushed to establish stronger support networks for their communities. Surveying the many unmet needs of first- and second-generation Puerto Rican families, and the continuing climate of prejudice that defined their experiences in the workplace, in schools, and in their neighborhoods, leaders with a variety of backgrounds—in labor and community organizing, in social work, and the law—and a range of political affiliations, from liberal to far left, began to imagine new possibilities for Puerto Ricans' inclusion in the life of the city. Some worked to expand access to the city's growing social service sector, building on or adapting organizations, like settlement houses, that had been founded in an earlier era or for different purposes or groups. Other leaders sought to develop new organizations from scratch, organizations whose missions were specific to the needs of Puerto Ricans and built on a community-based, participatory model. All this effort and innovation would produce, over the next decade, an enormous wave of social and political connection within and across Puerto Rican communities. Then, with the combined impact of new federal support provided by War on Poverty programs in the mid-1960s, and the explosion of social protest, Puerto Ricans would generate a new force of social change in their communities, with deep roots in social service networks and grassroots organizing.

Although sometimes accused of obstructing or coopting the efforts of more left-leaning organizations in Puerto Rican communities during the 1960s, the Migration Division—with offices in New York, Chicago, Philadelphia, Camden, and Hartford—remained one of the central hubs of networking and support for most organizing efforts in the community. Together with the Congreso de Los Pueblos, led by Gilberto Gerena Valentín, the New York office of the Migration Division worked with dozens of other organizations in the community of various types, helping to build their reformist and organizational capacity; Migration Division offices in other cities engaged in similar collaborations. In addition to providing needed services to Puerto Ricans who were struggling to find housing or employment, Migration Division staff generated important connections to a growing network of social workers and other social service professionals whose primary client population was Puerto Rican.

Because an increasing number of these professionals in the 1960s were Puerto Rican themselves, the dynamic within the social service sector began to shift. Now, rather than outsiders solving the problems of a needy migrant population, it was young Puerto Rican professionals working with members of their own communities to address the problems of poverty and marginalization Puerto Ricans faced. Although the number of Puerto Ricans attending college was still very small in 1960, many of the second-generation youth who had earned bachelor's and master's degrees began to enter the social service sector as professionals and managers. Many of them were determined to serve their growing community not just by rising through the ranks of existing agencies, but by starting their own organizations in order to fill gaps in the provision of services and to create more effective bridges to their communities. For instance, a young social worker named Agustín González left a job at Catholic Charities in New York City and with a group of Puerto Rican social workers founded the Puerto Rican Family Institute in 1960, which provided general casework and advocacy but also offered training in parenting skills and arranged for foster care when necessary. González believed that, despite the support provided by the Migration Division offices, there was a need for more services to help "preserve migrant families" and help care for the children of those families, especially during their most stressful first few years in the city.[40]

Young Puerto Rican leaders like González were beginning to develop a variety of creative models for leadership and community organizing, beyond simply the provision of social services. One of these was the Hispanic Young Adult Association (HYAA), later renamed the Puerto Rican Forum, based on the vision of about 20 ambitious, young, and well-educated Puerto Ricans. The founding group included many who would become lifelong leaders of their communities—academics, judges, and directors of other organizations—including Antonia Pantoja, Frank Bonilla, Maria Canino, John Carro, and others. The HYAA and the Forum were modeled on the NAACP and the American Jewish Committee, both well-established civil rights organizations whose leadership provided mentoring to their young Puerto Rican counterparts. The Migration Division also provided early support, as did New York's Committee on Inter-Group Relations, of which some of the Forum's founders were members.[41]

Antonia Pantoja later described the Puerto Rican Forum as a "think tank" that would launch more focused campaigns and organizations. While so many other organizations and social scientific studies of Puerto Ricans in that era focused on problems and defects, Antonia Pantoja and her collaborators sought to capture the hopefulness and striving of Puerto Ricans in the U.S. Indeed, within several years, Forum members had created two organizations that would have an enormous impact on Puerto Rican communities around the country. The Puerto Rican Association of Community Affairs (PRACA), founded in 1956, sought to solidify a network of socially engaged young Puerto Ricans interested in leadership, primarily in New York. The second organization that emerged from the Forum was the one that would stand as the most enduring, and the one with the broadest reach: Aspira, from the Spanish verb *aspirar*, "to aspire," was founded in 1961 to help Puerto Rican students graduate from high school and college. By 1970, there were scores of Aspira chapters in over a dozen cities around the country. [42]

Mobilization for Youth (MFY) was another youth-oriented organization that became an important incubator of Puerto Rican leadership in the 1960s, although it was not founded by Puerto Ricans or to serve the Puerto Rican population in particular. MFY, established in 1962 in New York City's Lower East Side, began as a program to address juvenile delinquency, but quickly expanded to spearhead community organizing—a shift due, in part, to the inclusion of more Puerto Rican community members in its leadership. Ted Vélez, a City College graduate who had worked with Pantoja at East Harlem's Union Settlement in the mid-1950s, took a job at MFY in the early 1960s and helped move the organization in the direction of broad-based activism. (Vélez also helped found the East Harlem Tenants Council in 1962.) An analogous organization based in Harlem, known as HARYOU-ACT (Harlem Youth Opportunities Unlimited, which merged in 1964 with a group called Associated Community Teams) operated the largest and most visible programs for poor youth in New York City in the early 1960s. Founded in 1962 by psychologist, scholar, and activist Dr. Kenneth Clark, HARYOU-ACT sought to offer young people in Harlem alternatives to juvenile delinquency and gang activity, and attracted a new cadre of Puerto Rican social workers and other social service professionals.[43] Together, these organizations encouraged youth and aspiring leaders in marginalized communities to build a new agenda to challenge that marginalization.

By the mid-1960s, community organizers had begun to merge the growing leadership energy "from below" with the expertise of social service professionals. At the same time, serendipitously, the Johnson administration initiated a "War on Poverty" in the U.S., motivated by the increasingly obvious need to augment the country's new civil rights protections with economic opportunity; Johnson signed the Civil Rights Act in July 1964, and the Economic Opportunity Act six weeks later. Through the federal Office of Economic Opportunity (OEO), social programs that formerly had been funded privately or at the local or state level could now compete for substantial federal support. The OEO also generated enormous motivation to start new programs and organizations. All this meant that the entire landscape of social service work in urban settings changed quite suddenly. New York officials set up a Council against Poverty in May 1965, an expansion and reorganization of the Mayor's Council against Poverty, which had previously only distributed city funds, to manage the distribution of new federal grants.[44]

In cities across the U.S., what first seemed to be a windfall of federal cash (referred to colloquially as both "poverty funds" and "anti-poverty funds") landing in the hands of community leaders and social service professionals turned out to be a small pie divided into too many pieces. African American and Puerto Rican leaders, already accustomed to competing with one another for limited resources in the impoverished urban communities in which many of them lived, raced to create proposals to win a share of the new federal windfall. A number of new organizations quickly formed, or substantially expanded their services, in order to become eligible for OEO funds.

Some of the New York agencies awarded the first round of grants from the OEO, like HARYOU-ACT, had existed prior to 1965, and had been funded until that point by the city and private donors. With HARYOU-ACT already mired in an internal power struggle, which had led Dr. Clark to step down as its chairman in 1964 (the *New York Times* called it "easily the most controversial and the most unorthodox of the antipoverty programs"), the largest share of the new poverty funds went to two Harlem-based organizations, the East Harlem Tenants Council and Massive Economic Neighborhood Development (MEND). "The struggle for power is edging out the struggle against poverty," noted one of New York's social service directors, sardonically. That comment may have been over-stated; but the infusion of resources into poor communities did indeed generate conflicts over different visions about how to solve social problems.[45]

On the other hand, in some cases the competition for federal dollars inspired collaboration between leaders of African American and Puerto Rican organizations. One of the most successful of the grassroots organizations in Puerto Rican New York in the 1960s involved collaborations across ethnic lines in the communities it served, the Lower East Side and East Harlem. The Real Great Society (RGS) was the brainchild of Carlos "Chino" García, former leader of a gang called the Assassin Lords, who began in the early 1960s to recruit other gang leaders to fight poverty in their immediate communities. For Chino, the anti-poverty imaginary of the Johnson administration was both a point of depar-ture and a false claim to be criticized. "We don't see any signs of a Great Society around here," he said.

> If life is going to change on these streets, we have to work together and change it. No one is going to do it for us. President Johnson has this idea of the Great Society. We need our own thing. We need the *Real* Great Society.[46]

Social workers, teachers, and anti-poverty workers worked with Chino and his collaborators to develop the organization between 1964 and 1965, and soon, with several small grants, they recruited 50 volunteers to run the "University of the Streets," which initially provided after-school courses including English, Puerto Rican history, karate, jewelry making, music, and photography for 800 children. After a major riot in East Harlem in 1967, and with additional grants from the Office of Economic Opportunity and the Ford Foundation, the organi-zation expanded uptown, and would go on to play a central role in the activist world of Puerto Rican communities in New York and beyond during the late 1960s. "The kind of fight we were looking for was right on our streets," said Angelo González, co-founder of RGS.[47]

The competition for funds created a new source of conflict not just between social groups, but also within them. Just after the Economic Opportunity Act was passed, a cadre of young Puerto Rican leaders assembled an ambitious proposal to form what they called the Puerto Rican Community Development Project (PRCDP), which would serve as a clearinghouse for community programs. The planning for the PRCDP was led by already prominent community leaders: Antonia Pantoja and several other members of the Puerto Rican Forum, labor and community organizer Gerena Valentín, and social work innovator Manny Díaz. Despite the clear mandate to "strengthen Puerto Rican organizational life," as Pantoja put it, and to foster grassroots community involvement in the process, ideological divisions quickly developed among the leadership. Pantoja stepped away from the PRCDP almost immediately, after criticizing its evolution into "a network of social service entities" with too much influence from the Migration Division. Manny Díaz led the organization for several more years, although Gerena Valentín noted in his memoir that the PRCDP soon became a patronage network under the influence South Bronx power broker Ramon Vélez.[48]

Another set of tensions about anti-poverty funds came from projects that involved collaboration between community leaders and "outsiders." With increasing opportunities to win external funding via the War on Poverty, neighborhood organizations that had once operated on small disbursements from the city, supplemented by volunteer labor, were now able to hire professional social service staff.[49] Major national foundations—the Rockefeller and Ford Foundations, most notably—had joined the federal government in the mid-1960s in offering money to help alleviate poverty and the social unrest it produced.[50] As sociologist Félix Padilla observed about Puerto Rican Chicago in this period, "Community organizing for Puerto Ricans now came to mean more than just activism and protest . . . [I]t also included working through the system or using the system's institutions as mechanisms of social change."[51] Invariably, though, grassroots leaders saw the problems in their communities from a vantage point entirely different than that of city officials and police, or university and foundation administrators, and efforts at collaboration were often complicated by these vast differences of perspective.

Work and Economic Life: Labor Organizing

Much of the "working through the system" was also happening in the labor movement, which by the mid-1950s had become, along with the Migration Division, the most productive site for Puerto Ricans' anti-discrimination activism in that decade. Puerto Rican and other Spanish-speaking activists were able to enhance their visibility in the labor leadership through a series of labor protests and organizing drives led by New York area unions during the late 1950s. Several of the more progressive unions had active civil rights committees that helped mobilize membership and generated funds to back organizing efforts led by Black and Puerto Rican labor organizations. A key result of these developments was that Puerto Rican labor activists developed productive collaborations with labor leaders. Together they were able to enforce non-discrimination rules, support the integration of Puerto Rican workers into the labor movement, and pursue policy goals shared by low wage workers.

Not all of the momentum gained by Puerto Rican workers in this era was the result of union organizing per se. By the early 1960s, Puerto Ricans were finally breaking into public employment and clerical work in significant numbers (as African Americans had begun to do at least a decade earlier), allowing a growing proportion of Puerto Rican workers to move away from manual labor and low wage service work. However, nearly half of the Puerto Rican population continued to work in factories, many of them connected to the garment industry, and others in the many food, leather, electrical, and metalwork factories that dotted New York and other cities' industrial areas. Thousands of Puerto Ricans living in the mid-Atlantic and Midwestern states also continued to do agricultural work in rural areas.

Agricultural workers were not unionized, but there was increasing awareness on the part of Puerto Rican labor leaders in urban areas that their campaigns for the rights of Puerto Rican workers needed to address those beyond the large urban centers. In one important case involving migrant farm workers in New Jersey, leaders of New York's Puerto Rican Merchants Association, the Spanish-language press, and the Migration Division strenuously protested assertions by a state Superior Court judge that Puerto Rican farmworkers were to blame for creating "rural slum conditions." They called for investigations into the living and working conditions of Puerto Rican farmworkers in New Jersey, and staged a protest rally in Freehold, New Jersey that turned into a "victory celebration." When New Jersey governor Robert Meyner ultimately fired that Superior Court judge for his "improper conduct" directed at Puerto Ricans, a group called the Brotherhood of Hispanic Workers wrote a public letter celebrating the judge's dismissal and protesting his statements: "As Americans, we declare that the appeal to racial hatred is the complete negation of the democratic spirit, and appeals to fascist and confused emotions [are] . . . anti-Christian."[52]

While labor issues did increasingly gain the attention of community leaders, including Migration Division representatives as well as radical nationalists, communists, and other leftists, it was within the unions that Puerto Ricans made their most successful efforts at challenging discrimination in this era. Between the mid-1950s and the early-1960s Puerto Ricans were at the center of labor movement efforts to fight racketeer-run unions, which were unions operated by bosses who relied on extortion, fraud, or other corrupt practices, often in collusion with organized crime. The major industrial and service unions, including the

TABLE 2.1 Puerto Rican Employment by Sector, 1950 and 1960

	Born in Puerto Rico		Puerto Rican Parents	
	1950	*1960*	*1950*	*1960*
Total Males Employed	46,275	118,288	3,585	9,096
% Occupation				
Professional, Technical & Kindred	2.4	1.8	5.4	7.4
Managers, Officers & Proprietors	5.5	3.7	4.4	4
Clerical, Sales, & Kindred	9.2	11.4	20.5	23.8
Craftsman, Foremen & Kindred	11	10.8	11.9	16.3
Operatives & Kindred	37.4	45.2	35.4	29
Non-household Service	29.3	21.1	16.3	12.5
Household Service	0.1	0.1	0	0.2
Laborers except Farm & Mine	5	5.7	6	6
Farm Laborers & Foremen	0.1	0.3	0	0
Total Females Employed	31,730	61,225	2,955	5,893
% Occupation				
Professional, Technical & Kindred	1.7	2.6	5.6	6.3
Managers, Officers & Proprietors	1	1.1	1.2	1.7
Clerical, Sales, & Kindred	6.4	12.1	39.4	56
Craftsman, Foremen & Kindred	1.7	1.9	2	1.7
Operatives & Kindred	80.8	74	40.9	24.4
Non-household Service	5.7	6.7	8.6	8.7
Household Service	1.6	0.8	1.7	0.5
Laborers except Farm & Mine	1	0.8	0.5	0.6
Farm Laborers & Foremen	0	0	0	0

Credit: United States Bureau of the Census. *U.S. Census of Population, 1960. Subject Reports. Puerto Ricans in the United States*. Final Report. U.S. Government Printing Office, Washington, D.C. 1963. Table 11.

American Federation of Labor–Congress of Industrial Organizations (AFL-CIO), organized major strikes and recruitment campaigns in this era, which led to the incorporation of tens of thousands of new members, including many Puerto Ricans, and resulted in some improvement of the very low wages of low skill factory workers.

By the late 1950s, a small cadre of Puerto Rican labor leaders was beginning to apply pressure from inside the unions more systematically while also establishing alliances with other organizations, especially Jewish and African American groups. One of these leaders was George Santiago, whose story illustrates the convergence of union, community, and anti-discrimination efforts for the Puerto Rican community during this period. Santiago arrived in New York as a young migrant in 1946, and after starting work wiring lamps at one of the many electrical factories, he joined the Local 3 of the International Brotherhood of Electrical

Workers (IBEW). After serving in the military during the Korean War, Santiago returned to the factory and also started taking college courses. Soon after Mayor Wagner named a Committee on Exploitation of Workers in 1957, to coordinate multiple city offices in processing workers' complaints, Santiago became the first Puerto Rican committee member. He would continue to play a leadership role in connecting labor and other issues throughout the 1960s, and with other Puerto Rican labor leaders, Santiago would co-found the National Association of Puerto Rican Civil Rights, the first formal Puerto Rican civil rights organization primarily led by labor organizers.[53]

Throughout these years, expansion in Puerto Rican membership in garment workers' union locals also contributed to the strengthening of the International Ladies' Garment Workers' Union (ILGWU), the largest union in New York City with about 235,000 members in its many locals by 1965.[54] The opportunity to join the ILGWU was especially transformative for the tens of thousands of Puerto Rican women who worked as dressmakers and sewing machine operators; Puerto Rican men also worked in the garment industry in packing, transportation, and pressing.

The ILGWU had a reputation as one of the more progressive, inclusive unions, and was an important base of support for Puerto Rican workers dating back to the 1930s. Yet by the 1950s ILGWU leadership at the top had ossified into a bureaucracy tightly controlled by longtime president David Dubinsky. With the ILGWU's increasingly obvious failure to protect its lowest-paid workers and to promote African American and Latina/o workers to leadership positions, NAACP Labor Director Herbert Hill referred to the union as "Dubinsky's Plantation."[55]

Nevertheless, within the union locals and at the shop level, where most of the common union business was done and working class leaders formed, Puerto Rican membership and leadership thrived. Indeed, most Puerto Rican workers remembered the ILGWU locals as a source of pride and mobilization, and as a space that respected and celebrated their cultural differences while bringing working class people of different cultures and races together in solidarity.[56] Historians Carmen Whalen and Altagracia Ortiz document this participation in their writing on the ILGWU's 1958 general strike. An important exemplar of the opportunities many Puerto Ricans found in the ILGWU was Frida Montalvo, who migrated to New York in the early 1930s and became a sewing machine operator. After joining the ILGWU Dressmakers' Unions (Local 22) in the 1930s, Montalvo worked with fellow dressmaker Rafaela Valledares to establish Agujas de Oro ("golden needles"), a club of Spanish-speaking garment workers. A tireless community activist, Montalvo also went on to cofound one of New York's largest Puerto Rican hometown associations, the Cabo Rojenos Ausentes, and she participated in school reform and Democratic party politics throughout the 1960s.[57]

Another key focus of Puerto Ricans' union activism was in the fight to create a municipal minimum wage in New York City. As a result of coordinated labor and civil rights mobilizations by Black and Puerto Rican activists by 1960, the

TABLE 2.2 Puerto Rican Annual Family Incomes, New York City, 1959

	Total Population		Non-white		Puerto Rican		White non-Puerto Rican	
	Numbers	*Percentage*	*Numbers*	*Percentage*	*Numbers*	*Percentage*	*Numbers*	*Percentage*
All families	2,079,832	100	263,963	100	140,389	100	1,675,480	100
Under $1,000	72,853	3.5	16,567	6.3	9,670	6.9	46,616	2.8
$1,000 to $1,999	102,220	4.9	21,615	8.2	12,942	9.2	67,663	4
$2,000 to $2,999	141,642	6.8	33,147	12.6	24,867	17.7	83,628	5
$3,000 to $3,999	195,771	9.4	43,549	16.5	27,998	19.9	124,224	7.4
$4,000 to $4,999	233,399	11.2	39,134	14.8	21,417	15.3	172,848	10.3
$5,000 to $5,999	272,970	13.1	32,951	12.5	15,891	11.3	224,128	13.4
$6,000 to $6,999	231,879	11.2	23,740	9	10,344	7.4	197,795	11.8
$7,000 to $7,999	184,151	8.9	16,533	6.3	6,532	4.7	161,086	9.6
$8,000 to $8,999	148,692	7.1	11,853	4.5	4,004	2.9	132,825	7.9
$9,000 to $9,999	111,832	5.4	8,109	3	2,375	1.7	101,348	6
$10,000 and over	384,423	18.5	16,755	6.3	4,349	3.1	363,319	21.7

Credit: Nathan Kantrowitz and Donnell Maynard Pappenfort. *1960 Fact Book for the New York-Northeastern New Jersey Standard Consolidated Area: The Non-White, Puerto Rican, and White Non-Puerto Rican Populations.* New York: Graduate School of Social Work, New York University, 1966, 31.

Central Labor Council (which coordinated all AFL and CIO unions in the city) put forward a proposal for a city minimum wage of $1.50, when the current state minimum was $1.00. The leader of the Central Labor Council charged in public hearings that city officials needed to support the measure because "the city is full of corrupt businessmen working in agreement with racketeer unions." Mayor Wagner did support the measure as an anti-poverty effort that would benefit low wage workers, many of whom were Black and Puerto Rican. The fight was then taken to the state level, supported by labor leaders and grassroots members of the "Citizen's Committee for a $1.50 Minimum Hourly Wage in New York State," led by longtime African American labor leader A. Philip Randolph. The conservative state legislature only agreed to increase the minimum wage to $1.15 (and it would take until 1970 to increase the minimum wage to $1.50)—a major defeat for the Black and Puerto Rican labor alliance that emerged around this issue.[58]

However, even such failed labor struggles managed to expand the arena for substantial collaborations between Black and Puerto Rican leaders and organizations. In addition to the largely unsuccessful campaign to raise the minimum wage, another collaborative movement in the early 1960s was the fight to unionize workers in private hospitals, most of whom were Black and Puerto Rican workers paid very low wages. This effort mobilized sectors from the old left and broad sectors of the labor movement, who helped create mass support for a series of strikes in 1961–1962 that ultimately led to the acceptance of the hospital workers' union. Joseph Montserrat, Director of the Migration Division, co-chaired the "Committee for Justice to Hospital Workers" with A. Philip Randolph. The Migration Division held meetings to support the strike, putting out flyers in Spanish, while the Congreso de los Pueblos and the Council of Puerto Rican and Spanish American organizations mobilized their memberships for the picket lines and rallies. The Spanish press also gave the protests and strike major coverage, calling for people to come out in support. [59]

As all of these examples illustrate, the landscape of labor was changing dramatically by the early 1960s. However, while many Puerto Ricans employed in the industrial and service sectors had experienced at least modest increases in their wages in the preceding decade, the prospects for younger people entering the labor market were still grim. Many high skill trade-based occupations were blocked by racist practices of the unions while the only growing sector of the New York economy was in white collar employment in the finance, insurance, and real estate industries (the "FIRE" sector). Most Puerto Rican youth, especially men, were not well positioned to enter this world because of their limited educational prospects. Black and Puerto Rican leaders focused mostly on expanding opportunities for workers in high skill trades, especially in construction, the other growing sector. They built broad coalitions with liberals and city officials to demand that doors to hiring and training open, emphasizing the civil rights dimension of these opportunities, with a particular impact on young people.

Another important coalition developed through a series of meetings in 1963 between community leaders and bankers "concerning employment of Negroes and Puerto Ricans." Convened by the city's attorney general and its Civil Rights Bureau, the meeting brought leaders of private banks together with city council members, representatives from the American Jewish Congress, the West Side Committee on Civil Rights, the NAACP, and the Migration Division to discuss hiring practices and discrimination in major industries including banking and insurance. Several years ahead of federal legislation, a 1960 state statute had allowed for prosecution of employers for denying opportunities or access to public facilities because of race, color, or creed, establishing that lack of diversity at a workplace could constitute proof of discrimination. When the attorney general threatened the banks with prosecution, they agreed to conditions set by the State Commission on Human Rights. The agreement, the details of which were hammered out at the 1963 meetings, promised that the banks would provide data, advertise vacancies, and increase the hiring of Blacks and Puerto Ricans. The bankers wanted to avoid quotas or percentages, while community leaders concluded that declaring a nondiscrimination policy and the end of discrimination was not enough.[60]

By the early 1960s, Puerto Rican and Black workers also found common ground in their efforts to get hired for construction jobs, which were sought after as high skill manual labor that came with wages four to five times the going factory wage. But unions traditionally controlled their training and apprenticeship programs, which meant they controlled who got hired—and funneled most construction jobs to white workers. In fighting against this exclusion, Puerto Ricans joined in with the longstanding efforts of varied Black civil rights organizations like the Negro American Labor Council (NALC), Congress of Racial Equality (CORE), and the NAACP to challenge racist practices of the construction unions. A few companies opened their apprenticeship programs throughout the 1960s, and by the 1970s had trained a new generation of Puerto Rican and Black workers. Electricians' unions opened up their trades, but steelworkers, bricklayers, carpenters, painters, and plumbers resisted. This resulted in many legal, political, and physical conflicts, and city efforts at breaking past these barriers which began in the early 1960s yielded only marginal results.

The city government began to take some measures to improve conditions, establishing and eventually enforcing minimums of minority hires for construction work paid with public funds (and later for small business contracts too). But these measures of minimal "affirmative action" were resented and fought against by white workers and many unions. Sometimes picket lines and attempts to stop construction would lead to confrontations and physical fights. One notorious conflict, the first of a long number of legal and political battles over this question, began when three plumbers, one of them Black and two Puerto Rican, challenged the practices that excluded them from the plumbers' union. Under pressure from leaders at the National Association for Puerto Rican Civil Rights, the NAACP, and the Mayor's office, the AFL-CIO forced the plumbers' union local to allow the workers to take the entry test. When they passed, the number of "non-whites" increased to 20 in a membership of 4,100. A 1965 report from the Human Rights Commission, "Bias in the Building Industry," found "a pattern of considerable exclusion within construction industry, effectively keeping Blacks and Puerto Ricans from participating in the economic life of the city." The commission asserted it would hold the city as well as industry contractors and unions responsible for ensuring that the rules of fairness be followed.[61]

Together, Puerto Rican and African American labor leaders addressed workplace conditions, minimum wage standards, and government welfare and labor policies, and worked to define these efforts as civil rights issues. While most of this work was done within unions, increasingly union leaders began to connect with larger community and civil rights organizations as well as government agencies. In 1961, for example, Harlem congressman Adam Clayton Powell organized hearings by the House Committee on Education and Labor to focus on racial discrimination within the garment industry and the International Ladies' Garment Workers' Union. Framed explicitly around discrimination against Black and Puerto Rican workers, the hearings brought national attention to the fierce, ongoing debate about the means, goals, and direction of advancement of "minorities" within the labor movement.[62]

Civil Rights and Leadership: Building Coalitions in the 1960s

By 1960 Puerto Ricans had gained a tremendous amount of experience in labor, political, civil rights, and community organizations, even if many of their goals to achieve recognition and representation remained elusive. Part of that experience involved collaborating with African American leaders and learning from their strategies. Indeed, by the early 1960s, intersections with the northern Black civil rights movement substantially influenced the burgeoning Puerto Rican movement, and one of the key questions debated by Puerto Rican leaders and organizations was how much they should align their own campaigns for civil rights with those of African Americans.

There were increasing—and increasingly obvious—opportunities for collaboration by the early 1960s. Puerto Rican activists helped mobilize a large Puerto Rican contingent from New York and New Jersey to attend the 1963 March on Washington for Jobs and Freedom, a mobilization coordinated by the Congreso de los Pueblos, with less publicized support from the Migration Division. Thousands of Puerto Ricans joined 250,000 other demonstrators to demand improved access to jobs and an end to employment discrimination through federal government action. That mobilization had produced a new coalition of Puerto Rican leaders by the fall of 1963, who sought to maintain the momentum from the March on Washington to organize a broad-based civil rights campaign in the Puerto Rican community. They called for a voter registration drive, quality education, an open housing policy, expanded job training and youth employment opportunities, and elimination of the English literacy test. Boasting that Puerto Ricans were racially integrated and free of racial prejudice, organizers asserted that Puerto Ricans were "living proof that integration can work."[63]

In late 1963, when two Puerto Ricans were shot to death inside a police patrol car, a group of leaders including Gerena Valentín, Paul Sánchez, José Morales, Mario Abreu, and Joseph Salguero spearheaded the creation of the National Association for Puerto Rican Civil Rights (NAPRCR), announcing Puerto Ricans' intention to demand justice using the same language as their African American allies. The NAPRCR was born in the heat of negotiations between police and community leaders, and its immediate goals were to push for investigations of police abuse and the creation of a civilian complaint board; but it did not limit itself to civil rights problems related to police. The organization also got involved in struggles for fair labor practices and other anti-discrimination efforts. The NAPRCR quickly became among the most active Puerto Rican organizations of this period. Although formed in New York, the group was intended to be national in scope and solicited participation by leaders in other cities; and although it never became a mass membership organization, its 300 or so leaders used their prominence and their preexisting networks to mobilize people for protests and meetings in various cities throughout the 1960s and 1970s.[64]

Police abuse again defined civil rights activism and sparked protests in New York City in early 1965, not long after a major riot in Harlem that would come to mark the real beginning of a decade of riots. The nation's shock over the massive, multi-day riots in the largest African American communities of New York (Harlem) and Los Angeles (Watts), during the summers of 1964 and 1965, had exacerbated the preexisting mutual suspicion between police and residents of Black and Latino ghettos. In this tense moment, over a span of just two months, four Puerto Rican prisoners were found dead in their prison cells in New York City. Police reports in each case stated that the prisoner had hung himself with a shirt or a scarf in the precinct holding cell, each within 30 minutes of being locked up. Frustrated that almost two years of negotiations between Puerto Rican leaders and police department officials had seemed to accomplish little, the NAPRCR once again pressured city officials and the police department, and managed to produce an agreement to establish regular communication between community representatives and police captains and a commitment to increase the number of Latino officers on the police force.[65]

This cyclical pattern, involving incidents of police abuse followed by remonstrations by Puerto Rican leaders and promises by police department or city officials, left leaders and community members skeptical about the prospects for civil rights gains. Police-community relations continued to worsen as youth in particular became more rebellious and intolerant of police abuse during the 1960s. Officials in large cities—where attempts to create summer jobs, training programs and entertainment for youth were never adequate—began to fear the "long hot summers" that would release thousands of working class unemployed youth into neighborhood streets. Given the intensifying pattern of confrontation between ghetto residents and police, both groups were now driven to escalate a conflict at the slightest provocation.

The leadership of urban Puerto Rican communities everywhere now redoubled their push for representation, trying to turn frustration over Puerto Ricans' lack of power into productive political action. This was driven not only by the desire to avoid violence but also because they understood the growing economic problems of the poorest youth in their communities. In New York, where the Puerto Rican community had been working for decades to elect more representatives, several Puerto Rican candidates had been elected to the New York state assembly by 1964, and that year marked the election of the first Puerto Rican member of the city council, Carlos Rios. The same year, Herman Badillo was named Commissioner of Housing Preservation and Development by Mayor Wagner. These leaders were all involved in the NAPRCR, which accomplished an unusually seamless coalition of liberal and leftists in the community. Many of them had worked together on campaigns for equal employment and fair housing in the 1940s or 1950s and shared a certain trepidation about the increasingly militant rhetoric coming from younger sectors of the both the African American and Puerto Rican communities.[66]

Along with battles over fair housing and equal employment, the struggle for an adequate education for their children had been a central focus of Puerto Ricans' demand for civil rights in the U.S. dating back to the 1930s. By the early 1960s, parents and community leaders, concerned about equal treatment of Puerto Rican children in schools, began to frame their expectations in the now highly politicized language of civil rights. In much the same way that union activity and workplace struggles began to unite Puerto Ricans and African Americans in new ways by the early 1960s, the shared concern over equality in education also brought Puerto Ricans and African Americans together in civil rights collaborations that would come to shape the way many activists and leaders in that era pursued justice for their communities.

Much of what was accomplished in the labor sector in this era was incremental and received little attention from major newspapers or the wider public. School-related protests were another matter: when African American and Puerto Rican activists in New York City decided to tackle the problem of school segregation in the early 1960s, they planned a massive, citywide boycott in February of 1964 that garnered front page coverage in newspapers across the country. Parents and community leaders resented the Board of Education's failure to take adequate steps toward integration nearly ten years after the Supreme Court's 1954 decision that "separate but equal" schools were unconstitutional. Meanwhile, civil rights leaders Reverend Milton Galamison and Gilberto Gerena Valentín, who had just helped found the NAPRCR, approached national civil rights leader Bayard

Rustin about planning a large-scale action to force the hand of the New York City Board of Education. Galamison and Gerena Valentín had both participated in the 1963 March on Washington—of which Rustin was a key organizer—and asserted that the time was right to draw attention to the rights of Black and Puerto Rican children in the urban north.[67]

The plan was embraced enthusiastically by members of Puerto Rican and African American communities across the city. Migration Division officials organized meetings to encourage parents and other community members to support the boycott, and Gerena mobilized his fellow activists in the Congreso and in the NAPRCR. By all measures the boycott was a resounding success: 45% of students (up to 92% in some predominantly African American schools) and 8% of teachers did not attend classes, and 2,600 picketers marched in front of 300 of the city's 860 schools despite 20-degree temperatures. Counting the number of total participants—those who marched and those who stayed home—Rustin called it the largest civil rights protest in the nation's history. (The 1963 March on Washington had drawn 250,000, who, unlike the school boycotters, all convened in one place.)[68] Puerto Rican leaders considered the boycott a success not just because it called attention to the failures of city officials to meet the needs of students in poor neighborhoods, but also because it publicized the fact that Puerto Rican communities suffered from the same failures of justice as African American communities. Puerto Ricans, too, were fighting to claim civil rights.

This message was proclaimed even more loudly a month later, when Gerena Valentín staged a follow-up march to demand improvement of facilities for Puerto Rican schoolchildren. The silent march of about 2,000 convened at City Hall in Manhattan, crossed the Brooklyn Bridge, and then rallied in front of the Board of Education office in Brooklyn. Reverend Galamison joined Gerena Valentín in addressing the crowd, along with a dozen other speakers, including Migration Division head Joseph Montserrat as well as representatives of Jewish and labor organizations. Their messages tied the demonstration to the multi-racial movement that produced the February boycott. According to the *New York Times* in its front-page coverage, some of the Puerto Rican speakers also "shouted that the Puerto Rican civil rights movement had come of age." [69]

Parents and other residents of Black and Puerto Rican neighborhoods saw the 1964 school boycott as a success in terms of the publicity they generated for the issue of inequality in schools. And just a few months after the boycott, their grievances were given even wider public legitimacy when the Supreme Court issued its opinion on another high-profile school desegregation case. "The time for mere 'deliberate speed' has run out, and that phrase can no longer justify denying these children their constitutional rights," wrote the court in its affirmation of the plaintiffs, a group of Black children denied admission to an all-white public school in Virginia. Such arguments gained substantial momentum over the next few years, in both legal and activist circles.[70]

The assertions by Puerto Rican leaders following the 1964 school boycott—both that a Puerto Rican civil rights movement already existed, and that it had "come of age"—may have been premature. But their confidence and determination signaled a new momentum for coordinated action, and also served as a challenge: it was time for Puerto Ricans to organize mass actions as African Americans had so successfully done for the past decade. The silent march was a model that would soon be replicated in other Puerto Rican communities in other cities. A few days after the Brooklyn demonstration in 1964, a similar silent march was organized by Philadelphia's Council of Spanish Speaking Organizations to protest police abuse, involving 175 participants who had trained in nonviolent tactics. After the march, a committee of five Puerto Rican leaders met with the city's chief of police. Similar meetings of the Jersey City Council of Spanish Speaking Organizations called attention to local cases of brutality and harassment, and connected them to a growing national trend of civil rights protest.[71]

Conclusion

By the mid-1960s, hundreds of Puerto Rican organizations in over a dozen cities, with the participation of tens of thousands of citizens and a leadership base that ranged from liberal to radical, had indeed begun to lay down the foundations of a civil rights movement. The difficulties, tensions, and even tragedies of adjusting to life in the U.S. for half a million migrants in the previous generation were balanced in part by accomplishments, along with an increasingly loud set of demands: for more security and equality in the workplace, for greater educational access for their children, for voting rights, political representation, and protections against police abuse. In these years Puerto Rican communities developed mature social, labor, and political organizations with strong leaders and strengthening regional and even national ties. The social programs of the anti-poverty organizations funded by city and federal budgets might have had mixed results in terms of lifting people out of poverty, but they, too, helped produce organizations and leadership that pushed forward the civil rights struggles of the 1960s. They also legitimized and encouraged popular participation in the resurgent liberal state that was partially responsible for these programs—a dynamic similar to the formation of leadership in leftist organizations of earlier decades.

The Migration Division, which created a strong base for Puerto Rican demands in labor, politics, and civil rights in the 1950s, had become an even more powerful platform in the early 1960s, with highly visible director Joseph Montserrat working extensively with other Puerto Rican leaders in other cities who represented a variety of ideological and institutional backgrounds. The cultural dimensions of Puerto Rican activism also served to anchor the community's struggle for civil rights in the U.S. This was a burgeoning moment of cultural nationalism, and part of its appeal was that it provided a strong foundation from which to navigate the complexities of race and class in a society in which democratic liberalism delivered inconsistently on its promises of equality. Conceptions of Puerto Rican culture or ethnic identity varied within communities—depending on age, economic status, geographic origins, and other factors—but a sense of ethnic and national solidarity surged during the 1960s, sparking the creation of what would become, indeed, a Puerto Rican movement.

Notes

1 United States Census Bureau. *Puerto Ricans in the United States: Social and Economic Data for Persons of Puerto Rican Birth and Parentage.* Washington, D.C.: U.S. Government Printing Office, 1960.

2 "The Growing Importance of the Puerto Rican Minority in New York City," n.d. [1958], Jesús Colón Papers-CPRS Series III Box 2 Folder 1.

3 "Harriman and Rockefeller Meet at Puerto Rican Fete." *The New York Times,* 8 Sept. 1958. Note that Rockefeller's attention to Puerto Rican voters seemed to pay off: an estimated 25% of Puerto Ricans in the Bronx voted for the Republican candidate. "Minorities Voted in G.O.P. Direction." *The New York Times,* 5 Nov. 1958, 27.

4 "Jose Ramos Lopez, 79, Former Assemblyman." *The New York Times,* 6 Nov. 1993.

5 Puerto Rican National Merchants United to Wagner, "Puerto Ricans Need Recognition," 26 Feb. 1956, Mayor Wagner Papers—LGCC Box 276 Folder 3217 Roll 149.

6 Thomas, Lorrin. *Puerto Rican Citizen: History and Political Identity in Twentieth-Century New York City.* Chicago: University of Chicago Press, 2010, 183–6; Wakefield, Dan. *Island in the City.* Boston: Houghton Mifflin, 1959, 265; Rev. Rubén Dario Colón, et al., "Press Release," 27 July 1953, Jesús Colón Papers-CPRS Series VI Box 1 Folder 9. "Slum Complaints: A Frustrating Problem." *The New York Times,* 20 Jan. 1964.

7 Flyer, Jesús Colón Papers-CPRS Folder 9 Box 15; "Identifican Boricua como lider rojo NY." *El Diario de Nueva York,* 17 Nov. 1959; Flyer, "Contestación al 'Diario' de Nueva York," Jesús Colón Papers-CPRS Box 25 Folder 6; Wakefield, Dan. "Politics and the Puerto Ricans: Getting out the Vote in Spanish Harlem." *Commentary* 25 (March 1958): 226–36; Lumen Román was a journalist for La Prensa who was involved in Liberal and Democratic party politics and in labor issues. Memo from John Carro, Assistant to Mayor Wagner; 15 Aug. 1963, Mayor Wagner Papers-LGCC Box 277 Folder 3222.

8 Council of Spanish-American Organizations, 4th Annual Meeting, 14 April 1956, Covello Papers-HSP Series X Box 105 Folder 3; Colón, "The Growing Puerto Rican Minority in New York City," Jesús Colón Papers-CPRS Series III Box 2 Folder 1; "Vote Drive Urged on Puerto Ricans." *The New York Times,* 17 April 1955, 77; "Vote Drive Begun by Puerto Ricans." *The New York Times,* 10 Aug. 1960, 25. An estimated 35,000 voted in the 1952 presidential elections, out of a population that could yield around 250,000 voters; Letter from HH Bonilla to Wagner, 21 Nov. 1956, Mayor Wagner Papers-LGCC.

9 "Puerto Rican Fights State Literacy Law." *The New York Times,* 7 Aug. 1960, 1; Juan Cartagena. "Puerto Ricans and the 50th Anniversary of the Voting Rights Act of 1965." http://latinojustice.org/JuanOpina/puerto_ricans_and_the_50th_anniversary_of_the_voting_rights_act_of_1965. A 1957 *Herald Tribune* article said that Puerto Ricans' registration campaigns that year had yielded 85,000 new voters. "New York Puerto Ricans: Their position Is Improving," *Herald Tribune,* 21 Oct. 1957, Vertical File, "Puerto Ricans—1950s–60s," NYCMA; Fitzpatrick, Joseph P., *Puerto Rican Americans: The Meaning of Migration to the Mainland.* Englewood Cliffs, NJ: Prentice-Hall, Inc., 1971, 57.

10 "Vote Drive Begun by Puerto Ricans." *The New York Times,* 10 Aug. 1960, 25. "City Spanish Vote at a Record High." *The New York Times,* 2 Nov. 1960, 30.

11 Schmitt, Edward R. *President of the Other America: Robert Kennedy and the Politics of Poverty.* Amherst: University of Massachusetts Press, 2010.

12 https://www.loc.gov/rr/hispanic/congress/badillo.html; González: "Few Played as Big a Role in Community as Herman Badillo." *New York Daily News*, 3 Dec. 2014.

13 José Cruz, personal communication with Lorrin Thomas, 12 Oct. 2014. "Mayor's Reforms Face Harlem Test." *The New York Times*, 19 Nov. 1961, 45.

14 *Nueva Voz*. Sept 1965, 3:31; "Youngest Commissioner, Herman Badillo Rivera." *The New York Times*, 17 Nov. 1962, 12; "Voting Gain Made by Puerto Ricans." *The New York Times*, 23 Nov. 1963, 46. Gerena Valentín, Gilberto. *Gilberto Gerena Valentín: My Life as a Community Organizer, Labor Activist, and Progressive Politician in New York City*. New York: Center for Puerto Rican Studies, Hunter College, 2013, 104.

15 This support was rewarded by Kennedy's appointment of two Puerto Ricans to the State Department, a process that was boosted by Puerto Rico's value to the U.S. in the context of U.S. attacks on the Cuban revolution and resulting in confrontations with the USSR in the early 1960s.

16 José Cruz, personal communication with Lorrin Thomas, 12 Oct. 2014.

17 "A Blind Judge Is Sworn by State Supreme Court." *The New York Times*, 13 Dec. 1975.

18 "City's Puerto Rican Voters Appear Heavily Pro-Johnson, but G.O.P. Believes It can Cut the Margin." *The New York Times*, 15 Sept. 1964, 22. "Philadelphia Primary Election Balloting at a Glance." *Philadelphia Inquirer*, 30 April 1964, 4.

19 The district that had been called the 16th became the 18th in 1963, but the lines did not change. "Democrats Split over Redistricting." *The New York Times*, 9 Aug. 1962, 1. "Harlem G.O.P. Candidates Score Redistricting Suit of Democrats." *The New York Times*, 30 July 1962, 24.

20 "Se piden policías e inspectores de sanidad hispanos para Harlem." *La Prensa*, 6 Sep. 1927, 4; "Un puertorriqueño, casi adolescente, es acusado de la muerte de un compañero." *La Prensa*, 6 April 1928, 1; Vega, *Memoirs*, 54. Interview with Félix Loperana, conducted by John Vásquez, 22 Nov. 1974, *Pioneros* Project, LIHS.

21 See, for example, "West Side Cops Beat 3 Puerto Ricans," *Daily Worker*, 21 July 1950 Jesús Colón Papers-CPRS Series X Clippings Folder 5; "Cops Beat Puerto Rican Youth in Murder Frame-up." *Daily Worker*, 8 Jan. 1953 Folder 6; "NAACP Meeting to Protest Increasing 'Police Brutality'." *New York Amsterdam News*, 8 Oct. 1949; "Charge Police Use 'Mad Dog Tactics.'" *New York Amsterdam News*, 5 Aug. 1950.

22 "Report on Police Brutality against the Negro and Puerto Rican People." [n.d.] Jesús Colón Papers-CPRS Series III Box 9 Folder 14; "Excerpts from Report of Mayor's Committee on Puerto Rican Affairs in New York City," 26 Feb. 1953, Leonard Covello Papers-HSP Series X Box 110 Folder 15; "What the City Does Right." *New York Post*, 29 July 1953, Clippings, Jesús Colón Papers-CPRS Box 36 Folder 6; "The Police and the Puerto Ricans." *New York Post*, 28 July 1953.

23 "Charge Cop Beat Up Puerto Rican Youth." *New York Amsterdam News*, 7 Feb. 1953, 1.

24 Fraser, Gerald. "Surpless Frowns on Hyphenated-Americans, Scores Puerto Ricans." *New York Amsterdam News*, 23 Aug. 1952, 17; "Bartell Demands Anti-Puerto Rican Judge Be Ousted." *The Militant*, 18 Aug. 1952.

25 "The Growing Importance of the Puerto Rican Minority in New York City," n.d. [1958] Jesús Colón Papers-CPRS; *New York Post*, 10, 11, 13, 14, 15, 16, 17 Feb. 1955.

26 *El Mundo*, 20 Jan. 1956; 26 Sept. 1956; 7 July 1958; "The Growing Importance of the Puerto Rican Minority in New York City"; 250 had been recruited by 1957 and 300 by 1964. "Dealing with Delinquents," Letter to the Editor. *The New York Times*, 31 May 1957; Senior, Clarence. "The Puerto Ricans in New York: Progress Note." *International Migration Review* 2, no. 2 (spring 1968): 73.

27 Darien, Andrew T. *Becoming New York's Finest: Race, Gender, and the Integration of the NYPD, 1935–1980*. New York: Palgrave Macmillan, 2013, 86; *NY World Telegram and Sun, 12 Oct. 1954*.

28 "Cervantes Society IWO Youth Condemn Attack on Puerto Ricans in New York," *Fraternal Outlook*, Jan. 1949; "The Growing Importance of the Puerto Rican Minority

in New York City"; On more positive representations of relations with police, see Carlos de Jesús's documentary film, *That Old Gang of Mine* (de Jesús, 1996).

29 "Greenpoint Residents Launch Fight on Race-Riot Hoodlums." *New York Amsterdam News*, 13 Aug. 1949; Rand, Christopher. *The Puerto Ricans*. New York: Oxford University Press, 1958, 90–1; "Youths Seized in Slaying." *The New York Times*, 24 July 1953.

30 Schepses, Erwin. "Puerto Rican Delinquent Boys in New York City." *The Social Science Review* 23 (March 1949): 51–61.

31 "Liebowitz Sued on Jury's Inquiry: Illegal Directive on Puerto Rican Migration Laid to Judge—Writ Is Sought." *The New York Times*, 6 Nov. 1959, 19; Darien, *Becoming New York's Finest*, 85.

32 Martin, John Bartlow. "Crime Without Reason." *Saturday Evening Post*, 5 Nov. 1960. Lilia Fernández discusses this case and the *Saturday Evening Post* article briefly in *Brown in the Windy City: Mexicans and Puerto Ricans in Postwar Chicago*. Chicago: University of Chicago Press, 2012, 158; we thank her for drawing our attention to this case.

33 Martin, "Crime Without Reason." 21.

34 *La Prensa*, 10 October 1957. Navarro, Félix C. *Historia de la comunidad puertorriqueña de Nueva York*. Mexico, D.F.: B Costa-Amic, 1971.

35 See articles in *El Diario*, 25 March 1957; *New York Post*, 25 March 1957. *El Diario*, 29 March 1957. *El Diario*, 1 April 1957.

36 Johnson, Marilynn S. *Street Justice: A History of Police Violence in New York City*. Boston: Beacon Press, 2003, 232; Darien, *Becoming New York's Finest*; Migration Division, Annual Report, 18 June 1964, OGPRUS-CPRS Box 2596, Folder 1.

37 Gilberto Gerena Valentín, City of New York Commission on Human rights, to Commissioner Howard Leary, 28 Sept. 1966, Goddard Riverside Community Center, Series IV, Executive Director files, Sub Series 1 Tom Wolfe Box 68 Folder 4 police programs, Operation Friend 1964–66; "Operation Friend; Report on a Precinct Project to Smash the Barrier Between Police and the Public." *New York World-Telegram* and *The Sun*, 10 Sept. 1965.

38 "The 'No-Knock' and 'Stop and Frisk' Provisions of the New York Code of Criminal Procedure," *St. John's Law Review* 38 no. 2 (1964) Article 12; "Frisking Assailed by Liberties Union." *The New York Times*, 24 March 1965, 50.

39 See Chapter 3, pp. 76–82.

40 Sánchez Korrol, Virginia. "In Their Own Right: A History of Puerto Ricans in the U.S.A." In Jiménez Núñez, Alfredo, Nicolás Kanellos, and Claudio Esteva Fabregat, eds., *Handbook of Hispanic Cultures in the United States*. Houston; Madrid: Arte Público Press; Instituto de Cooperación Iberoamericana, 1994.

41 Pantoja, Antonia. *Memoir of a Visionary, Antonia Pantoja*. Houston: Arte Publico Press, 2002, 72–9.

42 Pantoja, *Memoir of a Visionary*, 90–109; Lapp, Michael. "Managing Migration: The Migration Division of Puerto Rico and Puerto Ricans in New York City." Ph.D. Dissertation, Johns Hopkins University, 1991, 295–300; Herbstein, Judith F. "Rituals and Politics of the Puerto Rican 'Community' in New York City." Ph.D. Dissertation, City University of New York, 1978.

43 Sonia Lee, *Building a Latino Civil Rights Movement*, ch. 3, 134; Joel Schwartz, "The New York City Rent Strikes of 1963–1964." *Social Service Review*, no. 4 (1983): 545. "The Troubles of Haryou." *The New York Times*, 13 Oct. 1965, 36. On conflict between Clark and Harlem Congressman Clayton Powell see Block, Andrew. "Community in Action: The Central Harlem Experience in the War on Poverty, 1963–1968." Thesis, Vassar College, 2005; Gottehrer, Barry, ed. *New York City in Crisis*. New York: D. McKay Co., 1965.

44 "Poverty Council Increased to 100, Including 32 Poor." *The New York Times*, 28 May 1965, 1; "Brooklyn Antipoverty Program Is Set." *The New York Times*, 26 July 1964, 42, talks about the Mayor's Council Against Poverty. "City Reorganizes Drive on Poverty." *The New York Times*, 12 May 1965, 1; "Poverty Council Backs Bundy Plan," 26 Nov.

1967, 78. The Poverty Council had 28 members, half of them representatives of public and private education and social service agencies, labor, business, and religious groups. The other half were residents of neighborhoods served by the anti-poverty program. The earliest controversy surrounding the new Poverty Council had to do with its initial failure to include representatives from "deprived" neighborhoods.

45 Weekly Report, Employment Program, 10 July 1964, OGPRUS-CPRS Box 2948 Folder 6; Lee, *Building a Latino Civil Rights* Movement, 147–9; "Poor to Choose in East Harlem." *The New York Times*, 6 March 1966, 69; "City Reorganizes Drive on Poverty." *The New York Times*, 12 May 1965, 1.

46 Aponte-Parés, Luis. "Lessons from El Barrio–the East Harlem Real Great Society/Urban Planning Studio: A Puerto Rican Chapter in the Fight for Urban Self-Determination." In Rodolfo D. Torres and George N. Katsiaficas, eds., *Latino Social Movements: Historical and Theoretical Perspectives: A New Political Science Reader*, v, 209. New York: Routledge, 1999.

47 Blank, Joseph P. "The Real Great Society." *National Civic Review* 57, no. 11 (1968): 561–6.

48 Pantoja, *Memoir of a Visionary*, 114–99; Gerena Valentín, *Gilberto Gerena Valentín*, 185–8; "Group Organizes Puerto Rican Aid." *The New York Times*, 7 Nov. 1964, 29; "Puerto Rican Aid Killed A-borning." *The New York Times*, 4 March 1965, 21; "Split Emphasized by Puerto Ricans." *The New York Times*, 16 March 1965, 22. See Chapter 3, p. 91.

49 See, for example, Padilla, *Latino Ethnic Consciousness*, 104, 123–5.

50 "Columbia Aids 7 Poverty Projects but Harlem Group Insists on Community Decisions." *The New York Times*, 12 May 1968, 68.

51 Padilla, Félix M. *Puerto Rican Chicago*. Notre Dame, IN; London: University of Notre Dame Press, 1988, 193.

52 *El Diario de Nueva York*, 18 Jan. 1956. FBI, PIP SJ100-4014, Volumes 24 and 25. "Judge's Removal Upheld in Jersey: State Supreme Court Rules Unanimously Lloyd Had Not Acquired Tenure Driscoll Appointment Cited New Judges Not Covered," Clipping. 11 January 1956, OGPRUS-CPRS Box 2921 Folder 16.

53 IBEW Local 3, "Those who have come our way," no date, Santiago Iglesias Educational Society Papers-IBEW Local 3 Box 2 Folder 3.

54 Laurentz, Robert. "Racial/Ethnic Conflict in the New York City Garment Industry, 1933–1980." Ph.D. Dissertation, State University of New York at Binghamton, 1980, 365–6.

55 Benin, Leigh David. *The New Labor Radicalism and New York City's Garment Industry: Progressive Labor Insurgents in the 1960s*. New York, London: Garland, 2000, 89. Sparks, Selma. "Dubinsky's Plantation." *Liberator* 3, no. 1 (Jan. 1963), 3–4, 6.

56 Whalen, Carmen Teresa. "'The Day the Dresses Stopped': Puerto Rican Women, the International Ladies Garment Workers' Union, and the 1958 Dressmaker's Strike." In Vicki Ruiz and John R. Chávez, eds., *Memories and Migrations: Mapping Boricua and Chicana Histories*. Urbana: University of Illinois Press, 2008; Ortiz, Altagracia. "'En la aguja y el pedal eche la hiel': Puerto Rican Women in the Garment Industry of New York City, 1920–1980." In Altagracia Ortiz, ed., *Puerto Rican Women and Work: Bridges in Transnational Labor*. Philadelphia: Temple University Press, 1996; Ortiz, Altagracia. "Puerto Rican Workers in the Garment Industry of New York City, 1920–1960." In Robert Stephenson and Charles Asher, eds., *Labor Divided: Race and Ethnicity in United States Labor Struggles, 1835–1960*. Albany NY: State University of New York Press, 1990; Katz, Daniel. *All Together Different: Yiddish Socialists, Garment Workers, and the Labor Roots of Multiculturalism*. Goldstein-Goren Series in American Jewish History. New York: New York University Press, 2011.

57 Frida Montalvo, OGPRUS-CPRS Box 2596; Interview with Eddie González, 31 Jan. 2007, Oral Histories-CPRS; "Women Offering Shoes for Pupils: Puerto Rican Club Aims to Cut Truancy Among Needy." *The New York Times*, 27 July 1964; "She Embraced Puerto Rican Heritage." *Orlando Sentinel*, 20 Dec. 2009.

58 "Minimum Wage Law Suit Filed." *New York Amsterdam News*, 19 Jan. 1963. "$1.50 Minimum Pay Is Made Law Here: Mayor, in Signing Measure." *The New York Times*, 16 July 1964; "Morris Iushewitz." *The Militant*, 30 March 1964; "Minimum Wage: $1.60 an Hour." *Industrial Bulletin*; Freeman, Joshua Benjamin. *Working-Class New York: Life and Labor since World War II*. New York: New Press, 2000.

59 Flyer from Montserrat to Estimado Amigo, 11 July 1962, OGPRUS-CPRS Box 2847 Folder 15; Committee flyer, 18 July 1962, OGPRUS-CPRS Box 2847 Folder 15; Fink, Leon Greenberg Brian. *Upheaval in the Quiet Zone: A History of Hospital Workers' Union, Local 1199*. Urbana: University of Illinois Press, 1989; Lee, *Building a Latino Civil Rights Movement*; Ralph Rosas to Joseph Montserrat, Weekly Report; 18 July 1962, OGPRUS-CPRS Box 2555 Folder 4.

60 "Notes on first meeting of Westside bank representatives and community leaders," 26 June 1963, OGPRUS-CPRS Box 2057 Folder 7.

61 New York City Commission on Human Rights. "Annual Report—Commission on Human Rights." New York: Commission on Human Rights, 10–11; New York City Commission on Human Rights and Michael L. Vallon. *Bias in the Building Industry: An Updated Report, 1963–1967*. New York: The Commission, 1967; "Plumbers Agree to a Wagner Plan to End Walkout." *The New York Times*, 1964, 1. "3 Negros Pass Plumbers Test." *The New York Times*, 7 Aug. 1964; "3 Plumbers Flunk Test." *Daily Defender*, 20 May 1964; "The Plumber's Dispute," *Daily Defender*, 21 May 1964; "Labor Board to Review Plumbers," *New York Amsterdam News*, 8 August 1964; "Meany Supports Bronx Plumbers," 15 May 1964; "N.L.R.B. Rules Union Plumbers Cannot Boycott Nonmembers." *The New York Times*, 6 June 1965. "Report from human rights commission," OGPRUS-CPRS Box 2032 Folder 13.

62 Parmet, Robert D. *The Master of Seventh Avenue: David Dubinsky and the American Labor Movement*. New York: New York University Press, 2005; United States. Congress. House. Committee on Education and Labor. Ad Hoc Subcommittee on Investigation of the Garment Industry. Investigation of the Garment Industry Hearings before the United States House Committee on Education and Labor, Ad Hoc Subcommittee on Investigation of the Garment Industry, Eighty-Seventh Congress, Second Session, on Aug. 17, 18, 23, 24, Sept. 21, 1962. Washington, D.C.: U.S. Government Printing Office, 1962; Jonas, Gilbert. *Freedom's Sword: The NAACP and the Struggle against Racism in America, 1909–1969*. New York: Routledge, 2005; Lee, *Building a Latino Civil Rights*.

63 Montserrat quietly arranged for the Migration Division to pay for the buses. Interview with Eddie González, 31 Jan. 2007 by Lillian Jiménez, Oral History Collection-CPRS. "New York Puerto Rican Leaders' Statement and Program on Civil Rights." OGPRUS-CPRS box 3029. The press conference, held at the Hotel Manhattan, listed supporters including Joseph Montserrat, Gerena Valentín, labor leader Paul Sánchez, Assemblyman Frank Torres, Assemblyman Carlos Rios, Brooklyn community leader Antonia Denis, Liberal Party leader Irma Vidal Santaella, and city commissioner Herman Badillo.

64 *The New York Times*, 16 Dec. 1965. Joseph Montserrat to Frank Zorilla, 7 May 1964, OGPRUS-CPRS Box 2948 Folder 2; Fourth anniversary dinner to Ralph Rosas, 8 May 1970, OGPRUS-CPRS Box 2875 Folder 9; Montserrat to Zorilla, 14 April 1965, OGPRUS-CPRS Box 2948, Folder 6; Montserrat to Zorilla and Petroamérica Pagán de Colón, 7 Feb. 1964; Weekly report, OGPRUS-CPRS Box 2948 Folder 2.

65 "Deputy Police Position Announcement." *The New York Times*, 12 July 1965; "4 Cell Hangings Distress Police." *The New York Times*, 31 March 1965, 43. "Police Picketed over Killing of 2." *The New York Times*, 22 Nov. 1963, 31; "Accord Reached on Puerto Ricans." *The New York Times*, 18 Jan. 1964, 48; "'I Don't Think the Cop Is My Friend.'" *The New York Times*, 29 March 1964, SM28.

66 See Gerena Valentín, *Gilberto Gerena Valentín*, 121. Some Black leaders in New York commented that there were sectors of the Puerto Rican community that liked being "lumped with blacks in demand for better opportunities." Hickey, Neil, and Ed Edwin. *Adam Clayton Powell and the Politics of Race*. New York: Fleet Pub. Corp., 1965.

67 There was a school boycott in Chicago in fall 1963, but it did not involve the Puerto Rican community. "Boycott Cripples City Schools; Absences 360,000 Above Normal; Negroes and Puerto Ricans Unite." *The New York Times*, 4 Feb. 1964, 1; "Education and Race: School Boycott Stirs Mounting Controversy in Some Northern Cities." *Wall Street Journal*, 28 Feb. 1964, 1; "School Boycott Is Newest Civil Rights Weapon in Northern States." *Chicago Daily Defender*, 13 April 1964, A4.

68 "Boycott Cripples City Schools; Absences 360,000 Above Normal; Negroes and Puerto Ricans Unite." *The New York Times*, 4 Feb. 1964, 1. The *Times* clarified that the figures for both students and teachers who did not attend classes should be adjusted to account for the typical daily absentee rate: 10% for students, 3% for teachers.

69 "1,800 Join March for Better Schools for Puerto Ricans." *The New York Times*, 2 March 1964, 1.

70 *Griffin v. School Board of Prince Edward County*, 377 U.S. 218 (1964).

71 Joseph Montserrat to Frank Zorilla, 5 March 1964, OGPRUS-CPRS Box 2948 Folder 1.

3

MASS MOBILIZATIONS FOR SOCIAL JUSTICE, 1966–1973

Introduction

In the 1960s, in a handful of cities in the United States, Puerto Rican activism and politics suddenly became visible. In part this was because of the escalation of violent protest exploding out of urban ghettos around the country by mid-decade; Puerto Ricans were among the angry protagonists in this drama. As important, though, were Puerto Rican activists' steady, persistent efforts to build momentum in their defense of equal rights in U.S. society. A diverse and expanding group of leaders and activists fought for civil rights protections against police abuse, lobbied for labor equality and fair and decent housing, and pushed for community control of schools and equal access to higher education. Some also campaigned for Puerto Rican independence.

A few activists had talked about an incipient Puerto Rican "movement" by the early 1960s. But it was in 1966, following several days of riots in Chicago's largest Puerto Rican community, that the phrase became official, when the African American daily *Chicago Defender* announced in a headline that the "Puerto Rican Movement" had won the support of one of the city's major African American organizations. This mass mobilization, growing steadily and connected by a strengthening sense of Puerto Rican identity, did indeed constitute a "Freedom movement"—as the *Defender* phrased it—and generated a foundation of social and legal activism that would extend through the 1970s.[1]

The majority of the participants in the movement were young, and had been born or at least grown up in the U.S. A disproportionate number had attended college, and many were trained as social workers or worked in social service agencies, learning from older professionals and experienced labor leaders in the broad networks of post-war liberalism. The organizations and coalitions formed by these leaders intersected in many ways with those led by African Americans, often with significant support from whites and institutions and government agencies. Puerto Rican leaders were not only influenced by national and local African American civil rights and Black Power struggles, but in many cases trained or held membership in organizations led by African Americans. This ongoing dialogue with African American leaders, which had started in the 1950s, shaped the engagement of Puerto Ricans with other (mostly white) allies in liberal institutions and among government, labor, and social service leadership.

Among the biggest changes in the late 1960s involved how the community responded to conflicts about treatment of "minorities"—especially minority youth—by police, and this became one of the central issues that sparked political participation in the late 1960s. In the streets of the impoverished ghettos and public housing projects, young Puerto Ricans became radicalized as they viewed the experience of police abuse through a new lens, informed by ideologies of Black Power and the overall politicization of racial conflict. Riots also played a significant role in this shift, sharpening responses in the community even if also creating new rifts, especially across generational lines.

From the perspective of Puerto Rican residents of poor neighborhoods in New York, Newark, Chicago, and many other declining cities of the deindustrializing north, the intensifying street conflict in that decade was not a *cause* of their communities' decline. It represented, rather, a logical *response*—to violence inflicted on their communities by police, and to a growing sense of despair as poverty, scarce jobs, low wages, and crumbling housing were compounded by failing schools, gang violence, and intensified social marginalization. The Puerto Ricans who were galvanized into action in that era may or may not have described themselves as part of a new movement. However they described their engagement, these activists were creating or participating in campaigns for justice to address a variety of specific issues, some new and some decades old, that mobilized tens of thousands of their compatriots and dramatically changed the social and political identities of all Puerto Ricans in the U.S.

Civil Rights and Leadership: Collaboration and Emerging Crisis

The conventional explanation for the national epidemic of urban riots in the mid- to late-1960s, the one resorted to by many policymakers at the time, was that they were an expression of frustration over the limited gains of the early civil rights movement and the War on Poverty, motivated by the explosion of Black Power ideology after Malcolm X's assassination in 1965. In fact, though, outbreaks of "ghetto violence," as police and the media tended to refer to these incidents, were becoming common in poor urban areas across the country already by the early 1960s, and they are best understood as a response to accumulated experiences of police brutality and harassment in Black and Latino neighborhoods, exacerbated by the suffering that resulted from entrenched poverty.[2]

Police abuse was one of the primary civil rights issues around which Puerto Rican community organizers mobilized in the 1960s. Incidents of police brutality had spurred frequent protests in the 1950s; then, after an especially horrific police shooting case in 1963—when two Puerto Rican men were shot in the back of a patrol car—community and labor organizers founded the National Association for Puerto Rican Civil Rights (NAPRCR). Within a few years, the goals of the NAPRCR would be tested as community leaders in both Chicago and New York confronted full-scale riots in their cities' Puerto Rican neighborhoods, both sparked by incidents of police brutality.

It was in Chicago that the first major riot in a Puerto Rican community took place during the summer of 1966, and the upheaval commanded national news coverage. Ironically, the riot exploded on the last night of "Puerto Rican Week," a celebration convened by Mayor Richard Daley in an effort to show appreciation for the city's newest migrant group. After police shot and wounded a young Puerto Rican man during a foot chase, officers claimed that the man, Arcelis Cruz, had wielded a gun at an officer, but witnesses disputed that account. Protests erupted as bystanders attempted to help Cruz and were treated roughly by police, some of whom used dogs to manage the crowds. During three nights of rioting, police shot at and hit at least seven Puerto Rican men in their efforts to "restore order."[3]

The explosion had been more or less predicted by some observers. Commenting on the escalating tensions between police and residents in one of Chicago's largest Puerto Rican communities, an editorialist for the publication *El Puertorriqueño* had warned in 1965, "The time will come when we will have war on Division Street because of a lack of understanding between the police and our people." A year before that, in 1964, a youth worker on Chicago's West Side, where many Puerto Ricans lived, noted that " . . . police repeatedly roughed up youths, forced them to remove scarves they wore on their heads, tore up their cigarettes, confiscated their money, and subjected them to verbal abuse." That same summer Puerto Ricans also rioted against similar abuse in Perth Amboy, New Jersey and North Collins, New York.[4]

Immediately after the riot, one reporter for the African American *Chicago Defender* wrote that suddenly, both the city administration and "the [African American] civil rights movement" were "wooing" Puerto Ricans in the city as they tried to placate or collaborate with them. Another report in the *Defender* described the affirmation of support by the city's African American West Side Organization (WSO) for the "Puerto Rican Freedom movement." "Job discrimination, inadequate housing, and unfair treatment by police are all problems common to both people," said a WSO leader.[5] Although it was not uncommon for activists in either group to note the shared concerns of Puerto Ricans and African Americans, this brief report was notable for its use of the term "Puerto Rican movement." At this point, in 1966, the "Negro movement" had become a household phrase (and was just beginning to give way to a new term, the

"Black movement"), but Puerto Ricans were not typically credited with creating their own movement until some years later. This report on the aftermath of the Division Street riot forecast a new expansion of Puerto Ricans' campaigns for civil rights.

Puerto Rican activists certainly intended to make the most of this moment in the spotlight, highlighting the need for an organized response from both community leaders and local government. A Chicago-based community organizer in his forties, Juan Díaz, spearheaded the creation of a group called the Spanish Action Committee of Chicago (SACC, still in existence over 50 years later), to raise a unified voice with which to make demands of Chicago's Mayor Daley. SACC was inaugurated by a march and rally, identified by observers as the first such public protest organized by Chicago's Puerto Rican community. New Yorker Ted Vélez, of the East Harlem Tenant's Council, traveled to Chicago to join the march and show the "solid support from the New York community"; other New York activists also converged on Chicago that summer.[6]

More conservative Puerto Rican leaders in Chicago were nervous about the sudden radicalization, as were Chicago police. A surveillance report of Puerto Rican organizations from that summer (police had begun infiltrating a variety of organizations funded by the Community Action Program earlier in the year) notes that its author, an officer in the Intelligence Division, "launched an all-out anti-Ted Vélez, anti-Juan Díaz campaign amongst the original committee members of subject organization [SACC], with emphasis on the subversive into-nations."[7] What stands out here is that the Chicago police had assembled detailed knowledge of Puerto Rican activists in other cities—Ted Vélez, in this case—and were working explicitly against collaborative efforts by Puerto Rican leaders in different parts of the country.

In a national climate of fear and mounting racial tensions, the Division Street riot was soon overshadowed by riots in African American neighborhoods in Cleveland and Detroit, also in 1966. Throughout that summer in New York City, clashes between youth and police were visibly escalating, reaching the point of small-scale riots in Puerto Rican areas of the South Bronx and in the East New York and Brownsville sections of Brooklyn, although few of these incidents made national news. Puerto Rican leaders around the city understood the level of pressure that was building in these communities. It was not a coincidence that, earlier in 1966, a coalition of Hispanic leaders—largely Puerto Rican, but including heads of organizations representing other Latin American groups too—held a series of meetings with newly elected Mayor Lindsay, seeking "to convey grievances and community development proposals to City Hall."[8]

Labor and community organizer Gilberto Gerena Valentín, who helped convene this coalition, told the Mayor he was "shock[ed] at the seeming inability of your administration to find qualified Puerto Ricans to fill policy-level positions in the city's government." Within two months, newly elected Mayor Lindsay had named Gerena Valentín as director of the Business and Employment

Division of the City's Commission on Human Rights, along with several others offered positions in his administration. Gerena Valentín had become a somewhat controversial figure by this point. He was among the New York Puerto Rican community's best known figures, with leadership positions in two of the most high-profile organizations, the Puerto Rican Day Parade committee and the Congreso de los Pueblos. Recently, he had been accused of earlier ties to communist groups, which did not worry other members of the non-communist left, but did concern some mainstream leaders.[9]

Gerena Valentín and other organizers convinced the Mayor's office to sponsor a conference in spring 1967 to discuss the range of problems confronted by New York's Puerto Rican communities: decent housing, fair employment, educational achievement, access to social services, and the increasingly strained relations with police. One of the main goals of the conference was to coordinate efforts to address these problems; the other was to increase the visibility of the Puerto Rican community. As various leaders pointed out, the items on the agenda were issues Puerto Ricans had been pressing city officials to address (in New York as well as in Chicago) for many years. Repeating his admonition to the Mayor from the previous year, Gerena Valentín proclaimed, in his concluding remarks, "there is no representation of our community in the Mayor's Cabinet, yet we comprise 12% of the City's population . . . There is not a single Puerto Rican as a full paid commissioner."[10] Puerto Ricans' invisibility—and the associated lack of political power and representation—remained one of the community's most pressing challenges.

The annual Puerto Rican Day Parade, which would take place six weeks after the 1967 conference, was one way the community tried to challenge such invisibility, and had been doing so for the previous decade. Gerena Valentín served as head of the Parade's planning committee, which was one of Puerto Rican New York's liveliest organizations in that era, populated by a revolving array of high profile community leaders. The theme the committee chose for that year was "War on Poverty," even though this was a slogan whose hopefulness was already beginning to fade. Since Johnson had declared the nation's War on Poverty three years earlier, the flurry of city-level and community-level action, funded by the federal government, seemed to be doing little to slow the mounting frustration and anger in Black and Latino communities.

A month after the 1967 Puerto Rican Day Parade in New York City, a young Puerto Rican man was shot to death by an off-duty officer, who said the youth had been wielding a knife. Street protests developed into a full-blown riot that shook Puerto Rican East Harlem for three days. Young Puerto Ricans roamed the neighborhood in large groups, taunting police and instigating further conflict with them. Hundreds of community leaders organized dozens of community meetings to try to halt the violence. In an effort to reduce the scale of the rioting and minimize the violence, Mayor Lindsay ordered police not to shoot rioters or looters and visited the neighborhood repeatedly to try to end the confrontations.

Still, police killed two people during the riot (and denied responsibility until later faced with ballistics evidence), with many arrests, burnt police cars, and substantial property damage.[11]

By 1960s' standards, this riot was relatively contained and not as destructive as many others, but the Mayor's office took it seriously. City officials also began to acknowledge that some of both Mayor Wagner's and Lindsay's efforts at strengthening Puerto Rican communities had been ineffectual and insufficient. In the aftermath of the riots, Puerto Rican civil rights and community leaders, with Gerena Valentín once again playing a prominent role as chairman of a new 60-person planning committee, seized the opportunity to make sharp and concrete demands on city and federal agencies for more funding for housing, education, and community programs, and for more attention to problems of discrimination and marginalization.[12]

Puerto Rican leaders also pushed for more representation in city and state government. Although positions of real power were slow to materialize, one of the notable outcomes of the recent pressure was the appointment in June 1968 of Josephine Nieves, a former leader of the Puerto Rican Forum and the Puerto Rican Community Development Program, to direct the regional Office of Economic Opportunity, covering New York, New Jersey, and New England. This was a powerful position, as Nieves took charge of distributing $140 million annually for all programs supported by federal anti-poverty funds: Community Action Programs, Head Start, Legal Services, and various youth programs, including Job Corps.[13] Another important appointment was Félix Cosme, a social worker and former Migration Division program manager, who was named deputy commissioner of the New York City Human Resources Administration.[14]

The day after East Harlem's riot ended, and as a massive riot still raged in Detroit's largest African American community, President Johnson convened a National Advisory Commission on Civil Disorders (later referred to as the Kerner Commission), to study the causes of the scores of riots that had shaken dozens of U.S. cities in the previous several years. The commission's report, produced a few months later, characterized the riots as "racial disorders," famously declaring that "our nation is moving toward two societies, one black, one white—separate and unequal." The fact that this characterization excluded Chicanos and Puerto Ricans, who had played a major role in the decade's urban uprisings in their respective regions, was not particularly surprising to Latino leaders—and underlined the urgent need for increased visibility and more effective organizing in their communities.[15] Just weeks after the publication of the Kerner Commission report, in April 1968, Martin Luther King, Jr. was assassinated. At that point, even the commission's more accurate insights could do little to halt the momentum of social unrest expressed in urban riots, and the summer of 1968 would see even more extensive rioting around the country, including in Puerto Rican neighborhoods all over the Mid-Atlantic.

Another important action in the growing Puerto Rican movement that year was Puerto Ricans' participation in the 1968 Poor People's Campaign, organized by the Southern Christian Leadership Conference (SCLC) in the months before Dr. Martin Luther King's assassination. Gilberto Gerena Valentín recalled in his memoir that Dr. King convened dozens of leaders "of different races and ethnic groups" for a planning meeting in Atlanta in March 1968, which King and the SCLC referred to as the Minority Group conference. East Harlem Tenants' Council leader Ted Vélez was part of the delegation from New York, along with Frank Espada, former director of the City Community Development Agency, and Gerena Valentín, who was by then a member of the New York City Human Rights Commission and had been the primary organizer for Puerto Ricans' participation in the 1963 March on Washington. Hundreds of Puerto Ricans from various cities in the U.S. also joined in the planning effort, pledging "to make meaningful steps to fulfill nonviolence and uplifting programs for which that great black leader stood."[16]

According to Gerena Valentín, there were "differences of opinion," both among participants in the Minority Group conference and among other leaders, about how to create a partnership between African Americans and Puerto Ricans. This was especially difficult in New York City, where, as Gerena Valentín pointed out, Blacks and Puerto Ricans had begun to compete, bitterly in some cases, for access to federal War on Poverty funds. Although "the idea of 'everyone pulling together' seemed a little over-optimistic," recalled Gerena Valentín, the heterogeneous mix of marchers made the most of "the opportunity to take our demands directly to Washington and to present our cause to the rest of the nation and the world." Puerto Rican planners created a smaller Puerto Rican march as part of the national protest, to draw attention to specific Puerto Rican needs. Their demands for reform and change were also exemplified by a rumor that Puerto Ricans would stage a citywide strike, which did not ultimately happen.[17]

Tensions remained high all over the city. Rioting erupted during the summer of 1968 in New York's Puerto Rican communities, extending from the South Bronx to the Lower East Side to Coney Island—and well beyond New York too: riots shook Puerto Rican communities throughout urban New Jersey, including Perth Amboy, Elizabeth, Camden, Paterson, Passaic, Jersey City, Hoboken, Trenton, New Brunswick, and Newark; and in Philadelphia, Hartford, and New Haven too.[18] In many cases, these were rebellions in which Puerto Rican and African American youth joined together in violent protest, or rioted side by side in neighboring communities. Although such explosions seemed to take white leaders and officials by surprise, African American and Latino leaders understood that the era of active, persistent rebellion against police authority would continue as long as the provocations continued.

The New York police deployed a specialized riot unit, the Tactical Patrol Force, which caused intense resentment in the neighborhoods they descended upon at the first sign of unrest. In one leaflet distributed in the Lower East Side in July 1968, community activists proclaimed: "We are not animals . . . We do not need the Tactical Police Force [*sic*] in our neighborhoods to show our human dignity." A year later, the consecutive years of summer riots were a major topic of concern during New York's contentious Democratic mayoral primary. In a meandering essay he wrote for the *New York Times* to broadcast his candidacy (alongside eight other Democratic contenders), writer Norman Mailer picked apart the city's growing sense of social "breakdown," concluding that "our fix is to put the blame on the blacks and Puerto Ricans. But everybody knows that nobody can really know where the blame resides."[19]

Corrupt police certainly deserved a part of the blame; the role of corruption in the ongoing problem of police brutality was unveiled in New York City in 1971, when a scandal forced Mayor Lindsay to organize a special commission to investigate the problem. Former Migration Division Director Joseph Montserrat was appointed to the five-person body, which examined every form of police corruption except the use of violence and excessive force. A Black former police officer reported years later to a researcher that "the dudes that are taking the brothers' money are the dudes that are breaking the brothers' heads."[20]

Despite the substantial gains achieved by Puerto Rican by the end of the 1960s—in terms of programs developed, funding accumulated, protests organized, and even a few key political appointments secured—leaders and activists acknowledged that they needed direct electoral representation at the top positions in order to continue strengthening their communities. Gerena Valentín convened a large conference in early 1969 to "stress the Puerto Rican political role" in general and in the upcoming mayoral election. It was reportedly a great success in terms of generating visibility for the community. "We want to radicalize the Puerto Rican community here to obtain first-class citizenship," Gerena Valentín said. A few months later, he was fired from his position on the Human Rights Commission, allegedly for using his office to support his run for city council and for "inflaming and dividing the community" instead of conciliating or building bridges.[21] Gerena Valentín responded with a hunger strike. The organizing momentum he helped generate would continue, especially through the National Association of Puerto Rican Civil Rights, but Gerena Valentín no longer could serve as a direct intermediary with city officials.

Electoral Politics: Political Pressure and Militancy

Just before the New York City mayoral election in the fall of 1969, journalist Alfonso Narváez took the measure of Puerto Rican political representation in the *New York Times* with the headline "Puerto Rican Prospect: 10% of population, 0% of political power." Narváez reached this conclusion after interviewing Migration Division head Joseph Montserrat and community organizer Frank Espada, who attributed Puerto Ricans' lack of electoral success throughout the

1960s partly to demography—the group's median population age was 19, which meant that relatively few Puerto Ricans were old enough to vote. Montserrat and Espada also cited a lack of coordination within the community to run candidates that could garner adequate support and not compete against one another.[22]

In addition to these challenges, community leaders in the late 1960s blamed both city and national officials for the paucity of political influence achieved by Puerto Ricans in the U.S. At a meeting with New York Mayor Lindsay in the fall of 1966—just a few months after Chicago's Puerto Rican community had experienced a riot—local leaders objected strenuously to city officials' tendency to look to island officials and representatives of the Migration Division for advice about the Puerto Rican migrants' communities in the U.S. The years of increasingly widespread protest over police abuse and civil rights violations had generated new modes of organization and forged powerful connections within the community—and those who created that momentum expected to be consulted by local officials who were becoming increasingly concerned about "unrest" in poor communities.[23] On the other hand, Puerto Rican community leaders recognized they had not yet produced the kind of political strategy and influence that could protect a large and impoverished migrant community. Most agreed that it was representation by elected Puerto Rican leaders, not merely a handful of appointed "advisors" on Puerto Rican affairs, that would enable a powerful response to the socioeconomic slide that was gathering speed by the mid-1960s.

Previous generations had made various efforts to use electoral politics to attain the group's fair share of influence at the local level; but during the charged years of the late 1960s, the achievement of visibility and leverage in city and regional politics came to seem essential to Puerto Ricans' survival. While it was an exaggeration to assert that the group held "0%" of political power in the city, the achievement of political influence remained elusive despite some key gains earlier in the decade. Puerto Ricans in New York had managed to elect four Puerto Ricans to the state assembly in New York by 1965, which scholar José Cruz refers to as "the watershed year," and sent their first representative, Robert García, to the state Senate in 1967. But that success seemed to stall quickly, and Puerto Rican leaders still voiced frustration about remaining under-represented and unheard. Beyond New York, where close to a million Puerto Ricans lived by 1970, political momentum built up far more slowly. Camden elected a single Puerto Rican city council member in the 1960s, and Philadelphia had a Puerto Rican member of the state assembly, but in both cities the real breakthrough into city politics did not happen until the 1980s. Likewise, in both Chicago and Hartford, Puerto Ricans managed to get a few city appointments by the 1970s, but would not see major appointments or candidates elected to significant offices until the 1980s.[24]

Even as more Puerto Rican leaders in this era threw enormous energy into electoral politics, the necessity of focusing on their communities' dire problems of everyday life often took precedence. In other words, aspiring politicians were required to strike a delicate balance between addressing immediate community concerns and pursuing larger political ambitions. The career of lawyer and politician Herman Badillo in the late 1960s and early 1970s exemplifies some of this tension and illustrates the shifting dynamics and the growing momentum of Puerto Rican political empowerment in New York City in that decade.[25] (Similar patterns would be seen in cities with smaller but significant Puerto Rican communities—Chicago, Philadelphia, Hartford, Camden, and Newark—in the 1980s.) Badillo served as borough president of the Bronx from 1965 to 1969, an elected office analogous to deputy mayor for each respective borough. In that role, Badillo was widely praised, and seemed poised for continued achievement in politics.

Indeed, Badillo stepped down as Bronx borough president in 1969 in order to compete in the Democratic mayoral primary, alongside eight other contenders (which dwindled down to six by the time of the election). He lost, earning a respectable percentage of the vote. The following year, though, Badillo campaigned to serve as U.S. Congressional representative for his South Bronx district and won, becoming the first Puerto Rican representative in the U.S. Congress. Badillo's district was one where the Puerto Rican voting bloc had grown substantially during the 1960s, although that growth was mostly proportional, not numerical. In that decade, the terrible conditions in the South Bronx, including tenement fires, violent crime, and shuttered business districts, caused many residents to flee if they could afford to do so. Puerto Ricans comprised a majority of those who stayed—about 55,000 of 80,000 registered Democrats, by one contemporary estimate—and fell into in the "working poor" category. Most of the remainder were African Americans living in equally poor conditions just north of the Puerto Rican neighborhoods. As bad as this scenario was for residents, it also created a new political challenge: with a more homogeneous ethnic base, there emerged a growing number of Puerto Rican leaders seeking political office, which generated both productive competition and bitter conflict in the district.[26]

After his first term in Congress, Badillo was challenged in the Democratic primary in 1972 by Manuel Ramos, who had served in the state assembly since 1970. Ramos claimed Badillo had weak credentials as a true representative of the Puerto Rican community. Ramos charged that Badillo, who lived in the Bronx's only upper-middle class enclave and whose wife was Jewish, was not "Puerto Rican enough." Badillo did not deny that he did not define himself only as a Puerto Rican politician; he had worked steadily throughout his career on building coalitions with other liberal, progressive leaders who represented the two largest minority groups in New York, Jews and African Americans. In responding to Ramos's attack, Badillo's strategy was to focus not on identity but on ideology and policy positions. Having openly criticized New York's Governor Rockefeller for mishandling the violent prisoner uprising at the state's infamous Attica prison in 1971—Badillo went to Attica during the incident to serve as a witness and enforce respect for prisoners' rights—Badillo in turn accused Ramos, who supported Rockefeller and his tough-on-crime approach, of being out of touch with their community's larger political goals. "If Ramos were sent to Congress he would be more conservative than Nixon," said Badillo.[27]

In spite of such taunts about his loyalty to Puerto Rican people, Badillo at the time of his Congressional win was seen as a singularly powerful force in the rising tide of "minority" politics in the city. State Senator Robert García, who won his seat in 1967, remarked that, "for Puerto Ricans, Herman Badillo is like Jackie Robinson . . . [His success] goes beyond mere charisma. It's political magic." On the other hand, echoing Ramos's claims, many Puerto Rican activists accused Badillo of pandering to the political mainstream rather than concerning himself with the preoccupations of many of his Puerto Rican constituents. Gilberto Gerena Valentín, the labor activist and civic leader, frequently served as a bridge between leftist grassroots organizations and city officials, and in this case criticized Badillo for refusing to participate in a Unity conference of Spanish-speaking activists in Arlington, Virginia in 1971.[28] This kind of position put Badillo increasingly at odds with many politicized Puerto Ricans in New York, especially young voters who supported a more militant nationalist ideology.

In the absence of support from a growing number of his left-leaning constituents, it was not just persistence and charisma, magical or otherwise, that gave Badillo an edge in the political field. Badillo had two other important things going for him. First, he was never in his long career associated with corruption or cronyism (unlike some of his rivals, including Ramón Vélez and, later, Robert García). Second, Badillo's congressional victory involved very good timing. The reconfiguration of his South Bronx district in time for the 1970 election almost certainly helped his candidacy. Many Puerto Rican leaders denied some city officials' claims this was now "a truly Puerto Rican district," but at the very least, the question of Puerto Rican voters' political empowerment had been validated by the redistricting debate. And, nearly a decade after their first scuffle over redistricting in New York, Puerto Rican leaders now also had the federal government on their side.[29] In 1970, Congress passed a series of amendments to the 1965 Voting Rights Act, one of which stipulated that the Justice Department would investigate the districting lines of any county in which fewer than half the eligible population had registered or voted in the 1968 elections.[30] The goal was to open up to public scrutiny the process by which politicians decided which voters belonged in which districts, to curb the customary practice of "gerrymandering"—drawing district lines in such a way that minority or opposition voters were divided. The practice of gerrymandering had hindered the political empowerment of most poor Black and Latino communities, which should have grown in proportion with their increasing numerical strength in many cities during the 1960s.

Efforts to adjust district lines for U.S. congressional and New York state assembly, and city council districts produced mixed results and continued to inspire debate and disagreement during the 1970s. After his district was redrawn again in advance of the 1972 election, Badillo himself worried about the efficacy of a congressional district that combined voters in Puerto Rican areas of East Harlem, the Bronx, and Queens. Controversy also erupted over the New York city council's 1972 plan to redraw its districts, which the *New York Times* called a "bad and inadequately debated scheme," despite its admirable goal "to expand minority group representation on the council." (In 1972, the 37-member council had only two African American members and no Puerto Ricans or other Latinos, despite comprising 32% of the population.) As stipulated in the 1970 Voting Rights amendments, the United States Justice Department got involved, asserting in its 1974 ruling that several New York districts had been gerrymandered in order to "curtail the representation of blacks and Puerto Ricans."[31]

Although the simple math of larger constituencies could not guarantee political recognition, Puerto Rican leaders, determined to amplify their voice, worked hard to harness the growing demographic pressure within their communities. Districts with a majority or plurality of Puerto Rican voters began to appear on the electoral maps of a handful of northeastern cities, as well as Chicago. Even as Puerto Rican leaders struggled to mobilize voters, their growing constituencies influenced city and state officials to make appointments (non-electoral positions) of Puerto Ricans to significant posts. For instance, in 1972, Chicago's Mayor Daley appointed the first Special Assistant for Hispanic affairs, Myriam Cruz. At the same time, Illinois Governor Richard Ogilvie appointed a new Special Assistant for Latino Affairs. During the same year—surely not a coincidence—an organization called Puerto Ricans Organized for Political Action had mounted a successful class action voting rights case insisting that Chicago voters had a right to access to elections materials in Spanish.[32]

Another notable electoral victory for Puerto Ricans happened in Miami in 1973, when Maurice Ferré, son of a successful Puerto Rican industrialist and nephew of the island's incumbent governor, won the city's nonpartisan contest for mayor.[33] Ferré had served in the Florida State House in 1967–68, representing a largely Cuban district. Cubans were just beginning to vote in notable numbers as many of them naturalized by the late 1960s, and although their pro-business and anti-Castro leanings typically translated to allegiance to Republicans, Ferré's Hispanic Caribbean roots and his family connections to a successful industrial and real estate business (based in Miami, Puerto Rico, Panama, and Venezuela) seemed to ease conservative Cubans' doubts about his political affiliation.[34] When Ferré won the mayoral race five years later, analysis of election returns suggested that turnout rates among "Latin" voters—most of them Cuban—was far higher than among other ethnic groups in the city, giving Ferré a winning edge.

Once in office, Ferré made a case for representing Hispanics beyond just his Miami constituents. At an event celebrating the Cuban American Chamber of Commerce in Chicago, Ferré called for the creation of a national organization for the political and economic advancement of Hispanics, citing the paucity of political representation for Latinos in cities like Chicago despite their numerical strength. He also decried the limited gains provided by legal and policy protections, compounding Latinos' lack of power to demand change through legislative means. "There is no organization to demand the rights of a New York Puerto Rican boy who drops out of school because he doesn't understand English . . . There is no Hispanic urban league, no N.A.A.C.P. or B'nai B'rith," said Ferré. "The only weapon that 15 million Spanish-speaking Americans have is political pressure and militancy. The time is now," he urged.[35] Indeed, Puerto Ricans around the country in the 1970s would take up the gauntlet.

Work and Economic Life: Reaching for Stability

By 1970, migrant and second-generation Puerto Ricans constituted nearly 15% of the New York City population and had well established communities in about 30 other cities. In New York, a third generation added to these numbers, uncounted by the census and including thousands of children from mixed marriage. Migration from the island had slowed greatly during the 1960s, and included substantial "reverse migration," in which migrants returned to the island, usually for retirement or because they preferred to raise their children in their homeland. Modest gains in income by the mid-1960s meant that fewer Puerto Ricans were poor and many had attained modest working class incomes. In many cities, the Puerto Ricans who had become most economically successful began moving into more middle-class neighborhoods, away from communities where their poorer compatriots still lived; this class division became especially visible in New York City.

A central question concerning Puerto Ricans' economic status around 1970 was whether the War on Poverty and its associated programs had actually improved conditions for the poorest in the community. Even for historians examining the evidence, the answer is not clear. During the 1960s a booming economy had lifted about half of the country's poor white population out of poverty by raising wages and lowering unemployment, but only marginally reduced the poverty rate for Puerto Ricans and Blacks. One of the few careful studies of poverty in the 1960s found that in 1968, after a decade of gains, a staggering 28% of Puerto Rican and Black working families (excluding retirees above 65 years) were still poor and another 13% were categorized as low income. 36% of working families were moderate and modest income earners. Poverty clearly had been reduced, but Blacks and Puerto Ricans in New York City still represented 75% of all people categorized as poor. Puerto Rican families tended to be larger, which increased the burdens of poverty. In-migration also compounded Puerto Ricans' poverty outcomes as a group, since newer migrants nearly always started at the lower end of the income scale.[36]

As the War on Poverty faltered, and the availability of jobs and steady incomes declined with deindustrialization, the availability of welfare became a social justice issue. New York's "generous" welfare payments, especially to working poor with children, grew tremendously during the 1960s but could barely compensate for the low wages earned and the increasing numbers of unemployed. In New York City, welfare caseloads doubled between 1964 and 1969 and the amount of cash grants also increased significantly. The National Welfare Rights Organization (NWRO), with its New York chapter led by Frank Espada, was partially responsible for the demand that increased funding be provided to the working poor. The NWRO also encouraged and trained the thousands of qualified poor to apply for benefits they were not receiving. In part because of the increased awareness of eligibility, welfare use by Puerto Ricans increased to 35% of the population by 1970, and included mostly assistance to low wage working parents with children.[37]

In spite of these high levels of poverty recorded in the late 1960s, most Puerto Ricans had in fact seen some increase in their income during the decade. A large minority of the Puerto Rican community in New York City was middle class or earned high enough wages to escape poverty. In addition to benefiting from the determined efforts of labor leaders and union members, Puerto Ricans in the 1960s saw some modest increases in the occupational categories that enabled middle class status: skilled workers, small business owners, professionals, and white collar workers. However, most Puerto Rican communities outside New York City lacked such class heterogeneity. In New Jersey, for example, 68% of Puerto Rican earners were considered low income, while a whopping 63% were "operatives" or "laborers." In Massachusetts, 75% worked in low wage service and manufacturing.[38] New York's more middle class Puerto Rican population made for a striking contrast.

The Puerto Rican community in New York City was becoming more socio-economically stratified, however. Most of those who made big economic gains during the 1960s were either long-established migrants or U.S.-born, not recent migrants who struggled with English or who had low educational levels.[39] Skilled unionized workers continued to secure higher wages, two to three times as much as recent migrants. Many of the industries where the latter group worked, including the garment industry, were in a slow decline both in terms of numbers of jobs as well as stagnant wages at the lower ends of the pay scales. Younger second-generation Puerto Ricans avoided this sort of work, but for thousands of adult migrant women the slow decline of the garment industry in New York was the basis for an employment crisis that would bottom out by the early 1980s.

Deindustrialization accelerated dramatically during the 1970s. Between 1970 and 1974, 44,000 jobs were lost each year in New York City, the same number of industrial jobs lost during the entire 1960s. This represented a catastrophic loss of opportunities for all low income New Yorkers, and it hit Puerto Ricans especially hard. (And the worst was yet to come, by the late 1970s.)[40] Decline in industry was accompanied by the loss of more than 300,000 retail jobs as well. Youth unemployment, already high, soared, while total unemployment nearly doubled between 1968 and 1973.[41] For young and middle-aged women, the unemployment rate was around 9%, slightly higher than the overall rate for men, although older women's unemployment rate was only 3.8%.[42] In the early 1960s, the poorest workers had been aided by a growing economy, modest gains in construction jobs, and increases in welfare payments and federal investments of the War on Poverty; but new unemployment trends erased most of the gains that had been made by 1968.

Although the proliferation of Puerto Rican protest organizations would come to define the community's activism in the late 1960s and early 1970s, along with a renewed emphasis on electoral politics, much of the civil rights work of that era on behalf of Puerto Ricans continued to be grounded in the labor movement. Union activists pushed for equal access and opening work opportunities for Puerto Ricans in higher paying, higher status employment sectors that often remained closed to them. In pushing for access and opportunity in the labor market, Puerto Ricans were able to rely on foundations built mostly through the efforts of Jewish labor organizations and the early African American movement in the 1940s and 1950s. Issues of work and wage equity became more visibly connected with government policy efforts to lift urban minority populations out of poverty, including new measures to combat bias and discrimination based on race, national origin, religion, or ethnicity.

Because so many of the social and economic issues of this era were debated in urban contexts, the ongoing challenges faced by Puerto Rican workers in rural areas got relatively little attention. Farm work was a steady part of the economy and the flow of Puerto Ricans seasonally to the farms of the east coast continued yearly, having increased to about 40,000 annually by 1967. While migrant workers, who usually lived in camps or on the farms themselves, frequently encountered racist or nativist verbal attacks by local residents, relations with police were worse: they routinely abused migrant workers verbally and limited their physical mobility with low intensity harassment. Anthropologist Ismael García Colón has examined one important example of this sort of conflict, involving farm workers in North Collins, New York. In July 1966, hundreds of farmworkers in North Collins, pushed to their limit, gathered with bricks, bats, and other weapons and challenged local authorities to a violent confrontation if they did not agree to resolve migrants' problem with the police. The confrontation led to interventions by officials from the Migration Division and the New York Labor Department. In a rare acknowledgment that the origin of the problems was not with the migrant workers, the chief of police and other police officers were indicted, though later found not guilty by a local jury.[43]

In some regions, especially New York, New Jersey, Connecticut, and Massachusetts, members of nearby urban-based labor organizations responded to conflicts of this kind with supportive gestures towards farm workers. The New York State American Federation of Labor–Congress of Industrial Organizations (AFL-CIO) council supported full time organizers who helped non-unionized workers to clarify their demands and to push local and state officials for legislation that would provide improved working conditions. Puerto Rican labor organizers, representing the national and state organizations of the AFL-CIO, worked in upstate New York and Long Island to help Spanish-speaking farm workers demand better wages and conditions and gain access to government services. Paul Sánchez was one such representative. During the 1950s, he had worked in electrical factories and had become an active member of the youth and civil rights efforts of the International Brotherhood of Electrical Workers (IBEW), then, along with other Puerto Rican IBEW leaders in the 1960s, helped organize taxi drivers in the Bronx and spent time in California working with the United Farm Workers (UFW). Upon his return, Sánchez was assigned to work with farmworkers in upstate New York.[44]

The rise of the United Farm Workers (UFW), founded by Chicano labor organizer Cesar Chávez in California in 1962, provided a model for attempts to organize farm workers nationally and at the local level, motivating civic groups and unions in other sectors to help migrant workers. In Springfield, Massachusetts, a letter to the editor of the Springfield *Union* admonished Americans to learn why Spanish speakers were showing up in the area to work and reminded them how little they knew about Puerto Rico. "How can [anyone] say that Puerto Rican farm workers enjoy working in the heat as if they were inhuman beasts of burden?" Noting the difficult conditions on the island and the challenges met by labor unions there, the letter writer reminded readers that any effort to improve wages and conditions for Puerto Rican workers in Puerto Rico and in Massachusetts was to "help themselves at the same time."[45]

During the early 1970s, the U.S. branches of the Puerto Rican Socialist Party (PSP), along with church-based activists helped form various organizations to provide services to the seasonal farm workers. They organized short-lived farm worker organizations in New Jersey and Connecticut; the efforts were difficult to sustain given the transient status of the workers and their physical dispersion. A surge of support in 1973 to help form a union for the Puerto Rican farm workers got the attention of the Puerto Rico Department of Labor. The Puerto Rican Legal Defense and Education Fund (PRLDEF) and the American Civil Liberties Union also supported the union drive, although by 1977 these organizing efforts had withered, a result of staunch opposition from the growers and internal differences over strategy.[46]

Another important area of labor activism in the 1960s that converged with the core demands of Puerto Rican (and African American) civil rights organizations was the development of training and employment programs for youth, through collaborations between local and national officials. Youth employment and training programs were a key part of the anti-poverty organizations created by Puerto Rican leaders after the mid-1960s. In New York, many programs emphasized community-based training programs but when the city's focus shifted from community-centered programs to a more centralized model, the youth training components wavered and only achieved modest gains. The mixed results of this strategy contributed to the more dramatic and militant radicalization of poor youth after 1968. The career of Manny Díaz exemplifies this trajectory. Díaz, an activist social worker and a member of the Puerto Rican Forum and Director of the Puerto Rican Community Development Project, served in the late 1960s and early 1970s as deputy commissioner of New York's newly created Department of Manpower and Training. By the late 1960s the city's anti-poverty efforts, managed by the Manpower and Training agency, had shifted from relying on local community organizations and councils to centralized programs that enhanced the skills and social capital of the poor.[47] This transition helps explain why, after nearly a decade, the youth-oriented programs—even the ones directed by Puerto Ricans—had problems reaching significant sectors of the community.

Motivated by the slowly worsening industrial job markets for low wage workers in the Northeast skilled Puerto Rican industrial workers reached a peak of high wages and integration with the labor movement in the late 1960s. In 1969 New York's Central Labor Council (CLC)—a coordinating committee for most unions in New York City, representing hundreds of thousands of workers— permitted the inclusion of a Hispanic Labor Committee (HLC) on its advisory council. A significant impetus for the advancement of Puerto Rican leadership had come from the strongest unions, those with the highest-skill workers, like the IBEW. Paul Sánchez, the IBEW organizer who also worked to unionize Puerto Rican farm workers in upstate New York, had represented the IBEW in the CLC earlier in the 1960s. With his experience as a co-founder of both the Santiago Iglesias Society (an organization of Hispanic workers within the IBEW), and of the National Association of Puerto Rican Civil Rights, where he worked with Gilberto Gerena Valentín, Sánchez became a prominent union leader who successfully lobbied, over the course of a decade, for the creation of the HLC.[48] The recognition achieved by the HLC represented an acknowledgement by the union leadership of the now vast number of industrial workers who were Spanish-speaking. Formal incorporation would provide Spanish-speaking workers with access to citywide resources. It also gave them some political clout; the CLC's Civil Rights Committee became an important citywide player that coordinated political work with similar committees in hundreds of union locals throughout the city.

In seeking a place within an older and more conservative union leadership by about 1970, Puerto Rican labor leaders in New York City faced a major obstacle: the perception that they made militant demands and approached negotiations with rebelliousness and a confrontational style. The staid union hierarchy was struggling to process the effects of the radicalizing Black Power movement and a growing white opposition, particularly the racial divisions and white backlash following the city's 1968 teachers' strike.[49] The teachers' strike generated tremendous conflict within the CLC. Since the teachers' union was dominated by white leadership and members, most of them opposed to Black and Puerto Rican communities' efforts to introduce "community control" into the city's schools, progressive unions and Black and Puerto Rican leadership demanded that the CLC help end the teachers' strike and support the community demands. After initially supporting the strike, most Black and Puerto Rican union officials concluded that the purpose of the strike was "to wipe out" and "cripple" the community control efforts; they staged a 50-person sit-in at the CLC offices to force the issue.[50]

Conflicts abounded in the heterogeneous union movement, as members navigated terrain marked by racial and ethnic tensions. Black and Puerto Rican workers fought to democratize the hierarchy of the International Ladies' Garment Workers' Union (ILGWU), and Transit Workers' Union (TWU) complained of an entrenched white leadership that made little space for the majority Black and Puerto Rican rank and file. Within the TWU a well-organized insurgency, calling itself the Rank and File Committee for a Democratic Union, organized to push for equality and access to the union's higher paying jobs. They supported an NAACP lawsuit against the union and the transit authority that claimed that Blacks and Puerto Ricans were systematically excluded from higher paying jobs. The car repair shops, for example, where the highest paying job categories were found, continued to be nearly completely white, despite the fact that Black and Puerto Rican workers comprised two thirds of the TWU membership. District 65, a union known for its militant recruitment of Puerto Rican and Black workers and promoting them to leaders, actually withdrew from its parent union and the AFL-CIO for its refusal to "provide 'aggressive and progressive leadership' in organizing millions of low paid Negro and Puerto Rican workers."[51]

Labor continued to be an area of major civil rights activism during the late 1960s and early 1970s. Unions mobilized votes and harnessed hundreds of thousands of dollars in contributions to organizations working for Black and Puerto Rican rights. From within the labor movement, activists pushed for higher paying skilled jobs, especially in construction, and for opening training programs for youth. They also made a firm commitment to advancing Black and Puerto Rican leaders to the highest ranks of the union hierarchy. Many labor activists also extended their vision of social justice beyond the labor unions. The International Brotherhood of Electrical Workers built the Electchester apartment complex in Queens, where many Puerto Rican electrical workers bought their first apartments; Local 1199 also supported the construction of city-funded housing for its workers, promoting a strong ideology of multi-racial solidarity and "unionism [as] a way of life." [52]

Community Organizing: Housing and Community Development

By the tumultuous midpoint of the 1960s, Puerto Ricans in New York City could look back on a long history of community organizing, and in smaller cities, many of their compatriots were starting to build strong grassroots community organizations of their own. Observing the shift toward Black Power within the

African American movement and the urgency of the claims expressed by the rioting in urban ghettoes (including riots in Puerto Rican communities in Chicago
and New York), Puerto Rican leaders devoted more and more attention to what
was happening in "the streets." The War on Poverty brought both federal funds
and official recognition to community organizing efforts, expanding the possibilities of that grassroots work. On the other hand, access to funds also produced
new sources of competition and, at times, acrimony within the communities
with most to gain from the offerings of the Office of Economic Opportunity
(OEO). Housing and other quality of life issues remained a constant and increasingly central issue in Puerto Rican communities—not just in New York, where
community organizers had accumulated decades of experience in addressing
housing problems, but also in cities with smaller and more recent Puerto Rican
communities, including Philadelphia, Boston, and Chicago. By the early 1970s,
social service and community organizations were more and more defined by their
emphasis on housing.

In Chicago in the late 1960s Puerto Rican community leaders faced a particular problem as they sought to make use of the new funds provided by the
OEO during the years after the 1966 Division Street riots. Allegedly, those
who sought Community Action Program grants, or even jobs in the agencies funded by those grants, needed the blessing of precinct captains, the local
representatives of Mayor Daley's powerful Democratic machine. The two
organizations that became most central in their communities in this era were
the Division Street Urban Progress Center (DSUPC) and the Spanish Action
Committee of Chicago (SACC), both founded in the weeks following the
riots.[53] Mayor Daley's Committee on Urban Opportunity (analogous to New
York's Poverty Council) eagerly authorized the grants to support social service work within the community that had so recently exploded. Some Puerto
Ricans were skeptical about Mayor Daley's commitment to changing the social
and economic dynamics that left Puerto Ricans as a group among the most
vulnerable in Chicago; it was a skepticism that served as motivation for many
community leaders. Hector Franco, for example, a young social worker hired
by the DSUPC, later recalled:

> . . . it was just a matter of weeks after being out in the field that I came to
> the conclusion that the Center was not capable of correcting any of these
> problems [with employment, housing, welfare, and health care]; that the
> Center was established to quiet down the noise that we were making that
> summer. So we began to organize the people.[54]

In New York, the problems surrounding post-riot organizing had more to do
with competition among recently established community organizations, each
of which sought to maximize visibility within the city's increasingly crowded
landscape of social service providers and to win federal anti-poverty grants. The

most intense rivalry developed between two agencies in East Harlem, where the largest concentration of Puerto Ricans still resided. The East Harlem Tenants' Council (EHTC) was a robust organization founded in 1962 by Puerto Rican activists to guide residents through housing problems and to mobilize opposition to urban renewal approaches that harmed poor communities like East Harlem. The other organization, Massive Economic Neighborhood Development (MEND), had been founded in 1965. Puerto Rican activist and founding board member Humberto Cintrón had succeeded in securing money for MEND from the first round of grants from the OEO's Community Action Program. When EHTC leaders accused MEND of representing "not the poor, but the established social work agencies," MEND countered that its flexible structure, with ten separate divisions based around Harlem, enabled its leadership to engage community members in planning projects in their immediate neighborhoods. In 1966, city officials awarded half its budget of federal anti-poverty funds to MEND, and only about 15% to EHTC.[55]

In spite of its struggles for funding, the East Harlem Tenants Council was without a doubt the largest and most powerful of the housing organizations led by Puerto Ricans in the 1960s, and it appears as an important player in many of the social dramas in that era (and not just in New York—Ted Vélez, one of EHTC's founders, was investigated by the Chicago police department as an alleged instigator of that city's Puerto Rican riots in 1966). EHTC participated in planning the most ambitious project in the fight for low income housing in New York in this era, a massive housing development project in East Harlem called the Taíno Towers. The development, named for the original inhabitants of the islands of Puerto Rico and Hispaniola before the arrival of Europeans, consisted of four high rise towers between Second and Third Avenues, containing 656 low rent units. EHTC leaders worked with city officials and several New York-based banks to piece together the funding, which included grants from the Model Cities program and a low interest federal mortgage, reaching final approval in 1971. Yolanda Sánchez, a member of the EHTC board of directors, played a key coordinating role in the project, and later described herself to historian Roberta Gold as a "kid who grew up on welfare . . . now in charge of a $40 million housing project." "The sixties was a whole different world," remarked Sánchez.[56]

Indeed, by 1970, activists in various poor neighborhoods in New York City had begun organizing tenants, nearly all of them Puerto Rican and African American, to participate in rent strikes and tenant takeovers of buildings abandoned by landlords or those slated for "redevelopment" by the city, involving plans that made little or no provision for displaced low rent tenants. The rent strike was a strategy, first used in New York City by aggrieved tenement residents in the early 20th century, to force landlords or the city to take responsibility for substandard housing. The largest rent strike of the early 1970s, involving about 1,000 tenants, was organized by Black Panthers and Young Lords along with other housing activists in Ocean Hill-Brownsville, the community that became synonymous with Black and Puerto Rican radicalism after its takeover of the local schools in 1967.[57]

Tenants who gave up on uninhabitable apartments for which they had leases, and moved instead into abandoned buildings without a lease, were known as squatters, and by the late 1960s, hundreds of poor New Yorkers took this approach to demonstrating their frustration over the city housing crisis. The most high-profile action of the squatters' movement, so called by participants and critics alike, took place in Manhattan in an area designated as the West Side Urban Renewal Area. Organizers called the campaign Operation Move-In and recruited over 150 families. Given the publicity surrounding the campaign, and the intense politicization of housing at this moment, the city was forced to back off from threats of eviction and negotiate a relocation plan. For Puerto Rican activists, another important outcome of the squatters' movement on the Upper West Side was the formation of El Comité, a mostly-Latino collective of "Vietnam veterans, factory and construction workers, the unemployed, and former gang members" that took over a vacant storefront on Columbus Avenue in 1970 and began organizing in support of squatters' rights. Most members of El Comité were actively involved in other political struggles, including community control of schools, the Puerto Rican student movement, and Puerto Rican independence.[58]

Puerto Rican housing activists based on the Lower East Side also made their mark during this era. Ernesto Martínez, who had worked on the staff of Vito Marcantonio, the East Harlem congressional representative in the 1930s and 1940s, started an organization in the late 1960s called the Coalition for Human Housing. It was the first Latino-run housing organization in the Lower East Side—dominated by Puerto Rican women, according to the *New York Times*— and the Coalition's mission was to push back against urban renewal plans to replace low income housing with middle class apartments and condominiums. Under Martinez's leadership, the Coalition oversaw the creation of 1,600 subsidized housing units by the early 1970s.[59]

Each of these groups connected Puerto Ricans to the broader struggle against displacement in their communities. Displacement was an increasingly common experience for Puerto Ricans in many U.S. cities during the 1960s, and it worsened tremendously by the early 1970s, when the Bronx and other areas suffering from neglect and arson were literally burning. Rent strikes and seemingly anarchic squatting actions became connected to coordinated efforts to support the poor and challenge the treatment particularly of minority communities. What these stories also show is the substantial impact of anti-poverty programs on housing activism, as they contributed funding for both major redevelopment projects, like Taino Towers, as well as smaller community improvement initiatives. Even the organizations that cast a much smaller shadow made their mark, both by fighting to improve their communities' actual structures and by helping reshape the social landscape of the cities in which they struggled.

In Boston, the development of Puerto Rican community organizations in the 1960s followed a distinctive pattern, due to the group's small population there and its relatively recent arrival. Unlike its counterparts in New York and Chicago, Boston's Puerto Rican community was largely comprised of recent migrants, many of whom had come to Connecticut and Massachusetts initially as farm workers in the 1950s, but who made the shift in the 1960s to better paid factory work in the Boston area. They had had little opportunity for community organizing before the mid-1960s. But then, influenced by both activism and rioting in the Puerto Rican communities in Chicago, New York, Newark, and Philadelphia between 1966 and 1968, and boosted by funding from the OEO, Boston Puerto Ricans engaged in a flurry of community organizing, just like their counterparts in other cities.

By the mid-1960s, the South End of Boston, with its crumbling 19th century housing stock, had transitioned from a poor neighborhood of European and Jewish immigrants to a Black and then a Puerto Rican ghetto. When the new pastor of an Episcopal church in the South End heard from his Puerto Rican neighbors about the impact of housing problems in their area—negligent absentee landlords, lack of heat and working appliances, arson—he hired a Puerto Rican community organizer to help coordinate the community's response to the city's impending urban renewal plans. By 1966, that collaboration produced El Concilio de Acción (Council for Action), identified as Boston's first Puerto Rican community action organization, which focused primarily on housing issues in this era. Nearby, African American activists in the same neighborhood organized the South End Tenants Council as a response to the threat of urban renewal, and in 1969, their Puerto Rican neighbors organized the Tenants Emergency Committee (TEC) to represent their sector of the community. The TEC provided more than just a bulwark against gentrification. With the help of some VISTA volunteers, it also offered GED and English classes and a health clinic staffed with bilingual doctors. Around the same time, in Jackson-North Bay, another Puerto Rican community in Boston, La Unidad Hispana came together "to represent Spanish speaking people in Jackson and North Bay and help them solve their problems."[60]

According to one sociologist who wrote about Boston's early Puerto Rican community, much of the community activism in this era in Boston grew out of the church. In addition to the South End Episcopal church that first sponsored El Concilio, there were Catholic parishes in Puerto Rican communities that also initiated or gave support to community organizing projects in the late 1960s. Other accounts of Puerto Rican activism in Boston emphasize the ways the growing Puerto Rican struggle for fair housing attracted young activists from elsewhere in the region, many of them students, who sought to connect local problems to a broader focus on leftist ideology and Puerto Rican nationalism, much as their counterparts in New York City were doing at that time. After incidents of police abuse sparked rioting following the annual Puerto Rican Festival in Boston's South End, local organizing networks expanded into more political realms, including the creation of a chapter of the Puerto Rican Socialist Party (PSP) in Boston.[61]

Still, the core of Puerto Rican activism in South Boston remained anchored in issues of economic justice. Members of the TEC organized a welfare rights group, Madres Por Welfare, which was an increasingly common focus of grassroots community organizing in poor communities by the late 1960s.[62] Indeed, such groups came to comprise what was soon called the welfare rights movement. Although the movement in its most formal phase only lasted six or seven years—its primary organization, the National Organization of Welfare Rights (NOWR), folded in the early 1970s—this network of activists added a new dimension to the understanding of poverty in the U.S. by insisting on the rights of poor people to receive adequate government assistance. Leaders of Mobilization for Youth in New York City, together with Puerto Rican community organizer Frank Espada, had responded to what they saw as an obvious need in their communities by creating a Welfare Recipients League in 1964.[63] The goal was to provide information, advocacy, and support to individuals and families navigating the various public assistance programs sponsored by the city and by the federal government—and to people who qualified for such programs but were not receiving them. After a number of Welfare Recipients Leagues spread to poor neighborhoods across the city, Espada helped organize the Citywide Coordinating Committee of Welfare Groups in 1966. By 1967, they had joined with activists doing similar work promoting welfare rights in cities and created the National Welfare Rights Organization (NWRO), which collaborated with welfare rights groups and activists in over a dozen cities, staging a convention and rally with over a thousand participants in Washington in summer 1967.

Adding to the momentum and visibility of the NWRO was the Poor People's Campaign planned by Dr. Martin Luther King, Jr. and the Southern Christian Leadership Conference to take place during the spring and summer of 1968. (Dr. King was assassinated several weeks before the first scheduled actions of the campaign.) As with most grassroots advocacy organizing, the NWRO, a large national network, was only the most visible player in welfare rights activism. Puerto Ricans engaged in their own community-based welfare rights work alongside and in collaboration with the NWRO. In 1968, Gerena Valentín and Joseph Montserrat filled 100 buses bound for Washington, D.C. from New York City to participate in a Puerto Rican March on June 8 as part of an extended Poor People's Campaign that lasted for much of the summer of 1968. To mobilize participants in the weeks leading up to the march, organizers staged rallies in New York City, Philadelphia, and Boston; in Camden, Trenton, Vineland, and a handful of cities in northern New Jersey; in a dozen cities in Connecticut; in Chicago and a few smaller cities in the Midwest; and even in Los Angeles, San Francisco, and Miami.[64]

By 1969, the NWRO claimed 30,000 members, the majority of whom were recipients of Aid for Mothers with Dependent Children (AFDC, the entitlement program most commonly referred to as "welfare"). *Wall Street Journal* reporter Jonathan Spivak, in a piece titled "Why Do the Welfare Rolls Keep Rising?," asserted that the NWRO's strategy "is to create conflict and confrontation by 'sit-ins' and 'marches' on local welfare headquarters," though Spivak neglected to mention the consistent lobbying in Washington and efforts to gain the attention of congressional representatives voting on policy that affected federal entitlements. Spivak concluded that "its publicized successes—usually gaining 'special' extra grants for furniture or clothing—probably have attracted more of the poor to public assistance."[65] After campaigning consistently on behalf of welfare recipients for nearly a decade, the NWRO crumbled under financial pressure as mayors, governors, and the Nixon administration rolled back many public assistance programs in the early 1970s.[66]

Another notable event in Puerto Ricans' nascent welfare rights activism during that period was a hunger strike staged by Jack Agüeros, who was appointed in 1968 by New York's Mayor Lindsay as deputy commissioner of the city's Community Development Agency, which distributed funds to anti-poverty service-providing agencies. When Agüeros was notified that his probationary contract would not be extended due to a failure to file income tax returns for several years earlier in the decade, he initiated a hunger strike in his office a few blocks from City Hall. Over the course of five days of fasting (during which Agüeros drank water and coffee), Lindsay's deputy mayor negotiated with the Citywide Puerto Rican Action Committee, a consortium of leaders working in community, anti-poverty, and city agencies. Agüeros asserted that his action was not primarily about restoring his own job; he wanted to use the publicity surrounding his firing to demand that Mayor Lindsay give Puerto Ricans representation on the Board of Education, the Model Cities Advisory Committee, the Civil Service Commission, and the city Housing Authority. The Lindsay administration made a commitment to meet Agüeros's demands, validating the concern of "the Puerto Rican community . . . with matters of education, housing, and employment in the public sector."[67] Lindsay did indeed follow through with many important appointments including at Lincoln Hospital, the Housing Authority, the Board of Education, the City Planning Board, the Civilian Review Board, and various judgeships.

Education and Community Organizing: Community Control of Schools

Puerto Rican community leaders in New York had played an active role in educational issues dating back to the 1930s, but it was the boycott in 1964, to protest the persistent inequality in schools attended by the city's Puerto Rican and African American students, that marked the beginning of a new era of education-based activism in Puerto Rican communities. However much the boycott succeeded in giving more voice to supporters of integration in New York, the de facto segregation in northern urban schools was intransigent and produced many layers of disadvantage for Black and Puerto Rican students. In 1966, half the students in New York's schools were African American (30%) or Puerto Rican (20%), but each group only comprised a tiny proportion (3.6% and 1.6%, respectively) of those graduating from academic high schools; most Puerto Rican and Black high school students attended vocational programs. The vast majority attended schools where there were a quarter of the number of licensed teachers as at "top" (white) schools, and where teachers earned substantially lower salaries.[68]

With those frustrations motivating them, many activists redoubled their organizing efforts, asserting that what Black and Puerto Rican children really needed was not integration but rather the radical restructuring of the city's schools. The push by community activists for greater participation in the leadership, decision making, and everyday operation of their communities' schools intensified in 1966. That fall, parents and activists protested the outcome of a newly created Intermediate School (I.S. 201) in East Harlem, which the Board of Education had promised would attract an integrated student body. Many of the picketers pointed out that the school was only "integrated" if integration was taken to mean both Black and Puerto Rican students; with the school situated in the heart of East Harlem, no white parents had applied to enroll their children.[69]

As with the 1964 school boycott, leaders of national organizations offered their public support to this new chapter in the push for equality in the schools. Stokely Carmichael of the Student Nonviolent Coordinating Committee (SNCC) joined the demonstrators, as did members of the Black Panthers, along with representatives of community organizations like MEND and the East Harlem Tenants Council. The community's goals could only be accomplished, they said, through "community control"—a rallying cry that activists borrowed from a phrase popularized by Black Panthers' founders Bobby Seale and Huey Newton as they responded to police brutality by demanding "community control of police," then expanded the call to community control of all local institutions, including schools. By December 1966, a group of activists expressed its frustration by staging a two-day takeover of a Board of Education building, calling for the "People's Board of Education." Milton Galamison, a Presbyterian minister and a leader of the 1964 school boycott, was elected president of the People's Board of Education, alongside vice president Evelina López Antonetty, a field organizer for the Puerto Rican Community Development Project and longtime community activist from the Bronx.[70]

Earlier that year, Antonetty had founded a parent advocacy organization, United Bronx Parents (UBP), running it on a shoestring budget until it got funded by the OEO and was able to expand its reach to neighborhoods beyond the South Bronx. Tapping into the zeitgeist, with a focus on direct engagement of community members, Antonetty built an organization that empowered parents, children, and their communities—not just by providing training and resources but also, according to historian Adina Back, by providing Puerto Rican parents with "the language of rights and power [and] the statistics to back up their analysis."[71] As one report later explained:

> The basis on which United Bronx Parents was founded was that of providing democratic participatory mechanisms for community people, and devolving power to parents in their relationships with schools through teaching them to think critically and act independently and effectively.[72]

Antonetty and her colleagues at UBP quickly began to play a central role in the expansion of education-related activism in the late 1960s, not just around New York City but also nationally, through consultations and publications about parent advocacy and bilingual education. UBP was part of a growing network of organizations pushing hard to set agendas for change based on community members' input, rather than based on the assessments of outside policy makers.

Mayor Lindsay responded to the takeover of the city's Board of Education in 1966 by convening a committee to make recommendations about structural changes to the city's school system. The Mayor's Panel on the Decentralization of the New York City Schools was chaired by McGeorge Bundy, a former National Security Advisor in the Kennedy and Johnson administrations, who had just become president of the Ford Foundation. Antonia Pantoja, a founder of the Puerto Rican Forum and Aspira, represented the Puerto Rican community on the five-member panel that became known as the "Bundy Commission," which also had one African American member, Benedetta Washington, a director of the city's Job Corps program. The Bundy Commission was tasked with producing a plan to divide the city's school districts, serving 1,100,000 students in 900 schools, into smaller units that would enable more effective management and more involvement from parents and community members.[73]

After several months of intensive investigation, the commission produced a report of more than 100 pages that recommended the Board of Education double the number of school districts it currently operated and restructure those districts to be controlled by newly established Community School Boards. Parents would have substantial input in the composition of the Community School Boards, which would be given the power to appoint and remove community superintendents. In making this recommendation, the commission said it was responding to "the deep and legitimate desire of many communities in the city for a more direct role in the education of their children." The Bundy Commission report emphasized the need for participation by the communities, and their right to "shared authority" over their schools. Although the Bundy report avoided the language of "community control"—instead referring to the proposed changes as "decentralization," the Board of Education's preferred term—the report implied that the actual goal of decentralization was, indeed, to confer on communities a substantial degree of control over their schools.[74]

Albert Shanker, the powerful and vitriolic head of the city's powerful teachers' union (the United Federation of Teachers, or UFT), resented the UFT's lack of representation on the Bundy Commission and pressured Mayor Lindsay to modify the report's recommendations to allow the Board of Education to retain more of its power over the new districts. A compromise plan emerged that would enable the creation of three "demonstration" districts, in East Harlem and the Lower East Side in Manhattan and in the Ocean Hill-Brownsville area of Brooklyn, beginning in 1967. In each of these districts, elected community boards would replace the district's former school board, which had consisted of administrators primarily in an advisory role.[75] One of the community boards' central goals was control over the hiring of principals and teachers. More to the point, board members—now comprised of parents and leaders from the surrounding community—wanted the freedom to hire African American and Puerto Rican principals and teachers.

Bitter conflicts arose almost immediately between the community boards and the UFT, whose overwhelmingly white membership saw the boards' hiring goals as a threat. "The issue of community control has become intermeshed with the issue of racial quotas in hiring and has led to bitterness and conflict between [the teachers' union and the community]," noted a report on UBP's role in the push for community control. In September 1967, when the UFT went on strike over a contract issue, parents in Black and Puerto Rican communities kept their schools open, defying the union. UFT president Shanker dismissed the community control movement as merely signifying "the raw anger that surges through the slums." When the community board of Brooklyn's Ocean Hill-Brownsville community district transferred 17 white teachers out of the schools in 1968, Shanker and the UFT retaliated by calling a series of strikes, the longest of which lasted five weeks.[76]

This breakdown in the basic functioning of the city's entire massive school system triggered action by the New York State legislature, which in 1969 passed a decentralization law that effectively shut down the three experimental districts by significantly changing the structure of the community boards. The new law divided the school system into 32 community (elementary) school districts and six high school superintendencies. These were restructured districts that enabled some community input, with representation by elected boards that would appoint all administrators, grant tenure, and hire and fire administrators, but did not have power to hire and fire teachers— acceding to the UFT's most central demand.[77]

Although the community control "experiment" (as its less committed supporters tended to call it) did not succeed in any of the enduring ways that its proponents had hoped for, Puerto Rican leaders, activists, and parents certainly gained from their participation in the movement. One of the most crucial lessons, which labor and housing activists were also learning in the late 1960s, was about productive collaborations with African Americans. Although their struggles were not the same in any of these arenas—bilingual instruction, for instance, was a priority for Puerto Rican education activists—Puerto Rican leaders modeled some of their tactics on the well-tested movement strategies used by African American leaders like Bayard Rustin and Reverend Galamison. Leaders and participants alike learned the power and the momentum generated in the demand for more than a token say in the way institutions operated in their communities.

The most effective leaders of this era managed to strike a balance between optimism—emphasizing the gains Puerto Rican communities had made in terms of empowerment during the 1960s—and a realistic assessment of the momentous challenges that remained. In 1968, Aspira commissioned educational consultant Richard Margolis to visit the seven U.S. cities with the largest Puerto Rican populations (New York City, Chicago, and Philadelphia; Newark, Hoboken, and Paterson, New Jersey; and Bridgeport, Connecticut) and produce a report on the state of education for Puerto Rican children in those school systems. Margolis summed up his conclusions in the title he and Aspira leaders gave to the report: *The Losers: A Report on Puerto Ricans and the Public Schools*. In his introduction to the report, Aspira director Louis Nuñez explained that, because "America has not yet made [the] commitment" to help every child fulfill his or her potential, "all of us have been 'the losers.'" Margolis's report emphasized positive steps, though, describing programs that provided bilingual instruction, encouraged student retention, and mediated between school administrators and parents. In concluding his prefatory remarks, Nuñez emphasized optimism: "With pride in our Puerto Rican heritage and with faith in the American dream, we now have an opportunity to make our children the winners."[78]

The opportunity Nuñez cited was expanding because of activism, and because Puerto Ricans had begun to make advances in leadership positions. For example, after Jack Agüeros's hunger strike in New York City in 1968, and the advocacy of his demands by fellow members of the Citywide Puerto Rican Action Committee, two Puerto Ricans were invited to join the New York City Board of Education. Joseph Montserrat former director of the Migration Division, took over as president of the Board of Education in 1969. At the same time, Puerto Ricans in New York accomplished a major surge in local support for bilingual education, aided by the U.S. Congress's authorization of the first Bilingual Education Act in January 1968. Louis Fuentes, principal of P.S. 155 in the Ocean Hill-Brownsville demonstration district, started a bilingual program in 1968; the same year, the first bilingual school, P.S. 25, was established in the Bronx.[79]

In cities like Chicago and Philadelphia, which had substantial Puerto Rican communities by 1970, but not enough voting strength by that point to elect their own political representatives, engagement in school politics was an early proving ground. Responding to a 1971 report by the Chicago Council on Urban Education that more than 71% of Puerto Rican students dropped out of high school, activists in Chicago founded an alternative high school for Puerto Rican youth in Humboldt Park in 1972 (it was later named Dr. Pedro Albizu Campos High School, and still exists). Puerto Rican students in Philadelphia, pushing back against the tendency of high school counselors to steer Puerto Rican students away from application to college, started their own program to support Puerto Rican children who aspired to go to college. Hundreds of new chapters of Aspira clubs sprang up in a dozen cities in the late 1960s, attesting to the expanding power of ambition, hope, and anger among Puerto Rican children and parents during the activist era.[80]

Education and Community Organizing: The University and the Streets

Puerto Rican kids growing up in northern cities in the 1960s would have been acutely aware of the growing national debate about racial injustice, especially as it pertained to education. Although most of them probably experienced little of the violent realities of integration in their own cities, they would have seen dramatic television images of Black children and college students walking stoically through jeering white crowds toward the doors of newly desegregated schools. Puerto Rican youth in New York had witnessed, and in some cases participated in, the 1964 school boycott in their city, and then watched the push for educational equality in their neighborhoods grow into a movement for community control. Certainly, as the gains of that movement in Manhattan seemed to be unravelling by the 1969–70 school year (the third demonstration district, Ocean Hill-Brownsville, would be dismantled the following year), older students observed the inability of urban schools to serve the needs of most poor students, and they saw the fallout from activists' efforts to change the status quo. For the thousands of young Puerto Ricans entering college in the late 1960s, the vast majority of them the first in their families to do so, witnessing the battering of aspirations for desegregated schools or community participation in education during that era showed them the necessity of changing institutions from within.[81]

Puerto Rican students' own local experiences would fit into a larger picture of campus activism in the late 1960s. All over the country, since the start of the decade, students at colleges and universities had been agitating against campus administrations on issues ranging from military recruitment and academic freedom to urban renewal and racial discrimination. Demands to increase admissions of Black and Latino students, and to institute academic programs in Black, Chicano, and Puerto Rican Studies, became the focal point of groups of campus activists starting in the late 1960s and lasting up through the early 1970s. Across the campuses of the City University of New York (CUNY), groups of Puerto Rican students had begun organizing a citywide Puerto Rican Student Union in 1967, just after the riot in El Barrio, to add their voice to debates about "fixing" social problems. As their Black and Chicano peers at San Francisco State University (SFSU) begin to demand greater access and representation, a new collective of Puerto Rican students, PRISA (Puerto Ricans Involved in Student Actions) collaborated with ONYX, the Black students' association, to map out a strategy for protests on their own campus, CUNY's flagship City College.

Now referring to themselves more broadly as the "Black and Puerto Rican Student Community," student leaders staged a dramatic occupation of the campus in April 1969, which led to scores of protests and a handful of takeovers at various other CUNY campuses. Boycott leaders demanded the same kinds of institutional changes that students at SFSU had recently succeeded in negotiating: the creation of degree-granting programs in Black and Puerto Rican Studies, with the authority to set graduation requirements and participate in faculty hiring; and more equitable representation in enrollments of Puerto Rican, African American, and low income students. Puerto Rican activists highlighted the very low rates of college graduation: the 1960 census had shown only 2,500 Puerto Rican college graduates living in New York City (and about 9,500 with some college), out of a population of 612,000. Before the strike was ended by court order, the "rebel occupants" succeeded in shutting down—"liberating"—the campus for two full weeks, renaming it the "University of Harlem."[82]

Protesters succeeded in persuading CUNY officials to accede to most of their demands. The administration had already begun planning to implement an open admissions policy for the entire university system in 1975, which would mean that every high school graduate in New York City would be guaranteed a place at least one of the 15 senior colleges and community colleges in the system. In response to the protesters' demands, however, the CUNY administration agreed to enact the policy change immediately, starting with those who applied in the 1969–70 academic year and would matriculate in 1970.

This version of "open admissions" did not address one of the students' key demands, which was proportional representation of Black and Puerto Rican students at CUNY, especially at the more prestigious four-year colleges in the CUNY system, including City College. During the 1968–69 academic year, although Black students made up about 30% of the population of New York City high schools and Puerto Rican students about 20%, only 8% of freshmen admitted to CUNY schools were Black and 3.3% were Puerto Rican, and the percentage at City College was even lower. The strike leaders' demand was that the university enact a "dual admissions" policy, which would require 50% of freshman admissions (mirroring the roughly 50% of city high school students who were Black and Puerto Rican) to come from "disadvantaged" schools, without regard to academic performance. The CUNY faculty senate rejected this plan, proposing instead that a smaller number of students (about 300 per year) be admitted from disadvantaged schools with modified academic standards.[83] As a result of the compromise policy on open admissions, the proportion of Black and Puerto Rican students increased substantially: during the first year of the new policy, they comprised around 30% of entering students, and that proportion continued to rise slightly during the 1970s.[84]

The Black and Puerto Rican Student Community managed to accomplish a tremendous amount in a very short time, capturing the attention of political leaders, the media, and candidates in the city's mayoral race, who would be competing in the primary election in May. In fact, the crisis at City College was debated extensively by the candidates in the Democratic primary, a large group of contenders that included writer Norman Mailer, who had spoken out against blaming "blacks and Puerto Ricans" for the city's troubles, and Bronx borough president Herman Badillo, the first Puerto Rican to run for mayor. Several of the opponents of the students' admissions proposal (every mayoral candidate except Mailer opposed the idea) dubbed the plan "slum admissions," and rejected it as a "quota system." Badillo, the only candidate whose major constituency included some of the students in question, offered a more careful critique, saying forcefully that the place to start pushing for opening educational access was attacking the "dual system" of education that impeded Black and Puerto Rican kids—pushing many toward the vocational diploma that so many of them graduated with, as opposed to an academic diploma that would help them get into college.[85]

Aside from admissions policy changes, the other major demand of the protesters was the creation of degree-granting programs in Black Studies and Puerto Rican Studies. On this score, faculty and administrators at City College and throughout CUNY were generally receptive. They supported the creation of Black and Puerto Rican Studies programs or departments at 17 of its 19 senior college and community college campuses. The first degree-granting program in Puerto Rican Studies was already in place by fall of 1969; the Center for Puerto Rican Studies, the first research center dedicated to scholarship on Puerto Ricans, was founded in 1973 at Hunter College. Another concession by the CUNY administration was the creation of several new community colleges to better serve students in "disadvantaged areas," including Medgar Evers College in Brooklyn and Hostos Community College in the Bronx, the first CUNY campus designed to serve a primarily Puerto Rican student body.

Campus protests like those at the CUNY schools succeeded in part because they were part of a growing national trend. Student activism to press for racial justice—equal opportunity and inclusion for Black and Latino students on college campuses—was commanding major attention around the country. Officials pressured to respond included not just university and college administrators, who were beginning to take seriously the demand for programs in Black Studies, Chicano Studies, and Third World Studies, but also leaders at institutions like the Ford Foundation and the National Endowment for the Humanities, which in 1969 awarded substantial funds to Yale, Princeton, and Rutgers to develop Black Studies programs.[86]

Not all campus activists were equally successful, however. In Chicago, Latino students at the University of Illinois Chicago Circle Campus UICCC pressed the administration and demonstrated to demand more inclusive admissions of students from their communities. Puerto Ricans and Mexican Americans together comprised about 15% of the city's population, but Puerto Rican students made up barely half of 1% of the students at UICCC. Militant student leaders accused the institution, established nearly a decade before in a neighborhood that had been home to a large Latino population, of hypocrisy in its mission:

> The school was built after our people were forced to move from the area where Circle Campus stands. When it was built, the white *politiqueros* stated that Circle Campus was going to be an urban university. In other words, for people living in the city.[87]

To whatever degree student protesters succeeded in forcing their institutions to change, one very powerful aspect of their legacy was that they commanded substantial support and engagement from their own communities. As one student leader, Eduardo "Pancho" Cruz, told a reporter, "You have to understand that we came directly from communities that had riots . . . there was police brutality . . . community control . . . teachers striking. They were behind us." The fight over changing admissions policies to enable access by poor and disadvantaged students was, indeed, a fight to connect their communities to the academy. As one activist student had asserted during the strike at San Francisco State, "there is a need to use our student status to help those who don't have it."[88] In Chicago, Puerto Rican students, together with other Puerto Rican residents of the city's North Side neighborhoods, pushed for the establishment of community outreach centers on college campuses, in part to provide educational opportunities for the many community residents who had limited formal education.[89]

Activists on college campuses pushed successfully for the creation of a wide range of new educational programs in this period—which did not generate opportunities for Puerto Rican students to "study themselves," as one critic complained during the CUNY takeover in 1969. Programs in Puerto Rican Studies (and Black and Chicano and Third World Studies) were structured around the conviction the whole society would benefit from a more inclusive study of the histories and cultures of all Americans. "Taking ownership of Puerto Rican history," as one of the founders of the Center for Puerto Rican Studies later put it, pushed practitioners in the academy to reach out to people outside the university and also made this history accessible to people outside the academy, within and beyond Puerto Rican communities. The idea of creating research centers for Puerto Rican Studies had in fact been explored earlier in the 1960s by members of the Puerto Rican Forum, who sought "a means of uncovering vital information about Puerto Ricans, Puerto Rican social patterns, culture, history, migration, needs, and problems as well as other vital data about the Puerto Rican community."[90] Their proposal illustrates how adult members of the Puerto Rican Forum and the radical youth leading the CUNY strikes several years later had the same sense of how to achieve enduring change for Puerto Ricans in the U.S.

Asserting its goals in 1972, the committee that formed Hunter's Center for Puerto Rican Studies explained, "We must continue to seek a place within the university from which to articulate the social and intellectual problems of our community while reaffirming the intent to define and control our own intellectual agenda." The new academic programs created new possibilities for asking intellectual questions about Black and Latino people in the U.S. that did not focus primarily on "pathologies" at the expense of other aspects of their social, cultural, and political lives. Puerto Ricans were especially vulnerable to these academic distortions, since they could not claim a published canon of work by Puerto Rican scholars in the U.S., unlike both Chicanos and African Americans, both with established historical and literary traditions that could be deployed against the "deficit model" that predominated in many academic disciplines. Puerto Rican Studies programs began to train students and scholars who could respond to and rebut the many characterizations of their group as primarily a "problem" in American society.[91]

Puerto Rican Studies scholars criticized those who continued to publish work about Puerto Ricans based on thin data and generalizations about pathological behavior. A primary example was that of the well-known and politically liberal historian Oscar Handlin, who analyzed Puerto Ricans' socioeconomic stagnation in his 1959 book *The Newcomers: Negroes and Puerto Ricans in a Changing Metropolis*. In attempting to explain the sources of their social disadvantages, Handlin decried Puerto Ricans' political "apathy," their lack of "associational life," and the "tragically rare" instances of Puerto Ricans who were "willing and able to exercise creative leadership." He closed by warning that "frustration and bitterness may convert this group feeling into a narrow, self-defeating hatred of the outsiders. There are demagogues among the Negroes and nationalist agitators among the Puerto Ricans ready to take advantage of such a turn of events." Handlin may have believed wholeheartedly his assertion that inequality, if left unchecked, would "compromise our democratic life," but he also asserted, in so many words, that those most hurt by that inequality could not be trusted to participate in its vanquishing.[92]

Just over a decade after the publication of Handlin's book, as the movement of Puerto Rican youth was still exploding in 1970, sociologist Nathan Glazer and Senator Daniel Patrick Moynihan published a new edition of their 1963 book *Beyond the Melting Pot: The Negroes, Puerto Ricans, Jews, Italians, and Irish of New York City*, adding a new introduction in which they pilloried young Puerto Ricans for their "militant" actions at CUNY the year before. At the same time, partially contradicting their accusations about the students' aggressive activism, Glazer and Moynihan wrote the students off as insignificant historical actors, incapable of developing their own political analysis: "The radical white college youth, who are now so influential in the mass media, will try to convince [Puerto Rican youth] that they are 'colonized.'"[93]

Puerto Rican youth needed no "convincing" that they were "'colonized.'" Those who were not themselves born on the island were either the children or grandchildren of people born in the United States colony of Puerto Rico. The other falsehood in Glazer and Moynihan's assertion concerned the dynamics of political education among the nation's youth: young Puerto Rican activists were most often the ones educating "the radical white college youth" about American and global colonialism and racism, rather than the other way around.[94]

Community Organizing and Nationalism: Activists, Leftists, and Youth

"It was a world of revolution, and we didn't want to miss out," recalled Mickey Meléndez, one of the leaders of the New York Young Lords, about the organization's founding in 1969.[95] He was referring to actual worldwide events—student revolts in Paris and elsewhere around the globe, struggles for liberation across the Third World, demonstrations for democracy throughout Latin America—but revolutionary ferment was happening in the U.S. too. In poor urban Puerto Rican communities of New York City, in Chicago, Philadelphia, Hartford, Newark, Camden, and beyond, conditions of crumbling neighborhoods and suffocating invisibility galvanized many young Puerto Ricans into political protest and drew them into a burgeoning activist movement.

While some older Puerto Rican leaders lamented Puerto Ricans' continued lack of political influence despite their growing numbers throughout the 1960s, young activists seemed more confident about their group's growing empowerment. It was the youth that confronted most directly the ways that police, city officials, and other disgruntled whites blamed Puerto Ricans (along with African Americans) for the era's mounting problems—crime, delinquency, and general degradation of the social order—and it was young activists who created the most visible force of change within their communities. Acknowledging the early signs of such momentum, a Chicago newspaper referred to the existence of a "Puerto Rican movement" following the 1966 riots there. By the late 1960s, young Puerto Ricans in various cities began founding new organizations to tackle in radical ways the inequalities they perceived in housing, police-community relations, educational access, and healthcare. They brought a powerful, driving energy to the converging demands for justice that now came from every sector of Puerto Rican organizing, generating a mass mobilization that produced what was, indeed, a Puerto Rican movement.

Although it was a movement with a largely youthful face, it is important to recall that credit for its foundation had to be shared with leaders who came of age in the 1950s and forged new leadership paths related to civil rights issues, labor unions, and police-community relations. In New York, the oldest and largest

Puerto Rican community, a disproportionate number of the young activists who emerged in the late 1960s and 1970s got their start in organizations founded by this earlier generation of leaders. Some of these incubators were radical community organizations created in the early 1960s—Mobilization for Youth, the East Harlem Tenants Council, and MEND—started or led by Puerto Ricans in their twenties or thirties. But the leadership and example of older longtime activists was crucial. Gilberto Gerena Valentín, Manny Diaz, Evelina López Antonetty, José Morales, Antonia Pantoja, and many others had been organizing in their communities for well over a decade (or even, in Gerena Valentín's case, since the early 1940s) by the time young radicals began to come together to form what came to be called the Puerto Rican movement.

One of the most important training grounds for young leaders of the Puerto Rican movement, Aspira, did not fit the mold of the radical community organizations that had begun proliferating in the 1960s. Founded by young adult members of the Puerto Rican Forum in the early 1960s, Aspira had grown throughout the decade, providing academic support and leadership development to Puerto Rican youth and pushing them toward higher education. (Aspira continued to thrive through the 1970s and beyond, and still exists today.) By the late 1960s, Aspira was sometimes criticized from the left as imposing an assimilationist model on its members, since it promoted a conventional path to success in American society; it was based on a premise of maximizing "professional and technical talent in the community," as a group of leftist researchers described it in the 1970s. On the other hand, in that era many "Aspirantes" transitioned readily from their high school Aspira clubs into some of the many radical organizations forming in their communities, and some of the clubs themselves became incubators of nationalism and community activism.[96]

Whatever the details of their background, the young Puerto Rican activists of this era took seriously the idea of "maximum feasible participation of the poor," as the federal Community Action Program described the goal of collaborations with community members. They also worked toward the maximum feasible participation of the young. Groups like the Real Great Society (RGS) created new roles for youth in their communities, with a vision of redemption not just for the people seeking help but also for the people offering it.[97] Many of the young people who worked as teachers for the RGS program University of the Streets, for example, were high school dropouts or former gang members, now offered the chance to share their inspiration and knowledge on their own terms. In fact, the two founders of RGS had been members of a street gang in the Lower East Side before deciding that the most compelling battle for power was not the kind fought with fists and knives.

A similar motivation around the same time led José "Cha Cha" Jiménez, head of the Chicago street gang the Young Lords, to turn his gang into an organization that would serve its community. After spending time in prison in 1967, where he met Black Panther Fred Hampton and studied works by Malcolm X and Puerto

Rico's famous nationalist Pedro Albizu Campos, Jiménez became determined to share what he had learned with his friends from the streets. Over the next year, he sought guidance from Black Panthers and worked to turn the Young Lords gang into the Young Lords Organization (YLO), whose first campaign was a fight against urban renewal and rising rents in one of Chicago's Puerto Rican neighborhoods, Lincoln Park.

Radicalized by the shooting death of a Young Lord by an off-duty police officer in the spring of 1969, the YLO pushed further in its challenges to Chicago institutions that it saw as upholding patterns of injustice in the city. With a multi-racial group of leftist organizations including the Poor People's Coalition (PPC) and seminary students, the YLO members occupied a Presbyterian seminary in 1969 when its leaders declined to fund the PPC's plan for low income housing and public services in the Wicker Park and Lincoln Park neighborhoods. The seminary was targeted for its role in supporting the displacement of Puerto Ricans from the neighborhoods through the city's urban renewal process. The YLO's most high-profile action was the occupation of a Methodist church in the center of Lincoln Park's Puerto Rican community in June 1969, where Young Lords staffed an array of free social services—daycare, a food and clothing bank—and organized a health clinic, where they coordinated care by volunteer doctors, nurses, and medical students. They called it the People's Church, and, with the help of the pastor, the church became the YLO headquarters for two years.[98]

By this point in the 1960s, activists around the country, especially those organized around racial justice movements, the New Left, and the anti-war movement, had established powerful nationwide networks. News of radicals' bold actions traveled fast. By the summer of 1969, a number of New York activists, who had either met Cha Cha Jiménez or read about his organization in the Black Panther newspaper, got his permission to start a New York chapter of the Young Lords. Most of the founders of the New York branch were college students and graduates who wanted to combine their goals of radical community building with Puerto Rican nationalist politics. Pablo "Yoruba" Guzmán, who graduated from the Bronx High School of Science (one of New York City's elite public magnet high schools), had just finished his first year at the State University of New York in Old Westbury when he joined forces with Felipe Luciano, a self-described "street poet" and sometime college student, Richie Pérez, a leader of the Puerto Rican Student Union at City College, and Juan González, who had graduated a few years earlier from Columbia. Iris Morales, a recent City College graduate who was teaching at the Academy for Black and Latino Education (ABLE), a grassroots school that offered high school equivalency classes, joined the Young Lords' leadership shortly after its founding.[99]

Structurally, both branches of the Young Lords Organization—and the branches that would form within the next two years in Philadelphia, Newark, Camden, and Hartford—modeled themselves after the Black Panther Party (BPP), led by a central committee comprised of various "ministers" and guided by an ideological platform called the "Thirteen Point Program" (the BPP had a Ten Point Program). The Black Panthers, organized in Oakland, California in 1966, drew in thousands of young Latinos as well as African Americans. Beyond racial and economic justice, it was the Panthers' commitment to "self-determination" that resonated most powerfully with radicalized Puerto Rican youth (and other Latinos and African Americans who joined the group)—and that the Young Lords sought to formalize in their own Thirteen Point Program. Indeed, the language of self-determination captured better than any other formulation the goals of personal dignity, group recognition, and political sovereignty that young people of color pursued through their organizing in this era. The New York Young Lords who drafted the Thirteen Point Program probably had not read the flyers produced by a group called the Third World Liberation Front during SFSU's campus strike a few months earlier, but the message was almost identical: "We demand SELF-DETERMINATION—the right of a people to determine their own needs . . . and their own destiny."[100]

This cross-fertilization of radical ideas was happening not just on the streets—or in prisons, as in the radicalization experience of Cha Cha Jiménez—but in high schools as well. Many people who joined the Young Lords had attended SNCC or Black Panther meetings as high school students, in some cases because they were unaware of activist Puerto Rican groups and in other cases because they already identified as Afro-Puerto Rican. Pablo "Yoruba" Guzmán, a member of the Young Lords' central committee, explained how he saw the movements' connections, recalling that "before people called me a spic, they called me a nigger." Iris Morales, the Young Lords' Deputy Minister of Education, joined a Black Power organization in high school, because, she said, "I saw things in terms of black and white, and given that choice, it was very clear to me that my choice was black not white." She explained what motivated her cohort at CUNY—almost all of them the first in their families to attend college—in the late 1960s: "we were marginalized, and we tended to stick together united by common experiences of poverty and racial oppression." [101]

Energized by the successful Black and Puerto Rican student movement that spring and by the example of the Chicago Young Lords' Peoples' Church, the New York Young Lords announced themselves at an event in Tompkins Square Park on July 26, 1969, a celebration of Fidel Castro's first military assault 16 years earlier on Cuban dictator Fulgencio Batista, later commemorated as the "July 26 Movement." The message about their political DNA was clear: the Young Lords would serve as a new revolutionary force to challenge the status quo and remake their city's Puerto Rican communities. Within six months, the organization had attracted a thousand members and achieved citywide fame for its occupation of an East Harlem church that they briefly turned into the "People's Church" (until they were forced out by court order; they established a different People's Church the following year). The New York Young Lords also initiated a variety of community public health campaigns, most notably concerning the dangers of lead paint, and they also initiated a takeover of a failing public hospital in the Bronx, Lincoln Hospital, to dramatize the dire need to improve healthcare services in poor communities.

Not surprisingly, it was the Young Lords' campaign against police brutality that brought the organization into most direct confrontation with city officials and law enforcement. After a Young Lords member died in police detention in early 1970, the YLO staged a mass demonstration, and countless other protests were mounted on a smaller scale for the same reason. Spontaneous rioting against police abuse had continued to erupt in hundreds of poor urban communities across the country throughout the late 1960s and into the early 1970s. When Puerto Rican Hartford exploded after a white police officer was acquitted of manslaughter for the shooting of a 19-year-old Puerto Rican man following a traffic violation, several Puerto Ricans were shot by police during the rioting, and one of them died. Rioting also broke out in the summers of 1970 and 1971 in Puerto Rican communities in New Bedford, Massachusetts, in Waterbury, Connecticut, and in Camden, New Jersey, all sparked by incidents of police brutality. Added to the explosiveness of these events was the uprising of Black and Puerto Rican prisoners in the "Tombs"—New York City's infamous downtown jail—in 1970, and the catastrophic Attica uprising in 1971, which resulted in the deaths of 43 prisoners after Governor Rockefeller authorized state police to open fire on the protesters.[102]

Amid these continual incitements to radicalization, additional branches of the Young Lords formed in 1970 and 1971 in Philadelphia, Newark, Camden, and Hartford, each with a distinct local character. In some cases, new chapters emerged from a pre-existing radical group that decided to transform itself into part of the Young Lords organization; the founders of the Philadelphia Young Lords, for example, had been part of a group called the Young Revolutionaries for Independence before allying with the Young Lords in 1970. As the Young Lords expanded geographically, however, with their magnetic public image drawing in thousands of new members, the group's leadership was struggling to manage a growing rift within the ranks over strategy and ideology. Although the Lords' most visible and successful actions focused on local problems—police brutality, healthcare provision—a strong faction of the leadership wanted to engage directly in the nationalist struggle on the island. In 1972, the Young Lords started branches in Puerto Rico, but quickly recognized that they had miscalculated. Rafaela Colón, originally of the Philadelphia branch, recalled, "We were definitely out of tune with the movement in Puerto Rico" and concluded, "the fact is, going to Puerto Rico . . . [was] like Columbus discovering something that's been discovered."[103]

The Young Lords only survived as an organization for a couple of years after their attempt to expand to Puerto Rico, a tactical problem that was compounded by significant internal strife caused by some leaders' turn to ultra-left Maoist politics. Some of the members who remained began to focus on the Young Lords' commitment to advancing socialism in the U.S., many of them taking jobs in factories in order to deepen their connection to the Puerto Rican working class and soon creating an offshoot organization, the Puerto Rican Revolutionary Workers Organization (PRRWO). The Young Lords formally disbanded by 1973, and the PRRWO would fall apart by 1976.[104] Some former members blamed the Young Lords' demise on infiltration by the FBI, of which there is ample evidence. But others also emphasized the organization's internal fault lines: big questions of ideology and strategic goals, exacerbated by failures of leadership and interpersonal conflicts.

Although the organization was short-lived, and its end was contentious, the Young Lords made an indelible mark on their communities and on their cities, and shaped others' perception of Puerto Ricans far beyond their communities. As Pablo Guzmán wrote 30 years later,

> Ask any Latino professional who advanced in government or the corporate world between, say, 1969 and '84, and you'll be told they owe part of their opportunity to the sea change in perception that [the Young Lords] inspired. We helped raise the understanding, first among Latinos and then the society at large, that Puerto Ricans possessed a culture on par with anyone's.[105]

On the other hand, to Puerto Rican activists who participated in other organizations and other parts of the movement, it may have seemed that the Young Lords' high visibility obscured their connections with and reliance on other groups—or that the Young Lords simply stole the limelight, especially in terms of the historical recognition they have received.

In fact, the Young Lords had often collaborated with and relied on the work of other young contemporaries, through groups like El Comité, which forged strong connections to New York City's housing and labor activist networks that became useful for various Young Lords campaigns. (It is also important to note that, as the Young Lords were fragmenting in the early 1970s, El Comité managed to reformulate its mission and remained active for another decade.[106]) Likewise, when the Young Lords got involved in a conflict over labor practices and service provision at Lincoln Hospital in the Bronx and achieved a brief but high-profile takeover of the hospital, they were in fact joining an ongoing struggle that had been waged for months by the existing healthcare workers' union, Local 1199. A leftist insurgency within the union, the Health Revolutionary Unity Movement, had been challenging the 1199 hierarchy. What the Young Lords added to the situation was their capacity to mobilize a large political base of young people: the *New York Times* reported that "hundreds of teen agers came to the hospital . . . 'to see what was happening and to see what we could do.'" The fact that these actions were internally mired in ultra-leftist politics that would soon crash and burn was irrelevant to the larger community that urgently needed better health services.[107]

Accounts of the Puerto Rican movement usually describe the vitality and range of the organizing by young Puerto Ricans in the late 1960s, with its many storefront operations and student groups that began building a movement before the Young Lords formed in 1969. But once the most prominent organizations of any movement become the focus of its historical narrative, some of the richness, variety, and creativity of participation tends to get lost. One example of a group overshadowed by the Young Lords' ability to capture headlines in New York City (and beyond) in the early 1970s was the Ghetto Brothers, a much smaller organization of former gang members that was activating a similar agenda of Puerto Rican empowerment and community transformation in the South Bronx. The Ghetto Brothers started as a street gang in the 1960s, but after one of their lieutenants was killed in 1971, leader Benjy Meléndez convened a "peace meeting" of a number of gangs, at which he announced that the Ghetto Brothers were no longer a gang, "we're an organization, we want to help black and Puerto Rican brothers." "We are being oppressed by the North American Yankee," he said. "We the Puerto Ricans should rise up and defend ourselves . . . "[108] The Ghetto Brothers produced a record album in 1971, *Ghetto Brothers Power*, but their real work was in community politics, and the group worked hard to put out fires in the South Bronx during the years of its greatest destruction by arson and neglect. Meléndez led the Ghetto Brothers in numerous collaborations, including with the Black Panthers and various Puerto Rican nationalist groups. Within a few years, Meléndez took a job with United Bronx Parents, carrying with him the legacy of the radical and transformative grassroots organizing of the Puerto Rican movement.[109]

Conclusion

Puerto Rican activists who embraced the politics of the left, including racial and economic justice and Puerto Rican independence, greeted the 1970s with a surge of powerful energy and a widespread belief that the Puerto Rican movement would keep growing. While they were motivated, still, by frustrations about the oppression their community continued to face after more than a decade of protest, they also felt the force of hope coming from many sectors of their community and connecting many urban communities across the Northeast and midwestern U.S. Although the most visible group of the Puerto Rican movement, the Young Lords, came apart in the early 1970s, and many smaller groups (Real Great Society, El Comité) either dissolved or reconstituted in that decade, Puerto Rican activists in other realms, including academics, the arts, electoral politics, and legal advocacy, gained ground throughout the 1970s. They managed to create a new relationship between "the academy" and "the streets"—connecting teachers and students in community-based classes held in storefronts to those who worked and studied on the campuses of Columbia and City College, Princeton and UConn—which made for powerful and enduring achievements that continued well beyond the Puerto Rican movement of the early 1970s.

Most activist groups of their era, including the Young Lords, built on the legacies and examples of older leaders who had been organizing their communities for decades. These included members of the traditional left, many with connections to the labor movement of the 1940s and 1950s; nationalists, whose political roots reached back to the Puerto Rican community of the 1920s; and social service professionals, whose participation in dozens of city agencies and institutions had grown dramatically during the 1950s. In addition to the guidance from older leaders, Puerto Rican youth also watched and developed insights from the exploding African American struggles for equality as well as the ideals of other Caribbean revolutionary movements.

Building on this foundation of diverse but interconnected sources of inspiration for change, Puerto Rican leaders in the late 1960s and early 1970s managed to accomplish some of what they hoped for, particularly achievements in education, in labor, and more generally in the expanded visibility of their struggles. But they also faced frustrating limitations. Even as Puerto Rican communities produced hundreds of new leaders, organizers found it difficult to build enduring political organizations or to gain a solid foothold in local political networks; state and national political party organizations continued to ignore Puerto Rican participation. In terms of economic gains, the War on Poverty proved transient, and did little to stabilize poor neighborhoods. Despite the convergence of liberals' and radicals' determination to reduce poverty, the many innovations in job training, minimum wage campaigns, and anti-discrimination and welfare policies were still failing the poorest third of the community. With the growing impact of deindustrialization and a looming fiscal crisis in many cities, along with a mounting white backlash in response to recent legal and policy changes promoting racial equality, Puerto Ricans confronted a new constellation of social and economic challenges by the mid-1970s. For thousands of leaders and activists energized by the *despertar boricua*, the Puerto Rican awakening, the 1970s would be a decade of reckoning.

Notes

1 "Puerto Rican Movement Gets WSO Support." *Chicago Defender*, 30 June 1966, 20.
2 Lauria Santiago, Aldo A. "A Chalk Line on Third Ave: Policing and Puerto Rican Riots." Manuscript, 5–7. Thompson, Heather Ann. "Understanding Rioting in Postwar Urban America." *Journal of Urban History* 26, no. 3 (2000): 391–402.
3 Fernández, Lilia. *Brown in the Windy City: Mexicans and Puerto Ricans in Postwar Chicago.* Chicago: University of Chicago Press, 2012, 167; Padilla, Félix. *Puerto Rican Chicago.* Notre Dame, IN: University of Notre Dame Press, 1988 144–55; Staudenmaier, Michael J. "Between Two Flags: Cultural Nationalism and Racial Formation in Puerto Rican Chicago, 1946–1994." Ph.D. Dissertation, University of Illinois at Urbana-Champaign, 2016. Staudenmeir cites the use of dogs as especially angering to the young men. Staudenmaier, "Between Two Flags," 111–12, 164–5.
4 "2 Sides 'Wooing' Puerto Ricans." *Chicago Daily Defender*, 20 June 1966, 3; Andrew Diamond quoted in Fernández, *Brown in the Windy City*, 163; García Colón, Ismael. "Claiming Equality: Puerto Rican Farmworkers in Western New York." *Latino Studies*

6, no. 3 (2008): 269–89; "Puerto Ricans Stage Riot in Perth Amboy." *Chicago Daily Defender*, 2 Aug. 1966, 4.

5 "2 Sides 'Wooing' Puerto Ricans." *Chicago Daily Defender*, 20 June 1966, 3; "Puerto Rican Movement Gets WSO Support." *Chicago Daily Defender*, 30 June 1966, 20.

6 "1st Puerto Rican Protest March, Rally Set Today." *Chicago Daily Defender*, 28 June 1966, 4; Gilberto Gerena Valentín, Sept. 1980, Oral History Collection-CPRS.

7 Padilla, *Puerto Rican Chicago*, 174.

8 "Hispanic Leaders Form New Group." *The New York Times*, 14 March 1966, 21.

9 "Puerto Rican Leader Named to City Rights Post." *The New York Times*, 2 May 1966, 15; "Civil Rights Leader Denies Link to Reds." *The New York Times*, 20 Feb 1964, 13; "15 Puerto Rican Leaders Are Rated in Study Here." *The New York Times*, 1 June 1966, 118.

10 Office of Mayor John Lindsay, "Puerto Ricans Confront Problems of the Complex Urban Society: A Design for Change," 15–16 April 1967, Vertical File, "Puerto Ricans," NYCMA; Gerena Valentín, "Recommendations Regarding Civil Rights, Discrimination, Voter Registration, and Police-Community Relations," 349–50, Vertical File, "Puerto Ricans," NYCMA.

11 "2 Killed, 12 Hurt in Violence Here." *The New York Times,* 25 July 1967; "Disorders Erupt in East Harlem; Mobs Dispersed." *The New York Times,* 24 July 1967.

12 "Causes Pondered by Puerto Ricans." *The New York Times*, 25 July 1967, 18.

13 "Woman Heads Antipoverty Unit." *The New York Times*, 4 June 1968, 31.

14 "Poverty Job Goes to Puerto Rican." *The New York Times*, 7 Aug. 1968, 88.

15 "Text of Summary of Report by National Advisory Commission on Civil Disorders." *The New York Times*, 1 March 1968, 20.

16 Gerena Valentín, Gilberto. *Gilberto Gerena Valentín: My Life as a Community Organizer, Labor Activist, and Progressive Politician in New York City.* New York: Center for Puerto Rican Studies, Hunter College, 2013; Organizing Committee PRCamp, "Draft of press release," OGPRUS-CPRS Box 3473 Folder 27.

17 Gerena Valentín. *Gilberto Gerena Valentín*, 199–200. "5,000 Join Rally of Puerto Ricans." *The New York Times,* 27 May 1968, 20; Mantler, Gordon Keith. *Power to the Poor: Black-Brown Coalition and the Fight for Economic Justice, 1960–1974.* Chapel Hill: University of North Carolina Press, 2015. "Puerto Ricans Here Deny Strike Threat." *The New York Times,* 17 June 1968, 36.

18 Lauria Santiago, Aldo A. "A Chalk Line across Third Ave." Manuscript; "Negroes, Puerto Ricans Battle in Philadelphia." *Chicago Daily Defender*, 19 Sept. 1968, 5.

19 Mailer, Norman. "Why Are We in New York?" *The New York Times*, 18 May 1969.

20 Knapp Commission. *The Knapp Commission Report on Police Corruption.* New York: G. Braziller, 1973; Armstrong, Michael F. *They Wished They Were Honest: The Knapp Commission and New York City Police Corruption.* New York: Columbia University Press, 2012, 92.

21 "Parley Planned by Puerto Ricans." *The New York Times*, 21 Feb. 1969, 46. "Puerto Rican Militant." *The New York Times*, 18 July 1969, 38; East Harlem Coalition for Community Control, 17 July 1969; Julio Morales, Director to Lindsay, Mayor Lindsay Papers-LGCC Box 90 Folder 1671.

22 "Puerto Rican Prospect: 10% of Population, 0% of Political Power." *The New York Times*, 15 Oct. 1969, 30. "Brief Personal Biography of Frank Espada," García Papers-CPRS Box 58 Folder 7.

23 Henry Raymont, "Mayor Will Seek More Advice Here on Puerto Ricans." *The New York Times*, 23 Jan. 1967, 1; Lindsay to Pantoja, 26 Sept. 1967, Mayor Lindsay Papers-LGCC Box 94 Folder 1714; Pantoja to Lindsay, 15 Feb. 1967, Lindsay Papers-LGCC Box 94 Folder 1714; "Mayor Will Seek More Advice Here on Puerto Ricans." *The New York Times*, 23 Jan. 1967, 1.

24 José Cruz, personal communication to Lorrin Thomas, 12 Oct. 2014. Luis Cardona, *The Coming of the Puerto Ricans.* Washington, D.C.: Unidos Publications, 1976; James Jennings and Monte Rivera. *Puerto Rican Politics in Urban America.* Westport,

CT: Greenwood Press, 1984. Uriarte-Gaston mentions an unnamed Puerto Rican candidate for the state legislature in Massachusetts in 1968 (Uriate-Gaston, Miren. "Organizing for Survival: The Emergence of a Puerto Rican Community." Ph.D. Dissertation, Boston University, 1988, 188).

25 See Chapter 2, pp. 45–6, 66.

26 "8 New House Members Split Evenly in Outlook." *The New York Times*, 5 Nov. 1970, 30.

27 "Badillo-Ramos Contest Centers on Who Is More Puerto Rican." *The New York Times*, 13 June 1972, 45; Badillo, Herman and Haynes, Milton. *A Bill of No Rights: Attica and the American Prison System*. New York: Outerbridge and Lazard, 1972; Thompson, Heather Ann. *Blood in the Water: The Attica Prison Uprising of 1971 and Its Legacy*. New York: Knopf Doubleday Publishing Group, 2016, 90, 108, 142–3.

28 "Badillo-Ramos Contest Centers on Who Is More Puerto Rican." *The New York Times*, 13 June 1972, 45. "Puerto Rican Leftist Disputes Badillo on 'Unity' Conference." *The New York Times*, 3 Nov. 1971, 40. Schneider, Cathy. "Political Opportunities and Framing Puerto Rican Identity in New York City." In Hank Johnston, ed., *Frames of Protest: Social Movements and the Framing Perspective*. Lanham, MD: Rowman & Littlefield, 2005, 170–1.

29 See Chapter 2, pp. 44–5.

30 "Creation of a New 'Puerto Rican' District Stirs Controversy." *The New York Times*, 22 Jan. 1970, 24. See also José Cruz in *Boricuas in Gotham*, 49; "Leaders Assess Court's Decision on District Lines." *The New York Times*, 6 Jan. 1974, 1.

31 "Puerto Rican Leaders Say Remapping Cut Power." *The New York Times*, 9 Feb. 1972, 80; José Cruz in *Boricuas in Gotham*, 49; "Lopsided Redistricting." *The New York Times*, 19 Jan. 1973, 32; "3rd Council Redistricting." *The New York Times*, 26 Sept. 1973, 45; "Leaders Assess Court's Decision on District Lines." *The New York Times*, 6 Jan. 1974, 1; "The Grand Old Bipartisan Trick, the Gerrymander." *The New York Times*, 7 April 1974, 206.

32 Lucas, Isidro. "Puerto Rican Politics in Chicago." In Jennings and Rivera, eds., *Puerto Rican Politics*, 108; Culliton-González, Katherine. "Time to Revive Puerto Rican Voting Rights." *Berkeley La Raza Law Journal*, 2008, 39–42.

33 A nonpartisan election is one in which there is no requirement that each of the major parties is represented.

34 "Cubans' Vote Felt in Miami Election." *The New York Times*, 18 Nov. 1973, 47; "Hispanics Create Action Coalition." *The New York Times*, 30 June 1975, 15.

35 "Hispanics Create Action Coalition." *The New York Times*, 30 June 1975, 15.

36 Gordon, David M. "Poverty, Welfare, and Income Maintenance: Income and Welfare in New York City." *The Public Interest*, no. 16 (1969): 64–88.

37 Morris, Charles R. *The Cost of Good Intentions: New York City and the Liberal Experiment, 1960–1975*. New York: Norton, 1980; Kornbluh, Felicia Ann. *The Battle for Welfare Rights: Politics and Poverty in Modern America*. Philadelphia: University of Pennsylvania Press, 2007, 23, 45; "Now It's Welfare Lib." *The New York Times*, 27 Sept. 1970; Fitzpatrick, Joseph P. *Puerto Rican Americans: The Meaning of Migration to the Mainland*. Englewood Cliffs, NJ: Prentice-Hall, 1987, 155.

38 United States Commission on Civil Rights. *Puerto Ricans in the Continental United States: An Uncertain Future: A Report*. Washington, D.C.: U.S. Commission on Civil Rights, 1976, 56.

39 Powers, Mary G., and John J. Macisco. *Puerto Ricans in New York City, 1970. Labor Force Characteristics and Migration Experience of the Puerto Ricans*. Rio Piedras, P.R.: Social Science Research Center, University of Puerto Rico, 1981; McCauley, Margaret A. "A Study of Social Class and Assimilation in Relation to Puerto Rican Family Patterns." Ph.D. Dissertation, Fordham University, 1972.

40 In 1970 33% of Puerto Rican men and 39% of women were machine operatives in "light" (labor intensive) industrial work sites. United States Commission on Civil

Rights, *Puerto Ricans in the Continental United States: An Uncertain Future*. Washington, D.C.: U.S. Commission on Civil Rights, 1976, 52.

41 Morris, *The Cost of Good Intentions*.

42 United States Bureau of Labor Statistics, and Horst Brand. *Characteristics of the Unemployed: Bedford-Stuyvesant, Central Harlem, East Harlem, South Bronx*. New York: U.S. Bureau of Labor Statistics, Middle Atlantic Regional Office, 1970.

43 "Puerto Rico Acts to Protect Labor." *The New York Times*, 30 April 1967, 70; García Colón, "Claiming Equality: Puerto Rican Farmworkers in Western New York."

44 Michael Luis Ristorucci, "Some observations on the Hispanic Labor Committee, the Labor Movement, and post-World War II Latino labor activism in the metropolitan New York Area," Research paper for Harry Van Arsdale Junior Memorial Foundation, 2002; *Those who have come our way . . . Honoring Leaders in Civil Rights Struggle* (IBEW, no date); Paul Sánchez, "Daily activity reports," 1962–1967, AFL-CIO Archive RG28-002 Series 5 File 34/8; Paul Sánchez, 1968–1972, AFL-CIO Archive RG28-002, Series 5, File 34/9. Puerto Ricans were well represented among taxi drivers by the early 1970s. Taxi driving was a higher pay alternative to factory work, albeit with longer hours and higher risks. A 1970s strike drew support from students and radical organizations. Hodges, Graham Russell. *Taxi!: A Social History of the New York City Cabdriver*. Baltimore: Johns Hopkins University Press, 2007.

45 CL Kurrier, to the editor, *Springfield Union*, no date; clipping. USNARA RG 126 Records of the Office of Territories-Central files 1951–1971 Box 356 Folder PR-Population 4-2 Immigration and Emigration.

46 Left pro-independence activists insisted on a politicized organization in a way that alienated many of the workers themselves. Bonilla-Santiago, Gloria. *Organizing Puerto Rican Migrant Farmworkers: The Experience of Puerto Ricans in New Jersey*. New York: P. Lang, 1988.

47 "City's 2nd Generation Puerto Ricans Rising from Poverty." *The New York Times*, 23 April 1968, 49; Block, Andrew. "Community in Action: The Central Harlem Experience in the War on Poverty, 1963–1968." Senior thesis, Vassar College, 2005; Herbstein, Judith F. "Rituals and Politics of the Puerto Rican 'Community' in New York City." Ph.D. Dissertation, City University of New York, 1978; Lee, Sonia S. and Ande Díaz "'I Was the One Percenter': Manny Díaz and the Beginnings of a Black-Puerto Rican Coalition." *Journal of American Ethnic History* 26, no. 3 (2007): 52–80.

48 *Those who have come our way . . . Honoring Leaders in Civil Rights Struggle* (IBEW, no date).

49 See p. 101 of this chapter.

50 "Negro Unionists Threaten Revolt: Leaders of Minority Groups Protest Teachers' Strike." *The New York Times*, 14 Nov. 1968, 39. "Race Meant More Than a Union Card." *The New York Times*, 24 Nov. 1968. Freeman, Joshua Benjamin. *Working-Class New York: Life and Labor since World War II*. New York: New Press, 2000; Michael Luis Ristorucci, "Some Observations on the Hispanic Labor Committee, the Labor Movement, and Post-World War II Latino Labor Activism in the Metropolitan New York Area."

51 Freeman, Joshua Benjamin. *In Transit: The Transport Workers Union in New York City, 1933–1966*. Philadelphia: Temple University Press, 2001, 332–33; "Bias Laid to Transit Body and T.W.U." *The New York Times*, 22 May 1971, 29; "Retail Workers Sever Union Ties." *The New York Times*, 17 April 1969, 1; Phillips, Lisa Ann Wunderlich. *A Renegade Union Interracial Organizing and Labor Radicalism*. Urbana: University of Illinois Press, 2013.

52 "Group in Newark Seeks Bias Study." *The New York Times*, 21 Jan. 1970, 57. "1199, A Union with a 'Soul'," *The New York Times*, 22 March 1970; Fink, Leon. "Bread and

Roses, Crusts and Thorns: The Troubled Story of 1199." *Dissent* 33, no. 2 (1986): 179–88; First National City Bank of New York. *Poverty and Economic Development in New York City*. New York: The Bank, 1968.

53 Padilla, Félix. *Puerto Rican Chicago*. Notre Dame, IN: Notre Dame University Press, 1987, 159–60.

54 *Ibid.*, 163–4.

55 "Poor to Choose in East Harlem." *The New York Times*, 6 March 1966, 69; "Causes Pondered by Puerto Ricans." *The New York Times*, 25 July 1967, 18.

56 Joel Schwartz, "The New York City Rent Strikes of 1963-1964." *Social Service Review*, no. 4 (1983): 545. Gold, *When Tenants Claimed the City*, 230.

57 Gold, *When Tenants Claimed the City*, 183–5; "Rent Is Withheld in City Tenements." *The New York Times*, 8 Nov. 1970, 53.

58 "Squatters Cast Doubt on Housing Plans." *The New York Times*, 11 Oct. 1970, 324; José E. Velázquez, "An Interview with Members of El Comité-MINP." In Andres Torres and José Velázquez, eds., *The Puerto Rican Movement*. Philadelphia: Temple University Press, 1998, 88–92; Muzio, Rose. *Radical Imagination, Radical Humanity: Puerto Rican Political Activism in New York*. Albany: State University of New York Press, 2017.

59 Gold, *When Tenants Claimed the City*, 231; "Residents Protest Plan for Housing." *The New York Times*, 16 July 1968, 24.

60 Uriarte-Gaston, 144, 150, 164–5, 176, 183, 196, 198; Matos Rodríguez, Félix V. "Saving the Parcela: A Short History of Boston's Puerto Rican Community." In Carmen Teresa Whalen and Víctor Vázquez-Hernández, eds., *The Puerto Rican Diaspora: Historical Perspectives*. Philadelphia: Temple University Press, 2005.

61 Moreno de Toro, Angel A. Amy. "An Oral History of the Puerto Rican Socialist Party in Boston, 1972–1978." In Torres and Velázquez, eds., *The Puerto Rican Movement*, 246–9; Uriarte-Gaston, 136–7.

62 Uriarte-Gaston, 164–5.

63 Kornbluh, Felicia. *The Battle for Welfare Rights: Politics and Poverty in Modern America*. Philadelphia: University of Pennsylvania, 2007, 14, 25–6.

64 Will Lissner, "5,000 Join Rally of Puerto Ricans." *The New York Times*, 27 May 1968, 20; "Puerto Ricans Here Deny Strike Threat." *The New York Times*, 17 June 1968, 36.

65 Jonathan Spivak, "Why Do the Welfare Rolls Keep Rising?" *Wall Street Journal*, 24 April 1969, 18.

66 Kornbluh, *The Battle for Welfare Rights*, 60–1.

67 "High Poverty Aide Starts Fast after Dismissal." *The New York Times*, 29 June 1968, 33; "Ousted Poverty Aide Ends Fast after Mayor Backs His Aims." *The New York Times*, 4 July 1968, 8; "City's 2nd Generation Puerto Ricans Rising from Poverty." *The New York Times*, 23 April 1968, 49. Agüeros later directed the Museo del Barrio and became one of the community's most celebrated writers. Maldonado, Adál Alberto, Louis Reyes Rivera, and Julio Rodríguez. *Portraits of the Puerto Rican Experience*. Bronx: IPRUS, 1984.

68 Vázquez, Hector, "Puerto Rican Americans," *Journal of Negro Education* 38 (summer 1969): 247–56; see 248, 250.

69 "Harlem Factions United on School." *The New York Times*, 23 Sept. 1966, 24.

70 "Petition Statement for Community Control of Police. Summary of Police Control Amendment that Must Be Established in the Cities and Communities of America to End Fascism," in *The Black Panther* (14 June 1969), reprinted in Philip S. Foner, ed., *The Black Panthers Speak*, Philadelphia: Lippincott, 1970, 179; De Jesús, Anthony and Madeline Pérez. "From Community Control to Consent Decree: Puerto Ricans Organizing for Education and Language Rights in 1960s and '70s New York City." *Centro Journal* 21, no. 2, (2009) 7–31; Charmichael, Stokely, "What We Want." *The New York Review of Books*, 22 Sept. 1966, 5–6, 8; Purnell, Brian. *Fighting Jim Crow in the County of Kings the Congress of Racial Equality in Brooklyn*. Lexington: University Press

of Kentucky, 2013; Taylor, Clarence, and Milton A. Galamison. *Knocking at Our Own Door: Milton A. Galamison and the Struggle to Integrate New York City Schools.* Lanham, MD: Lexington Books, 2001.

71 See Katznelson, *City Trenches*, p. 155; Back, Adina. "Parent Power: Evelina López Antonetty, the Unite Bronx Parents, and the War on Poverty." In Annelise Orleck and Lisa Gayle Hazirjian, eds., *The War on Poverty: A New Grassroots History, 1964–1980.* Athens: University of Georgia Press, 2011, 185.

72 "The Setting of United Bronx Parents' Work: Summary Description of the South Bronx" UBP-CPRS Box 2 Folder 14 (quotes from pp. 325, 327).

73 "Bundy Will Head Panel on Schools." *The New York Times*, 30 April 1967, 1; "Bundy Panel Asks Community Rule for City Schools." *The New York Times*, 8 Nov. 1967, 1.

74 Bundy report, "Reconnection for Learning," 2–3 and passim. The report was issued just before the start of a three-day Conference on Race and Education in Washington, D.C., sponsored by the U.S. Commission on Civil Rights, during which Bayard Rustin pushed for more collaboration on those issues between African Americans and both Chicanos and Puerto Ricans. "Negro-Puerto Rican Alliance Urged," *Chicago Daily Defender*, 21 Nov. 1967, 9. See also David Blumenthal, "City Education on the Verge of Revolution," *Harvard Crimson*, 13 June 1967.

75 "Lindsay Modifies School Reforms Urged by Bundy." *The New York Times*, 5 Jan. 1968, 1. "Harlem Proposes a Special Panel to Operate I.S. 201." *The New York Times*, 3 Oct. 1966, 1; "Action Demanded in I.S. 201 Dispute." *The New York Times*, 22 Oct. 1966, 17; "Cleric Accused City of 'Harassing' I.S. 201 Board." *The New York Times*, 9 Dec. 1968, 53.

76 "Cleric Accused City of 'Harassing' I.S. 201 Board." *The New York Times*, 9 Dec. 1968, 53; United Bronx Parents [n/d] UBP-CPRS Box 2 Folder 14, p. 25; "Sympathy Hinges on Neighborhood: Affluent Area Backs Union, Harlem Supports School." *The New York Times*, 13 Sept. 1967, 34; "Volunteers Help to Run Schools." *The New York Times*, 14 Sept. 1967, 52. "He Leads His Teachers Up the Down Staircase." *The New York Times*, 3 Sept. 1967, 150; Martin Mayer, "The Full and Sometimes Very Surprising Story of Ocean Hill . . ." *The New York Times*, 2 Feb. 1969, SM18.

77 De Jesús and Pérez, "From Community Control to Consent Decree," 6–31, 19.

78 Louis Nuñez, introduction, *The Losers: A Report on Puerto Ricans and the Public Schools.* U.S. Department of Health, Education, and Welfare, Office of Education, May 1968.

79 De Jesús and Pérez, "From Community Control to Consent Decree," 14, 16–17, 21; "'Self-Made' New Yorker Heads Puerto Rican Migration Agency." *The New York Times*, 9 Feb. 1970, 50.

80 Isidro Lucas, Council on Urban Education, *Puerto Rican Dropouts: Numbers and Motivation.* Washington, D.C., Office of Education, Bureau of Research, 1971; Margolis, *The Losers*, 8, 14.

81 A Senate subcommittee report on school violence, compiled in 1969, documented a sharp rise in violent crime taking place on school grounds between 1964 and 68. This was a report by the Senate Subcommittee on Juvenile Delinquency, headed by Senator Thomas Dodd. "Authority Shift Asked in Schools." *The New York Times*, 14 Jan. 1970, 50.

82 New York State Division of Human Rights. *Puerto Ricans in New York State, 1960–69.* New York, 1969; U.S. Commission on Civil Rights. *Puerto Ricans in the Continental U.S.: An Uncertain Future.* Washington, D.C., 1976, 119; "Court Order Ends C.C.N.Y. Blockade by 250 Students." *The New York Times*, 6 May 1969, 1.

83 "Faculty Rejects C.C.N.Y. Dual Plan." *The New York Times*, 30 May 1969, 1.

84 There are discrepancies in enrollment data reported in newspapers and other reports. A high estimate came from "Entrants Put Minority Groups' Rolls at 33%." *The New York Times*, 14 Sept. 1970, 1; a slightly lower estimate can be found in Iver Peterson, "As CUNY Cuts Back, Those Who Suffer Most Are the Minorities." *The New York Times*, 21 Dec. 1975, 179. In 1969, CUNY had 5,425 Puerto Rican undergraduates

(4% of enrollment) but by 1974 the number was 16,352 (7.4%); see U.S. Commission on Civil Rights, *Puerto Ricans in the Continental US: An Uncertain Future*, 119.

85 Mailer, "Why Are We in New York?"; "Candidates Score Dual Admissions for City College." *The New York Times*, 26 May 1969, 1.

86 "Black Studies Programs." *Chicago Daily Defender*, 26 July 1969, 8.

87 "Chicano-Boricua Union at University of Illinois Chicago Circle Campus 1974–75," quoted in Lilia Fernández, "Mexicans, Puerto Ricans, and Latino/a Alliances," presented at the annual meeting of the Latin American Studies Association, San Juan, Puerto Rico, 28 May 2015.

88 "'Where We Come From,' Strikers Represent Their Communities," *San Francisco Chronicle* [n.d.], San Francisco State Strike Collections-SFSU Archive Box 3 Folder Clippings.

89 Fernández, "Mexicans, Puerto Ricans, and Latino/a Alliances."

90 Pérez, Nélida. "Two Reading Rooms and the Librarian's Office: The Evolution of the Centro Library and Archives," *Centro Journal* 21, no. 2 (fall 2009): 199–220; Frank Bonilla, "Rethinking Latino/Latin American Interdependence." In Frank Bonilla et al., eds., *Borderless Borders: U.S. Latinos, Latin Americans, and the Paradox of Interdependence.* Philadelphia: Temple, 1998; Ortiz Márquez, Maribel. "Beginnings: Puerto Rican Studies Revisited," *Centro Journal* 21, no. 2 (fall 2009), 177–96. Puerto Rican Forum. *A Study of Poverty Conditions in the New York Puerto Rican Community.* New York: 1970, 77.

91 Pérez, Nélida. "Two Reading Rooms and the Librarian's Office: The Evolution of the Centro Library and Archives," *Centro Journal* 21, no. 2 (fall 2009): 200–21, 200.

92 Handlin, Oscar. *The Newcomers: Negroes and Puerto Ricans in a Changing Metropolis.* Cambridge, MA: Harvard University Press, 1971, 111.

93 Glazer, Nathan and Daniel Patrick Moynihan. *Beyond the Melting Pot: The Negroes, Puerto Ricans, Jews, Italians, and Irish of New York City.* Cambridge, MA: MIT Press, 1970; Lorrin Thomas, *Puerto Rican Citizen: History and Political Identity in Twentieth-Century New York City.* Chicago: University of Chicago Press, 2010, 225–7; Briggs, Laura. "La Vida, Moynihan, and Other Libels: Migration, Social Science, and the Making of the Puerto Rican Welfare Queen." *Centro Journal* 14, no. 1 (spring 2002): 74.

94 See, for example, "Conferencia de estudiantes condena intervención de EU en Puerto Rico." *El Imparcial*, 9 Jan. 1967, Jesús Colón Papers-CPRS Series X Box 2 Folder 8; Teach-In on Puerto Rico, flyer, 13 July 1967, Jesús Colón Papers-CPRS Series VI Box 21 Folder 7.

95 Meléndez, Miguel. *We Took the Streets: Fighting for Latino Rights with the Young Lords.* New York: St. Martin's Press, 2003, 87–9.

96 Pantoja, *Memoir of a Visionary*, 93–109; History Task Force, *Labor Migration Under Capitalism*, 52. See, for example, Carmen Vivian Rivera, "Our Movement, One Woman's Story." In Torres and Velázquez, eds., *The Puerto Rican Movement*, 203.

97 See Chapter 2, pp. 56–7.

98 Jeffries, Judson. "From Gang-Bangers to Urban Revolutionaries: The Young Lords of Chicago," *Journal of the Illinois State Historical Society* 96, no. 3 (2003): 291; Young Lords Party and Michael Abramson, *Palante.* Chicago: Haymarket Books, 1971.

99 Morales, Iris. "¡Palante, Siempre Palante!" in Torres and Velázquez, eds., *The Puerto Rican Movement*, 211–12. Luciano was also a member of the Original Last Poets.

100 The Young Lords and Abramson, *Palante*, 150; "ON STRIKE!!" [n.d. (1969)], San Francisco State Strike Collections-SFSU Archive Box 3 Folder: Third World Liberation Front.

101 Iris Morales attended SNCC, NAACP, and Human Relations Club meetings while at Julia Richman High School, Columbia Oral History interview with Ron Grele, 19 Nov. 1984, 19–20; "Young Lords Win Church Battle." *New York Amsterdam News*, 3 Jan. 1970, 1; Aspira, "Sixth Puerto Rican Youth Conference, 15 Feb. 1964, Points to Ponder," Covello Papers-HSP Series X Box 102 Folder 2.

102 *The New York Times*, 3 Aug. 1966; *El Diario/La Prensa*, 3 Aug. 1966; *El Diario/La Prensa*, 5 Aug. 1966; *El Diario/La Prensa*, 2 Aug. 1966; "Violencia contra los Boricuas." *El Tiempo*,

2 Aug. 1966; *The New York Times*, 9 July 1968; *The New York Times*, 6 July 1968; *El Diario/La Prensa*, 8 Aug. 1966; Jorge Colón to Ralph Rosas, Activity Report, 24 July 1967, OGPRUS-Centro Box 3046 Folder 9; *The New York Times*, 19 Aug. 1970; *The New York Times*, 2 Aug. 1970; *The New York Times*, 20 Aug. 1971; *The New York Times*, 21 Aug. 1971; *The New York Times*, 24 Aug. 1971; Rodríguez-Morrazani, "Political Cultures of the Puerto Rican Left in the United States." In Torres and Velázquez, eds., *The Puerto Rican Movement*, 45–6.

103 Carmen Whalen, interview with R. Colón, in Whalen, "Bridging Homeland and Barrio Politics," 119.

104 Fernández, Johanna. "The Young Lords and the Social and Structural Roots of Late Sixties Urban Radicalism." In Clarence Taylor, ed., *Civil Rights in New York City: From World War II to the Giuliani Era*. New York: Fordham University Press, 2011, 141–60. Guzmán, Pablo. "La Vida Pura: A Lord of the Barrio." In Torres and Velázquez, eds., *The Puerto Rican Movement*, 171–2; Subcommittee to Investigate the Administration of the Internal Security Act and Other Internal Security Laws of the Committee on the Judiciary, United States Senate, *The Puerto Rican Revolutionary Workers Organization: A Staff Study*. Washington, D.C.: U.S. Government Printing Office, 1976.

105 Guzmán, "La Vida Pura," 158.

106 See Chapter 4, pp. 136, 139, 148.

107 "HRUM Sums up Hospital Organizing." *The Guardian*, 27 Dec. 1972; "When the Union's the Enemy: An Interview with Cleo Stivers." *Jacobin*. 22 July 2014. "Young Lords Seize Lincoln Hospital Building." *The New York Times*, 15 July 1970. Hoffman, Lily M. *The Politics of Knowledge: Activist Movements in Medicine and Planning*. Albany: State University of New York Press, 1989, 124–5; Mullan, Fitzhugh. *White Coat, Clenched Fist: The Political Education of an American Physician*. Ann Arbor: University of Michigan Press, 2006, 185–7; "Lincoln Hospital: Case History of Dissension That Split Staff." *The New York Times*, 21 Dec. 1971, 1.

108 "Flyin' Cut Sleeves" directed by Henry Chalfont and Rita Fecher (1993); "South Bronx Gang Seeks Peace Role." *The New York Times*, 4 Dec. 1971, 63.

109 "Flying' Cut Sleeves"; Fernández, *Brown in the Windy City*, 172.

4

CIVIL RIGHTS IN THE ACTIVIST DECADE, 1974–1980

Introduction

In 1973, the *New York Times* ran a front-page story by reporter Martin Tolchin with the sensational headline "A Jungle Stalked by Fear, Seized by Rage." The descriptions conjured images of a conflict zone in the Third World, although the area Tolchin had visited was just few miles from the newspaper's Manhattan offices—the South Bronx.

> Fire hydrants are open, even in this biting cold weather—town pumps that provide the sole water supply for drinking washing and sanitation for thousands of tenants . . . packs of wild dogs pick through the rubble . . . a drug pusher is murdered by a youth gang . . .

Tolchin got his most dramatic quote from Harold Wise, founder of a local health center, who called the South Bronx "a necropolis—a city of death." Alongside his descriptions of an apocalyptic landscape, Tolchin deployed statistics to clinch the case: 40% of the community's 400,000 residents received welfare, 30% of adults were unemployed, 20,000 were drug addicts and 9,500 were gang members. 20% of houses the houses lacked water, and 50% lacked heat half the time.[1]

Indeed, these were the years when Tom Walker, a police officer who later became captain, worked in the 41st Precinct—nicknamed Fort Apache—and soon began chronicling his experiences in a book that became the controversial movie, *Fort Apache, the Bronx*. Conditions in the Puerto Rican community in the Bronx were arguably worse than in any other neighborhood in New York City. The community was literally "burned out": slum landlords, who had squeezed rents out of their unmaintained apartments for over a decade as the area declined, found they could collect on federally subsidized insurance after burning down their own buildings—with few questions asked and little fear of prosecution. In New York City, arson and uncontrolled fires exploded in the mid-1970s with 33,000 in the South Bronx in 1974 alone; this was during the city's fiscal crisis, when many fire stations were closed due to budget cuts.[2]

The burned out South Bronx got national attention, especially after President Carter visited the neighborhood in 1977, but the story was similar in the poor neighborhoods in many of the decaying cities of the Northeast where Puerto Ricans lived. The small city of Camden, located across the river from Philadelphia, where Puerto Ricans had started settling in the mid-1940s, experienced a decline in the 1970s that rivaled that of the South Bronx. By 1970 Camden had lost half of its manufacturing jobs, leading to municipal bankruptcy and urban blight. After the city was rocked by Black and Puerto Rican riots protesting police brutality in the early 1970s, Camden's decline accelerated. Former Mayor Angelo Errichetti later recalled looking out his car window as he drove to his first day of work at Camden's city hall in 1973.

> The Pride of Camden . . . was now a rat-infested skeleton of yesterday, a visible obscenity of urban decay . . . The years of neglect, slumlord exploitation, tenant abuse, government bungling, indecision, and short-sighted policy had transformed the city's housing, business and industrial stock into a ravaged, rat-infested cancer on a sick, old industrial city.[3]

Though many tried, it was—and still is—difficult to portray the enormity of the crisis faced by the poor and working class people of the large industrial cities of the north during the late 1970s, the very same cities that had attracted over 95% of Puerto Rican migrants since the start of the 20th century. Trends that had been brewing since the 1950s spelled disaster for many in the Puerto Rican communities in U.S. cities by the 1970s. Deindustrialization, the relocation of industry to places where real estate and labor costs were cheaper, along with its associated flight of urban white middle class residents, fueled the growth of the suburbs, exacting a great cost to cities and their inhabitants but especially to those in poor communities who already suffered from decades of racially discriminatory housing policy. Burned out and decaying buildings and a spike in street crime were only the most visible problems of the ballooning urban crisis. Illegal drug use, school violence, rising dropout rates, and persistent unemployment added up to a bleak future for ghetto residents.

As economic "stagflation" wracked the country by the mid-1970s, poor Black and Latino communities in Bridgeport, New Haven, Newark, and Philadelphia became shadows of the bustling neighborhoods they once were. The near-bankruptcy of New York City in 1975 and the austerity crisis that resulted led to massive cuts in basic services and tens of thousands of public sector layoffs. The city's faltering economy also resulted in a catastrophic failure of maintenance in

TABLE 4.1 Puerto Rican Population by City, 1970 and 1980

City	1970	1980
NYC	817,712	860,552
Chicago	79,582	112,074
Philadelphia	26,948	46,990
Newark	27,663	39,732
Jersey City	16,325	26,830
Hartford	8,631	24,615
Patterson	12,036	24,326
Bridgeport	10,046	22,146
Boston	7,335	19,379
Camden	6,566	14,799
Cleveland	8,104	14,153
Los Angeles	10,116	13,835
Miami	8,800	12,320
Springfield		12,298
Perth Amboy		11,025
Rochester	5,916	10,545
Passaic	6,853	10,539
Yonkers		9,096
Buffalo	6,090	9,085
Vineland		8,976
Union City		8,103
Lorain	6,031	8,033
Elizabeth		7,675
Milwaukee		7,708
San Francisco		5,174
Bethlehem		4,904
Allentown		4,279

Source: Rivera-Batiz, Francisco L., Carlos Santiago, and National Puerto Rican Coalition. *Puerto Ricans in the United States: A Changing Reality.* Washington, D.C.: National Puerto Rican Coalition, 1994, 22.

its enormous public housing sector as well as the general destruction of inner city housing. As a result, the Puerto Rican community experienced major difficulties rooted in the simultaneous decline of both the industrial and public sectors of the economy as well as public policies aimed at facilitating social mobility and welfare.

When efforts at recovery began in the late 1970s, low income Puerto Ricans were not well positioned to take advantage of labor market improvements, as most of the growth took place in city employment, construction, and financial services—all sectors in which Puerto Ricans were grossly underrepresented, either because of discriminatory hiring or the requirement of specialized education and training. By 1980 Puerto Rican communities faced a massive crisis of employment and income, and poverty rates had increased to 30% (and 37% for women). Puerto Rican communities had bifurcated by this point into distinct sectors. The most vulnerable included younger and older residents, more recent migrants, and those with less education, while a significant minority, around 30% of Puerto Ricans in the U.S., had achieved middle class status via stable jobs and income, and a high school diploma or a college degree. Like some other residents of Newark, Hartford, New York, and other crisis-ridden cities, middle class Puerto Ricans were likely to move to the suburbs—or to migrate further, to Florida or even back to Puerto Rico, which experienced a significant return flow of migrants during the 1970s.

Whereas the 1960s had ended with a blaze of youthful energy for change, the 1970s appeared to be marked by the smoldering ashes of ghetto tenements—and their residents' dreams of better lives for their children. Yet this metaphor, while an accurate reflection of so many accounts of urban Puerto Rican communities in that decade, only captures a certain dimension of their experience. Only about half of Puerto Ricans in the U.S. lived in densely impoverished urban neighborhoods in the 1970s; and the persistence or resurgence of poverty in those years did not mean that Puerto Ricans were quietly accepting their circumstances. After decades of creative organizing for equity in education, housing, employment, city services, and political representation—efforts that became more visible and confrontational by the late 1960s—dedicated activists persisted in their work throughout the 1970s. Indeed, in spite of the decline in the momentum of some of the most visible groups that had comprised the heart of the early Puerto Rican movement, grassroots activism in Puerto Rican communities flourished throughout the 1970s. The many social service and advocacy groups that had been founded by the early 1970s, together with a new crop of national policy organizations, shared a durable energy to build on the momentum created by the *despertar boricua*, the Puerto Rican awakening.

Puerto Rican leaders in the U.S. began the decade facing a more challenging reality, but now could rely on well-practiced strategies and a network of mature organizations that increasingly rejected the 1960s' polarization between "liberal" and "radical"perspectives. With varied approaches, Puerto Ricans continued to fight for equal rights and against discrimination. Some used the arts as a way to critique society and build community; many remained dedicated to the goal of Puerto Rican independence, expressing their nationalism in a wide variety of ways, from poetic invocation to armed insurrection. The people who carried this Puerto Rican movement through the 1970s were an even more heterogeneous group of activists than those who participated in previous eras of the Puerto Rican civil rights struggle. In the early years of the movement, it was the young radicals who got the most attention—and who, indeed, first proclaimed the creation of a singular movement. But the longer phase of the Puerto Rican movement engaged people of different generations working in diverse organizations and extending their work into new areas of advocacy, particularly a growing focus on equal educational access (through bilingual instruction), voting rights, and affirmative action in both employment and admission to colleges and universities. All of them continued working to expand rights and opportunities, making concrete the goals of real social change.

Community Organizing: Networks of Grassroots Support

By the early 1970s, the "organization and political mobilization of the discontented," as South Bronx organizer Evelina Antonetty characterized the era's activism, was everywhere visible in urban Puerto Rican communities. The number of organizations serving Puerto Ricans in U.S. cities had exploded during the 1960s, a mobilization that sprang from many different bases and centered on education, housing, and labor issues. These new organizations were bolstered by the spirit of engagement that animated many sectors of each city's Puerto Rican community, aided by collaborators from outside those communities, and supported by the infusion of War on Poverty funds during the mid-1960s. Some of these organizations developed out of pre-existing social service organizations that had over time become primarily Puerto Rican in terms of staff and leadership as well as clientele. There was no single defining feature of the Puerto Rican community organizations that thrived during the 1970s. Most offered multiple kinds of services and advocacy, while some organizations focused on a particular category of issues, like housing or education.

Although the size of New York City's Puerto Rican community meant that it boasted the largest number of activist groups, other cities also experienced a Puerto Rican movement on their own scale, shaking up the social and political dynamics that had kept Puerto Rican communities in a state of largely invisible suffering for a generation. In many of those smaller cities, rapid ethnic succession had transformed old immigrant neighborhoods during the 1960s, with an exodus of white residents to suburbs and an influx of Latinos and African Americans. In this era, it was not uncommon for new community organizers to get their start working in neighborhood settlement houses (many of them founded in the early 20th century to serve the European immigrants of that era) or other community social service agencies found in virtually every poor and working class urban neighborhood. With the help of federal funds supporting anti-poverty and job training work, these networks of organizations, sometimes established as "community development corporations" during the 1960s, continued to provide services to the urban poor despite increasing struggles for funding during the late 1970s and early 1980s.

In Chicago, the Association House, a settlement house established at the turn of the 20th century to serve European immigrant communities around Wicker Park and Humboldt Park, had provided support to new Puerto Rican residents of the area in the 1950s. By the 1970s, the Association House became such a central base for Puerto Rican community organizers that when Chicago's city hall cut its funding, the community mounted a major demonstration to protest the cuts. Similarly, the Chicago Commons Association, built to provide support for Eastern European immigrants of West Town and Humboldt Park in 1894, served as an incubator of the Latino Institute, an advocacy organization founded jointly by leaders of the Puerto Rican and Mexican communities in Chicago in 1974.[4] In Philadelphia, the Friends Neighborhood Guild, established by Quakers in 1879, served the Puerto Rican community that grew around it in the 1950s and, two decades later, helped foster networks of community development that incorporated both Puerto Rican activists and non-Puerto Rican social service professionals.[5]

In New York City, the large and heterogeneous Puerto Rican community (which numbered 860,000 people by 1980) had developed independent organizational structures that were decades old by the 1970s, and in several Puerto Rican neighborhoods in Brooklyn and Manhattan, the historic settlement houses remained central to the community support networks. In the Bronx, however, where much of the housing had been built to accommodate middle class Manhattan residents moving "up" into the northern borough in the early- and mid-20th century, there were few preexisting social service organizations to aid the residents who remained after the area's downward economic slide during the 1960s. Casita Maria, founded in East Harlem during the 1930s, relocated to the South Bronx in 1961 as thousands of Puerto Ricans began migrating to that borough. With a mix of public and private funding, Casita Maria expanded its programs to include homeless services, violence prevention, gang intervention, and teen pregnancy intervention to help manage the growing social and economic crisis in the area.[6]

The largest Puerto Rican community social service organization of this era, the Hunts Point Multi-Service Center (HPMSC), was founded in the South Bronx in the late 1960s by Ramon Vélez, a former community organizer for the Migration Division. HPMSC closely resembled its early 20th century predecessors in that its services were dedicated to the full range of needs of recent migrants: housing, job placement and training, an emergency food bank, child care, and healthcare. Vélez became expert in winning funds flowing from the federal War on Poverty, and by the end of the decade he had developed a vast array of programs and businesses that earned him wealth and power—as well as multiple indictments (though no convictions) for misuse of public funds.[7]

With such a broad range of operations that served such a large number of needy people—including newcomers who, thanks to their citizenship, could vote—Vélez became the head of a social service network that was the kind of "patronage-client system of the distribution of wealth and power" that activists like Evelina López Antonetty explicitly rejected. Vélez was able to leverage his influence over his South Bronx community into a term on city council in 1974–76, although he failed in a bid to displace rival Herman Badillo from the South Bronx congressional seat in 1976. Referred to by many as the "baron" or the "emperor" of the South Bronx, Vélez's empire was not, however, the only game in town in the 1970s. His chief rival in that decade was an Italian

American priest and community activist, Father Louis Gigante, who was also a charismatic community leader and a city councilman, representing a neighboring South Bronx district. Gigante, who referred to Vélez as a "poverty pimp, and a community eater," had a reputation for working well with younger activists, and on many community actions in the early 1970s, he collaborated with members of the Young Lords and El Comité, along with a growing number of young activists who had left street gangs in order to devote their time to helping their communities.[8]

The career of one such politicized former gang leader, Benjamin Meléndez, who headed the Ghetto Brothers gang during the early 1970s, exemplified the young radicals' rejection of Vélez's poverty empire. Shortly after leaving the gang, Meléndez took a job at United Bronx Parents (UBP), the organization Evelina López Antonetty had founded in the mid-1960s during the fight for community control of public schools, and stayed with the organization for 30 years. In line with young militants of that era, like the Ghetto Brothers, Antonetty fought for "the right to control our own life and the conditions in which we live" and to change the way Puerto Ricans were recognized as social actors. "Puerto Rican people, my people," she wrote, "are longing for the day when our children and the children of other minorities can sing 'My Country 'Tis of Thee' and stand and feel it without saying under their breath, 'except for me.'" As UBP expanded well beyond its Bronx roots throughout the 1970s, Antonetty kept her focus on education, working to transform schools and expand parents' sense of empowerment in advocating for their children. Given the "oppressive system" that most Black and Puerto Rican school children were exposed to, said Antonetty, "it is . . . not surprising that an approach which stresses organization and political mobilization of the discontented would be one which could thrive in this environment."[9]

UBP was by the early 1970s a powerful force in New York City grass-roots politics, serving schoolchildren and their families in the Puerto Rican South Bronx, and active in education issues and neighborhoods well beyond that geographic base. Through Antonetty's leadership, according to a report from the mid-1970s, "United Bronx Parents has managed to coordinate its case advocacy work with class advocacy, political action, organizing, parent education, and programmatic work [to a degree] greater than we have seen in a good number of other community-based advocacy programs." Although Antonetty remained in the South Bronx throughout her career and continued to focus on the parents and families of that community, she adapted her commitment to participatory community empowerment to create a vision of much broader advocacy throughout the 1970s and 1980s. She served on dozens of boards of social service and educational organizations in the New York City area and worked nationally as a consultant.[10]

In New York City, an extended fiscal crisis, precipitated by a tax base eviscerated by deindustrialization and white flight plus a rising demand for services by needy residents, plunged poor communities into two decades of seemingly unremitting poverty and unemployment accompanied by drug addiction and street violence. Conditions in most other cities with growing Puerto Rican populations were not much better. Housing remained the primary issue—a problem of both justice and survival—that continued to animate Puerto Rican communities as urban renewal produced intensifying patterns of displacement and exacerbated insecurity in ghetto neighborhoods. In the dozen or so cities with growing Puerto Rican populations in the 1970s, housing activism continued to attract a broad base of participation, engaging young and old, radicals and conservatives, priests and housewives.

As in previous eras, the economic and racial dynamics that underlay housing struggles also produced broad political connections that extended well beyond that particular issue. El Comité, for example, had been founded in the late 1960s to address housing problems in Manhattan, but soon adopted a broader agenda that combined community justice and Puerto Rican independence. By 1975, the organization changed its name to El Comité-MINP (Movimiento de Izquierda Nacional Puertorriqueño, or Puerto Rican National Left Movement), balancing its focus on community activism in the U.S. with support for Puerto Rican independence. Even as it evolved and expanded, the organization continued to serve as an anchor in the fight against urban renewal in the various cities where El Comité-MINP chapters formed. Likewise, chapters of the Puerto Rican Socialist Party (PSP), though founded to fight for Puerto Rican independence, collaborated on fair housing campaigns in various cities and also had its U.S.-based members push within the organization for a focus on U.S. working class struggles as opposed to a sole focus on island independence.[11]

According to historian Roberta Gold, the "big picture" of housing activism in New York City shifted dramatically in the 1970s, and her argument could be extended to other cities—San Francisco, Chicago, Boston—where struggles for fair housing dominated grassroots politics in the poor neighborhoods where Puerto Ricans tended to live. Gold writes that even though many radical community organizations worked in the 1960s to address "the minimum standards of modern urban living" in New York City, including basic healthcare, clean streets, and lead-safe residences, none of these efforts changed what she calls "the lynchpin of slum economics, which was New York's dearth of affordable housing." Around 1970, though, following a surge in evictions in poor neighborhoods throughout the city, that lynchpin began to weaken, as "a new breed of activists, organized squatters, embarked on the 'liberation' of housing itself."[12]

The surge in tenant organizing in the 1970s had a powerful impact in several New York City neighborhoods with large Puerto Rican populations. In Williamsburg, a group of activists—many of whom had participated in protests on behalf of Puerto Ricans during the 1968 citywide school strikes—founded a new organization, Los Sures, to deal with the problems of abandonment and arson and to push for Puerto Ricans' equal access to public housing. It was widely understood that in Williamsburg, where Hasidic Jews were the majority, Puerto Ricans were actively excluded from lists of applicants to some of the city's afford-able housing projects. Los Sures collaborated with other community activists, including some members of the PSP, to ensure that Puerto Rican residents were given equal access to public housing; the group also helped manage rehabilitation projects that would provide upgraded housing for Puerto Ricans and other poor residents of Williamsburg. In the Lower East Side, Puerto Rican tenants' associa-tions managed to rehabilitate a number of city-owned buildings in the 1970s and early 1980s, creating a bulwark against developers who sought to capitalize on skyrocketing real estate values in an impoverished neighborhood. As sociologist Janet Abu Lughod observed, "Housing was the one issue that always galvanized Lower East Siders into action . . . This is a neighborhood whose unity has been forged in contest."[13]

Puerto Ricans in Chicago engaged in similar struggles against urban renewal and gentrification, and against arson as well. Adjacent to the heavily Puerto Rican Division Street community was Wicker Park, a neighborhood that was beginning to be gentrified by developers in the mid-1970s. As a rash of build-ing fires swept through the Division Street and Humboldt Park communities in those years, just as they had done in the South Bronx, Puerto Rican residents feared that the fires were a tactic to push poor residents out of an area that developers had targeted for their own expansion. In 1976, a coalition of over 30 Latino organizations in Chicago pressed Mayor Daley's office to take action. In response, the city established a special arson investigation team that, together with the community's vigilance, was able to substantially reduce the problem of arson. Another outcome was the establishment of a new Community Housing Education Corporation, enabling community leaders and residents to plan their own renewal and rehabilitation in ways that would strengthen the Division Street neighborhoods. Their approach to community revitalization was remarkably suc-cessful: the Humboldt Park community continues to be one of Chicago's most vital mixed-class neighborhoods, where a wide range of community-managed services—youth programs, cultural resources, public health initiatives—flourish along with a powerful community pride.[14]

Boston's Puerto Rican neighborhoods also continued to see substantial pro-tests about housing in the 1970s, along with very effective organizing to address the problems. In 1974, as they struggled to stop the planned demolition and redevelopment of their community, organizers of the Puerto Rican-led Tenants Emergency Council changed the group's name to Inquilinos Puertorriqueños Unidos (United Puerto Rican Tenants). Under the banner of "community con-trol," the group was able to negotiate plans for a housing project that would replace the decrepit buildings in their neighborhood. Inquilinos Puertorriqueños Unidos helped design a housing project, called Villa Victoria, that consisted of a low-rise "village" with a central plaza and two-family townhouses, reproducing some of the characteristics of small town life in Puerto Rico. The project became a national icon for successful public housing design and also provided a model for cultural and social considerations in the use of public funds to subsidized housing. When a group of mostly white gentrifiers mounted a lawsuit to stop the project, the activists who had helped create Villa Victoria emerged victorious. The first 190 units were completed in 1979, and 6,000 applicants, the majority of them Puerto Rican, applied for residence there.[15]

Many campaigns for housing reform had less happy endings than that of the Villa Victoria community. Housing activists in East Harlem, led by the East Harlem Tenants Council, had convinced New York City officials in the late 1960s to build an affordable housing complex in the city's largest Puerto Rican neighborhood. Rents for the Taino Towers apartments (named after the indigenous people of the Caribbean islands conquered by the Spanish) would be set at rates proportional to family size and income, and subsidized at up to 80%, the same formula used in other public housing projects. In nearly every other respect, the planners of the development intended for its design to differ from typical public housing. Taino Towers would offer amenities like balconies and laundry facilities, as well as a gym, a swimming pool, college classroom space, a health clinic, and a day care center, all available to the surrounding community—affirmations of dignity for residents who were used to living far below the standards of New York's affluent middle class. Activists and planners secured the input of federal funds from Federal Housing Authority (FHA) and the federal office of Housing and Urban Development (HUD), as well as a number of New York City banks, and builders broke ground in 1972. With backing even from moderate Republican politicians, the project was widely viewed as a promising model for other community-developed projects.[16]

The project was delayed, however, by a combination of the city's fiscal crisis and the developers' demands for higher profits to offset the rampant inflation of that era, and it was not until 1979 that the first several hundred families were finally able to move into Taino Towers. Further complications developed when HUD tried to take control of the project and convert it to middle class housing, a strategy intended to prevent defaulting on loan payments during the long project delays. Community activists persisted, though, and retained control of the complex; when the buildings opened, there was a waiting list of 7,000 applicants, the vast majority of them low income households with Section 8 vouchers.

Some aspects of the planners' vision succeeded—the health clinic served as a major regional center for low income New Yorkers—but many others remained problematic. The size of the complex was seen as a detriment to the immediate neighborhood in an otherwise decrepit area, and maintenance was always a problem. For many critics, the "bloated," "sprawling," over-budget project was a symbol of everything that was wrong with liberal public spending on low income housing. One letter to the *New York Times* estimated that the 650 families could have been provided with private market housing and lifelong incomes instead of building the Towers. Ronald Reagan, then governor of California, attacked the project as luxury housing for "slum dwellers." After a 15-year process of planning, lobbying, and building, even many leftists and liberals came to see Taino Towers as a cautionary example of how activist goals could be distorted by the complexities of public policy, fiscal politics, and social inequalities in U.S. society.[17]

Work and Economic Life: Labor Activism for Equality

By the end of the 1970s, Puerto Ricans as a group had achieved some significant economic gains: professional, para-professional, and white collar employment had increased dramatically since the 1950s, and high- and middle-income Puerto Ricans now comprised a larger share of the population. But the gains were skewed. Puerto Ricans were still overwhelmingly working class, and a substantial percentage of the population still lived in poverty. Like in other periods, labor activists in the late 1970s continued to focus on improvement in public sector employment and construction, pushing for access to jobs that were still largely unavailable to Puerto Ricans. Unions continued to struggle for better wages and conditions, although as industrial and service unions began to lose membership and bargaining power, this was a defensive battle. The old industrial and service sectors of the urban economies had been decimated by deindustrialization, budget cuts, and further movements towards an automated and globalized economy in which low skill and manufacturing workers were no longer as necessary. Only public sector unions, like the American Federation of State, County, and Municipal Employees (AFSCME), were able to combat more effectively the conditions of austerity and fiscal crisis, as public services and administration were in increased demand.

Puerto Ricans made some important advances through labor activism during the 1970s. Additional connections between labor and other areas of advocacy developed during these years, and the organizations of the Puerto Rican "new left" invested more time and energy in the working class struggles happening in both factories and farms. The radical group El Comité-MINP, for instance, in addition to its work in community housing, educational access, and nationalist politics, collaborated with labor activists to stage protests at construction sites to draw attention to discriminatory hiring. The U.S. chapters of the Puerto Rican Socialist Party (PSP) mobilized in support of striking factory workers and helped organize Puerto Rican farmworkers in Connecticut and New Jersey.[18]

The most substantial gains for Puerto Rican workers during the 1970s were achieved by Puerto Rican labor leaders who, through persistent pressure (in many cases begun in the 1950s), achieved more visible positions of leadership within industrial unions, including the International Ladies' Garment Workers' Union (ILGWU) and unions of electrical workers. But it was in public employment and the service and health sectors that Puerto Rican workers advanced the most. These areas of the economy experienced a recovery during the late

1970s and leadership gained ground, in part because their unions were increasing in membership, bargaining power, and militancy in the difficult economic terrain of the 1970s. Puerto Ricans had a particularly strong presence in the unions that represented workers in the building services and garment industries, as well as hospital workers, hotel and restaurant workers, public administrators, and teachers.

Nevertheless, these gains were limited, and not just because the majority of Puerto Rican activists and labor leaders during the 1970s remained at mid-level positions. The 1970s was also the decade when industrial decline hit bottom all around the country; and it is an understatement to say that low skill minority industrial workers bore the brunt of this decline. After years of relatively stagnant wages, roughly half of the industrial jobs disappeared from the cities of the Northeast during this decade. New York, for instance, went from having 950,000 manufacturing jobs at the end of the 1960s to 500,000 by 1980.[19] At the same time, federal and state investment in public services—housing, education, health care, employment training—declined just as the needs of low wage workers increased, while inflation spiked in the second half of the decade.

By 1976, a federal report noted that Puerto Rican households in the U.S. had a lower per capita income than any other group, and they suffered unemployment rates roughly three times higher than whites.[20] Paradoxically, at the same time that the U.S. Civil Rights Commission was pointing out with alarm the poverty conditions that prevailed within the Puerto Rican community, policies promoting equity and affirmative action in the educational and corporate world began to open doors for a small but significant minority of Puerto Rican youth, creating the foundation for a stronger middle class. But this was a slow process and its results only became visible in retrospect. During the late 1970s most Puerto Ricans were struggling to survive within the ruins of their increasingly devastated cities, with few options for improvement.

The terms under which devastated neighborhoods would be rebuilt, and the question of who would benefit from the process and results of this reconstruction, became contested within Puerto Rican communities. By 1980 $350 million had been allocated to rebuild the devastated South Bronx, and Puerto Rican workers, including many residents of the Bronx itself, wanted jobs in the reconstruction efforts. Herman Badillo, the South Bronx's former congressman, who also served from 1978–79 as Ed Koch's deputy mayor, complained that radical groups like the United Tremont Trades (UTT) and Black Economic Survival (BES) created unnecessary conflicts because "they want *their* blacks and Puerto Ricans hired" and ignored those already on the job.[21] In some instances, disrupting the work sites was a tactic used by these groups and at least in one case a fight between UTT and members of the International Brotherhood of Electrical Workers (IBEW) members was averted by police.

United Tremont Trades, organized in 1976, was a South Bronx organization led by Julio Muñoz that sought investment in the reconstruction of the South

Bronx as well as jobs for local Black and Puerto Rican workers. UTT ran training workshops and helped ex-prisoners find work. Backed by a membership of 500 workers, UTT leaders complained of the continued dominance of construction jobs by "white" unions and contractors. With the assistance of HUD and the federal Department of Labor, UTT managed to win a number of lawsuits for back pay because of race-based wage differentials. Picketing was another important strategy that contributed to some success in increased hires of Black and Puerto Rican construction workers. Sometimes protests turned violent; for example in 1978, when UTT members picketed midtown Manhattan building sites to protest their exclusion from construction jobs, they were attacked by white workers with steel pipes.[22]

The group El Comité-MINP also worked with Black and Puerto Rican labor groups in New York to demand construction jobs from developers, unions, and the city. El Comité-MINP organized the Frente Obrero Unido, which sought to organize Puerto Rican workers at worksites and unions for improved conditions and access, involving a number of former members of the Young Lords as well as members of the U.S. chapters of the PSP.[23]

The 1970s also saw continued efforts to organize into unions the thousands of permanent and seasonal Puerto Rican farm workers who labored in fruit and vegetable farms and canneries in New York, Connecticut, and New Jersey. The successes and militancy of the United Farm Workers (UFW) during the late 1960s and the resurgence of Puerto Rican leftist organizations contributed to these efforts. The American Federation of Labor–Congress of Industrial Organizations (AFL-CIO) and many of its member unions invested resources in upstate New York, sending full time organizer Paul Sánchez to assist local farm workers (he also helped organize the grape boycott of the UFW in California). Even Puerto Rico's government sought to encourage the unionization of the farm workers by inviting various unions in 1976 to organize them. Despite some improvements, however, most of these efforts failed, largely because the conditions of the workers themselves and interference from employers did not allow consistent organizing.

During the 1970s, more aggressive legal and policy action by the federal government based on the Equal Employment Opportunity Commission (EEOC), mandated by the 1964 Civil Rights Act, offered Puerto Ricans an additional set of tools for securing access and rights in the workplace. Puerto Ricans had participated in and also benefited from the older and larger African American struggles for equity, and federal-level policies like affirmative action and legislation enforcing equality of opportunity were an important source of protection. Also driving these policies was advocacy for women's rights as gender became an officially designated protected class; indeed, Puerto Rican women benefitted concretely from the combination of race- and gender-based legal protections. Affirmative action was often criticized on the presumption that it was a "quota system" that designated specific numbers of jobs (or spots in college admissions) to presumably unqualified members of a distinct demographic. The reality was far more complicated, however.

By the mid-1970s the federal government and many states had established anti-discriminatory practices and regulations through the EEOC and state anti-discrimination commissions, which sought to ensure equitable opportunities and the removal of barriers for minority employees, contractors, and students. These innovations were not simply the enacting of anti-discrimination legislation; that had happened, piecemeal, since the 1940s. What was new was the legal commitment of presidential administrations and Congress to reducing the blatant exclusion of women, Blacks and other minorities from the world of elite education and skilled work, high pay, and middle class and professional employment and contracting. Pressure from Black civil rights leaders, especially the NAACP, resulted in corporations with massive public contracts, especially those in the defense industry, diversifying what were often nearly 100% white labor and administrative workforces. The corporate world and elite educational institutions began to assume some responsibility for inclusion and diversity, and opened the doors, for the first time in many cases, to high skilled, managerial, and executive positions for many Blacks and Puerto Ricans. A similar process took place with federal employment, as more rigorous standards for detecting and enforcing discrimination were put in place with often vigorous lawsuits to enforce goals. In education, Black and Puerto Rican students entered elite academic institutions in large numbers for the first time, including many who came from low income families.[24]

Efforts at enforcing equal employment rules since the 1960s had been opposed by the AFL-CIO and independent unions by preventing injured parties (those who claimed they had been kept from access to training, employment, or union membership) from suing for discrimination. Piecemeal efforts at opening employment for Blacks and Puerto Ricans (and sometimes also women) with legal, educational and civic action from activists and state government continued throughout the 1970s.[25] Particularly resistant were many of the construction trades unions which, because of the high skill level and the peculiarities of the contracting system, controlled most of the hiring in the construction sector. In New York City, it did not help that the construction industry itself crashed with the city's financial struggles, with little new office building construction between 1974 and the early 1980s.[26] In 1970 the Steamfitters' Union, after years of agreeing to train and recruit "non-white" members, shut out trained Puerto Rican and Black applicants, motivating several of the rejected applicants to mount a legal challenge to the union's decision. Drawing support from militant labor organization Harlem Fightback along with Columbia University's Employment Project, the plaintiffs' 1971 lawsuit was successful; by 1977, the union had 30% minority membership.[27] With the power of the federal government as co-plaintiff, affirmative action legislation finally provided some muscle to support the efforts of workers and their allies.

Still, even many successful demands for access and inclusion by the Puerto Rican community led to limited results. Lawyer Patria Nieto Ortiz was a second generation New Yorker, a graduate of Barnard College and NYU law school whose parents worked in factories, whom Mayor Koch appointed to serve as director of New York City's Human Rights office in early 1978. Soon after her appointment, however, Nieto Ortiz confronted obstacles in trying to investigate the status of Puerto Rican and other minority employees within city agencies. She also challenged the city's compliance with equal opportunity employment laws, even threatening to subpoena Mayor Koch himself. Nieto Ortiz resigned within a few months of her appointment, commenting that "My experience shows that the Koch administration is not sensitive to issues involving discrimination, [and] they are uncomfortable around any other ethnic group than themselves."[28]

Describing the status of the Puerto Rican community during the 1970s poses certain challenges, as new middle-class sectors consolidated and a growing number of Puerto Ricans—like Nieto Ortiz—gained positions of visibility, status, and influence in business and government. With an increasing presence as well in health, education, public service, and skilled labor occupations, thousands of Puerto Ricans achieved more comfortable incomes in the 1970s. But at the same time a significant proportion of the community experienced stagnant if not deteriorating conditions due to declining incomes, crumbling inner cities, failing schools, and drug related violence—conditions that would only worsen through the early 1980s.

Education and Community Life: Students, Intellectuals, and Artists

The mobilization for change in Puerto Rican communities in the 1970s was not limited to fixing the social and economic problems of the ghetto, which is how the agenda of the Puerto Rican movement of that era typically has been defined. Having come of age during a decade when equality in education at all levels was a primary goal, young Puerto Rican scholars, students, writers, and other intellectuals in the 1970s agitated for change on a broad scale, demanding attention to Puerto Rican communities and their cultures and history and pushing for inclusion in the nation's educational and cultural institutions. Simultaneously, a loosely assembled group of Puerto Rican poets, performers, and other artists in many cities were forging a new dimension in the struggle for visibility, recognition, and equality, creating centers for performance and artistic collaboration that served as community cultural spaces where images and conceptions of Puerto Ricanness could be generated in an empowering environment and shared with the public. Acting both individually and in community, these activists were animated by a set of ideas that were not primarily or explicitly political—but that would have a real and lasting impact on the empowerment of their communities, their cities, and on American society more broadly.

College students and other young Puerto Ricans took the lead in demanding institutional change, gaining substantial momentum in their cause in the early 1970s. Within a few years of the first campus protests organized by Latino and African American students in the late 1960s, dozens of colleges and universities had adjusted their admissions procedures and goals, and enrollments reflected a demographic shift underway. The New Jersey Department of Higher Education reported that enrollment of Puerto Ricans at the state's public colleges and universities had tripled, on average, between 1968 and 1972; similar spikes were reported at several of New York City's community colleges. One important outcome of the protests at the City University of New York (CUNY) was the creation of a handful of new community colleges to better serve students in poor areas of the city, most of which had large African American and Puerto Rican populations. Eugenio María de Hostos Community College, founded in 1970 in the Bronx, was the first of these schools geared primarily toward Puerto Ricans. Boricua College, independent of the CUNY system and founded by Victor G. Alicea in 1974, was designed to offer college degrees to non-traditional students, most of them Puerto Rican.[29]

Such expansion in New York City was partly an answer to the higher enrollments that resulted from CUNY's 1970 open admissions policy, but it also represented a response to the question of social accessibility and cultural relevance—making the idea of higher education meaningful to people who may not have imagined its value, or its possibility, before the push for more open access. The impact of these new programs and campuses reverberated far beyond the university and changed the relationship between the university and the communities that surrounded them. In 1970, only about 5,000 students who identified as Puerto Rican, out of a U.S. student population of 1.8 million, were enrolled in US colleges; ten years later the percentage of Puerto Ricans with college degrees had more than doubled, growing from 2.2% to 5.5%.[30]

Alongside this major sociological shift in the landscape of higher education, the other key outcome of the campus protests was their intellectual legacy, particularly the proliferation of degree-granting programs in Black Studies and Puerto Rican Studies. Whereas the opening of admissions policies at CUNY (and many other universities) was controversial, most faculty and administrators throughout the CUNY system were receptive to the idea of creating academic programs that had the potential to challenge the marginalization of communities of color—both within and beyond the university. Likewise, when students at the University of Illinois in Chicago demanded the creation of what they described as "bilingual-bicultural" programs in Latin American Studies, administrators did not argue with the logic of the demand. Soon, Puerto Rican Studies programs were inaugurated at the main campus of the University of Illinois at Urbana-Champaign, at Loyola, and at Northern Illinois University. One of the founders of the Union for Puerto Rican Students at Northern Illinois University, Miguel Del Valle, explained:

We wanted to look at our roots, find things out about where we came from . . . There are many different sources [of strength] and one definite source was our own culture, that gave us a feeling of self-worth, made us feel we counted, that we were just as important as anyone.[31]

Puerto Rican Studies programs represented new sites of academic inquiry, pulling together scholars in a variety of fields, and created new possibilities for asking intellectual questions about Puerto Ricans that could be relevant both to their community and to the expansion of knowledge in all the disciplines in which Puerto Rican studies scholars were trained. Creators of these programs gained momentum in achieving their goals from a growing national trend; by the mid-1970s, dozens of colleges and universities had developed Black, Chicano, and Puerto Rican Studies programs, some of them supported by major higher education funders, including the Ford Foundation and the National Endowment for the Humanities. Even some elite colleges and universities, with tiny Puerto Rican student populations, began offering courses in Puerto Rican Studies. At Columbia, former Migration Division director Clarence Senior taught a sociology course in the 1970s on "the Puerto Rican migrant and the cultural, economic, educational, racial and political factors in his background." Supreme Court Justice Sonia Sotomayor recounted in her memoir, *My Beloved World*, how, as a student at Princeton in the mid-1970s, she solicited the help of history professor Peter Winn to design an independent study course on Puerto Rican history for a group of undergraduates, since none then existed.[32]

The proliferation of new programs called attention to the need for expanding the scope and depth of scholarship on Puerto Ricans. At the Center for Puerto Rican Studies at Hunter College in New York City, members of the History Task Force promoted a research agenda that would examine the structural basis of Puerto Rican poverty, contextualized in a history that paid close attention to the political economy of colonialism and migration. In doing so, these scholars confronted the impoverishment of earlier scholarship, criticizing other scholars for broadcasting over and over the "stale news of the stagnation of the poor." They insisted on opening to the academy ideas that were then avant garde: the persistent weight of colonialism; the powerfully transnational cultures of Latin American peoples in the U.S., and the far-reaching impact of a globalizing economy.[33]

One of the archivists at the Center for Puerto Rican Studies at Hunter College described how the idea of "taking ownership of Puerto Rican history" was a process by which activists challenged the historical silence about their people. In seeking out the memories of people in the surrounding communities,

. . . we were introduced to trailblazing individuals whose life stories were told not only in the oral histories but were also contained in the cabinets, drawers, trunks and boxes, where they kept their most precious belongings:

photographs, scrapbooks, programs, ticket stubs, letters, buttons and all those other items that chronicled their activities, their community participation, as well as their personal and family life.[34]

In the process of connecting the community's past with the academy, young activists and academics amassed ample documentation of how their own paths had been made possible by previous generations of leaders. Evelina López Antonetty, founder of United Bronx Parents, represented one such example. She attended Brooklyn College and Hunter College in the 1950s while working as a labor organizer, and 20 years after attending Hunter as an adult student, she returned to teach for the new Puerto Rican Studies program in the early 1970s. Antonetty lobbied to ensure that all Puerto Rican Studies programs in the CUNY system included courses on education, and she herself taught "the Puerto Rican Child in the American School."[35]

Puerto Rican Studies programs bridged the divide between campus and community not only by inviting experts who worked outside the academy—like Antonetty—to participate as instructors. They also sponsored countless initiatives that enabled community leaders, writers, visual artists, and others to come together in workshops and conferences, facilitating connections across the Puerto Rican community. In 1974, the Center for Puerto Rican Studies at Hunter hosted a conference on "Culture and the Puerto Ricans: Critique and Debate," a gathering of artists and intellectuals from Puerto Rico and New York. This was a seminal event in that it offered academic recognition of the importance of artistic production now commonly labeled "Nuyorican." A number of the conference invitees were members of an artists' collective called the Taller Boricua, founded a few years earlier in East Harlem as a community institution promoting work in visual and performing arts by Puerto Ricans in New York, many of whom were U.S.-born and called themselves Nuyorican. Also in 1974, artists and community leaders in Philadelphia founded the Taller Puertorriqueño, which quickly became the cultural center of the city's rapidly growing Puerto Rican community.[36]

The popularization of the term Nuyorican came from a 1964 book by the poet Jaime Carrero, *Jet Neorriqueño: Neo-Rican Jetliner*, a book of poems in Spanish and English. Inspired by the impact of their counterparts in the Black Arts Movement (which had emerged among writers and artists in the mid-1960s alongside the Black Power movement), many New York-based Puerto Rican visual artists, musicians, poets, playwrights, performers, and novelists began identifying as Nuyorican. The Nuyorican collective, which included many artists who lived in cities other than New York, embraced the language of cultural unity, offering an antidote to the rigid ideologies and fragmenting politics of Puerto Rican radicalism by the mid-1970s. In 1973, poet Miguel Algarín (who was also an English professor at Rutgers) opened a literary salon of sorts in his Lower East Side apartment, a space where he and his collaborators could invite other artists to perform and view one another's work. The Nuyorican Poets Café, as it became known, soon outgrew the apartment, and moved to a new location in "Loisaida," the Puerto Rican Lower East Side, institutionalizing a new phenomenon that, in the words of Angelo Falcón, "all came together in ways to create a new cultural sensibility/invention from the streets of Puerto Rican New York that would endure to the present."[37]

Like the members of militant Puerto Rican community organizations and the student activists and intellectuals of the era, many of these artists were inspired by Puerto Rican nationalism. But they also advocated for their communities in public life in ways that were not ideological. Nuyorican fiction writers, for instance, used storytelling to gain access to and visibility in the broader culture. Nicholasa Mohr, raised in the Bronx, achieved acclaim far beyond her community for her books *Nilda* (1973) and *El Bronx Remembered* (1975), which explored the everyday struggles and joys of her Puerto Ricans characters, whose lives were not defined by the crime and chaos featured in most newspaper stories of Puerto Rican communities in that era. "No complicated symbolism here, no trendy obscurity of meaning, no hopeless despair or militant ethnicity," noted one reviewer, praising Mohr's books, both of which won important literary awards. In 1974, playwright Miguel Piñero's *Short Eyes*, set in the prison world from which he had just emerged, won the New York Drama Critics Circle Award for best American play. It was a bitter irony—noted by many Nuyorican artists—that Piñero's play was then produced at Lincoln Center, just 15 years after a Puerto Rican neighborhood had been razed to make room for its construction.[38]

"The Nuyorican poet fights with words," wrote Algarín, indicating that most artists and writers who identified as Nuyorican rejected rigid political identities and avoided fixed positions. He argued that ideological flexibility was a strength of the movement, which he contrasted with the more rigidly political organizations of the decade, as in this anecdote: "A Young Lords Party member ran into Chino García, once leader of the Real Great Society, and said, 'Your politics stink,' and Chino replied, 'I think your politics are okay.' Both organizations are Nuyorican born . . . " While adherents of the movement tended to see their artistic production in a political context, many Nuyorican artists were not involved in traditional political activism. In conducting their struggles for justice outside the formal political arena, Nuyorican activists were not giving up on politics. They chose instead to comment on issues of power and injustice through their art—which enabled Puerto Ricans to set the terms of debate themselves.[39]

Puerto Rican Nationalism: Between Socialist Militancy and Anti-Colonial Violence

While many Puerto Rican artists in the 1970s embraced a non-ideological mode of activism, some Nuyoricans were committed to political activism. Felipe Luciano, for instance, was a member of the militant group of musicians called the

Last Poets before helping to found the Young Lords and serving on its central leadership committee. Elizam Escobar, a visual artist and writer connected to several Puerto Rican arts organizations in the 1970s, was also a committed member of a Puerto Rican nationalist group that embraced tactics of armed resistance. In 1980 he was charged with seditious conspiracy and sentenced to federal prison for his involvement in violent attacks by the nationalist group Fuerzas Armadas de Liberación Nacional, or Armed Forces of National Liberation (FALN).[40] Despite a small membership in the militant groups in the U.S. that actively fought for Puerto Rican independence, a general pro-independence ideology suffused Puerto Ricans' political activity throughout the 1970s, illustrating how powerfully Puerto Rican nationalism held sway over young activists and intellectuals during this period.

Most leftist Puerto Rican organizations in this era confronted the difficult balance of rights-oriented community activism with broader political goals of Puerto Rican sovereignty. El Comité, founded originally by activists working on local justice issues, especially housing, was restructured by its leadership in 1975 and renamed El Comité-MINP (Movimiento de Izquierda Nacional Puertorriqueño, or Puerto Rican National Left Movement). The new hybrid organization sought to maintain its engagement in issues affecting Puerto Ricans' daily life in the U.S. while also focusing on a socialist workers' agenda and the struggle for Puerto Rican independence. El Comité-MINP endured through the end of the 1970s but dissolved by 1982.[41]

The Puerto Rican Socialist Party (PSP) was another of the major radical Puerto Rican organizations of the 1970s that struggled to balance local commitments and political nationalism. Founded in Puerto Rico in 1972 as an explicitly Marxist reorganization of the nationalist advocacy group Movimiento Pro Independencia (MPI, founded in 1959), the PSP became the largest and most active of the Puerto Rican nationalist groups both on the island and in the U.S. in the 1970s. Unlike the Young Lords and El Comité-MINP, which had formed to address local justice issues first, the PSP was organized from the start around balancing "dual priorities," fighting simultaneously against the "superexploitation" of Puerto Ricans living in the United States with a commitment to end U.S. colonialism on the island. The majority of those who joined PSP were Puerto Ricans born and raised in the U.S., working class youth whose political awakening during the years of the Puerto Rican movement inspired them to seek out a "serious Marxist organization."[42]

For much of the 1970s, the PSP would maintain its original balance of local organizing and island nationalism. Its leaders planned campaigns to increase support for Puerto Rican independence but also, in the words of a former PSP leader, José Velázquez, devoted energy to "the basics: . . . workplace and union organizing, the struggle for democratic rights, expanding the Party's influence among high school youth, and recruitment of new members." In Philadelphia, the *Inquirer* reported that "strains of discontent colored this year's

Puerto Rican week . . . when the city's newly organized chapter of the Puerto Rican Socialist Party marched in the parade under the banner, 'Parade One Day, Hunger Every Day.'"[43]

Increasingly, the organization attracted activists seeking "a reaffirmation of Puerto Rican identity," "bridging differences" between their island and mainland compatriots. In so doing, the PSP attracted a membership that "reflected the entire range of the Puerto Rican community: young and old; Nationalists; post-1959 *independentistas*; young, mainland Puerto Rican radicals; and New York and non-New York Puerto Ricans." When the PSP organized a "National Day of Solidarity with the Independence of Puerto Rico" in October 1974, 20,000 people took part in the event at Madison Square Garden. During the Bicentennial celebrations in Philadelphia in 1976, the PSP staged a "Bicentennial without Colonies" demonstration that attracted thousands. (As political scientist Angelo Falcón observed, nationalists were not the only critics of Puerto Rico's colonial status; those who supported statehood, rather than independence, also lobbied the United Nations to add Puerto Rico to its list of "Non-Self-Governing Territories.")[44]

PSP chapters that formed in various cities—Chicago, Philadelphia, Hartford, Boston, and Newark, among others—created the central network of nationalist Puerto Rican political activism throughout the 1970s. Many of these chapters engaged in other issues that were important to their Puerto Rican communities as well, particularly related to housing and bilingual education. PSP organizers also lobbied extensively on behalf of Puerto Rican workers, in both urban areas and in the rural areas of New Jersey, Connecticut, and Massachusetts that attracted thousands of Puerto Rican farmworkers. In the arena of local electoral politics, though, according to political scientist José Cruz, the PSP's role could be problematic. Cruz's research in Hartford demonstrated that to the extent that PSP leadership focused on the outcomes of island elections, it "deviated the attention of many within the Hartford community from day-to-day issues," which in turn "prevented the PSP from developing a solid base of support among the masses, thereby undercutting its potential." By the end of the 1970s, the PSP's leadership could no longer agree on how to balance the competing priorities of homeland politics and the dire problems of the local community. After reaching a crisis point similar to that experienced by both the Young Lords and El Comité-MINP, the PSP disbanded in 1982, the same year as El Comité-MINP.[45]

A small number of *independentistas*, meanwhile, carried on the nationalist struggle as members of militant revolutionary groups that embraced violence as a revolutionary tactic. The detention of the surviving nationalist responsible for the 1950 attack on Truman (one of the two assailants was killed at the scene) and the 1954 attack on Congress, as well as other political prisoners, had remained a powerful symbol for nationalists. They also saw their political goals in a broader field of anti-imperialist activism, connecting their movement to ongoing anticolonial national liberation movements in Africa and Southeast Asia.

Most prominent among the U.S.-based Puerto Rican nationalist organizations was the FALN, which claimed responsibility for over 100 bombings in several U.S. cities between 1974 and 1983, resulting in five deaths and $3 million in damage. In 1975, the FALN took credit for bombing Fraunces Tavern in New York City, killing four and injuring 53.[46]

A less contentious and very popular campaign by a nationalist group in the 1970s was the mounting of the Puerto Rican flag on the crown of the Statue of Liberty in 1977, by the New York Committee to Free the Nationalist Political Prisoners, which sympathized with the FALN. The symbolic power of the Puerto Rican flag adorning this icon of American inclusion won the support of many Puerto Ricans, even those who did not endorse the cause of independence or opposed most forms of nationalist activism.[47] The same year, a group of FALN sympathizers in Chicago formed the Movement for National Liberation (Movimiento de Liberación Nacional, or MLN). At its peak, the MLN operated chapters in New York, Philadelphia, Boston, Hartford, and even San Francisco. Both the MLN and FMLN were targeted by the FBI and local law enforcement, and while most members embraced the defiance of law governing what they considered to be the "internal colony" of Puerto Ricans in the United States, this militant approach also made it difficult to attract a broad membership.[48] The FALN disbanded in 1980 after a series of arrests; the MLN still exists as a base of advocacy for Puerto Rican political prisoners.

Even as most of these nationalist groups declined by the early 1980s—through a combination of tactical and ideological divisions, as well as harassment, arrest, and infiltration by law enforcement—Puerto Rican voters and activists continued to support independence and advocated for the release of nationalists jailed for their political activities. For example, Bronx Congressman Robert García petitioned for the pardon of Puerto Rican political prisoners, a response to demands of his constituency, which included leaders of El Comité-MINP and PSP. In 1979 President Carter commuted the sentences of four nationalists responsible for the 1950s attacks. The symbolic power of a U.S. president taking an interest in the fate of Puerto Rican political prisoners was significant and testified to the growing influence of left-leaning Puerto Rican voters during that decade.[49]

Although nationalist activists alienated many mainstream Americans with their approach to demanding sovereignty, they contributed to the growing visibility of Puerto Ricans' demands for rights in this era. As more members of armed nationalist groups went to prison or went into hiding, campaigns to sever the political relationship between the island and the U.S. by force dwindled. Although many left-leaning but non-militant Puerto Ricans expressed ambivalence about electoral politics in general and suspicion about the motives of Puerto Ricans who aspired to elected office, some leftist leaders by the late 1970s sought to adjust their ideological agenda to explore the possibility of more mainstream empowerment through formal politics. Like members of earlier radical organizations in the 1930s and 1940s, activists trained in militant organizations sometimes went on to provide leadership to more mainstream electoral and organizational efforts. José Cruz notes that, "just as the PSP was blowing itself to pieces in Puerto Rico and New York" around 1980, ex-members of the group in Hartford capitalized on the moment when Puerto Ricans in that city "began to cash in on the political capital accumulated over two decades," shifting their focus to Democratic electoral politics.[50]

Electoral Politics: Politicians and Voters

The 1970s was, indeed, the decade when Puerto Rican leaders in cities like Hartford, Camden, Newark, Philadelphia, and Chicago began to see the possibility of achieving elected representation for their communities. Mass mobilization of residents and activists increased the visibility of issues important to Puerto Ricans, and coordinated pressure from Puerto Rican leaders and voters had resulted in bilingual ballots and increases in voter registration—all of which produced an expanded political power base. By the end of the 1970s, Puerto Ricans in New York City were 15% of population and the broader Latino population another 6%. In Boston, Puerto Ricans had become nearly 7% of the population and reached 19% in Newark.[51] Although there were only a small handful of elected Puerto Rican officials outside of New York City by that point, Puerto Rican communities in most cities had reached an important milestone en route to electoral successes: political appointments and positions in mayors' cabinets. In New York City, where Puerto Ricans had spent at least three generations trying to break into electoral politics, momentum had finally been consolidated, and this decade saw a major expansion in the number of elected officials.

As promising as these political advances were, this was a challenging moment for any group of newcomers to enter politics. Cities across the nation were in crisis from loss of jobs, racial conflict, deindustrialization, riots, white flight, and drugs. On the other hand, the crisis created political opportunity. Although some may have considered the South Bronx to be a "jungle" in the 1970s, it was there, in that decade, that the Puerto Rican community's most lively political contests played out. Herman Badillo was the Bronx's first native son of electoral politics, a leader whose early success could be attributed to a combination of ambition, skill, and the good fortune to enter politics when there were very few other Puerto Rican candidates to compete against.

Badillo's alleged lack of personal connection with voters—he was aptly described as a "political loner"—did not hold him back when he was the only game in town, but once other Puerto Ricans entered the field, Badillo was forced to defend the authenticity of his ties to Puerto Rican voters.[52] By the early 1970s, Badillo's biggest political challenge came from the South Bronx's powerful and magnetic Puerto Rican community leader, Ramon Vélez. Vélez used his role as manager of the Bronx's largest social service organization—and his influence over voters as a result of the thousands of patronage jobs he was said to control—to build a political fiefdom that would last for decades. This consolidation of his power produced an even more dramatic political rivalry on the streets of the South Bronx. Father Louis Gigante, an Italian American priest, was the charismatic leader of the other most important institution in the community—the church—and he competed with Vélez for anti-poverty funds, for control over local representation on projects like Model Cities, and for the loyalty of community residents. Both wound up serving on city council in 1973 to 1974, both winning election by enormous margins in their side-by-side Bronx districts. (Both had also run for election to the U.S. House of Representatives in 1970, campaigning against front-runner Badillo and at the same time competing violently against one another. Reportedly, each had hired "teams of thugs [who] roamed the streets with bats and chains to rip down one another's posters and workers rode around with shotguns that, according to both sides, were sometimes used.")[53]

Despite Badillo's visibility and early electoral successes, by 1976 his political power within the Puerto Rican community was indeed threatened by Ramon Vélez. Their rivalry became increasingly bitter, and as neighborhood deterioration caused population decline in the South Bronx—the 21st congressional district lost a full *half* of its registered voter population between 1974 and 1976—the balance of power shifted toward Vélez. The charismatic dispenser of patronage held more sway over the impoverished remaining residents of his district than did Badillo, the experienced politician who continually angled for a place in the mainstream. Vélez's popularity in his district was hardly affected by ongoing suspicions about corruption, particularly his management of the Hunts Point Multi-Service Center; in one federal investigation, he was cited for being unable to account for $1.6 million in annual spending. In fact, Vélez and his various community agencies were investigated multiple times between 1970 and the early 1990s, but he was never found guilty.[54]

Vélez's seemingly unshakable popularity was a source of great frustration for Badillo, who insisted that the structure of the citywide anti-poverty program, which helped fund Vélez's many businesses, "lends itself to theft." Badillo was soon vindicated—both by beating Vélez in the 1976 congressional primary, and by mayoral candidate Ed Koch's referring to Vélez as a "povertician," someone who manipulated his constituents via control of resources via community service organizations. Robert García, who had served three terms in the New York senate, took over Badillo's congressional seat in 1978 when the latter became deputy mayor to Ed Koch, who had won the election. García called himself a protégé of Badillo, at least early in his career, but managed to maintain what many saw as a stronger connection to the Puerto Rican community than Badillo had. García was the first Puerto Rican to serve in any state senate. For Puerto Rican constituents who followed island politics and supported the nationalist cause, the signature issue of García's first term in Congress was his push for the release of Puerto Rican political prisoners in 1979.[55]

In both electoral politics and political appointments, Puerto Ricans also saw more gender diversity in these years. In addition to the local pressures to enable minority representation in government, there was increasing national pressure to reduce barriers to women's participation in politics. New York City Mayor Koch may have regretted naming Patria Nieto Ortiz as director of the city's Human Rights Office in 1978, since one of her first acts in the job was to investigate the city's noncompliance with equal opportunity employment laws. Nieto Ortiz threatened to subpoena Koch himself, then resigned her post. The first Puerto Rican woman elected to Congress, Olga Méndez, was a psychologist and had been a New York City deputy commissioner before her electoral victory in 1978. Then a Democrat, Méndez easily won Robert García's seat in the 30th senate district, including East Harlem and the South Bronx, against a "Republican-Conservative," Roberto Acevedo. Méndez herself later switched to the Republican party.[56]

Although Chicago and Philadelphia were home to, respectively, the second- and third-largest Puerto Rican populations throughout the 1970s and claimed the longest-standing Puerto Rican communities outside of New York, their Puerto Rican voters were actually slower to achieve local and state-level representation than in some smaller cities—Camden, New Jersey and Hartford, Connecticut most notably—where the proportional population of Puerto Ricans grew substantially after 1970. In Chicago, Puerto Ricans' pattern of entry into electoral politics in this era was further differentiated by the fact that Puerto Ricans in Chicago were outnumbered by an older, more established Mexican American community. The combined Mexican American and Puerto Rican proportion of the city's population increased from about 7% to 14% between 1970 and 1980, with Puerto Ricans comprising roughly a quarter of that population. This meant that, as Puerto Ricans sought to become part of a "Hispanic" voting bloc, the first elected representatives would likely be Mexican, not Puerto Rican.[57]

In Philadelphia, meanwhile, no Puerto Ricans seemed poised to follow in the footsteps of the city's first Puerto Rican elected official—Germán Quiles, who won a seat in the state legislature in 1968 but failed in his 1970 reelection bid. Yet as the community mobilized more and more loudly around issues like housing and police brutality, elected officials began to pay attention. The *Philadelphia Inquirer* noted in 1974 that "strains of discontent" were visible in that year's Puerto Rican Week celebration in Philadelphia, when the city's chapter of the Puerto Rican Socialist Party (PSP) marched in the parade under the banner "Parade One Day, Hunger Every Day." "The Puerto Ricans are becoming more aggressive in making their objections known," concluded the reporter.[58]

At that time in Philadelphia, young Puerto Rican leaders were working to build political influence by establishing a coalition called the Puerto Rican Alliance, which sought to shape issues important to the Puerto Rican community, including injustices in public housing and incidents of police brutality.

Another "objection" of Puerto Rican leaders was the fact that Republican mayor Frank Rizzo had appointed only a single Puerto Rican in his administration, Oscar Rosario, to a relatively minor post as liaison with the "Spanish-speaking" in the city. In 1978, motivated by Rizzo's threat to change the city charter so he could run for a third consecutive term in 1980, the Puerto Rican Alliance worked with African Americans and progressive whites to challenge the proposed charter change. They also managed to double the voter registration among Puerto Ricans in the city by the 1980 election, paving the way for several electoral victories by Puerto Rican candidates in the early 1980s.[59]

Across the river in Camden, a much smaller city, a Puerto Rican community one third the size of its Philadelphia counterpart achieved even more concrete political gains by the end of the 1970s—in part because Puerto Ricans comprised nearly 20% of Camden's population by that point. Political momentum here, never a result simply of numbers, came also from productive relationships with local political leaders that strengthened in the wake of major rioting and political demonstrations motivated by incidents of police brutality in both 1971 and 1973. Camden had one Puerto Rican city council member throughout the 1960s, long before any other Puerto Rican community outside New York had any elected representatives, and a second was elected in 1975.[60]

After the 1973 riots, Camden's Mayor Errichetti appointed Puerto Ricans to several key positions in the city, including a deputy mayor and Model Cities director, and appointees to the housing authority, school board, and board of elections. Together, this cadre of Puerto Rican leaders came to be known as the "Committee of 12," described by a local journalist as a group of Puerto Rican "'apostles' . . . who have some leverage in deciding community needs." Puerto Ricans also made inroads into state-level politics. Camden lawyer Joseph Rodríguez was appointed to the State Investigating Committee, which monitored organized crime in the state. In Trenton, the capital, leaders from around the state convened the Puerto Rican Congress of New Jersey, which in the 1970s was the only state-level organization of Puerto Ricans in the country. Despite this increased visibility in policymaking, though, the immediate future did not necessarily inspire optimism. In the late 1970s, one Camden leader told a journalist, "For twenty years, you tell the people to vote, that they'll see some changes. They vote, and still the houses keep falling down."[61]

Puerto Ricans in Hartford followed a path of political engagement parallel to that of their compatriots in Camden, though marked by somewhat less success in electoral politics. Not coincidentally, their demographic paths in that decade were also remarkably similar: Puerto Ricans comprised under 6% of Hartford's population in 1970, but, due to a combination of migration (from both New York City and rural areas in Connecticut as well as directly from Puerto Rico) and white flight out of Hartford, they made up nearly 20% of the city's population in 1980. The first elected Puerto Rican official in Hartford was Marta Sánchez, who ran in 1973 for a seat on the board of education and won, despite her strong support for bilingual education, which was controversial outside the Puerto Rican community, and despite her own heavy accent, which one of her critics referred to as "broken English."[62]

During the same election year, Hartford's first Puerto Rican city council candidate, René Rodríguez, ran on the Republican ticket and lost—constrained by a dynamic that political scientist José Cruz calls "brokered representation," wherein party leaders decide how and when to tolerate the incorporation of those outside the machine. In a Democrat-dominated city of largely working class voters, Cruz notes, the opportunity Republicans gave Puerto Ricans offered little chance of success; Democrats were the gatekeepers of access. Indeed, a high-profile independent city council campaign by former Puerto Rican Socialist Party (PSP) leader Edwin Vargas was a spectacular failure in terms of his proportion of votes. As one of his supporters argued, though:

> The only way you can participate in this city is to challenge the machinery. We take the people out to vote election after election, and what do we get? Unemployment, discrimination, housing . . . I don't have to describe to you. So what do we have to lose?

It was not until 1979 that a Puerto Rican, Mildred Torres, made it to city council, and even that victory did not involve an electoral victory: Torres was appointed by the mayor, who needed to fill a vacancy in the middle of the election cycle.[63]

Even for successful Puerto Rican candidates, there was a limit to the political power they could attain as representatives of impoverished communities with minimal political clout. Indeed, Ramón Vélez enjoyed the recognition of other New York politicians for his power to mobilize the votes of his South Bronx constituency; but since his leadership emphasized solving immediate, local problems of people with virtually no social capital (and, evidence suggests, enriching himself and his cronies at the same time), it is hard to say what impact Vélez actually had beyond his district. Herman Badillo, cited by supporters for achievements like helping pass an $80 million funding plan for bilingual education in Congress, and for his role as a founding member of the Congressional Hispanic Caucus, pushed a more expansive rights agenda that gave him influence in a wider field. Yet even that relatively broad influence only extended so far: Badillo ran in every New York City mayoral primary election between 1969 and 1985, and never came close to winning.[64]

The pessimism expressed by leaders in both Camden and Hartford was real, driven by their disappointment when promised improvements on issues like jobs, housing, and educational opportunity did not materialize. Also real was the acute disappointment of those who supported Badillo and expected to reap greater benefits of investing in electoral politics—but instead observed the shaky commitment of non-Puerto Rican allies during New York's fiscal crisis of the 1970s. In spite of the many setbacks, though, Puerto Ricans continued to engage in the process of finding—or making—a "place at the table" in city politics. Puerto Ricans did manage to increase their visibility in the political arena in the 1970s and forced elected officials and policymakers to shift the way they approached issues like housing inequality, bilingual education, and police brutality—both in New York, where Puerto Ricans achieved some representation in the 1970s, and in cities like Chicago, Philadelphia, Camden, and Hartford, where such representation was fitful or did not quite materialize until the following decade.

One silver lining of the uneven path to political empowerment was that Puerto Rican leaders began to focus on influencing policy at least as much as achieving electoral representation. As a result of the influence they began to exert, other local officials, rather than simply identifying problems and proposing solutions from a vantage point outside of Puerto Rican communities, began to solicit the input of Puerto Rican leaders to help define the issues and establish goals to address them. And by the mid-1970s, Puerto Rican leaders and organizations were shaping policy at the national level too, a new visibility that could converge with and amplify their potential for electoral impact. This was the decade when the phrase "sleeping giant" came into regular use to describe what was seen as the latent voting power among Spanish-speakers in the U.S. The "giant"—the Latino electorate—had never actually been asleep, of course; it had, instead, been silenced, and was now raising its voice.[65]

Civil Rights and Community Leadership: Legal Activists and National Organizing

Puerto Ricans' expanding engagement in electoral politics was key to the gains they made as they lobbied for broader rights and recognition in the 1970s. However, the most important political force generated by Puerto Ricans in the 1970s, which produced the most immediate and most enduring impact on the group's civil rights, came through the creation of national organizations whose primary focus was the expansion of Puerto Ricans' legal rights in the 1970s. Leaders of heterogeneous Puerto Rican communities, representing a range of interests, created networks and coalitions that connected leaders and activists across regions and enabled them to collaborate to push forward an ambitious rights agenda by the mid-1970s. This organizing at the national level did not represent a rejection or dismissal of the importance of street-level grassroots activism of the late 1960s and early 1970s; rather, it illustrated the increased capacity of more conventionally structured Puerto Rican organizations to demand change. In a short decade, these leaders accomplished more, and on a larger range of issues—bilingual education, voting rights, affirmative action, gender equity—than U.S. Puerto Rican leaders in any previous era.

Of the many legal issues tackled by nationally organized Puerto Rican leaders in the 1970s, the right to bilingual instruction was the most publicly visible, the issue that got the most attention from non-Puerto Rican leaders and media.

Puerto Rican parents and community leaders had actually agitated for bilingual instruction dating back to the 1930s; and in the 1960s, the lack of bilingual education options had become an important driver of Puerto Ricans' demands for community control of schools. Parents and community leaders argued that, while urban school district bureaucrats had historically paid insufficient attention to Puerto Rican migrant children's transition to instruction in English, community leadership in the schools would facilitate the hiring of bilingual teachers and mandate some bilingual instruction, ensuring that children would be given the necessary tools to succeed academically.

By the late 1960s, bilingual programs had been created in many places where large numbers of Puerto Ricans settled, supported by local nonprofit organizations and some state funding. (The struggles to create bilingual programs for the primarily Mexican American Spanish-speaking children in California and the southwestern states followed a similar trajectory in the 1960s, but comprises a separate history that has been well documented.[66]) Established in settings ranging from impoverished urban schools to church basements, and serving children of business owners, factory workers, and migrant farmers, such programs helped build momentum for a growing group of lawyers and activists who were pushing the federal government to recognize its obligation to mandate the provision of bilingual instruction where needed. The legal and legislative foundation for these changes was somewhat confusing. The U.S. Congress had passed a comprehensive Bilingual Education Amendment in 1967, which allotted $7.5 million for the creation of bilingual programs around the country—but school districts were not required to create such programs, so the amendment did almost nothing to change the status quo. Even school districts with large populations of Spanish-speaking students could still easily evade the responsibility to provide bilingual instruction.[67]

Activists took up the gauntlet. In Chicago, Puerto Rican leaders pressured members of the Illinois legislature to draft a bill mandating bilingual education at the state level and managed to get it passed in 1973. Chicago's Latino Institute won a substantial grant that year from the Rockefeller Foundation to support its leadership development program, geared toward helping parents advocate for their childrens' bilingual education. The Parent Leadership Training remained one of the institute's important areas of focus throughout the 1970s. Parent Leaders facilitated bilingual councils at each school with a bilingual program—with a mandate from the Illinois Office of Education. In this way, the Latino Institute helped institutionalize extensive parent engagement in nearly 100 Chicago public schools with a Latino-majority population (though many of these schools were in predominantly Mexican, as opposed to mixed Mexican and Puerto Rican or Puerto Rican-majority neighborhoods).[68]

Aspira, which by the 1970s had expanded to over a dozen cities since its founding in 1961, continued its focus on supporting Puerto Rican high school students, especially those who hoped to go to college, and advocating for bilingual education was a central aspect of its mission. Aspira collaborated with the newly formed Puerto Rican Legal Defense and Education Fund (PRLDEF, founded in 1972) to initiate a class action lawsuit against the New York City Board of Education on behalf of its Hispanic students, who at that point comprised 25% of the city's 1.1 million public school students. The major result of this suit was a judicial consent decree, in 1974, which stipulated that New York City schools would implement transitional bilingual instruction to all Spanish-speaking children who needed it. The Board of Education established an Office of Bilingual Education in 1975, appointing as director Hernán La Fountaine, an educator with a long history of experience with bilingual education.[69] Similar cases were soon mounted—and won—by PRLDEF in Philadelphia, Long Island, and Connecticut.

PRLDEF had made its first mark through its work on educational access, but its mission was defined by a broader civil rights agenda. Modeled on the NAACP's Legal Defense and Education Fund, PRLDEF was founded by three young Puerto Rican lawyers who had been part of the surge of civil rights activism by Puerto Ricans in the 1960s. One founder, César Perales, worked as a legal advisor for the community organization Mobilization for Youth upon graduating from law school in 1965, and then went on to serve as a founding director of the Brooklyn Legal Services office, opened with War on Poverty funds in 1968. Before joining with lawyers Jorge Batista and Victor Marrero to found PRLDEF, Perales defended both the student protesters who shut down the City College of New York in 1969 and the Young Lords who, in 1970, occupied an East Harlem church to create a center for community services.[70]

Aside from access to bilingual education, the other key area of civil rights litigation pursued by the PRLDEF was voting rights, ensuring that non-English speakers had fair access to the ballot. State-level Puerto Rican advocacy organizations had laid the foundation for the campaign for voting rights in the 1960s. The first class-action suit on behalf of Puerto Rican voters was mounted by a group called the Puerto Rican Organization for Political Action (PROPA), based in Chicago. A federal court held in the case *PROPA v. Kusper* (1973) that Chicago officials were obligated to provide access to Spanish-language voting materials for those residents who requested them. Also that year, in *López v. Dinkins*, PRLDEF lawyers won a similar case mounted on behalf of Puerto Rican and Chinese voters in New York City; in 1974, in *Torres v. Sachs*, PRLDEF secured the guarantee that bilingual ballots would be provided in all New York City elections. Following those precedents in Chicago and New York City, PRLDEF won cases to establish bilingual election systems in Philadelphia, New York State, and New Jersey.[71]

In 1975, largely as a result of this body of case law, the 1965 Voting Rights Act was amended to ensure federal protection of voting rights for linguistic minorities. While these victories in voting rights cases accumulated in a short burst in the 1970s, Puerto Rican leaders had been doing the preliminary work of these struggles—especially related to the abolition of the literacy test—since the 1950s.[72] When the Voting Rights Act was passed in 1965, it contained a provision that prohibited the denial of voting rights of any person born in Puerto Rico on the basis of their inability to read, write, or understand English. Based on this precedent, a series of legal cases in Chicago, New York, and Philadelphia reaffirmed the Puerto Rican community's right to Spanish language ballots during elections, ultimately leading to the 1975 amendment that protected voting rights for other language minority groups.[73]

Another important development in institutional access for Puerto Ricans in the 1970s was affirmative action in college admissions. This policy emerged from roots very different from those of campus activism of the late 1960s but focused on similar goals: greater access by women and "minority" students (that is, members of ethnic/racial groups identified by the EEOC) to institutions of higher education. As many of the nation's Ivy League and elite universities and colleges opened their doors to their first female classes, they also welcomed their first large contingents of Puerto Rican students, drawn not just from the urban ghettos of the Northeast, but also from the small middle classes of the suburbs and the large middle and upper classes from the island itself. Supreme Court justice Sonia Sotomayor, who attended Princeton in the mid-1970s, declared once that she was a "perfect affirmative action baby." Having excelled in a prestigious Bronx Catholic high school, Cardinal Spellman, she landed in a very small group of Puerto Rican trailblazers at Princeton, graduating summa cum laude in 1976.[74] Not all affirmative action "experiments" were considered successful, and many students recruited to increase the representation of minority groups on nearly all-white campuses suffered from isolation or exclusion. On the other hand, many students admitted to college via affirmative action policies, Sotomayor included, created strong student networks to combat their social marginalization, and worked to change the institutions from within, to generate greater openness for those who would follow them.

Gender equity issues got far less attention in this era than bilingual education, voting rights, employment rights, or affirmative action in higher education. Yet Puerto Rican women activists pushed hard for equity in this area too in the 1970s. Puerto Rican women had campaigned for decades—in their own organizations and alongside men—for the rights of their communities. Some women leaders of some of the leftist organizations of the late 1960s and 1970s made gender politics an explicit topic of debate within their organizations. Women leaders in the Young Lords Organization, for instance, established a women's committee and worked to mentor other women in the Young Lords and educate the organization's men about issues of gender equality. Women involved in other activist groups in the 1970s were similarly focused on combining their grassroots political work with women's advocacy.[75]

In 1972, a group of activists established the National Conference of Puerto Rican Women (NACOPRW), based in Washington D.C., to promote "Puerto

Rican women's role as an agent of change" by advocating for women's political rights, improving their educational status, and expanding the number of women in the workforce. NACOPRW's focus on legislative and legal efforts for equity included helping found the National Committee on Pay Equity. One New York chapter of NACOPRW was created by a group of women who had been involved in East Harlem housing activism during the early 1970s and who were eager to connect their advocacy work to a national organization. One of these women explained that she sought to create a "separate subway line to feminism" for other Puerto Rican women during a time when many early feminist organizations were widely seen as failing to include issues important to women of color.[76] Despite its efforts to address concerns of Puerto Rican women of all class backgrounds, the mostly middle class leadership of the NACOPRW largely failed in its efforts to recruit working class women, even after establishing chapters in 17 cities.

Overall, coordinated action at the national level improved Puerto Ricans' prospects in the 1970s, especially in terms of defining and protecting civil rights, even though securing greater overall equality in the U.S. continued to be a slow and fitful process. In 1976, four years after holding hearings to investigate the "difficulties Puerto Ricans face in seeking jobs, education, and political opportunities," the U.S. Civil Rights Commission released its final report, *Puerto Ricans in the Continental United States: An Uncertain Future*, offering conclusions that validated what most Puerto Ricans already knew: the U.S. government had displayed "official insensitivity" to Puerto Ricans' needs, and this, "coupled with private and public acts of discrimination, has assured that Puerto Ricans often are the last in line for benefits and opportunities made available by the social and civil rights legislation of the last decades."[77]

Nothing could erase the impact of decades of social, economic, and political marginalization on Puerto Rican communities, or the burden of being relegated to a debased status as a racial minority in a historically racist society. Even if some of the disadvantages could be gradually reduced, the "bold action" promised by the federal government in the 1960s had not materialized enough to change most outcomes. Though many Puerto Ricans shared the sentiment Gerena Valentín expressed during the Civil Rights Commission's hearings in 1972—that "any fool could see" Puerto Ricans' "uncertain future"—most also appreciated the fact that the report painted a stark picture for a national public and policymakers who could see very little about Puerto Ricans at all. With this encyclopedic report based on extensive data, it became possible to demonstrate to a national audience the degree to which Puerto Ricans continued to experience serious problems in the U.S.[78]

Two related points in the 1976 report stood out above all. First, the Civil Rights Commission showed that the massive efforts by the federal government to reduce poverty in the previous decade had failed Puerto Ricans more than any other group (in 1975, Puerto Rican households had a lower per capita income than any other racial or ethnic group studied), largely because their differences from other impoverished Americans were poorly understood. "Those who designed and implemented the [anti-poverty] programs lacked, almost entirely, an awareness of the Puerto Rican community, its cultural and linguistic identity, and its critical problems," asserted the report's conclusion.[79] Second, the writers of the report underlined the damage done by the combination of this misapprehension and the prejudice Puerto Ricans faced in all facets of life in the U.S.: "official insensitivity, coupled with private and public acts of discrimination, has assured that Puerto Ricans often are the last in line for benefits and opportunities made available by the social and civil rights legislation of the last decades."[80] The report also urged that leaders and policymakers reduce educational disadvantage by increasing funds to needy children and training bilingual teachers. In other words, it recommended that the nation take action on most of the issues Puerto Rican activists had been working on in the previous two decades.

Taking the 1976 report's grave warning to the nation as an opportunity, in 1977, a group of Puerto Rican legal and policy leaders formed the National Puerto Rican Coalition (NPRC), based in Washington, D.C., and named Louis Nuñez as the first president. Nuñez, a veteran of the Korean War and City College graduate, began his activism with the Hispanic Youth Association, then became national executive director of Aspira (1967–72), served on CUNY's Board of Higher Education, supporting the establishment of Puerto Rican Studies programs, and was appointed to the U.S. Commission on Civil Rights in 1972. With the overall goal of improving Puerto Ricans' chances at economic stability, the NPRC established a handful of direct-service programs in cities with large Puerto Rican populations in order to provide support on issues like homeownership, higher education, and financial literacy. Although direct service was an important tool, the organization's primary mode of advocacy was through influencing policy: the NPRC assessed the impact on Puerto Rican communities of policies at the local, state, and federal levels, and, on the basis of its interpretations, applied pressure to adjust existing policies or develop new ones.[81] It was this kind of shift in Puerto Rican advocacy organizations that, building on the grassroots organizing that had sparked a movement, enabled activists in the 1970s to make lasting gains in securing civil rights for Puerto Ricans in the U.S.

Conclusion

The Civil Rights Commission's report on Puerto Ricans was published just as Jimmy Carter was elected president in 1976. Less than a year later, Chicago's largest Puerto Rican neighborhood exploded in the nation's worst riot of the decade. Within two years, chairman of the Commission Civil Rights Arthur Flemming accused the Carter administration of having "largely ignored" the report's warnings and blueprint for action. It was an African American policy leader and journalist, Roger Wilkins, who announced this accusation to the public, in a 1978 *New York Times* article titled "Puerto Rican Deprivation: A Call for Federal Action." Wilkins had consulted with Herman Badillo, then deputy mayor of New York City, who criticized the Carter administration for failing to enforce existing laws that should have helped Puerto Ricans, most notably the bilingual education legislation, and the Comprehensive Employment and Training Act (CETA), which provided for bilingual job training. PRLDEF president Jorge Batista seconded Badillo's critique, noting

> the Federal Government has tried to some extent [to enforce laws] . . . but the position of Puerto Ricans in center cities has deteriorated in the last 10 years. In terms of housing, education, and employment, the programs just aren't helping much. It's the same old story, except we're at the bottom now.[82]

President Jimmy Carter had witnessed Puerto Ricans' place "at the bottom" just a few months earlier, when he made a visit to the South Bronx. Already known as champion of human rights and "moral policy" both abroad and at home, Carter had driven in a limousine to the Charlotte Street area of the South Bronx after attending meetings at the United Nations in midtown Manhattan, where he had signed the U.N.'s International Covenant on Economic, Social, and Cultural Rights and its International Covenant on Civil and Political Rights. It was a bitter irony—surely not lost on the President himself—that Carter then traveled just a few miles from the U.N. to observe thousands of people suffering from a lack of many of the rights his administration championed elsewhere in the world.[83]

A week later, in the same area Carter had visited, a five-alarm fire in a vacant school building blazed on national television. The fire had begun an hour before the start of the second game of the 1977 baseball World Series, which was taking place in Yankee Stadium, just a few blocks from the fire. Sportscaster Howard Cosell was said to have announced, as the game got underway, "There it is, ladies and gentlemen, the Bronx is burning." This quote turned out to have been invented after the fact, based on a less quote-worthy exchange between Cosell and another newscaster about the fire. Yet the apocryphal phrase became iconic because it captured so well the everyday violence and unremarkable horror of life in the largely Puerto Rican South Bronx.[84]

Longtime community organizer and labor leader Gilberto Gerena Valentín later wrote that "Over the next few years the Carter administration—and the Koch administration in New York City—sat back and did nothing, despite the constant lobbying we representatives of the community did in Washington and downtown . . . ." During the 1980 presidential primary, Senator Edward Kennedy, running against incumbent president Jimmy Carter, made a strategic visit to Charlotte Street, the same beleaguered area of the South Bronx that Carter had toured several years earlier. Kennedy, taking an easy shot at his political opponent, assailed Carter for "failing to make good on his promises."

Republican candidate Ronald Reagan made essentially the same statement, and garnered a nearly identical headline from the *New York Times*, when he took his campaign entourage to Charlotte Street a few months later.[85]

All three candidates demonstrated for a national audience the national significance of the ongoing problem of Puerto Rican deprivation. That audience could see that the Bronx was burning, and they could read the statistics that showed the extent of Puerto Ricans' "falling behind." From nearly any quarter, they could hear laments and critiques of this group that had failed to achieve the American dream. What was mostly invisible outside the nation's Puerto Rican communities, what was not included in government statistical reports or in accounts of the nation's ongoing civil rights campaigns, was the vibrancy of Puerto Ricans' struggle for civil rights and recognition in the United States. The thousands of members of United Bronx Parents and scores of progressive community organizations like it in cities all over the country's Northeast and Midwest, the patrons and supporters of Camden's Twelve Apostles and other grassroots political organizations that put new pressure on old political machines, the students and faculty building Puerto Rican Studies programs at dozens of colleges and universities, the small but growing army of Puerto Rican lawyers determined to turn civil rights aspirations into civil rights laws, the Nuyorican poets and other thriving groups of artists who wrote and performed into existence a world of greater freedom and equality—all of these people had viable ideas about how to make Puerto Ricans' "uncertain future" more certain. But, on the eve of an era of smothering neoliberal ideology, when social spending, entitlements, and affirmative action programs would be increasingly slashed, some of those ideas were starved of oxygen and failed to thrive.

Notes

1 "The South Bronx: A Jungle Stalked by Fear, Seized by Rage." *The New York Times,* 15 Jan. 1973, 1.
2 Jonnes, Jill. *South Bronx Rising: The Rise, Fall, and Resurrection of an American City.* New York: Fordham University Press, 2002; Wallace, Deborah, and Rodrick Wallace. *A Plague on Your Houses: How New York Was Burned Down and National Public Health Crumbled.* New York: Verso, 1998.
3 As cited in Howard Gillete Jr. "The Wages of Disinvestment: How Money and Politics Aided the Decline of Camden, New Jersey." In Jefferson Cowie and Joseph Heathcott, eds., *Beyond the Ruins: The Meanings of Deindustralization.* Ithaca, NY: Cornell University Press, 2003, 147.
4 Lucas, Luis. "Puerto Rican Politics in Chicago." In Jennings and Rivera, eds., *Puerto Rican Politics,* 106; Félix Padilla, *Latino Ethnic Consciousness.* Notre Dame, IN: University of Notre Dame Press, 1988, 123–7; Puente, Silvia and Victor Ortiz. "The Latino Institute." In Gilberto Cárdenas, ed., *La Causa: Civil Rights, Social Justice, and the Struggle for Equality in the Midwest.* Houston: Arte Público Press, 2004, 55–79.
5 Cardona, Luis. *The Coming of the Puerto Ricans.* Washington, D.C.: Unidos Publications, 1976, 63.
6 http://www.casitamaria.org/history.

7 "Badillo Says City Hall 'Protects' Vélez." *The New York Times*, 28 Aug. 1976, 47.

8 Setting of United Bronx Parents' Work: Summary Description of the South Bronx"; quotes from p. 325, UBP-CPRS Box 2 Folder 14. "Badillo, in a Tough Race, Fighting for Political Life." *The New York Times*, 18 Aug. 1976, 19; "Gigante and Velez in Ring of Slum Politics." *The New York Times*, 19 Nov. 1973, 37; "Ramon Vélez, 75, 'El Jefe' of the Bronx." *The New York Times*, 8 Dec. 2008, B13.

9 "Evelina—Bkln," n.d., p. xi. UBP-CPRS Box 2 Folder 5; see also Lee, *Building a Latino Civil Rights Movement*, 1; The Setting of United Bronx Parents' Work: Summary Description of the South Bronx"; quotes from pp. 323, UBP-CPRS Box 2 Folder 14.

10 United Bronx Parents, UBP-CPRS Box 2 Folder 14; White House Conference on Children, *Report to the President*. Washington, D.C.: U.S. Government Printing Office, 1970.

11 Muzio, Rose. "The Struggle against 'Urban Renewal' in Manhattan's Upper West Side and the Emergence of El Comité." *Centro Journal* 21, no. 2 (fall 2009): 109–41; Velázquez, José E. "Another West Side Story: An Interview with Members of El Comité-MINP," in Andrés Torres and José E. Velázquez, eds., *The Puerto Rican Movement: Voices from the Diaspora. Puerto Rican Studies*. Philadelphia: Temple University Press, 1998. Moreno De Toro, Angel A. "An Oral History of the Puerto Rican Socialist Party in Boston, 1972–1978," in Torres and Velázquez, eds., *The Puerto Rican Movement*.

12 Gold, Roberta. *When Tenants Claimed the City: The Struggle for Citizenship in New York Housing*. Champaign: University of Illinois Press, 2014; Uriarte-Gaston, Miren. "Organizing for Survival: The Emergence of a Puerto Rican Community." Ph.D. Dissertation, Boston University, 1989; Fernández, Lilia. *Brown in the Windy City: Mexicans and Puerto Ricans in Postwar Chicago*. Chicago, London: University of Chicago Press, 2012; Contreras, Eduardo. *Latinos in the Liberal City: Politics and Protest in San Francisco*. Philadelphia: University of Pennsylvania Press, forthcoming.

13 Schneider, Cathy. "Political Opportunities and Framing Puerto Rican Identity in New York City." In Hank Johnston and John Noakes, eds., *Frames of Protest: Social Movements and the Framing Perspective*. New York: Rowman and Littlefield, 2005, 171–2, 175; http://www.southsideunitedhdfc.org/about-us/mission-history/; Abu-Lughod, Janet. *From Urban Village to East Village: The Battle for New York's Lower East Side*. Oxford: Blackwell, 1995, 38, 110.

14 Chicago Rehab Network, "Development without Displacement" (Chicago, April 1980), 14; http://www.chicagorehab.org/resources/docs/network_builders/1980s/development_without_displacement_april_1980.pdf.

15 Uriarte-Gaston, "Organizing for Survival," 254; Hubner, John. "Villa Victoria. Public Housing That Works," *Mother Jones*, Sept.–Oct. 1981, 14; Small, Mario Luis. *Villa Victoria: The Transformation of Social Capital in a Boston Barrio*. Chicago: University of Chicago Press, 2004.

16 "East Harlem's Troubled Taino Towers Set to Open." *The New York Times*, 9 Feb. 1979; Gold. *When Tenants Claimed the City*, 135.

17 Baldwin, Susan. "Taino: 'Dream' Housing for Poor Set to Open," *Citylimits.org*, 5 Jan. 2009; Aponte-Parés, Luis. "Lessons from El Barrio–the East Harlem Real Great Society/Urban Planning Studio: A Puerto Rican Chapter in the Fight for Urban Self-Determination." In Rodolfo D. Torres and George N. Katsiaficas, eds., *Latino Social Movements: Historical and Theoretical Perspectives*. New York: Routledge, 1999; "A Pilot Public Housing Complex in East Harlem Still Unfinished after 10 Years." *The New York Times*, 24 June 1981.

18 Cruz, José. "Puerto Rican Radicalism in Hartford, Connecticut." In Torres and Velázquez, eds., *The Puerto Rican Movement*, 73.

19 Fitch, Robert. *The Assassination of New York*. New York: Verso, 1993, Appendix 8.

20 United States Commission on Civil Rights. *Puerto Ricans in the Continental United States: An Uncertain Future: A Report.* Washington, D.C.: U.S. Commission on Civil Rights, 1976.
21 "Bronx Group Accused of Using Violence to Get Minorities Jobs." *The New York Times,* 6 Sept. 1979.
22 *Ibid.*
23 Muzio, "The Struggle against 'Urban Renewal' in Manhattan's Upper West Side and the Emergence of El Comité," *Centro Journal* 21, no. 2 (fall 2009): 109–41.
24 Golland, David Hamilton. *Constructing Affirmative Action: The Struggle for Equal Employment Opportunity.* Lexington: University Press of Kentucky, 2011. "Enrollment of Minorities in Colleges Stagnating." *The New York Times,* 19 April 1987.
25 Hamilton, Konrad Mark. "From Equal Opportunity to Affirmative Action: A History of the Equal Employment Opportunity Commission, 1965-1980." Ph.D. Dissertation, Stanford University, 1998, 236–8; Anderson, Terry H. *Pursuit of Fairness.* New York: Oxford University Press, 2004; Hill, Herbert. "Race, Ethnicity and Organized Labor: The Opposition to Affirmative Action." *New Politics* 1, no. 2 (1987): 31; Hill, Herbert. "Race and Ethnicity in Organized Labor: The Historical Sources of Resistance to Affirmative Action." *Journal of Intergroup Relations* 12, no. 4 (winter 1984): 5–50.
26 Fitch. *The Assassination,* Appendix 9.
27 Golland, David Hamilton. *Constructing Affirmative Action: The Struggle for Equal Employment Opportunity.* Lexington: University Press of Kentucky, 2011, Ch. 5.
28 "A Defender of Human Rights: Patria Orelinda Nieto-Ortiz." *The New York Times,* 27 Feb. 1978; "Human Rights Chairman Resigns after Dispute with Koch and Staff." *The New York Times,* 13 April 1978, A1; "Ex-Head of Rights Panel Disputes Reasons Given by Koch for Ouster: 'You Are Not the Highest'." *The New York Times,* 22 April 1978, 8; "Rights Head Forced Out." *New York Amsterdam News,* 15 April 1978, A1; "Black Women Urge Rights Unit Inquiry." *New York Amsterdam News,* 13 May 1978; "Official under Fire." *Newsday,* 11 April 1978, 4Q.
29 "A Kind of Higher Education: This Side of Paradise." *The New York Times,* 27 May 1973, 202; Alfonso Narváez, "Puerto Ricans at Colleges Triple." *The New York Times,* 14 Oct. 1972, 71; Meyer, Gerald. "Save Hostos: Politics and Community Mobilization to Save a College in the Bronx, 1973-78," *Centro Journal* 15, no. 1 (fall 2003), 73–97.
30 Compared to 40,000 college and university students out of a population of 2.7 million on the island. "Puerto Ricans Here Told to Aim High." *The New York Times,* 21 Dec. 1970, 37; Félix Matos Rodríguez. "Puerto Ricans in the United States: Past, Present and Future." Presented at the Regional Conference of the Council of State Governments. Fajardo, Puerto Rico, December 9 2013.
31 Padilla, *Puerto Rican Chicago,* 182–90.
32 "Black Studies Programs." *Chicago Daily Defender,* 26 July 1969, 8; Sotomayor, Sonia, *My Beloved World.* New York: Knopf, 2013, 149–51.
33 Ortiz Márquez, Maribel. "Beginnings: Puerto Rican Studies Revisited," *Centro Journal* 21 (fall 2009), 177–96; Flores, Juan. "Reclaiming Left Baggage: Some Early Sources for Minority Studies," *Cultural Critique* 59 (winter 2005): 187–207, 199; History Task Force, Centro de Estudios Puertorriqueños. *Labor Migration Under Capitalism.* New York: Monthly Review Press, 1980, 156.
34 Pérez, Nélida. "Two Reading Rooms and the Librarian's Office: The Evolution of the Centro Library and Archives," *Centro Journal* 21, no. 2 (fall 2009): 199–218, 209.
35 Hunter College of the City University of New York Department of Black and Puerto Rican Studies, Spring Semester Bell Schedule 1974. UBP-CPRS Box 2 Folder 9.
36 Ramírez, Yasmin. "Nuyorican Visionary: Jorge Soto and the Evolution of an Afro-Taíno Aesthetic at Taller Boricua," *Centro Journal* 17, no. 2 (fall 2005): 34; Jennings, James and Monte Rivera. *Puerto Rican Politics in Urban America.* Westport, CT: Greenwood Press, 1984, 150.
37 Mohr, Eugene. *The Nuyorican Experience.* Westport, CT: Greenwood Press, 1982, 116; Falcón, Angelo. "From Civil Rights to the 'Decade of the Hispanic'." In Gabriel

Haslip-Viera, Angelo Falcón, and Félix Matos-Rodríguez, eds., *Boricuas in Gotham: Puerto Ricans in the Making of Modern New York City*. Princeton, NJ: Markus Wiener, 2005, 91; "Puerto Ricans Express Pain and Joy in Poetry." *The New York Times*, 14 May 1976, 48.

38 "El Bronx Remembered." *The New York Times*, 16 Nov. 1975; Thomas, *Puerto Rican Citizen*, 193.

39 Algarín, Miguel and Miguel Piñero, eds., *Nuyorican Poetry: An Anthology of Puerto Rican Words and Feelings*. New York: William Morrow and Company, 1975, 24, 110, 111; Mohr, *The Nuyorican Experience*, 97.

40 Susler, Jan. "Unreconstructed Revolutionaries: Today's Puerto Rican Political Prisoners/ Prisoners of War." In Torres and Velazquez, eds., *The Puerto Rican Movement*, 147, 149.

41 Muzio, Rose. *Radical Imagination, Radical Humanity Puerto Rican Political Activism in New York*. Albany: State University of New York Press, 2017.

42 Velázquez, José. "The Puerto Rican Socialist Party, U.S. Branch." In Torres and Velázquez, eds., *The Puerto Rican Movement*, 51–52.

43 "Puerto Ricans Strive for a Spot in U.S. Sun." *Philadelphia Inquirer*, 20 Jan. 1974, B1.

44 Velázquez, José. "Coming Full Circle: The Puerto Rican Socialist Party, U.S. Branch." In Torres and Velázquez, eds., *The Puerto Rican Movement*, 52, 54; Falcón, "From Civil Rights to the 'Decade of the Hispanic'," 93; Cruz, "The Changing Socioeconomic and Political Fortunes of Puerto Ricans in New York," in *Boricuas in Gotham*, 48; Moreno de Toro, Angel A. "An Oral History of the Puerto Rican Socialist Party in Boston." In Torres and Velázquez, eds., *Puerto Rican Movement*, 257.

45 Moreno de Toro, Amy. "An Oral History of the Puerto Rican Socialist Party in Boston," 248, 251–3, 257; Cruz, "Puerto Rican Radicalism in Hartford, Connecticut," 79; Velázquez, "Coming Full Circle: The Puerto Rican Socialist Party, U.S. Branch," 52–63.

46 Falcón, "From Civil Rights to the 'Decade of the Hispanic'," 93; Lucas, Isidro. "Puerto Rican Politics in Chicago." In Jennings and Rivera, eds., *Puerto Rican Politics*, 107.

47 "30 in Puerto Rican Group Held in Liberty I. Protest." *The New York Times*, 26 Oct. 1977, 30; "Why We Took the Statue of Liberty," statement presented in court by the New York Committee to Free the Nationalist Political Prisoners, 22 Nov. 1977, Lourdes Torres Papers-CPRS Series IV Box 3 Folder 1.

48 Torres, Andrés. "Political Radicalism in the Diaspora." In Torres and Velázquez, eds., *The Puerto Rican Movement*, 9–10.

49 Gerena Valentín, Gilberto. *Gilberto Gerena Valentín: My Life as a Community Activist, Labor Organizer, and Progressive Politician in New York City*. New York: Center for Puerto Rican Studies, 2013, 273.

50 Velázquez, José. "An Interview with Members of El Comité-MINP," *The Puerto Rican Movement*, 97; Cruz, *Identity and Power*, 89.

51 Cruz, José. "The Changing Socioeconomic and Political Fortunes of Puerto Ricans in New York City, 1960-1990." In *Boricuas in Gotham*, 50; Massey, Douglas and Bitterman, Brooks. "The Paradox of Puerto Rican Segregation," *Social Forces* 64 (Dec. 1985): 306–31, 310.

52 See Chapter 3, pp. 84–5, on the challenge to Badillo's congressional seat in 1972 by Manuel Ramos, who accused Badillo of not being "Puerto Rican enough." "Badillo-Ramos Contest Centers on Who Is the More Puerto Rican." *The New York Times*, 13 June 1972, 45.

53 Schneider, "Political Opportunities and Framing Puerto Rican Identity," 169; "Gigante and Velez in Ring of Slum Politics." *The New York Times*, 19 Nov. 1973.

54 "Badillo, in a Tough Place, Fighting for Political Life." *The New York Times*, 18 Aug. 1976, 19. "Ramon S. Velez, the South Bronx Padrino, Dies at 75." *The New York Times*, 2 Dec. 2008.

55 "Badillo Says City Hall 'Protects' Veléz." *The New York Times*, 28 Aug. 1976, 47. "Badillo Threatens to Quit, but Yields." *The New York Times*, 11 April 1978, 1; "Badillo Criticizes

City Hall Shuffle: Cites Growth of Manhattan Power." *The New York Times*. 6 Aug. 1979, A1. "Robert García, the Winner in Bronx Race." *The New York Times*, 15 Feb. 1978, 22.

56 "A Defender of Human Rights: Patria Orelinda Nieto-Ortiz." *The New York Times*, 27 Feb 1978; "Human Rights Chairman Resigns after Dispute with Koch and Staff." *The New York Times*, 13 April 1978, A1; "Ex-Head of Rights Panel Disputes Reasons Given by Koch for Ouster: 'You Are Not the Highest'." *The New York Times*, 22 April 1978, 8; "Bronx Upset Victory Buoys Liberal Party." *The New York Times*, 13 April 1978.

57 "Irene Hernández, Ex-county Official." *Chicago Sun-Times*, 29 Sept. 1997. Hernández, who was Mexican-American, was appointed by Mayor Daly to the Cook County Board of Commissioners in 1974; the first Puerto Rican candidate was elected to Chicago city council in 1983. Padilla, *Puerto Rican Chicago*, 226. Campbell Gibson and Kay Jung, "Historical Census Statistics on Population Totals by Race, 1790 to 1990, and by Hispanic Origin, 1970 to 1990, for Large Cities and Other Urban Places in the United States," Population Division Working Paper No. 76. Washington, D.C.: U.S. Census Bureau, February 2005, Table 14, Illinois.

58 "Puerto Ricans Striving for a Spot in the U.S. Sun." *Philadelphia Inquirer*, 20 Jan. 1974, 1-B, 10B.

59 "Puerto Ricans Begin Drive for 'Brown People' Label," *Philadelphia Evening Bulletin* 27 Dec. 1970. Newspaper Clipping Collection-TUUA. See also Whalen, Carmen Teresa. *From Puerto Rico to Philadelphia: Puerto Rican Workers and Postwar Economies*. Philadelphia: Temple University Press, 2001, 235; Arnau, Ariel. "The Evolution of Leadership within the Puerto Rican Community of Philadelphia, 1950s-1970s." *The Pennsylvania Magazine of History and Biography* 136, no. 1 (2012): 53–81; Adams, Carolyn et al. *Philadelphia: Neighborhoods, Division, and Conflict in a Postindustrial City*. Philadelphia: Temple University Press 1991, 134; González, Juan. "The Turbulent Progress of Puerto Ricans in Philadelphia," *Centro Journal* 2, no. 2 (winter 1987–88), 35–41; Whalen, *From Puerto Rico to Philadelphia*, 237; Vázquez-Hernández, Victor. "From Pan-Latino Enclaves to a Community: Puerto Ricans in Philadelphia, 1910-2000." In Carmen Teresa Whalen and Victor Vázquez-Hernández, eds., *The Puerto Rican Diaspora: Historical Perspectives*. Philadelphia: Temple University Press, 2005, 102.

60 "Puerto Ricans Striving for a Spot in the U.S. Sun." *Philadelphia Inquirer*, 20 Jan. 1974, 1-B; "Where Dreams Die: The Hispanic Ghettoes of Camden." *Philadelphia Inquirer*, 30 July 1978, 1A; "Hispanics Find Little Strength in Numbers." *The New York Times*, 16 July 1978, E6.

61 "Where Dreams Die: The Hispanic Ghettoes of Camden." *Philadelphia Inquirer*, 30 July 1978, 1A.

62 Cruz, *Identity and Power*, 26 and *passim*.

63 *Ibid.*, 93, 110–1, 121.

64 "Badillo-Ramos Contest Centers on Who Is the More Puerto Rican." *The New York Times*, 13 June 1972, 45.

65 Godsell, Goeffrey. "Hispanics in the U.S.: Ethnic 'Sleeping Giant' Awakens." *Christian Science Monitor*, 28 April 1980; "It's Your Turn in the Sun." *Time*, 16 Oct. 1978.

66 See, for example, Blanton, Carlos Kevin. *The Strange Career of Bilingual Education in Texas, 1836–1981*. College Station: Texas A & M University Press, 2004; Brilliant, Mark. *The Color of America Has Changed: How Racial Diversity Shaped Civil Rights Reform in California, 1941–1978*. New York: Oxford, 2010.

67 Uriarte-Gaston, "Organizing for Survival," 225, 226, 232. The amendment was to the 1965 Elementary and Secondary Education Act.

68 Padilla, *Puerto Rican Chicago*, 212–4. Padilla, *Latino Ethnic Consciousness*, 125–6. See Latino Institute, *Annual Report: 1977*. Chicago: Latino Institute, 1977, cited in Puente and Ortiz, "The Latino Institute," *La Causa*, 63–4.

69 Falcón. "Commentary. From Civil Rights to the "Decade of the "Hispanic." In *Boricuas in Gotham*, 91; De Jésus. "From Community Control to Consent Decree."

70 "Legal Defense Unit Established Here for Puerto Ricans." *The New York Times*, 30 July 1972.

71 Culliton-González, Katherine. "Time to Revive Puerto Rican Voting Rights," *Berkeley La Raza Law Journal* 19 (2008): 101–42; Arnau, Ariel. "Suing for Spanish: Puerto Ricans, Bilingual Voting, and Legal Activism in the 1970s," Ph.D. Dissertation, City University of New York Graduate Center, 2018; 490 F. 2nd 575 *Puerto Rican Organization for Political Action et al. v. Stanley T. Kusper*, No. 73-1035, United States Court of Appeals, Seventh Circuit, 1973.

72 Culliton-González. "Time to Revive Puerto Rican Voting Rights," 27–70; Arnau, Ariel. "Put a Sticker on It: Civil Rights, Bilingual Voting and Puerto Ricans in Philadelphia in the 1970s." *Centro Journal* 27, no. 1 (spring 2015): 34–69.

73 Culliton-González. "Time to Revive Puerto Rican Voting Rights," 27.

74 "Sotomayor: In Her Own Words, on Tape." *The New York Times*, 11 June 2009.

75 See Morales, Iris. "¡Palante, Siempre Palante! The Young Lords." In Torres and Velázquz, eds., *The Puerto Rican Movement*, 217–19; Morales, Iris. *Through the Eyes of Rebel Women: The Young Lords 1969–76*. New York: Red Sugarcane Press, 2016.

76 Slavin, Sarah. *U.S. Women's Interest Groups: Institutional Profiles*. Westport, CT: Greenwood Press, 1995, 342–5; *Puerto Rican Women in the United States: Organizing for Change*, NACOPRW, Proceedings of Fourth Conference, Washington, D.C. 1977; Acosta-Belen, Edna. "National Conference on Puerto Rican Women." In Vicky Ruiz and Virginia Sánchez-Korrol, eds., *Latinas in the U.S.* Bloomington: Indiana University Press, 2006); Gold. *When Tenants Claimed the City*, 232–3.

77 "Puerto Rican Plight in U.S. Is Deplored." *The New York Times*, 14 Oct. 1976, 18.

78 "Puerto Rican Deprivation: A Call for Federal Action." *The New York Times*, 29 May 1978, A7.

79 *Ibid.*; U.S. Commission on Civil Rights, *Puerto Ricans in the Continental U.S.: An Uncertain Future*. Washington, D.C.: U.S. Government Printing Office, 1976, 144.

80 "Puerto Rican Plight in U.S. Is Deplored." *The New York Times*, 14 Oct. 1976, 18.

81 Adams, Florence. *Latinos and Local Representation: Changing Realities, Emerging Theories.* New York: Routledge, 2016, 72. NPRC, Inc., "Study to Assess the Impact of Federal Cutbacks on the Employment and Training Opportunities for Puerto Ricans," 5 vols. Washington, D.C.: National Puerto Rican Coalition, 1982; de los Santos, Alfredo, Jr. *Career Education, the Comprehensive Employment and Training Act of 1973 and the Spanish-Speaking.* 1974; Nuñez, Louis. "Reflections on Puerto Rican History: Aspira in the Sixties and the Coming of Age of the Stateside Puerto Rican Community." *Centro Journal* 21, no. 2 (fall 2009): 33–47; "Louis Nuñez, Champion of Puerto Ricans, Dies at 87." *The New York Times*, 7 May 2015.

82 Lauria Santiago, Aldo A. "A Chalk Line on Third Ave: Policing and Puerto Rican Riots." Manuscript; "Puerto Rican Deprivation: A Call for Federal Action." *The New York Times*, 29 May 1978, A7; Doeringer, P. B. *Jobs and Training in the 1980s: Vocational Policy and the Labor Market.* New York: Springer, 2013; Mirengoff, William and Lester Rindler. *The Comprehensive Employment and Training Act, Impact on People, Places and Programs: An Interim Report: Staff Paper.* Washington, D.C.: National Academy of Sciences, 1976.

83 See Gerena Valentín, *Gilberto Gerena Valentín*, 267; "Kennedy, in South Bronx, Says Carter Broke Aid Vow." *The New York Times*, 23 March 1980, 28; "Reagan, in South Bronx, Says Carter Broke Vow." *The New York Times*, 6 Aug. 1980, A16; "Carter, Ending Visit, Sees Decaying South Bronx," *Washington Post*, 6 Oct. 1977, 4.

84 "Millions Watch Fire on TV." *Washington Post*, 13 Oct. 1977, A13; Joe Flood, "Why the Bronx Burned." *New York Post*, 16 May 2010.

85 Gerena Valentín, *Gilberto Gerena Valentín*, 267.

5

DISPERSION AND MOMENTUM SINCE 1980

Introduction

By the 1980s, as the Puerto Rican population in the U.S. reached over two million—with vibrant communities across the Northeast, Midwest, Florida, and California—efforts for empowerment, recognition, and representation became more diverse and decentered. New migrants continued to arrive from the island during the 1980s, settling further from the core population centers of New York and New Jersey and creating communities in many smaller cities and towns in farther-flung states. Puerto Ricans fleeing the disastrous post-industrial centers of New York City, Newark, and a few other declining industrial cities contributed to the dispersion.[1] By 2010, ten states would have Puerto Rican populations of 100,000 or more; ten cities had over 30,000 Puerto Ricans, with expanding communities in Tampa, Orlando, Allentown, and Springfield growing closer in size to the still-growing populations of Philadelphia, Miami, Bridgeport, and Boston. More important perhaps were the new clusters of higher income residents in varied counties in Texas, Florida, North Carolina, Georgia, southern California, and Nevada.[2] A growing middle class of second generation Puerto Ricans, or those of more distant Puerto Rican descent, became more stable and integrated into heterogeneous middle class urban enclaves and suburbs.

Yet, because large sectors of the Puerto Rican population continued to experience varying levels of poverty or income insecurity, as well as failing educational systems, local efforts for improved access to quality education, housing, and anti-povertyservices continued to be important arenas for Puerto Rican activism after 1980, along with ongoing campaigns against discrimination and police abuse. Electoral politics became even more important for Puerto Ricans across all socio-economic levels, and Puerto Ricans in a number of cities

TABLE 5.1 Puerto Rican Descent Population in US Cities (20,000 or higher), 1990

City	Population
New York City	896,763
Chicago	119,866
Philadelphia	67,857
Newark	41,545
Hartford	38,176
Bridgeport	30,250
Jersey City	29,777
Boston	25,767
Springfield	23,729
Paterson	27,580
Camden	22,984

Source: PRLDEF, *Puerto Ricans Stateside 2000: A Demographic Overview*, n.d.

began to make their way into electoral politics after 1980. Despite the existence of national networks of leadership that communicated across urban centers, along with the emergence of new national organizations, no single organization emerged as the locus for these efforts. Instead, competing leaders with conflicting political dispositions—usually differing in their acceptance of liberal politics and sometimes led by recent migrants from the island—dominated the evolving Puerto Rican public sphere at different moments.

In large cities like New York, Newark, Philadelphia, Chicago, and Boston, former members of the radical organizations of the 1960s and 1970s had become journalists, lawyers, academics, and leaders of civic, cultural, and political organizations. More Puerto Ricans than ever before worked in higher education, including the founding or leadership of important centers for research and teaching. Younger Puerto Ricans grew up in more heterogenous urban environments, often in poor or working class barrios and mixed Latino and Black neighborhoods, participating in a varied social world enlivened by the struggles of the urban poor. These contacts with Dominican, Mexican, and African American neighbors, depending on the city and the region, opened new cultural and political possibilities, along with additional arenas of inter-Latino cooperation.[3]

Electoral Politics: Political Representation and National Organizing

Throughout 1980, the year that Ronald Reagan won the presidency and inaugurated a long decade of conservative leadership in the White House, pundits, journalists, and the public at large debated what looked like a new national trend: Hispanic voters, the "sleeping giant" of the American political system, were waking up—and their participation at the polls promised to change political outcomes around the country. This attention to the Hispanic vote was partly a result of the decade-long efforts of political strategists to win new voters after the acrimonious election of 1968. Republicans had begun actively courting Hispanic voters in 1969, and Democratic leaders followed suit in 1971; in 1972, during his reelection campaign, Republican president Richard Nixon convened a "brown mafia" to win Spanish-speaking voters.[4] Mexican Americans, politically organized in some areas of the Southwest since the 19th century, were the presumptive head of the giant; but Puerto Ricans, whose community activism in Chicago, New York, and elsewhere in the Mid-Atlantic commanded serious attention in the 1970s, seemed to comprise increasingly powerful appendages.

Puerto Ricans had slowly worked their way into electoral politics, starting in the mid-1960s in New York City and over a decade later in Chicago, Philadelphia, Camden, and Hartford. Even by the mid-1980s, though, voters in New York City—the largest Puerto Rican settlement in the United States, which numbered one million by 1985—had trouble maintaining their momentum. In 1986, only ten city and state elected offices were held by Puerto Ricans—the same number as in 1976. Robert García, who won the 21st congressional district in the Bronx in 1978, when Herman Badillo stepped down to become deputy mayor to Ed Koch, was still the only Puerto Rican representative in the U.S. Congress in 1985.[5] If hundreds of thousands of voters concentrated in the largest Puerto Rican city in the Americas outside of San Juan could not increase their direct political representation over time, how real was their role in the awakening of the "sleeping giant"?

One problem was Puerto Rican leaders' apparent ambivalence about where to invest the most resources in the service of political empowerment. Early experiences in the 1960s taught many to question how much merely electing one of their own could serve the complex needs of the community. Herman Badillo, who had achieved the most celebrated political successes since the 1960s, was seen by both Puerto Rican and establishment political figures as a kind of "lone wolf" who was not attached or beholden to the Democratic machine. On the other hand, by the late 1970s he was also seen by many Puerto Rican leaders as not particularly responsive to his community base, especially compared to some of the other Puerto Rican activists entering the political arena by the late 1970s. Badillo, who lived in the prosperous Riverdale neighborhood of the Bronx and was married to a Jewish woman, regularly had to defend himself against charges that he was not "Puerto Rican enough" to represent the constituency of the 21st district. Democratic mayor Ed Koch went so far as to assert that Badillo was "no more Puerto Rican than I am." To this slight, Badillo responded that Koch was a "petty racialist" who incited "racial divisiveness" in the city.[6]

At the other extreme was Ramon Vélez, a powerful presence in the South Bronx district where, since the 1960s, Vélez had built a career managing large community service organizations that successfully tapped into federal and state anti-poverty funds. Vélez and Badillo maintained a political rivalry that had become increasingly bitter throughout the 1970s.[7] During his first mayoral campaign in 1977, Ed Koch, concurring with Badillo's criticism of his Bronx rival, had criticized Vélez for abusing his influence over his impoverished constituents. Yet by the mid-1980s, after a falling out with Badillo, Koch apparently decided that Vélez's management of community funds was admirable. The mayor rewarded his Hunt's Point Multi-Service Center with over $200,000 to renovate the organization's headquarters in 1984, barely a year before Vélez navigated his way around another in a series of investigations of his mismanagement of millions in federal and state funds.[8]

Multiple allegations of legal and ethical violations against Vélez, none of which ever stuck, seemed not to trouble Governor Cuomo either; Cuomo accepted Vélez's endorsement during his 1986 reelection campaign. Such were the workings of the machine politics that Badillo had spent his political career trying to avoid. Badillo, who ran in every mayoral Democratic primary election between 1968 and 1985 without winning one, sought to find a place for Puerto Ricans in city politics that did not involve the kind of unprincipled deal-making that he accused Vélez of relying on. It seemed clear, though, that powerful politicians in New York in the 1980s were more receptive to Puerto Rican leaders who took the traditional machine-style approach than they were to those, like Badillo, who expected to be able to operate through a more direct relationship with their constituency.

One Puerto Rican politician in New York in the 1980s managed—with great success, at least for a time—to occupy a middle ground between the principled "outsider" and the well-connected but corrupt "insider." Robert García, who had served three terms in the New York State Senate, took over Badillo's congressional seat in 1978 when the latter became deputy mayor to Koch. García called himself a protégé of Badillo, at least early in his career, but also maintained what many saw as a stronger grassroots connection to Puerto Rican community. For politicized Puerto Rican constituents, the signature issue of García's first term in Congress was his successful push for the release of jailed Puerto Rican nationalists in 1979. García was also known as a coalition-builder, and served as the first Puerto Rican chair of the National Hispanic Caucus in Congress starting in 1981.[9] From there he led an effort at immigration reform, which was important as one of the first crossover political moments in which a Puerto Rican of national stature lobbied for reforms in support of non-citizen Latino immigrant communities. A representative of the still-beleaguered Bronx had to beat the odds to build such a strong and balanced foundation in national politics. García's constituents were hit exceptionally hard by his downfall in 1989, when he was convicted on charges of extortion and conspiracy in a minority defense contract scandal involving a Bronx company called Wedtech.[10]

Like Badillo, many Puerto Rican leaders became more conservative with age. Olga Méndez, elected as a Democrat in 1978 to represent East Harlem in the New York State Assembly (who would go on to serve 12 consecutive terms), was the first Puerto Rican woman elected to public office in the U.S. Criticized for being an opportunistic pragmatist by liberals, Méndez ultimately rejected the Democratic party for doing little for her constituency and became a Republican, although she continued to support liberal policies like low cost housing, increasing the minimum wage, sentencing reform, and equal access to education.[11] Despite the difference of her party affiliation, Méndez's political leadership resembled that of Badillo, García, and Vélez in certain ways, particularly in terms of her lasting commitment to the community's basic needs and her staunch but idiosyncratic liberal politics.

Whereas the end of the 1980s brought dashed hopes for Puerto Rican voters in New York—who, based on their momentum in the 1970s, had every reason to expect that they would lead the political charge in the "decade of the Hispanic"—in other cities with somewhat smaller and more recently established Puerto Rican communities, the decade's political outcomes were better. In Chicago in the early 1980s, the Puerto Rican population had reached 112,000, but there was only one Puerto Rican member of the city council, and one elected municipal judge; there were no Puerto Ricans in the Illinois state legislature nor representatives of Chicago in the U.S. Congress.[12] But reform coalitions with African American leaders that shook up the boss-controlled Democratic party, especially Mayor Harold Washington, helped elect Luis Gutiérrez as an alderman to the Chicago city council in 1986. After many successes in the city council, Gutiérrez was able to mobilize a majority of the Mexican American vote as well as the Puerto Rican vote, winning a seat in the U.S. Congress in 1992 and representing a new majority-Latino district in Chicago.[13]

Puerto Ricans in Philadelphia in 1980 would have described the same challenges as their peers in Chicago: low voter registration; electoral districting that made it unlikely or impossible for Puerto Rican voters to successfully back Puerto Rican candidates; and, most important, a political machine controlled by Democratic party bosses that made little room for Puerto Rican candidates.[14] However, as in Chicago, voters and leaders in Philadelphia saw an upswing in their impact during the 1980s. Mobilizing against conservative mayor Frank Rizzo's effort to change the city charter in order to run for a third term in 1978, young Puerto Rican leaders helped double the number of registered Puerto Rican voters in the city and laid the foundation for several important electoral victories by the mid-1980s. These included the elections of Ángel Ortiz, supported by a broad coalition of progressive voters and elected to city council in 1983, and Ralph Acosta, who won a seat in the state legislature in 1984.[15] In Connecticut, too, Puerto Ricans made some electoral gains in the 1980s as a result of focused efforts at voter registration and community-level political organization, including the Hartford city council during the 1980s. (Tough times and persistent community building, plus the politically focused Puerto Rican Action Committee of Connecticut, would pave the way for the election of Hartford's first Puerto Rican mayor, Eddie Pérez, in 2001.)[16]

Community Building: Organizing at the National Level

During a decade characterized by budget-cutting coservatism at the national level—which included a backlash against affirmative action specifically and anti-discrimination efforts in general, along with a rollback of support for minority communities—it was no small feat for Puerto Ricans as a group to achieve any political gains. In the smaller cities, where Puerto Ricans were making notable progress in political representation, as well as in New York, where they only managed to maintain the status quo, Puerto Rican communities around the U.S. were bolstered in this era by the expansion of several key organizations into national entities. To be sure, the foundations of this organizational base had been laid over the course of decades, with many of the organizations emerging out of the large Puerto Rican community in the New York metro area through political groups like the American Labor Party, the Puerto Rican Socialist Party, El Comité-MINP, the Young Lords, and a variety of community and civil rights organizations like Aspira, the Puerto Rican Forum, the National Coalition of Puerto Rican Civil Rights, the Puerto Rican Legal Defense and Educational Fund, and the state-based Puerto Rican Congress of New Jersey.

The regional and national scope of organizations grew through a strategy of expanding both their membership base and their connections with allies beyond Puerto Rican communities. By the early 1980s, the Puerto Rican Forum, which had been founded in 1957 by a group of young New York leaders, had expanded to eight cities around the U.S.—including Boston, Miami, Chicago, and Cleveland—and was renamed the National Puerto Rican Forum. It served tens of thousands of Puerto Ricans, particularly in supporting employment advancement.[17] Aspira, the organization that formed in 1961 to support young Puerto Ricans' school achievement, oversaw programs in a few cities by the early 1970s. Then in 1972 its leaders collaborated with the newly-formed Puerto Rican Legal Defense and Education Fund (PRLDEF) to demand in court for the right of Puerto Rican children to bilingual education—a fight that resulted in the 1974 Aspira Consent Decree, which forced the New York Board of Education to change its policies.[18] Through this effort, Aspira joined the growing ranks of Puerto Rican organizations with a voice in national policy debates on bilingualism, desegregation, and educational access. By the 1980s, Aspira operated various state-level offices, each coordinating the work of dozens of high school and community chapters, as well as national headquarters in Washington, D.C.[19]

PRLDEF, likewise, continued to be an important force in policymaking related to Puerto Ricans throughout the 1970s and 1980s, litigating and winning victories in voting rights, redistricting, equal employment, and educational opportunity.[20] Supported by nearly all the politically involved lawyers in the Puerto Rican community and modeled around the NAACP, PRLDEF counted

Supreme Court justice Sonia Sotomayor among its board members throughout the 1980s, as she advanced in her career from a prosecutor just out of law school to a federal appeals court judge.

The work of PRLDEF was especially important for Puerto Rican voters in Chicago in the early 1980s. Over the course of two decades, 14 Latino candidates (evenly split between Puerto Rican and Mexican American men) had sought election as aldermen in their Chicago wards, and in each case the candidates lost, having been refused the backing of the Democratic machine. One political scientist, writing a few years later, observed that the neighborhoods where most Puerto Ricans lived had been "carefully gerrymandered by the machine" so voters were unable to elect a single representative to city council. Relying on the census count of 1980 to make its case, PRLDEF joined with its Mexican American counterpart, the Mexican American Legal Defense and Education Fund (MALDEF), along with groups of African American voters and representatives of the Republican party, to mount a legal challenge to the legislative map constructed by the Democratic machine. The first Puerto Rican representative, José Berrios, won a seat in the Illinois General Assembly in 1982.[21] (Since the 1990s, PRLDEF has extended its work to include Latinos of various national origins and as a result changed its name in 2008 to LatinoJustice PRLDEF.)

Shortly after taking office in 1981, in the midst of a severe recession, President Reagan implemented a series of major budget cuts that had an especially brutal impact on the urban poor, many of whom had barely begun recovering from the industrial and fiscal crises of the 1970s. By 1983, the Reagan administration's austerity approach had encouraged large scale mobilizations from a variety of civil rights, labor, and racial or ethnic groups, including those representing Puerto Ricans. That year, the 20th anniversary of the historic 1963 March on Washington served as a powerful marker of the continuing struggles Puerto Ricans and other Latino groups that still relied heavily on underfunded public programs to offset the burdens of poverty and unemployment in the midst of recession. Now, though, two decades after the original March on Washington, Puerto Ricans were supported by large national organizations and political networks that were stronger and more diverse. Sixty-two Latino organizations, including dozens of Latino politicians, supported the march. "We are here today not only to lend support to our Afro-American friends but also because the right to jobs, peace and freedom strikes at the core of our Latin-American heritage. It is a vision of American shared by all people of conscience," announced José Rivera, a New York state legislator from the Bronx.[22]

Massive budget cuts at the local level also spurred responses. Activist Julio Pabón remembers how Puerto Rican organizations responded to New York City mayor Koch's attempts to explain and justify the large budget cuts on social programs in the devastated Bronx in 1980:

South Bronx activist attorney Ramón Jimenez and myself worked together with other friends and members of the Coalition in Defense of Puerto Rican & Hispanic Rights to come out and greet the mayor. Our plan was simple: we asked the mayor if he came to ask for our opinion and suggestions on the budget cuts, or did he come to tell us what he already cut? He said they already had made the cuts, but he came to explain the cuts and how they would take effect. We then told him he could not speak and got all the hundreds in attendance to agree with us and that was the end of Koch's quick South Bronx visit.[23]

Puerto Ricans continued to play a prominent role in the political battles over improving city public services. In 1987 they pushed Mayor Koch to reply to recommendations made by his own Commission on Hispanic Concerns that called for massive interventions to improve schools, housing, and economic development. Angelo Falcón, founder of the Institute for Puerto Rican Policy, concluded that "the mayor really nickeled and dimed our community."[24] Puerto Rican activists and organizations continued to fight against massive spending cuts in education and social services through the 1980s and 1990s, including large cuts by Republican New York State governor Pataki, which prompted acrimonious protests.[25]

A key goal that Puerto Rican organizations strived for in the 1980s, and partially achieved, was a mutually reinforcing relationship with Puerto Rican political leaders. This trend was exemplified early in the decade by the creation of two key lobbying groups, the National Congress for Puerto Rican Rights, formed in 1981 as a grassroots coalition focused on social and economic equality, and the Institute for Puerto Rican Policy (IPRP; its name was changed in 2006 to the National Institute for Latino Policy), founded in 1982 by political scientist Angelo Falcón.[26] In its first year, the IPRP published extensive reports on Puerto Rican voter registration and on their representation in government employment, both of which emphasized the need for city and state governments to take action to fix disparities that hindered the political empowerment of Puerto Ricans.[27]

The growth of organizations like these represented a major departure from the patterns of community empowerment predominant in the 1970s, when leaders like Ramón Vélez fostered a clientelistic relationship to his support base. Both the National Congress for Puerto Rican Rights and the IPRP sought to maintain close ties to people in the communities they represented, but they envisioned the goals of their work on the scale of shaping policy at various levels of governance. Although leaders continued to complain about both the lack of unity and the lack of mass membership in these organizations, they managed to develop models wherein highly committed leaders could respond to local needs and crises and create functional coalitions to address specific issues, while maintaining and expanding connections to Puerto Rican and other Latino leaders across the U.S.[28]

Puerto Rican policy leaders also began to take on the nationally debated issue of affirmative action in the 1980s. The Institute for Puerto Rican Policy's 1983 report "Simple Justice: Puerto Rican and Latino Government Employment in New York and the Failure of Affirmative Action," set the agenda for discussions of employment mobility and inclusion at the municipal level—a task that the National Institute for Latino Policy has continued to fulfill to this day. By the 1980s any politician seeking citywide office had to court Latino voters and appear to be responsive to this sort of data-driven criticism. During the 1980s Puerto Rican organizations also pushed for more Latino presence in many professional fields. In 1989, for example, the National Puerto Rican Forum and the National Hispanic Media Coalition filed a complaint with regulatory agency FCC about the near complete lack of Latinos employed at all levels in the media and especially in televised journalism.[29]

A consistent dilemma for leaders of Puerto Rican organizations in the U.S. has been the complexity of responding to the island's needs and problems. Puerto Rico's political status as an unsovereign U.S. territory and the migration flows that are a constant of Puerto Rican life—on the island and the mainland—continue to shape the diaspora's perceptions of its own rights and status in the U.S. Because of the continued ties of migrants and many of their children to the island but also because of the constant flow of people, culture, ideas, and money between Puerto Rico and the U.S., island politics and economics are often part of mainland activism. Critical island issues find echo in the diaspora and many activists, both pro-statehood and pro-independence, use their position within U.S. political and other institutions to lobby for their views. By the 1980s, these activists increasingly converged in their perception that Puerto Rico's political status was untenable and needed to be resolved. Ideology might separate nationalists, *independentistas*, statehooders, and supporters of the status quo, but often these differences are set aside when major crises affect the island.[30]

Among the most important issues unifying island and mainland activism in the 1980s and 1990s was the movement to push the U.S. Navy out of Vieques island, part of the Puerto Rican archipelago. Two thirds of Vieques was turned into a naval base during World War II, in conjunction with the construction of the massive Roosevelt Roads naval base on the main island. Starting in the 1970s, independence, socialist, and nationalist organizations joined together with local people, especially fishermen, to end the Navy's military activities and occupation of land. When a civilian worker was killed in 1999 by an accidental bomb drop, the movement to get the Navy out of Vieques intensified, with significant participation of the diaspora as well as many U.S. politicians, who put pressure on the Navy and the Democratic party. The Navy's complete withdrawal began in 2001 and ended in 2003 with the return of both Roosevelt Roads and Vieques to Puerto Rican and U.S. Parks Service ownership.[31]

Community Building: Anti-Gentrification Campaigns

Alongside the intensifying focus of Puerto Rican leaders on city and state politics and national policy debates, activism at the community level still defined the political engagement of most Puerto Ricans in the 1980s. Since the early decades of migration from the island, Puerto Ricans in the U.S. had struggled over access to housing; and although most residents of Puerto Rican communities by 1980 had lived in the U.S. for at least a generation, making them less vulnerable to exploitative landlords, the scarcity of decent and affordable housing remained one of the most central problems for Puerto Ricans in urban areas. The safety and stability of a family's housing situation had always depended on its income and the breadwinners' employment status; discrimination was also a factor. But starting in the 1980s, gentrification added a new dimension to many Puerto Ricans' housing troubles.[32]

The pressures of gentrification—spurred by developers' motivation for steeper profits in a deregulating market—were especially intense for residents in New York City's Lower East Side, because of its location in lower Manhattan near high-rent residential and office real estate markets. Puerto Rican community leaders there had worked throughout the 1970s and 1980s to create their own tenants' organizations and collaborated with other groups whose mission was to improve housing in poor neighborhoods. Along the way, the convergence of housing activism and Nuyorican cultural production generated a cohesive identity for the community that became widely known as "Loisaida," the Puerto Rican Lower East Side. Tenants' associations managed to rehabilitate a number of city-owned buildings in the 1970s and by the early 1980s created a bulwark against developers who sought to capitalize on skyrocketing real estate values in an impoverished neighborhood. In the spring of 1986, Mayor Koch—a cantankerous independent politician who for the most part had a contentious relationship with Puerto Rican leaders—went so far as to proclaim a "Loisaida Day," recognizing the "value added" to the community after local housing organizations renovated several decrepit buildings on Avenue C.[33]

But gentrification was usually a more powerful force than community action and cultural pride. By the 1990s, it had transformed Loisaida, a ghetto blighted by old housing, burnt out buildings and open-air heroin markets, into what developers began marketing as "Alphabet City," a trendy neighborhood that was primarily white. Nearly all the area's low income residents, including elderly eastern European immigrants along with their Puerto Rican neighbors, got pushed out; only the public housing residents on Avenue D remained as a reminder of the ethnic and class character of the neighborhood since the 1950s. Christadora House, a landmark building on Avenue B built as a settlement house for immigrants in 1928, became emblematic of the gentrification process when it was turned into expensive condominiums in 1988, "a conspicuous symbol of gentrification" amidst the still-blighted neighborhood. Residents who knew the building's history recognized its symbolic value, not just as part of the community's immigrant story but also in its second act as a Lower East Side base for Black Panthers, who rented space in the building (by then owned by the city) in the 1960s. For years after the condominiums were completed, Lower East Side activists staged regular anti-gentrification protests and confrontations with police across the street in Tompkins Square park.[34]

In the South Bronx, after two decades of landlord destruction, arson, and neglect by city officials, the remaining residents of the neighborhood, a majority of them Puerto Rican, received relief from the city when Mayor Koch invested nearly a billion dollars of federal and city funds in rebuilding large parts of the area. Father Louis Gigante, an Italian American priest with strong support in the Puerto Rican community, played an important role in the rebuilding through his remarkably successful organization, South East Bronx Community Organization (SEBCO), which he had founded in 1968. By 1981, SEBCO had built or refurbished 1,100 housing units in the Hunts Point area of the South Bronx. Demand for housing in the burnt-out South Bronx was intense; when SEBCO completed a new development of federally subsidized housing in 1981, as many as 4,000 people lined up to apply for 236 units. Participation in the rebuilding also took the form of collaborative organizing among neighborhood residents. A group of neighbors calling themselves "Los Desperados" organized in the Crotona section of the South Bronx to respond to the abandonment, crime, and arson in their community. They reclaimed housing for 1,000 people throughout the 1980s, and with support from Mayor Koch, collaborated with other citywide groups to rehabilitate additional housing.[35]

Nos Quedamos ("We Stay"), another activist group based in the South Bronx, fought for similar goals. Led by Yolanda García and supported by Bronx borough president Fernando Ferrer (elected in 1987 and the second Puerto Rican to hold that office), Nos Quedamos pressured the city to allow them to build community gardens in abandoned lots and transfer ownership of abandoned buildings for rehabilitation. After years of planning and organizing, and continuous demands by Ferrer for more funding and faster work, the group led the construction of hundreds of units of housing in the Melrose section of the South Bronx.[36] By the 1990s, entire burnt out areas had turned back into stable working class neighborhoods, with 20,000 apartments and nearly 5,000 houses refurbished or newly built and offered for rent or sale to mixed income residents. Puerto Ricans could count themselves among the "core of resilient people" who stayed and "proved the place was worth saving," as journalist Robert Worth described the South Bronx's renovators.[37]

Similar struggles over affordable housing and the cultural and ethnic character of neighborhoods played out in Spanish Harlem, *El Barrio*, where gentrification and commercial displacement slowly changed the cost of housing and the character of the business district. Market forces as well as lack of city action led to increased rents as physical conditions improved and new, mixed income housing replaced the burnt-out shells and empty lots that dotted the neighborhood before the 1990s. Anthropologist Arlene Davila has documented the efforts of community leaders to secure more attention from city agencies and to steer commercial development towards more inclusive models that would not displace the local poor Puerto Rican and Mexican communities.[38]

Local leaders and community groups in Brooklyn's Williamsburg neighborhood also confronted demographic change and gentrification in the 1980s and worked to protect their communities from the economic fallout. Los Sures was a group founded in the 1970s to promote low income housing and tenant organizing; as gentrification intensified in the 1990s, Los Sures created additional programs to support the community, including senior centers and a food pantry, and collaborated closely with nearby Hasidic organizations in developing jobs and housing for the poor of both communities. The absence of opportunities for young people in Williamsburg inspired former Young Lord Luis Garden Acosta to create El Puente in 1982, a center for education, health, and anti-gang programs that quickly became a national model for youth social service provision. As the gentrification of Williamsburg began in the 1990s, El Puente extended its work to the development of low cost housing as well. By the early 2000s, Los Sures and El Puente, along with many other community organizations, became community development corporations a formal classification that allowed them access to government and foundation support and recognition by city agencies.[39]

Puerto Ricans in other cities, including Chicago, Boston, and Philadelphia, engaged in similar activism, generating notable pushback against the forces of gentrification in their communities in the 1980s. After the Puerto Rican Humboldt Park area in Chicago lost thousands of units of housing in the 1980s, pressure from community groups spurred Mayor Harold Washington to call for an investigation of exclusion of Latinos from Chicago Housing Authority facilities. Anthropologist Gina Pérez has chronicled how, as part of these efforts, the newly formed Latinos United sued the Chicago Housing Authority and federal Department of Housing and Urban Development for discrimination in 1989. Other local efforts in the early 1990s included the creation of the "Paseo Boricua," a corridor along Humboldt Park's main thoroughfare, Division Street, that combined public space with symbols of Puerto Rican pride.[40]

In Boston, leaders of a South End tenants' organization, Inquilinos Boricuas en Acción, won financial support from a national housing organization to rebuild several blocks of residential and commercial properties in the 1990s. In Puerto Rican Philadelphia, the major force in housing activism was the Tenant Action Group (TAG), founded by Puerto Rican and Black leaders in the mid-1970s. TAG gained strength in the 1980s as it focused on political strategies—lobbying city council and state representatives, pressuring the city's Licenses and Inspections office—to take seriously the concerns and complaints of low income Philadelphia residents.[41] Similar organizing efforts animated Puerto Rican and mixed Latino communities in cities all around the U.S. in the 1980s, campaigns not only to solve concrete problems but also to open space for expressions of Puerto Rican working class identity and culture. By the 1980s, the struggling Puerto Rican neighborhoods in many cities were dotted with community gardens and DIY parks created by community residents from the empty lots left by razed abandoned buildings, often with official approval by city agencies. Community groups also erected *casitas*, or "little houses," built in the style of rural Puerto Rican dwellings—"icons of the Puerto Rican past"—and designed to be informal community gathering places. The result of these projects, the literal building of community, was enduring networks of small, community-controlled spaces, many of which remain proud symbols of small scale local activism by Puerto Ricans and their neighbors.[42]

Work and Economic Life: Catastrophe and Its Explanations

The most important driver of the political work of Puerto Rican leaders in the 1980s was the ongoing economic struggle of the poor within Puerto Rican communities. In a decade of triumphant conservatism and Reagan's "trickle-down" economic policy, major shifts in the American economy wound up playing a far more important role than electoral politics in determining how poor Puerto Ricans fared. The study of Puerto Rican poverty became a central focus of social science scholars in these years. Most analysts failed to notice how the emphasis on ethnic and racial categorizations obscured the staggering impact of collapsing urban economies, with dire consequences for all working class people.

The debate over the causes of Puerto Rican poverty was comparative, examining statistical measures of Puerto Ricans' lives in relation to those of other populations. At the start of the 1980s, Puerto Ricans ranked at the bottom of all other racial and ethnic groups in terms of income levels and labor participation rates.[43] By the mid-1980s, data showed that Puerto Ricans were faring steadily worse than other Hispanics—Mexican-Americans, Cuban-Americans, and Dominican-Americans—in macro-economic measures. This trend had begun to emerge during the 1970s; at the national level, Puerto Ricans with incomes under the federal poverty level increased from 30% to 37% between 1970 and 1980. Only 55% of Puerto Rican men and women in the U.S. were active in the labor force in 1980, compared to a national average labor force participation rate of 62%. Those figures worsened as industrial restructuring continued to create an urban "rustbelt" of closed factories and warehouses; the remaining industrial jobs were those that were low wage with no prospects for advancement. Industrial decline produced a massive displacement of Puerto Ricans (and other Latinos) throughout the urban Northeast as people tried to follow the disappearing promise of industrial jobs and greater economic security.[44]

Tracking outcomes for the group as a whole, these trends all but erased the gains made by U.S.-born Puerto Ricans who in the 1960s had made their way into the higher wage, skilled or white collar sectors of the service economy.

The early 1980s brought even worse numbers, when the Reagan recession of 1981–84 destroyed more jobs, lowered wages, and raised national unemployment rates to nearly 11%; for Puerto Ricans, unemployment reached over 20% and was even higher for Puerto Rican youth. In addition, massive cuts in social and educational spending at all levels of government reduced opportunities and the safety net available to the urban poor.[45]

Urban youth found themselves especially unprepared for the shifts in the economy, as their education—already compromised by the problems of poverty and failing schools—did not prepare them for entry into the growing areas of the economy like construction, insurance, real estate and finance—sectors that were also known for high levels of discrimination towards minorities.[46] Even for adults with workforce experience, many of these jobs were unattainable because they all had significant training requirements. The structure of welfare benefits encouraged low income young women to remain unmarried and remove male incomes from their household as a strategy to maintain welfare benefits for children, while stagnant wages and childcare costs encouraged many to reject minimum wage jobs. The persistent flow of migrants to and from Puerto Rico made tracking poverty more difficult and distorted the statistics for long-time residents of the U.S., as recent migrants consistently landed the lowest-paying jobs and took years to improve their conditions.

There were some improvements in income during the second half of 1980s, but in 1989, as in 1979, a third of employed Puerto Rican men earned incomes below the poverty level while real hourly wages increased only 3%. According to one labor economist's analysis, "The progress of the second part of the 1980s . . . had little effect on [Puerto Ricans'] decade-long economic position."[47] This new crisis of poverty, which hit women and more recent migrants from the island especially hard, produced multiple policy and grassroots responses, some of which would take years to yield any results. For activists and scholars, the worsening poverty of Puerto Ricans was deemed to be not only an economic problem but a civil rights crisis.

Journalists, policymakers, and scholars, including those working in the field of Puerto Rican Studies, increasingly focused on the downward socioeconomic slide of many Puerto Ricans during the 1980s. As economic suffering intensified in urban ghettos in the early 1980s—along with its attendant social costs, including drug abuse, drug-related violence, and incarceration—scholars began to debate whether a permanent "underclass" existed in the U.S. that had completely lost access to work. The debate was bitter, with the most vehement disagreement on the question of whether structural causes or individual behavioral factors—related to the so-called culture of poverty—should be blamed for the apparent intransigence of poverty in communities that seemed to experience only downward mobility. Two decades of steady economic hardship for Puerto Ricans in particular inspired scholars to ask whether there were any self-reinforcing disadvantages keeping Puerto Ricans locked in extreme poverty.

Scholars and commentators on the right relied on culture-based explanations of poverty and failed to consider the decline of local economies and schools in the Northeast and the effects of major losses in manufacturing jobs. In 1991, President Reagan's staff director of the U.S. Commission on Civil Rights, Linda Chávez, added a new degree of rancor to the debate with her book *Out of the Barrio: Toward a New Politics of Hispanic Assimilation*, which described Puerto Ricans as a "tragic and curious exception" to the growing successes of Latinos as a group nationwide. Citing statistics on welfare dependency and low marriage rates, and making a fuzzy case for a causal relationship between them, Chávez posited that it was Puerto Ricans' access to social benefits and anti-poverty programs, rather than the structural disadvantages of migration, poor education, and discrimination that caused their suffering. "Puerto Ricans have been smothered by entitlements," she asserted, "which should serve notice as a warning to other Hispanics." Chávez concluded that the Puerto Rican "exception" to Latino upward mobility was caused by cultural deficiencies of the Puerto Rican poor. Scholars who had studied the growth in poverty and the labor market problems of Puerto Ricans responded with a vigorous rebuttal to Chávez's flawed methods and culturalist blame-the-victim arguments.[48]

A more productive debate took place among scholars and policy analysts who noted with concern the increased poverty of large segments of the Puerto Rican community and tried various approaches to explain these dramatic increases. Sociologist Marta Tienda, a leading liberal voice in the "underclass debate," argued that "underclass" status was best understood as a function of long-term labor force withdrawal. She found that rates of Puerto Rican men's "chronic detachment" from the labor market were much higher and accelerating faster than that of Cuban and Mexican American men. Other scholars noted that much of the increase in poverty was explained by the continued arrival of low income workers from the island itself, where cyclical fluctuations and the harsher effects of the 1983 recession boosted emigration. When recent emigrants were excluded from the data, the poverty rate for Puerto Ricans was much lower, with significantly lower rates (nearly half) for U.S. born second generation Puerto Ricans and long-established migrants who arrived before 1970.[49]

In a field that by the 1990s grew to include hundreds of books and articles, scholars explored a variety of explanatory approaches. Economist Andrés Torres noted that Puerto Ricans were behind African Americans in the acquisition of federal, state, and local public sector jobs, especially white collar jobs that provided a path out of poverty and were somewhat immune to the decline in industrial employment. By the 1950s Puerto Ricans held postal, police, and civil servant jobs, but their numbers did not compare with African American gains in public sector employment, which had picked up momentum since the 1940s. A late start and language and educational barriers kept more Puerto Ricans in New York from entering public sector jobs after the city's recovery from its fiscal crisis of the mid-1970s.[50]

Most scholars agreed that the crisis of deindustrialization and the larger problems of the industrial cities of the Northeast hit women the hardest and pushed them out of the labor market. Puerto Rican women's participation in the workforce between 1950 and 1980 shifted from the highest measure among all racial and ethnic groups to one of the lowest in 30 years. There were many reasons why older women stopped working. Some retired, while many former factory workers found themselves ill-prepared for the demands of a white-collar economy that often discriminated against dark-skinned people with accents and working class origins.[51] Explanations for low incomes and unemployment among younger people pointed to the crisis-ridden urban school systems of New York, Newark, Philadelphia, Chicago, and other declining urban centers that scarcely prepared students for the new labor market or for higher education; no longer could they count on a living wage at a nearby factory, as many of their parents had. Additional challenges—residential segregation, early pregnancy, and the fact that welfare benefits were more accessible than decent employment—compounded the likelihood of long-term poverty for young adults. In summarizing the lessons of two decades of poverty studies, sociologist Hector Cordero Guzmán asserted that, in order for social scientists to explain the role of racial, ethnic, and class differences in the lives of poor people, they needed to move beyond analyzing "individual level attributes" (educational attainment, labor force participation, and wages), and look at "social disparities in material and cultural resources, differences in institutional practices, and differences in the structural level conditions that set the parameters under which individuals operate."[52]

Given the alarming increase in the poverty rate and the larger urban crisis, the absence of coordinated policies directed specifically at the urban poor amounted to a tragic failure. Federal anti-poverty programs were all but dead; job training programs like the Federal Comprehensive Employment and Training Act (1973–82) and the Job Training Partnership Act (1982–98) were underfunded and mostly ineffective. Confirmation of this neglect lies in its principal exception: food supplementation became the most critical federal intervention for the urban poor. At the state level, policy responses were also few but provided minimal relief with health services and low cost housing. Even liberal governors agreed that government did little to change the larger pattern. In 1985 New York Governor Cuomo convened a commission that issued a report confirming the dire conditions of urban minority populations, but the effort yielded no policies.[53] Puerto Ricans were left to respond to the crisis on their own and through their own efforts.

Work and Economic Life: Recovery through Labor Activism and Education

When the Center for Puerto Rican Studies founder Frank Bonilla co-authored "A Wealth of Poor: Puerto Ricans in the New Economic Order" in 1981, the prospects for most working class Puerto Ricans were bleak and the poverty crisis was creating havoc in their urban communities. According to Bonilla, Puerto Ricans were trapped between the structural changes of a capitalist economy and a shrinking welfare state. Bonilla's approach was useful as a frame for understanding the flow of people from the island and how crises in the U.S. affected the working poor. But in focusing on a structuralist framework, he too suffered from blind spots, merely hinting at strategies developed by Puerto Ricans themselves to recover from poverty and overcome the obstacles to their social mobility. As in previous decades, these efforts depended on the public sector, educational improvements, and the labor movement, and they relied on collective mobilizations as well as family-based efforts to combat economic insecurity. The recovery, in other words, would emerge from the diverse efforts of workers and their families as they reoriented themselves in a changing economic landscape.[54]

Bucking the worst of Bonilla's predictions in "A Wealth of Poor," Puerto Ricans did begin to experience a partial recovery from the extreme poverty they had experienced in the 1970s and 1980s. Puerto Ricans' poverty rate dropped from its peak of nearly 40% in the mid-1980s to 32% in 1990 and achieved its greatest decline to 25.8% by 1999.[55] The sources of these slow but significant improvements were varied. A growing economy brought significant gains in employment and incomes, which in turn helped bolster rates of high school and college graduation and para-professional training. The economic growth during the Clinton presidency (1993–2001) created favorable conditions for employment, wages, and social welfare spending; growth also improved the island's employment levels, which produced a decline in migration.[56] Public sector jobs recovered significantly, as did public sector unions. A growing service economy for the high-income urban demographic (which was now moving back into city centers) added additional job opportunities, especially in New York City.[57] During the years of sharp decline in the industrial economy of New York, New Jersey, and Connecticut, thousands of U.S.-born Puerto Ricans had moved to states with more job opportunities and better housing; and migrants from the island were also settling in more varied mainland locations with growing economies, in cities like Tampa, Los Angeles, Houston, and New Orleans.

The growing economy helped with Puerto Ricans' recovery, but so did the efforts of Puerto Ricans and their allies who continued to work with labor and civil rights organizations to improve their lot. For labor leaders in service, public sector, and health related unions in particular this growth created opportunities for organizing campaigns and wage improvements, especially in New York and New Jersey. Unions like the Service Employees International Union (SEIU), the New York Transit Workers Union, the Buildings Services Union, the Union of Needletrades, Industrial, and Textile Employees (UNITE), United Electrical, Radio and Machine Workers and the International Brotherhood of Electrical Workers (IBEW) continued to be important for tens of thousands of Puerto Ricans because of their continued struggle to gain better wages.

Latino membership, leadership, and employment in these unions increased dramatically during the 1990s. Latinos at this point comprised more than 10% of the nation's largest union, the American Federation of Labor–Congress of Industrial Organizations (AFL-CIO), and fought national AFL-CIO leaders for greater involvement in union leadership. This resurgence was perhaps strongest in New York City, and boosted the efforts of labor leaders like Eddie de Jesús, a longtime activist and former Young Lord, who established a labor task force through the National Council for Puerto Rican Rights to help consolidate the Puerto Rican presence in the labor movement. The career of Dennis Rivera, who became president of the National Health Care Workers' Union (Local 1199) in 1989, exemplifies the powerful possibilities of union leadership positions, as well as the importance of healthcare unions for Puerto Rican workers since the 1980s. Rivera migrated from the island in 1977 and worked as an organizer in Local 1199, also joining the National Council for Puerto Rican Rights. Under Rivera's leadership, the union improved wages in hospitals by 140% (the membership was 20% Latino in the early 1980s).[58] By the end of the 1990s, Puerto Ricans worked together with Mexican Americans, Central Americans, Dominicans, Cubans, and others to build new unions that merged together the shrinking membership of older labor organizations and fought to extend membership to workers in the increasingly low wage service economy.

Anti-discrimination advocacy work was also part of the story of the gains achieved by Puerto Ricans in the labor market in the 1980s and 1990s—despite declining federal support for work equity lawsuits since the Reagan administration. In New Jersey, a Puerto Rican lawyer was named in 1995 to direct the state's anti-discrimination office, which handled thousands of work and housing complaints yearly. More lawsuits were led by the principal Latino civil rights organization in the Northeast, LatinoJustice PRLDEF (formerly the Puerto Rican Legal Defense and Education Fund). The emergence of Puerto Rican law firms that work on employment, equity, and anti-discrimination cases also added to the growing network of advocacy for Puerto Rican workers. [59]

For a community that originated overwhelmingly in patterns of working class migration, access to education has proved to be the most critical path for Puerto Ricans' gains in mobility, security, and equity in the workplace. Gains were slow to accumulate, but high school graduation rates for Puerto Ricans, as well as most students served by underperforming urban schools in impoverished communities, improved steadily during the late 1980s and 1990s, especially for Puerto Ricans born in the U.S. as opposed to on the island. Educational attainment, a major predictor of income levels, increased from an average of 9.84 years in 1979 to 10.48 years in 1985 and 11.14 years in 1989. Between 1980 and 2000 the percentage of Puerto Ricans with some sort of post-high school education tripled, from 15.6% to 36%, while the percentage of adults without a high school education declined from 60% to 27%. These slow-paced but steady changes, marked in many areas by family movement towards school districts perceived as better, have improved the overall economic gains made by Puerto Ricans since the 1980s.[60]

Puerto Ricans' gains in the higher education arena went beyond access to degrees and social mobility. Students who pushed their colleges and universities to establish programs in Puerto Rican Studies in the late 1960s were not just interested in studying their own history; they also wanted the opportunity to study with sympathetic and supportive faculty in what were often alienating institutional settings. These goals matured during the 1980s, when larger numbers of Puerto Rican youth began pursuing college degrees, especially at public universities. On many campuses during the 1980s and 1990s, Puerto Rican activism combined with the emerging presence of other Latinos, especially Dominican and Mexican students, to continue to press for access. During this period, many programs and departments that had been founded in the 1970s as "Puerto Rican Studies" transitioned to become more inclusive of all Latinos in their curricula, students, and faculty.

Increasing the presence of Puerto Rican and other Latino faculty and staff in the academy has been a key dimension of student activist demands since the 1980s and 1990s, especially within the public universities of the Northeast. However, even at campuses of the City University of New York (CUNY)—the university system with the largest population of Puerto Rican students in the country—results were inconsistent and tended to concentrate Puerto Rican faculty in a small number of ethnic studies departments. Sociologist Felipe Pimentel directed an effort in the 2000s to pressure the CUNY administration to hire more Latino faculty as numbers had stagnated. His data shows that while the number of Puerto Ricans with PhDs increased and their presence in the academy at the national level grew significantly between the 1980s and 2000, the number of Puerto Rican faculty had declined within the CUNY system since the mid-1970s. With pressure from students, politicians, and various community leaders, the chancellor responded by creating a special hiring initiative that yielded modest results at the college level and a negligible impact at the graduate level.[61] Similar controversies played out in other public university systems where Puerto Ricans constituted a significant proportion of the student body, including Rutgers, the University of Connecticut, and the State University of New York.

Police Abuse and Community Response

The urban working class communities in which many Puerto Ricans lived had long suffered from blight and decay, gang violence and petty crime. During the 1980s and 1990s, with expanding illegal drug markets that emerged with the epidemic of crack cocaine and increasingly violent crime, conditions in these communities reached a crisis point. Police departments responded with aggressive "zero-tolerance" campaigns, which tended to heighten police brutality and produced a spike in civil rights violations; a related problem was the easy drug money that corrupted hundreds of officers and even entire police precincts. Amid the growing urban crisis, regular incidents of police violence in Black and Latino neighborhoods—most notably in large post-industrial cities with "majority minority" communities, but also in smaller cities and towns—brought increasing national attention to the issue. The Rodney King case, involving the brutal beating of an African American taxi driver in Los Angeles in 1991 and then the acquittal of the four officers involved, sparked a dramatic and deadly riot in 1992 that garnered international media coverage. In cases involving Puerto Ricans, swift reactions from Latino or Puerto Rican coalitions and civil rights organizations emphasized the community's long history of responding to police abuse.[62] Below, we offer a case study of Puerto Ricans' increasingly forceful response to police abuse in New York City, which joined with the chorus of voices around the nation demanding reform and legal action.

One of the incidents that served as a catalyst for the growing Puerto Rican community response during the 1980s was the August 1979 police killing of Luis Baez, a mentally ill man who spoke only Spanish. The community responded with large protests against police abuse led by an alliance of Black and Latino leaders. As was often the case, the police response to protest created more conflict. Leaders of PRLDEF and other civil rights organizations considered lawsuits especially after the police attacked with their cars, threw bottles, and aimed guns at peaceful demonstrators. Activists asked the Federal Department of Justice to probe the New York police department's patterns of abuse and civil rights violations, but a local grand jury refused to indict the policemen involved in the shooting, and FBI and federal civil rights investigations resulted in no charges.[63]

In 1981, motivated by the increase in violence and rights violations in Puerto Rican communities around the country, activists in New York City founded the National Congress for Puerto Rican Rights (NCPRR), with early leadership by former members of the Puerto Rican Socialist Party and former Young Lords Juan González and Richie Pérez. Although police brutality was the primary issue motivating the NCPRR, the group also participated in the 1983 March on Washington (the 20th anniversary of the historic 1963 March on Washington for Jobs and Freedom), in demonstrations against apartheid in South Africa, and against U.S. intervention in Central America throughout the 1980s. By 1983 the level of conflict with the police in New York City led to Congressional hearings on police abuse, which drew 500 people and dozens of testimonies, including participants from PRLDEF, the NCPRR, and the NAACP. Mayor Ed Koch and his police commissioner dismissed the complaints as exaggerated and politically motivated or claimed they had already been dealt with. Within a few years, the NCPRR opened chapters in several cities and became a prominent voice in debates about police brutality, lobbying for the suspension of abusive police officers and mobilizing public outrage over police shootings. [64]

Despite these responses, horrific incidents continued. One prominent case taken up by the NCPRR was the police killing of an unarmed 14-year-old, José Lebrón, in Brooklyn in 1990. Less than a year later, five police officers were indicted and found not guilty after they beat and choked an unarmed car theft suspect in Queens. Police claimed the suspect, Federico Pereira, aged 21, died from a cocaine-induced frenzy, but the state's medical examiner declared he had been by choked to death. Pereira's mother offered a wrenching description of the injustice:

> This was well orchestrated, a set up. I don't trust the judicial system, and those police officers who taunted me and called me names, they were delighted a person of color was killed. But what hurt me most were the Latino and African American cops who cheered right along with the white racist cops—that hurt me even more . . . These cops know that they have free rein to kill people of color and that they will never have to make restitution for their crimes—you can compare our police departments throughout this nation with the death squads in Central or South America. There's no true justice here for people of color.[65]

Two months later, when the largely-Puerto Rican Hispanic Society of the NYPD invited Pereira's stepfather, a popular musician, to perform at their annual scholarship dinner, the predominantly white Patrolman's Benevolent Union (PBU) decided to boycott the dinner. Hispanic Society leaders were careful to not brand the entire PBU as racists but noted that their membership included "devout racists." One leader expressed to a reporter his "surprise" that the federal Department of Justice had taken years to review police brutality complaints.[66]

Conflicts continued through the 1990s, with police shootings only the most visible part of the problem; residents of many neighborhoods reported feeling under siege by both street crime and the police. Responding to another shooting incident in 1992, New York resident Juan Gutiérrez complained to journalists that "the police consider this a drug slum . . . It's not like that. A lot of people sell drugs here. A lot of people live here and work here too. But they treat everybody the same. They have no respect." Another local businessman suggested that "they don't care about innocent people." The statements came on the heels of the police killing of Jose Uviles, a factory worker from Puerto Rico who was shot after he raised his hands to surrender after having stolen a car. When police tried to break up a memorial procession in his honor, some of his Bushwick, Brooklyn neighbors resisted by burning two police cars and setting dumpsters on fire and firing bullets in the air.[67]

Perhaps the most prominent case of these years was the killing of Anthony Baez (no relation to Luis Baez), who died as the result of an illegal chokehold while in police custody. Baez, a 29-year-old visiting from Florida, was playing football with his brothers in front of his family home in the Bronx on a December night in 1994 when he got into an altercation with police after the football hit a parked police car. Baez's brother was arrested during the confrontation that ensued, and when Baez protested his brother's arrest, he was restrained by Officer Francis Livoti, who put Baez in a chokehold until he was unconscious. Despite evidence that Baez, face down on the floor and handcuffed, could not breathe, police allowed him to lie unconscious for 15 minutes, ignoring pleas by his father for medical assistance. The judge concurred with Baez's father that his son had been "treated like a piece of meat" when shoved unconscious into a police car and allowed to die from trauma to his larynx and lack of oxygen.[68]

For years the Baez family demanded justice, without success. For Baez's father the problem was that

> when you tell police you know your rights, that's a problem, especially if you're Latino. They think because we are Latino we are not intelligent people. But my son, Tony, was a well-educated man . . . My kids all got education, and they treat us like criminals!

The Baez family asserted they were let down not just by city officials in general but by the Puerto Rican community's leaders and politicians. One of the few allies they found was the NCPRR, which devised a strategy of pressure, confrontation, and public shaming through two failed trials against Livoti.[69]

Finally, after a trial marred by police perjury, Officer Livoti was convicted for violating Anthony Baez's civil rights and sentenced to seven years in a federal prison. The city paid $3 million to the Baez family in compensation.[70] Even the *New York Times* agreed that the Livoti case was not an aberration, as claimed by Mayor Giuliani and the police commissioner, but provided evidence of "how violent behavior has been tolerated by the department's top echelons." This admission came after police commissioner Safir fired 106 officers for brutality, theft, and corruption. These practices led to multiple lawsuits over civil rights violations resulting in $87 million in payments between 1990 and 1995. Years later, Mayor Giuliani proposed naming a street after Anthony Baez, calling his killing "a terrible thing . . . [that] should never have happened."[71]

By the time Livoti killed Baez, the police abuse crisis of the 1980s and early 1990s had already led to intense pressure for a civilian review board, which Black and Puerto Rican activists had been calling for since the late 1950s. David Dinkins, New York's first Black mayor, elected in 1990, finally approved the Civilian Review Board (CRB) in 1993. Opposition by police to the creation of the board was swift and nearly unanimous. Thousands of officers, backed by the police union, demonstrated at City Hall, blocking traffic and shouting racial epithets; Rudolph Giuliani (elected mayor a year later, but at that time in private law practice) participated in the protest.

On the overall response to the creation of the CRB, Human Rights Watch reported that "police protested violently and engaged in actions, according to a police department report, that were unruly, mean-spirited and perhaps criminal." A few years later, the CRB's director, a Puerto Rican civil rights lawyer named Hector Soto, resigned from the position, citing lack of support from the mayor's office and the board's ineffectiveness. In 2001, Republican mayor Rudolph Giuliani—who had campaigned on a law-and-order platform—would acknowledge these problems and the lack of public confidence in the NYPD by turning the CRB into an independent civilian agency.[72]

Less than two years after the creation of the Civilian Review Board, another major case of police violence gripped Puerto Rican New York. Two robbery suspects, Anthony Rosario and Hilton Vega, were killed by 28 police bullets—all shots to their backs—inside a Bronx apartment. For nearly 15 years, Anthony Rosario's mother, Margarita Rosario, pursued prosecution of the police officers responsible. Through the press and in public forums, Ms. Rosario demanded explanations and prosecutions. Vigils and protests were held and murals were mounted; Rosario and her supporters were dismissed by the police commissioner as "a bunch of fools." A grand jury refused to indict but the Civilian Review Board found that the detectives had used unnecessary and excessive force, with evidence and testimony indicating that Rosario and Vega were shot once they surrendered and were face down on the floor. But, due to the political climate of the Giuliani administration—which was openly hostile to complaints about abusive policing in poor neighborhoods—the city in the end settled a civil lawsuit for $1.1 million in damages, avoiding public scrutiny and further investigation of the shootings.[73]

In these years of Giuliani's law-and-order offensive, hardline "zero-tolerance" policing meant that even minor crimes or nonviolent drug-related violations were treated as predictors of greater criminal offenses. This meant that Black and Latino working class neighborhoods were policed in a way that criminalized most young men, producing constant harassment by police. Despite the fact that crime rates were declining rapidly by the mid-1990s, both nationally and across New York City, the Giuliani administration adhered to its highly aggressive policing tactics. In late 1995, a few months after the shootings of Rosario and Vega, *El Diario-La Prensa* noted a 30% increase in the arrest of children and youth, mostly for minor offenses. With another headline pronouncing "*más brutalidad*" (more brutality), *El Diario-La Prensa* also announced the worsening of police abuse complaints, which had increased 32% in the first half of 1995. In one case, a Puerto Rican police officer reported he had been subjected to civil rights violations by other police in his own house in Staten Island. The situation in New York became so bad that Amnesty International carried out a special investigation and issued a harsh review of the violent practices of the NYPD and its failures to discipline abusive officers.[74]

For decades, Puerto Ricans and their neighbors in poor communities had suffered from aggressive and violent policing in addition to the crime and poverty that surrounded them. (Indeed, violent treatment by police was something that Puerto Rican migrants complained about as far back as the 1920s; one man, Félix Loperana, interviewed by an oral historian in the 1970s, asserted that "the police were the first who discriminated against us.") But the problem of police brutality took on a new urgency by the late 1980s and 1990s, exacerbated by the growing problems of drugs and gun violence. Even after significant declines in the drug trade and violent crime compared to the previous decade, the *New York Times* noted in 1998 the "continuing fear of police brutality in black and Hispanic neighborhoods."[75]

Hampered by the stigma of living in crime-ridden areas, relatives and activists often had difficulty in their pursuit of justice in individual cases. But, as these advocates generated an increasingly loud and visible protest movement against police brutality, they were joined by civil rights organizations and leaders. In 1999, the National Council of Puerto Rican Rights achieved a major gain in the campaign against police brutality when it won a lawsuit against the NYPD's elite Street Crimes Unit regarding its "stop and frisk policy." This case would turn out to be the first big victory in the legal challenge to the police department's practices of racial profiling, which would eventually be outlawed after a federal judge ruled them to be a violation of civil rights. Although the problem of police brutality may not have improved materially due to the increased media attention or to a series of legal victories related to racial profiling, Puerto Rican leaders and activists who had been working on police abuse issues since the 1960s (or even earlier) were moving toward the possibility for real change, in New York and around the U.S..[76]

Conclusion

The urban crisis that began in the 1970s and worsened during the 1980s resulted from familiar problems—poverty and unemployment, decaying housing and neglect by landlords and city officials, police abuse and violence—the impact of which was intensified by an expanded illegal drug trade and a rollback in public services during a severe recession followed by Reagan's austerity policies directed at the poor. Despite the seemingly endless challenges, residents of these neighborhoods pursued the same aspirations for a secure life that had motivated early communities of Puerto Rican migrants in New York City in the 1920s, and that continued to motivate all the later generations of Puerto Ricans that lived and worked all over the U.S. By the 1980s and 1990s, Puerto Rican activists and leaders had amassed decades of experience in advocacy for their communities and had created large networks capable of mobilizing support from many Puerto Rican and Latino communities, along with other non-Latino allies. Particularly with the help of a handful of national organizations created between the 1960s and 1980s, Puerto Ricans had achieved much greater recognition and some concrete legal and policy changes in a number of key areas, including voting rights, affirmative action, labor union leadership, educational equality and access, and campaigns against police brutality.

Another significant if less visible accomplishment in this era was the growing presence of Puerto Rican intellectuals and academics poised to gain a louder voice in the public sphere. Scholars connected to the field of Puerto Rican Studies had created archives and libraries to document the history of the Puerto Rican diaspora in the U.S., assembling personal and organizational papers and photographic collections donated by Puerto Ricans around the country. Challenging the limitations of mainstream disciplines, these scholars made pioneering contributions to understanding a variety of issues specific to Puerto Ricans, including colonial labor migration, bilingualism, and the history of U.S. colonial policy. Whereas few mainstream scholars had paid any attention to their work in the 1970s or even the 1980s, by the 1990s, Puerto Rican scholars began to get more credit for their contributions to social science, history, and cultural studies. Puerto Ricans now participated not just in national debates about issues concerning "the underclass" and "the culture of poverty," but also developed new intellectual understandings of issues like globalization, colonialism, and transnationalism. By the 1990s, Puerto Rican Studies scholars had built new connections to the broader field of Latino Studies, bringing their research into dialogue with scholars from related but distinct cultural and intellectual traditions.

In addition to forging greater connections with other Latino groups academically, Puerto Ricans also began to conceptualize connections with Latinos more broadly at the community and political levels. In both community- and national-level organizations, Puerto Rican professionals and activists found themselves serving an increasingly diverse (and often undocumented) Latino immigrant population, especially Mexicans and Central Americans. In Connecticut, New York, and New Jersey, where decades of activism by Puerto Ricans yielded significant gains, organizations like the Puerto Rican Family Institute and the Puerto Rican Action Committee continued to engage with the new Spanish-speaking immigrant populations, often adjusting their focus to match the needs of the new communities. PRLDEF changed its name in the early 2000s to LatinoJustice-PRLDEF, to better reflect the actual scope of its work. Likewise, the Institute for Puerto Rican Policy, founded in 1982, became the National Institute for Latino Policy in 2005.[77] In broadening their vision in order to extend services and advocacy to new communities, many of which had difficulty voicing their own demands because of lack of citizenship rights and extreme poverty, these organizations exemplified the expansiveness of the ongoing struggles for Puerto Rican rights.

Notes

1 "The Latinization of Allentown, Pa." *The New York Times*, 15 May 1994; Silver, Patricia. "Puerto Ricans in Florida." In Edwin Meléndez and Carlos Vargas Ramos, eds., *Puerto Ricans at the Dawn of the New Millennium*. New York: Centro, 2014, 62–81; Silver, Patricia. "Latinization, Race, and Cultural Identification in Puerto Rican Orlando." *Southern Cultures* 19, no. 4 (2013): 55–75; Otterstrom, Samuel M., and Benjamin F. Tillman. "Income Change and Circular Migration: The Curious Case of Mobile Puerto Ricans, 1995–2010." *Journal of Latin American Geography* 12, no. 3 (2013): 33–57; Duany, Jorge. "The Orlando Ricans: Overlapping Identity Discourses among Middle-Class Puerto Rican Immigrants." In Jorge Duany. *Blurred Borders: Transnational Migration between the Hispanic Caribbean and the United States*. Durham: University of North Carolina Press, 2011, 105–34.

2 Instituto de Estadísticas de Puerto Rico. *Puerto Rican Diaspora Atlas*, 2013.

3 See, for example, De Genova, Nicholas, and Ana Yolanda Ramos-Zayas. *Latino Crossings: Mexicans, Puerto Ricans and the Politics of Race and Citizenship*. London: Routledge, 2004; Dávila, Arlene M. *Barrio Dreams: Puerto Ricans, Latinos, and the Neoliberal City*. Berkeley: University of California Press, 2004.

4 Francis-Fallon, Benjamin. "Minority Reports: The Emergence of Pan-Hispanic Politics, 1945–1980." Manuscript; Kaplowitz, Craig. *LULAC, Mexican Amerians, and National Policy*. College Station: Texas A&M University Press, 2005; also *LULAC, Mexican Americans, and National Policy*, 150.

5 "Badillo's Run [for State Comptroller] Highlights Lack of Hispanic Gains." *The New York Times*, 12 Oct. 1986; "Rep. García: Bronx Figure with Following that is National." *The New York Times*, 11 April 1985, B1; "García is Battling Energetic Rival in Bronx." *The New York Times*, 13 Sept. 1988, B1.

6 In a book called *Politics* that he published as he campaigned for reelection in 1985, "Badillo Accuses Koch of Racism in His Criticism." *The New York Times*, 12 Dec. 1985.

7 Jonnes, Jill. *South Bronx Rising: The Rise, Fall, and Resurrection of an American City*. 2nd ed. New York: Fordham University Press, 2002.

8 "Poverticians Make Good Campaign Workers." *The New York Times*, 13 July 1985, 21; "South Bronx Development Agency Is Target of Investigation by City." *The New York Times*, 4 Feb. 1986, B3; "From Farm Boy to Social Worker." *The New York Times*, 14 May 1993.

9 "Rep. García: Bronx Figure with Following that is National." *The New York Times*, 11 April 1985, B1.

10 "In Bronx, Bitterness on García." *The New York Times*, 22 Oct. 1989, 34; "Robert García Dies at 84; Bronx Congressman Undone by Scandal." *The New York Times*, 26 Jan. 2017. García's conviction was later overturned on appeal, but the scandal ended his political career.

11 "Olga Méndez, East Harlem Senator, Is Dead at 84." *The New York Times*, 29 July 2009. "The Sparks of Senator Méndez." *The New York Sun*, 26 Oct. 2004.

12 "Why Philly Latinos Lack the Representation They Deserve." *Philly Voice*, 6 Feb. 2015. Jennings and Rivera, eds., *Puerto Rican Politics*. "In Miami, Puerto Rican Mayor Faces Politically Macho Cubans." *The Washington Post*, 25 Oct. 1981, A11.

13 Gutiérrez, Luis and Doug Scofield. *Still Dreaming: My Journey from the Barrio to Capitol Hill*. New York: W.W. Norton & Company. 2013, Chaps. 16–17; González, Juan. *Harvest of Empire: A History of Latinos in America*. New York: Penguin Books, 2011, 179, 184.

14 Arnau, Ariel. "Put a Sticker on It: Civil Rights, Bilingual Voting and Puerto Ricans in Philadelphia in the 1970s." *Centro Journal* 27, no. 2 (spring 2015): 34–69.

15 González, Juan. "The Turbulent Progress of Puerto Ricans in Philadelphia," *Centro Journal* 2, no. 2 (winter 1987–88): 38–41; Whalen, *From Puerto Rico to Philadelphia*, 237; Vázquez-Hernández, Victor. "From Pan-Latino Enclaves to a Community: Puerto Ricans in Philadelphia, 1910-2000." In Carmen Teresa Whalen and Victor Vázquez-Hernández, eds., *The Puerto Rican Diaspora: Historical Perspectives*. Philadelphia: Temple University Press, 2005, 102; "Boricuas en Filadelfia: un volcán a punto de estallar." *El Diario/La Prensa*, 4 July 1985; "Sigue el acoso a los hispanos en Filadelfia." *El Diario/La Prensa*, 5 July 1985.

16 "Registration Drive Targets Black, Puerto Rican Voters." *Hartford Courant*, 30 Oct. 1983, A1. For an encompassing review of Puerto Rican politics in Hartford see: Cruz, José E. *Identity and Power: Puerto Rican Politics and the Challenge of Ethnicity*. Philadelphia: Temple University Press, 1998 and Cruz, José E. "A Decade of Change: Puerto Rican Politics in Hartford, Connecticut, 1969-1979." *Journal of American Ethnic History* 16, no. 3 (1997): 45–80.

17 "Professor to Head Puerto Rican Agency." *The Hartford Courant*, 22 March 1983, B1.

18 De Jesús, Anthony and Madeline Pérez. "From Community Control to Consent Decree: Puerto Ricans Organizing for Education and Language Rights in 1960s and '70s New York City." *Centro Journal* 2, no. 2 (2009): 7–31.

19 Nuñez, Louis. "Reflections on Puerto Rican History: Aspira in the Sixties and the Coming of Age of the Stateside Puerto Rican Community." *Centro Journal* 21, no. 2 (fall 2009): 32–47.

20 "Strife over Aims and Leadership . . ." *The New York Times*, 2 Jan. 1984, 25.

21 Lucas, Isidro. "Puerto Rican Politics in Chicago." In Jennings and Rivera, eds., *Puerto Rican Politics*, 109–11.

22 "Latin Groups to join March on Washington." *New York Amsterdam News*, 13 Aug. 1983.

23 Pabón, Julio. "NYC Mayor Ed Koch Remembered by Latino Activist." *Huffington Post*, 2 April 2013; "'Common Sense Approach': Schools Were an Exception." *The New York Times*, 27 Jan. 1980, E6.

24 "Mayor's Response to Report on Hispanic Concerns Criticized." *The New York Times*, 10 March 1987.

25 "Llegaron los recortes." *El Diario/La Prensa*, 17 Dec. 1995; "Duro Contra Pataki." *El Diario/La Prensa*, 19 Dec. 1995.

26 "Puerto Ricans Foresee Gain in Political Power." *The New York Times*, 25 April 1983, B6. "Investigando a la comunidad: El Instituto para la política puertorriqueña ha cumplido trece años de hablarle con honestidad a los poderosos." *El Diario/La Prensa*, 6 Aug. 1995.

27 Calitri, Ronald. *Latino Voter Registration in New York City: Statistics for Action.* New York: Institute for Puerto Rican Policy, 1982; "Minority Caucus Stresses Voters' Role." *The New York Times*, 15 Feb. 1982.

28 "Puerto Rican Leader Says Movement Needs Unity." *The Hartford Courant*, 16 Dec. 1981.

29 IPRP. *Simple Justice: Puerto Rican and Latino Government Employment in New York and the Failure of Affirmative Action.* New York: Institute for Puerto Rican Policy, 1983. "PR Groups Filed Hiring Petitions Against 2 TVs." *New York Amsterdam News*, 3 June 1989.

30 See the Conclusion, pp. 198–9, for a brief discussion of Puerto Rico's economic crisis since 2006 and the catastrophe intensified by the two hurricanes in 2017.

31 McCaffrey, Katherine T. *Military Power and Popular Protest: The U.S. Navy in Vieques, Puerto Rico.* New Brunswick, NJ: Rutgers University Press, 2002; Ayala, Cesar J. and José L. Bolivar. *Battleship Vieques: Puerto Rico from World War II to the Korean War.* Princeton, NJ: Markus Wiener Publishers, 2011.

32 See Backstrand, Jeffrey R. and Stephen Schensul. "Co-Evolution in an Outlying Ethnic Community: The Puerto Ricans of Hartford, Connecticut." *Urban Anthropology* 11, no. 1 (1982): 9–37.

33 Mele, Christopher. "Neighborhood 'Burn Out': Puerto Ricans at the End of the Queue." In Janet Abu-Lughod, ed., *From Urban Village to East Village.* Cambridge, MA: Blackwell, 1994, 130–7; Sevcenko, Liz. "Making Loisaida: Placing Puertorriqueñidad in Lower Manhattan." In Augustín Laó-Montes and Arlene Dávila, eds., *Mambo Montage.* New York: Columbia, 2001, 300–13; Mele, Christopher. *Selling the Lower East Side: Culture, Real Estate, and Resistance in New York City.* Minneapolis: University of Minnesota Press, 2000.

34 Goldberg, Barry. "'The World of Our Children': Jews, Puerto Ricans, and the Politics of Place and Race on the Lower East Side, 1963-1993." Ph.D. Dissertation, City University of New York, 2017; "Arresta a 18 tras desaolojo." *El Diario/La Prensa*, 6 July 1995. Kayton. *Radical Walking Tours of New York City*, 93; "Condominiums Divide Angry Tompkins Square Residents." *The New York Times*, 26 Aug. 1988; Unger, Craig. "The Lower East Side, There Goes the Neighborhood." *New York Magazine*, 22 May 1984, 32–44; Maffi, Mario. *Gateway to the Promised Land: Ethnic Cultures on New York's Lower East Side.* Amsterdam: Rodopi, 1995, 31.

35 "Mortality on the Mind, A Legacy on the Agenda: Father G. Is Out to Preserve Rebuilt Bronx." *The New York Times*, 30 April 2001, B1; "Controversial Father Gigante Wins Applause." *The New York Times*, 15 July 1981, B1; "Once Desperate, a Bronx Housing

Group Earns Praise: Once Desperate, Group Earns Praise in Bronx." *The New York Times*, 30 Oct. 1987.

36 "State Grant Money to Spur Bronx Housing Development." *The New York Times*, 12 March 1998, B10; "A Renewal Plan in the Bronx Advances: Now the Hard Part: Finding Developers." *The New York Times*, 10 July 1994, R1.

37 "A Bronx Miracle." *The New York Times*, 12 March 1995. Worth, Robert. "Guess Who Saved the South Bronx." *The Washington Monthly*, 31 April 1999, 4. For background on the South Bronx's housing and economy see Flood, Joe. *The Fires: How a Computer Formula Burned Down New York City—and Determined the Future of American Cities.* New York: Riverhead Books, 2010; Jonnes, Jill. *South Bronx Rising: The Rise, Fall, and Resurrection of an American City.* 2nd ed. New York: Fordham University Press, 2002; González, Evelyn. *The Bronx.* New York: Columbia University Press, 2006.

38 Dávila, Arlene M. *Barrio Dreams: Puerto Ricans, Latinos, and the Neoliberal City.* Berkeley: University of California Press, 2004.

39 Rivera, Melissa and Pedro Pedraza. "The Spirit of Transformation: An Education Reform Movement in a New York City Latino/a Community." In Nieto, ed., *Puerto Rican Students in U.S. Schools;* "Williamsburg: un puente hacía el activismo social." *El Diario/La Prensa*, 27 Aug. 1995; Meléndez, Edwin. "The Economic Development of El Barrio." In Frank Bonilla et al., eds., *Borderless Borders: U.S. Latinos, Latin Americans and the Paradox of Interdependence;* Marwell, Nicole. *Bargaining for Brooklyn: Community Organizations in the Entrepreneurial City.* Chicago: University of Chicago Press, 2007; "Donde las papas queman." *El Diario/La Prensa*, 27 Aug. 1995; "Southside United/HDFC-Los Sures," http://www.southsideunitedhdfc.org/about-us/mission-history/.

40 Pérez, *The Near Northwest Side Story*, 136; Pérez, Gina M.. "The Other 'Real World': Gentrification and the Social Construction of Place in Chicago." *Urban Anthropology and Studies of Cultural Systems and World Economic Development* 31, no. 1 (2002): 37–68; Erika Gisela Abad. Interview with Juanita Irizarry. 21 Nov 2015. Oral History Collection-CPRS. Flores González, Nilda. "Paseo Boricua: Claiming a Puerto Rican Space in Chicago." *Centro Journal*, 13, no. 3 (fall 2001): 6–23.

41 Ribeiro, Alyssa. "'The Battle for Harmony': Intergroup Relations between Blacks and Latinos in Philadelphia, 1950s to 1980s." Ph.D. Dissertation, University of Pittsburgh, 2013, pp. 145–6.

42 "Boston Project Is a Showcase for Group That Help Rebuild Neighborhoods." *The New York Times*, 12 Nov. 1982, A16; Matos-Rodríguez, Félix V. "Saving the Parcela: A Short History of Boston's Puerto Rican Community." In Whalen and Vázquez-Hernández, eds., *Puerto Rican Diaspora, Historical Perspectives*, 200–26; Ribeiro, Alyssa. "'The Battle for Harmony': Intergroup Relations between Blacks and Latinos in Philadelphia, 1950s to 1980s." Ph.D. Dissertation, University of Pittsburgh, 2013, 143–6. Martínez, Miranda J. *Power at the Roots: Gentrification, Community Gardens, and the Puerto Ricans of the Lower East Side.* Lanham, MD: Lexington Books, 2010; Sciorra, Joseph and Martha Cooper. "'I Feel like I'm in My Country': Puerto Rican Casitas in New York City." *The Drama Review* 34, no. 4 (winter, 1990): 156–68. Flores-González, 16.

43 Wilson, William J. *When Work Disappears: The World of the New Urban Poor.* New York: Knopf, 1996; Wilson, William J. *The Truly Disadvantaged: The Inner City, the Underclass, and Public Policy.* Chicago: University of Chicago Press, 1987; Sugrue, Thomas J. *The Origins of the Urban Crisis Race and Inequality in Postwar Detroit.* Princeton, NJ: Princeton University Press, 2014. See Aranda, Elizabeth. "Struggles of Incorporation among the Puerto Rican Middle Class." *The Sociological Quarterly* 48, no. 2 (2007): 199–228.

44 See, for example, Barber, Llana. *Latino City: Immigration and Urban Crisis in Lawrence, Massachusetts, 1945–2000.* Chapel Hill: The University of North Carolina Press, 2017.

45 United States Commission on Civil Rights. *Puerto Ricans in the Continental United States: An Uncertain Future: A Report.* Washington, D.C.: U.S. Commission on Civil Rights, 1976; "Puerto Rican Deprivation: A Call for Federal Action: Urban Affairs." *The New York Times,* 29 May 1978. http://www.pewresearch.org/2010/12/14/reagans-recession/.

46 González, Juan. *Roll Down Your Window: Stories of a Forgotten America.* New York: Verso, 1995, 27–8.

47 Torres, Andrés. "Labor Market Segmentation: African American and Puerto Rican Labor in New York City, 1960–1980." *Review of Black Political Economy* 20 (1991): 59. Torres, Andrés. *Between Melting Pot and Mosaic: African Americans and Puerto Ricans in the New York Political Economy.* Philadelphia: Temple University Press, 1995. Bonilla, Frank and Ricardo Campos, "Puerto Ricans in the New Economic Order." *Daedalus* (1981): 155–6. Portes, Alejandro and Cynthia Truelove, "Making Sense of Diversity: Recent Research on Hispanic Minorities in the United States." *Annual Review of Sociology* 13 (1987): 359–85, 365. Enchautegui, Maria. "Education, Location, and Labor Market Outcomes of Puerto Rican Men during the 1980s." *Eastern Economic Journal* 19 (1993): 295–308.

48 Chávez, Linda. *Out of the Barrio: Toward a New Politics of Hispanic Assimilation.* New York: Basic Books, 1991, 152. Falcón, Angelo, and John Santiago. *The 'Puerto Rican Exception': Persistent Poverty and the Conservative Social Policy of Linda Chavez.* New York: The Institute, 1992. For a similar debate that contrasted West Indian origin Blacks and African Americans, see James, Winston. "Explaining Afro-Caribbean Social Mobility in the United States: Beyond the Sowell Thesis." *Comparative Studies in Society and History* 44, no. 2 (2002): 218–62.

49 Tienda, Marta. "Puerto Ricans and the Underclass Debate." *The Annals of the American Academy of Political and Social Science* 501, no. 1 (1989): 105–19. Acosta-Belén, Edna and Carlos E. Santiago. *Puerto Ricans in the United States: A Contemporary Portrait.* Boulder, CO: Lynne Rienner Publishers, 2006, Chap 5.

50 Torres. *Between Melting Pot and Mosaic*; Marzan, Gilbert. "Regional Variation in Socioeconomic Status among Mainland Puerto Rican Males: A Comparative Analysis." Ph.D. Dissertation, State University of New York, 2001.

51 *Ibid.*; Daponte, Beth Osborne. "Race and Ethnicity during an Economic Transition: The Withdrawal of Puerto Rican Women from New York City's Labour Force, 1960-1980." *Regional Studies* 30, no. 2 (1996): 151–66. Colón, Alice Warren. "The Feminization of Poverty among Women in Puerto Rico and Puerto Rican Women in the Middle Atlantic Region of the United States." *The Brown Journal of World Affairs* 5, no. 2 (1998): 263–81.

52 Cordero-Guzmán, Hector R. "Puerto Rican Poverty: A Review of the Main Trends and Proposed Explanations with an Emphasis on the New York Experience." 1996. Manuscript. See also Jennings, James. "Missing Links in the Study of Puerto Rican Poverty in the United States." William Monroe Trotter Institute Publications, no. 12 1995. For an excellent review of the literature with important historical and regional discussions see Baker, Susan S. *Understanding Mainland Puerto Rican Poverty.* Philadelphia: Temple University Press, 2002.

53 "Striving but Still Lagging: Puerto Ricans Wonder Why." *The New York Times,* 5 June 1986, B1.

54 Bonilla, Frank and Ricardo Campos. "A Wealth of Poor: Puerto Ricans in the New Economic Order." *Daedalus* 110, no. 2 (1981): 133–76.

55 By 2015, the poverty rate was down to 23%. Cruz, Jose. "Unfulfilled Promise: Puerto Rican Politics and Poverty." *Centro Journal* 15, no. 1 (spring 2003): 166; Center for Puerto Rican Studies, "Puerto Ricans in New Jersey, the United States, and Puerto Rico." 2015.

56 Center for Puerto Rican Studies, "Demographic Transitions: Settlement and Distribution of the Puerto Rican Population in the United States," 2013. Meléndez, Edwin and M. Anne Visser. "Low-Wage Labor, Markets and Skills Selectivity among Puerto Rican

Migrants. *Centro Journal* 23, no. 11 (fall 2011): 39–62; Rivera Batiz, Francisco L. "Puerto Rican New Yorkers in the 1990s: A Demographic and Socioeconomic Profile." In *Boricuas in Gotham*, 109.

57 Marzan, Gilbert. "Still Looking for That Else Where: Puerto Rican Poverty and Migration in the Northeast." *Centro Journal* 21, no. 1 (spring 2009): 101–17. New York's share of the total Puerto Rican descent population declined from 60% in 1970 to 23% in 2000 (Angelo Falcón. "De'tras pa'lante: Explorations on the Future history of Puerto Ricans." In *Boricuas in Gotham*).

58 Figueroa, Hector. "Puerto Rican Workers, a Profile." *NACLA Report on the Americas* Vol. 30 (Nov/Dec 1996): 29–30. Ocasio, Hector. "Portrait of an Organizer." *NACLA Report on the Americas* Vol. 30 (Nov/Dec 1996): 27–8; Fink, Leon. "Bread and Roses, Crusts and Thorns: The Troubled Story of 1199." *Dissent* 33, no. 2 (1986): 179–88; Fink, Leon and Brian Greenberg. *Upheaval in the Quiet Zone: A History of Hospital Workers' Union, Local 1199*. Urbana: University of Illinois Press, 1989; Foner, Moe and Dan North. *Not for Bread Alone: A Memoir.* Ithaca, NY: Cornell University Press, 2002, 103.

59 "Nombran a un hispano como director de derechos civiles." *El Diario/La Prensa*, 21 Sept. 1995.

60 Bergad, Laird W. and Herbert S. Klein. *Hispanics in the United States: A Demographic, Social, and Economic History, 1980-2005.* New York: Cambridge University Press, 2010, 199–203.

61 Pimentel, Felipe. "The Decline of the Puerto Rican Fulltime Faculty at the City University of New York (CUNY) from 1981-2002." *CENTRO Policy Brief* 2:3 (fall 2005).

62 Schneider, Cathy Lisa. *Police Power and Race Riots: Urban Unrest in Paris and New York.* Philadelphia: University of Pennsylvania Press, 2014. Chs. 1, 3; Solis, Carmen Leonor. "The Impact of Community Policing in New York City's Puerto Rican Communities." Ph.D. Dissertation, City University of New York, 2004.

63 "No Rights Violations Seen in 21 Shot Police Slaying." *The New York Times*, 11 July 1980; "Crowd of 100 Gathers Outside Police Station for Protest on Slaying." *The New York Times*, 25 Aug. 1979; "Man Wielding Scissors Is Killed as 5 Officers Open Fire." *The New York Times*, 23 Aug. 1979; "Baez Supporters Battled by Police." *New York Amsterdam News*, 1 Sep. 1979; "Demonstrators Say Police Caused Violence at Protest over Shooting." *The New York Times*, 29 Aug. 1979; "Police Ruled Not Liable in Killing." *The New York Times*, 21 Nov. 1979; "Black, Puerto Rican Groups Set a 'Hearing' on Police Clash." *Newsday*, 29 Aug. 1979; "Policeman Kills a Brooklyn Man Who Was Carrying a Putty Knife." *The New York Times*, 29 Sept. 1979; "Questions Swirl around a Fatal Shooting." *The New York Times*, 5 Jan. 1988; "When Mental Illness Meets Police Firepower." *The New York Times*, 28 Dec. 2003; "Murder, Racism Scar City." *New York Amsterdam News*, 1 Sept. 1979; "Hispanics Seek Probe into Brooklyn Cops Conducts." *The New York Times*, 6 Sept. 1979; "Federal Inquiry on Police Action at Protest Urged." *The New York Times*, 6 Sept. 1979; "Daughtry Announced People's Tribunal." *New York Amsterdam News*, 8 Sept. 1979.

64 "Police Brutality Charged at Forum: U.S. Panel Hears Allegations." *The New York Times*, 20 Sept. 1983.

65 "Residents Protest Cop Slaying of a 14-Year-Old." *New York Amsterdam News*, 10 Feb. 1990; "Officer Indicted in the Death of a 14-Year-Old in Brooklyn." *The New York Times*, 31 March 1990; "Killer Cop Acquitted." *New York Amsterdam News*, 4 April 1992.

66 "Black and Latino Cops Speak on Brutality, Racism, the PBU." *New York Amsterdam News*, 6 April 1991.

67 "A Fatal Shooting by Police Ignites Protest in Bushwick." *The New York Times*, 25 May 1992.

68 "The Threat of Police Perjury." Editorial. *The New York Times*, 30 Jan. 1998; "Former Officer Gets 7½ Years in Man's Death." *The New York Times*, 9 Oct. 1998; "Safir Dismisses Officer in Case of Illegal Use of Choke Hold." *The New York Times*, 22

Feb. 1997; "From Deadly Confrontation in Bronx to a Record Settlement." *The New York Times*, 3 Oct. 1998; "City Will Settle Suits on Death in Police Arrest." *The New York Times*, 2 Oct. 1998; "Safir Has Dismissed 106 Officers, 8 for Brutality." *The New York Times*, 6 Oct. 1997; "U.S. Asserts Police Officers Planned to Lie." *The New York Times*, 20 Aug. 2015; "U.S. Trial Evidence Shows How Police Protect Their Own." *The New York Times*, 26 June 1998; "Prosecutors Broaden Investigation into Police Brutality." *The New York Times*, 3 July 1998.

69 "Hispanos toma la fiscalia." *El Diario/La Prensa*, 12 Oct. 1995. "Giuliani Evita confrontación durante reunión en Brooklyn". *El Diario/La* Prensa, 18 Aug. 1995. "The NYPD Murder of Anthony Baez." *Revolutionary Worker* 962, 21 June 1998, http://revcom.us/a/v20/960-69/962/baez.htm; "Ahora se espera justicia." *El Diario/La Prensa*, 19 Oct. 1995. Interview with Richie Pérez. By Blanca Vazquez. Oral History Collection-CPRS.

70 "Ex-officer Guilty in Choking Death." *The New York Times*, 27 June 1998. "Se reabre el caso Livoti." *El Diario/La Prensa*, 15 Dec. 1995. Livoti's two partners were also dismissed from the force for providing perjured testimony after a third confirmed their conspiracy to lie about the events. "Antecedentes de violencia: Millionaria demanda contra la policía por la muerte de Anthony Baez." *El Diario/La Prensa*, 19 July 1995.

71 "Deeper Failures in the Livoti Case." Editorial. *The New York Times*, 15 Oct. 1998; "Disrespect a Catalyst for Brutality." *The New York Times*, 19 Nov. 1997; "Interview with Susan Karten, attorney for the Baez family." Edited by Kelly Anderson. AndersonGold Films, 2004; "Settling Suits for Brutality Rises in Cost." *The New York Times*, 2 Aug. 1995; "Mayor to Sign Bill Naming Street for Police Choking Victim." *The New York Times*, 17 April 2000.

72 "Human Rights Watch. *Shielded from Justice: Police Brutality and Accountability in the United States*. June 1998; "Officers Rally and Dinkins Is Their Target." *The New York Times*, 17 Sept. 1992; Renuncia Hector Soto." *El Diario/La Prensa*, 2 Nov. 1995; "Mas cambios en la junta." *El Diario/La Prensa*, 3 Aug. 1995; Hector Soto. "The Failure of Civilian Oversight." *Gotham Gazette*, 9 Oct. 2007; "Giuliani to Shift Police Discipline to Civilian Board." *The New York Times*, 27 Jan. 2001.

73 "Recomiendan acusar a policias." *El Diario/La Prensa*, 27 July 1995. "Bronx Mom of Teen Killed by Cops in 1995 Finally Gets Answers, and $1.1 Million." *New York Daily News*, 26 March 2009; "A Bronx Murder Mystery." *NY Press*, 27 Jan. 2004; "Victims' Families Sue New York City in Fatal 1995 Police Shooting." *The New York Times*, 6 March 2009. A documentary film "Justifiable Homicide" was made about this episode. http://www.realityfilms.net/.

74 Schneider. *Police Power and Race Riots: Urban Unrest in Paris and New York*; "De violencia en violencia." *El Diario/La Prensa*, 19 Nov. 1995. "En vigor el plan calidad de vida." *El Diario/La Prensa*, 26 Nov. 1995; Amnesty International, "Police Brutality and Excessive Force in the New York City Police Department." 1 June 1996, AMR/51/36/96.

75 Interview with Félix Loperana, conducted by John Vásquez, 22 Nov. 1974. *Pioneros* Project, LIHS-CPRS. "A Police Shooting." *The New York Times*, 10 April 1997.

76 "Permitted by Court, 1,000 March against Police Brutality." *The New York Times*, 23 Oct. 1998; "Aceptan denuncia de policía hispano." *El Diario/La Prensa*, 6 July 1995; "Lawsuit Seeks to Curb Street Crimes Unit, Alleging Racially Biased Searches." *The New York Times*, 9 March 1999, B3; "Judge Rejects New York's Stop-and-Frisk Policy." *The New York Times*, 12 Aug. 2013.

77 Olvera, Jaqueline. "Together but without Mixing: Mexican and Puerto Rican Relations in New Urban Destinations." Manuscript. For a review of the Connecticut experience see: Glasser, Ruth. *Aquí Me Quedo: Puerto Ricans in Connecticut*. Middletown, CT: Connecticut Humanities Council, 1997.

CONCLUSION

Rethinking the Struggle for Puerto Rican Rights

Throughout this book, we have shown that struggles over claiming and defining rights comprised a central theme of Puerto Ricans' experience in the U.S. in the 20th century. In assessing the meaning and implications of this history, it is important to distinguish between the continuities of struggle as a process of response—to racism and discrimination, to economic disadvantage and social exclusion—and the evolving intentions and goals that motivated that response. In other words, struggle may have been a constant for many Puerto Ricans who sought to make a life in the U.S. in the 20th century, but the motivations that guided them and the strategies they developed to meet the challenges at hand were constantly changing, partly in response to changing context. Economic opportunities shifted, alliances formed and broke apart, political winds blew in multiple directions, and racism and ethnic prejudice blocked opportunity in different ways in different settings.

In Puerto Ricans' evolving efforts to secure rights and resources and to live with dignity in the U.S., there were important continuities. As far back as the 1920s and 1930s, there had been campaigns by Puerto Ricans to secure decent housing, access to social services, fair wages, and educational access. The vast majority of these early demands for rights developed first in New York City, where Puerto Rican communities had laid down roots in the early 20th century; Puerto Ricans only began to settle in sizable groups in other cities and towns around the mid-1950s. By the mid-1960s, there were visible and increasingly vocal Puerto Rican communities in over a dozen U.S. cities. Members of the younger generations who had been born and educated in the U.S. began adding their voices to the older generation's demands for rights.

Also constant were the ways Puerto Rican migrants used their U.S. citizenship as a strategic resource, developing creative strategies to demand their rights as American citizens. While most migrants did not cling to naïve expectations that they would encounter social equality upon arrival in the U.S., many were hopeful that their status as U.S. citizens would mitigate some of their disadvantages as newcomers. This hopefulness ebbed over time, following nativist and racist responses to the mass migration of Puerto Ricans in the late 1940s and early 1950s, and then receded sharply during the 1970s and 1980s, as factory jobs and opportunities for employment left the cities where Puerto Ricans had settled. In response to both types of challenges, Puerto Ricans pursued political representation as a means of making their voices heard in public life and participated in the creation of policies that would support the survival of their communities.

During the 1960s, Puerto Ricans adapted their decades-long struggles to secure rights in the United States to the zeitgeist of the decade. Puerto Rican leaders gained momentum first by participating in anti-poverty programs of the mid-1960s, independent of organizations like the Migration Division or the Democratic clubs that had traditionally served as Puerto Ricans' organizational base. Then, joined by younger activists—many of them still teenagers—who were radicalized by the work of their peers in Black Power and Chicano organizations, Puerto Ricans across the political spectrum achieved a mass mobilization of their compatriots that peaked during the mid-1970s. New York and Chicago were the primary hubs of the movement, but Puerto Ricans in many smaller cities all over the Northeast joined in what became known as the *despertar boricua*, the Puerto Rican awakening.

By the early 1970s, the movement had united Puerto Ricans in new ways across class and generational lines. Even as Puerto Rican leftist and liberal activists debated their ideological differences, they often maintained a shared commitment to common goals, especially after the more militant organizations of the early 1970s dissolved. Older leaders who had been involved in the Puerto Rican community's earliest efforts in politics and the labor movement expressed gratitude for the energy and drive of the younger leaders, even though they did not always agree with their political style. These second-generation leaders had come of age in the 1950s and 1960s, and many of them had attended college, poised to embark on careers in politics, labor unions, grassroots organizing, legal advocacy, social services, and teaching. Even as many of these young leaders found paths into the middle class, they maintained connections to poorer members of their communities, including more recent migrants who tended to have less education and less economic security.

Although the movement receded after the mid-1970s, the principal drivers of the Puerto Rican mobilization—economic suffering and discriminatory treatment—continued to galvanize grassroots and labor activists along with intellectuals and professionals working in legal and social service fields. Through their work, many Puerto Rican activist networks became national in scope during the 1970s and 1980s. In fact, it was during the era following the decline of the most visible mass movement that activists began to accomplish the most substantial gains in civil rights protections and educational access. Among the most important legacies of this later stage of the Puerto Rican movement—the movement's "coda," perhaps—were a sharpened focus on securing legal protections for civil rights, particularly in the areas of voting rights and access to equal education for non-English speakers.

Another important achievement by the 1980s was that Puerto Ricans had secured at least a small foothold in local politics in half a dozen U.S. cities. This change, along with the impact of concrete gains in legal civil rights at the national level, produced a notable adjustment in the tenor and scope of organizing work by Puerto Rican leaders. The center of gravity of Puerto Ricans' activism began to shift away from a nationalist form of ethnic politics and toward a deeper engagement with policy issues and cultural politics that were more broadly Latino rather than specifically Puerto Rican, including language rights, higher education access, school quality, affordable housing, and fair policing. Although connections with other Latino groups were at times tense or begrudging, this building of alliances continued throughout the 1980s, with increasing solidarity on labor issues, immigrants' rights, and in protests against the Central American wars backed by the Reagan administration.

Scholarship was another key area of collaboration among Puerto Ricans and other Latinos in the 1980s. Although often marginalized in the academy, still, Puerto Rican scholars had begun to fortify their projects by collaborating across national origin boundaries with other Latino academics. Together, they created broader agendas for the study of Latinos in the U.S. at a time when the "culture wars" had generated a more open conversation about how power was distributed within institutions like the university. The idea of cultural citizenship that Chicano anthropologist Renato Rosaldo proposed in the early 1990s reflected the expansive vision of Latino Studies as a field: the goal to situate and analyze Latinas and Latinos as social and political actors in frameworks beyond the usual binary categories—citizen or noncitizen; black or white; migrant or settled; middle class and "assimilated" or poor and marginal. These dialogues provided a strong basis for the emergence of Latino Studies as a field by the early 1990s.[1]

Along with its central concern with Puerto Ricans' fights to protect their civil rights, this book also provides a general survey of Puerto Ricans' history in the U.S. since the 1940s. In crafting this survey, we have relied on the work of many other scholars whose research illuminates various aspects of the Puerto Rican experience in places beyond our own expertise, as we seek to draw out consistent themes and patterns across time and region. The historical literature on Puerto Ricans has grown tremendously just in the past decade and has begun to move beyond a narrow focus on specific places and time periods into work that is more comparative and relational, examining Puerto Ricans' experience as part of larger networks and issues of regional and national significance.

Still, historians' focused analysis of particular places and groups continues to be essential as the field expands. For example, the Puerto Rican experience in New Jersey, for decades the second largest state of settlement, remains largely unexamined; upstate New York settlements, including Albany, Rochester, and Schenectady have also not been studied.[2] A plethora of advocacy and social service organizations, many of them with significant archival collections at the Center for Puerto Rican Studies, still await study; so do the histories of youth employment and training programs in Puerto Rican communities in the decades after the 1960s, of Puerto Rican entrepreneurship and small businesses throughout the 20th century, and the work of Puerto Rican lawyers and their campaigns for voting rights. While the field has seen a few new publications on Puerto Rican radicalism in the 1960s and after, there is still a need for thorough histories of the complex movements in support of Puerto Rican independence in the same period. Puerto Ricans' extensive participation in the labor movement after the 1970s has not been explored, nor have their responses to the urban crises of the 1970s and 1908s.[3] *Rethinking the Struggle for Puerto Rican Rights* is a starting point, and we anticipate substantial growth in historical scholarship on Puerto Ricans in the coming decade.[4]

The Current Landscape and the Evolution of Puerto Rican Struggles for Rights

These new directions in the scholarship will keep evolving along with the changing goals and challenges of Puerto Ricans in the U.S., as the label "Puerto Rican" encompasses an even more diverse population in terms of regional, class, and generational identification. Two trends in particular promise to shape the ways Puerto Ricans in the U.S. continue to engage in the political and social issues that matter to them. The first involves changes in how Puerto Ricans identify themselves: with the highest out-of-group marriage rates of all Latinos, the category "Puerto Rican" includes tens of thousands of children of mixed families— Puerto Ricans who have children with partners who identify as white, African American, or other Latino. The children of these families are growing up with a variety of possible racial and cultural identities, and varied relationships to the island and to U.S. Puerto Rican communities. This is not a completely new phenomenon. Since at least the 1940s second-generation Puerto Ricans, especially women, married outside their group in large numbers. But the rate of intermarriage has risen sharply since the 1990s and will likely mean that political expressions of rights will be framed in pan-Latino or pan "minority" languages but also that many white-skinned people of Puerto Rican descent will identify as Puerto Rican only circumstantially.[5]

The other trend has to do with ongoing migration from the island to the U.S. Because of a resurgent economy in Puerto Rico during the 1990s, migration during that decade declined significantly. But that decline reversed sharply after the Puerto Rican economy took a sharp dive in 2006—largely the result of changes in U.S. tax law that produced a precipitous drop in investment in the island's major industries, losses that were then compounded by mounting debt from an unequal Medicaid reimbursement program and the recession that followed the United States' sub-prime mortgage crisis of 2007. In addition to producing a tremendous resurgence in the number of migrants to the U.S., the Great Recession in the U.S. also intensified a growing internal migration of Puerto Ricans already in the U.S., particularly southward to Florida, Georgia, Texas, and the Carolinas. Some of this migration is related to the Puerto Rican presence in the military, but most of it has been driven by the promise of jobs, decent schools, and cheaper housing.[6]

Puerto Rican communities in Florida have expanded most dramatically in recent years. In the decade after Puerto Rico's economic crisis began in 2006, the state's Puerto Rican population (which had grown steadily since the 1980s) almost doubled, from about 640,000 to over one million, with the majority of migrants settling in the central Florida counties surrounding Orlando. Overall, Puerto Ricans who have migrated to Florida—both from the island and from other U.S. states—have higher family incomes, lower rates of residential segregation, higher rates of educational attainment, and higher rates of business ownership than Puerto Ricans in any other state. In other words, more of them have achieved middle class status than their counterparts elsewhere in the U.S.

Yet inclusion and incorporation have presented challenges even for Puerto Rican migrants who are less economically vulnerable, as anthropologists Patricia Silver and Simone Delerme have amply documented in their work on Puerto Rican and Latino communities in the Orlando area. In one local controversy, a Puerto Rican county commissioner proposed the renaming of a former public golf course as a memorial to Puerto Rico's 65th Infantry, an all-volunteer regiment of the U.S. army whose soldiers fought and died in both World Wars and in the Korean War. In the rancorous debate that led up to the creation of the 65th Infantry Veteran's Park, opponents raised the same issues that Puerto Ricans have confronted elsewhere in the U.S. throughout the 20th century: unsure of Puerto Ricans' status as "Americans," many refused to include them in additional categories of belonging, like "veteran" or even "neighbor."[7]

Along with the impact of intermarriage and migration trends that are diversifying and expanding existing Puerto Rican communities, cultural and political shifts have created opportunity for connection with other groups in other ways. In the last two decades, Puerto Rican leaders, activists, artists, and intellectuals have increasingly asserted their group's presence as part of larger national debates over race, gender, sexuality, and class, often in collaboration with African American and other Latino groups. The Black Lives Matter movement has attracted substantial participation by Puerto Ricans, whose motivations come from a range of political and identity positions. Activist and writer Rosa Clemente, for example, has written extensively about her identification as Afro-Latinx, a Puerto Rican woman who is also part of the African diaspora. Although they are American citizens no matter where they are born, Puerto Ricans have also been very active in organizations that support immigrant rights and the broad range of justice issues related to U.S. Latinos, many of whom are undocumented. Latino Rebels, a group of media activists founded in 2011 by Puerto Rican-born Julio Ricardo Varela, defines its audience and subject—"U.S.-Latino communities"—as capaciously as possible, generating solidarity across boundaries that typically separate Latinos by nation, race, and class.[8]

In 2018, as we conclude this book, an unprecedented crisis grips Puerto Rico, threatening the lives and livelihoods of Puerto Ricans on the island and substantially affecting Puerto Ricans in the U.S. whose families and histories have roots in their homeland. After two massive hurricanes hit the island in September 2017, the historic destruction and infrastructure collapse—combined with the island's decade-old economic crisis—triggered an enormous new wave of migration estimated at 250,000 in just the first six months after the storms. The majority of these migrants left the island in desperation, not because they planned or desired to relocate to the U.S., and their path of return is uncertain: Puerto Rico's government and public sector is bankrupt and austerity measures from the Financial Oversight and Management Board, imposed in a colonialist fashion by the Obama administration and Congress, have done nothing to reverse the evisceration of the island's economy.[9]

These overwhelming problems have produced at least one silver lining: a seismic movement of solidarity with the island on the part of U.S.-based Puerto Ricans. Members of the diaspora have wired millions of dollars to family and to aid groups on the island, they have created new support and advocacy networks, and they have founded their own reconstruction organizations, harnessing social media and applying enormous pressure on elected officials and federal government agencies to provide both immediate and long-term aid to the island. Outstripping previous responses to a handful of other major natural disasters and political crises on the island in the last century, the stateside Puerto Rican community has tapped into its power to mobilize essential resources in support of the island, despite continued disagreements over the best future for Puerto Rico's political status. In many ways, in fact, this response by U.S. Puerto Ricans represents yet another engagement in their long history of struggle for rights, recognition, equal standing—this time not for their ailing urban communities or neglected migrant labor settlements, but for the survival of their homeland. The goal of this book has been to make concrete and visible the ways Puerto Ricans have fought for inclusion and strategized to participate fully and equally in the plural society of the United States—and continue to do so even after 100 years as U.S. beleaguered citizens.

Notes

1 Cabán, Pedro A. "Puerto Rican Studies and Political Economy." In M. Sánchez and A. Stevens-Arroyo, eds., *Toward a Renaissance of Puerto Rican Studies*. Highland Lakes, NJ: Atlantic Research and Publications, 1987, 73–8; Cabán, Pedro A. "Moving from the Margins to Where? Three Decades of Latino/A Studies." *Latino Studies* 1 (2003): 5–35; Cabán, Pedro A. "Puerto Rican Studies: Changing Islands of Knowledge." *Centro Journal* 21, no. 2 (fall 2009): 256–81; Cabán, Pedro A. "From Challenge to Absorption: The Changing Face of Latina and Latino Studies." *Centro Journal* 15, no. 2 (fall 2003): 126–45.

2 Olga Wagenheim (professor emerita at Rutgers University) organized the New Jersey Hispanic Research and Information Center at Newark Public Library with the help of Ingrid Betancourt and Yesenia López. Laurie Lahey has written about cross-racial alliances in Camden ("'The Grassy Battleground': Race, Religion, and Activism in Camden's 'Wide' Civil Rights Movement." Ph.D. Dissertation, George Washington University, 2013; "'Too Much Singing:' Christianity and the Limitations of Nonviolence in the Ghetto." *New Jersey Studies: An Interdisciplinary Journal* 1:1 (2015), 152–79); Jiménez de Wagenheim, Olga. "From Aguada to Dover: Puerto Ricans Rebuild Their World in Morris County, New Jersey, 1948 to 2000." In Whalen and Vázquez-Hernández, eds., *The Puerto Rican Diaspora*.

3 See Arnau, Ariel. "Put a Sticker on It: Civil Rights, Bilingual Voting and Puerto Ricans in Philadelphia in the 1970s." *Centro Journal* 27, no. 1 (spring 2015): 34–69. Fernández, Johanna. "The Young Lords and the Social and Structural Roots of Late Sixties Urban Radicalism." In *Civil Rights in New York City: From World War II to the Giuliani Era*. New York: Fordham University Press, 2011, 141–60. Lee, Sonia S. and Ande Diaz, "'I Was the One Percenter': Manny Diaz and the Beginnings of a Black-Puerto Rican Coalition." *Journal of American Ethnic History* 26, no. 3 (2007): 52–80. Lauria Santiago, Aldo A. "A Better Life: Puerto Rican New York—A History of Class, Work, and Struggle, 1920–1970." Manuscript.

4 Much of this work centered on dialogues and collaborations initiated by the History of Puerto Ricans and Latinos in the U.S. Working Group organized by Lauria Santiago in 2009.

5 Fitzpatrick, Joseph Patrick. "Intermarriage of Puerto Ricans in New York City." *American Journal of Sociology* 71 (January 1966): 395–406; Fitzpatrick, Joseph P., and Douglas T. Gurak. *Hispanic Intermarriage in New York City, 1975*. Monograph Series—Hispanic Research Center Monograph No 2. New York: Hispanic Research Center, Fordham University, 1979. Aquino, Gabriel. "Puerto Rican Intermarriages: The Intersectionality of Race, Gender, Class and Space." Ph.D. Dissertation, State University of New York at Albany, 2011.

6 Franqui-Rivera, Harry. "Puerto Rican Veterans and Service Members' Wellbeing and Place within the Diaspora." In Edwin Meléndez and Carlos Vargas-Ramos, eds., *Puerto Ricans at the Dawn of the New Millennium*. New York: Centro Press, 2014; Franqui-Rivera, Harry. "Military Service: Migration and a Path to Middle Class Status." In Edwin Meléndez and Carlos Vargas-Ramos, eds., *The State of Puerto Ricans*. New York: Centro Press, 2016. Newkirk, Vann. "The Historical Exclusion Behind the Puerto Rico Bankruptcy Crisis," *The Atlantic*, 2 May 2017.

7 Delerme, Simone. "65th Infantry Veteran's Park: Contested Landscapes and Latinization in Greater Orlando." *Southern Cultures* 23, no. 4 (winter 2017): 116–25; Delerme, Simone. "Reflections on Cultural Capital and Orlando's Puerto Rican and Latino 'Elite.'" *Centro Journal* 29, no. 3 (fall 2017): 74–96; Patricia Silver and William Vélez, "'Let Me Go Check Out Florida': Rethinking Puerto Rican Diaspora." *Centro Journal* 29, no. 3 (fall 2017): 98–125, 119. Silver, Patricia. "Sunshine Politics: Puerto Rican Memory and the

Political in New Destinations," *Centro Journal* 29, no. 2 (summer 2017): 4–37. Aranda, Elizabeth, and Fernando I. Rivera. "Puerto Rican Families in Central Florida: Prejudice, Discrimination, and Their Implications for Successful Integration." *Women, Gender, and Families of Color* 4, no. 1 (2016): 57–85.

8 Rosa Clemente, "Who is Black?" 10 June 2001, http://rosaclemente.net/who-is-black/.

9 Duany, Jorge. "El éxodo Boricua a la Florida antes y después del huracán María." Florida International University, 2018; Centro Research Brief. "Post-Hurricane Maria Exodus from Puerto Rico and School Enrollment in Florida." 2017; Feldman, Noah. "Puerto Rico's 'Colonial' Power Struggle," *Bloomberg*, 8 July 2015. Meléndez, Edwin. "The U.S.'s Neglect of Puerto Rico Has Never Been Benign," *Global Americans*, 3 Oct. 2017 https://theglobalamericans.org/2017/10/neglect-puerto-rico-never-benign/.

BIBLIOGRAPHY

Abramson, Michael. *Palante: Young Lords Party*. Chicago: Haymarket, 1971.

Abu-Lughod, Janet. *From Urban Village to East Village: The Battle for New York's Lower East Side*. Oxford: Blackwell, 1995.

Acosta-Belén, Elena and Carlos E. Santiago. *Puerto Ricans in the United States: A Contemporary Portrait*. Boulder, CO: Lynne Rienner Publishers, 2006.

Adams, Carolyn et al. *Philadelphia: Neighborhoods, Division, and Conflict in a Postindustrial City*. Philadelphia: Temple University Press 1991.

Adams, Florence. *Latinos and Local Representation: Changing Realities, Emerging Theories*. New York: Routledge, 2016.

Algarín, Miguel and Miguel Piñero, eds., *Nuyorican Poetry: An Anthology of Puerto Rican Words and Feelings*. New York: William Morrow and Company, 1975.

Allport, Gordon W. *The Nature of Prejudice: A Comprehensive and Penetrating Study of the Origin and Nature of Prejudice*. Garden City, NY: Doubleday, 1954.

Anderson, Terry H. *Pursuit of Fairness*. New York: Oxford University Press, 2004.

Aponte-Parés, Luis. "Lessons from El Barrio--the East Harlem Real Great Society/Urban Planning Studio: A Puerto Rican Chapter in the Fight for Urban Self-Determination." In Rodolfo D. Torres and George N. Katsiaficas, eds., *Latino Social Movements: Historical and Theoretical Perspectives*. New York: Routledge, 1999.

Aquino, Gabriel. "Puerto Rican Intermarriages: The Intersectionality of Race, Gender, Class and Space." Ph.D. Dissertation, State University of New York at Albany, 2011.

Aranda, Elizabeth. "Struggles of Incorporation among the Puerto Rican Middle Class." *The Sociological Quarterly* 48, no. 2 (2007): 199–228.

Aranda, Elizabeth, and Fernando I. Rivera. "Puerto Rican Families in Central Florida: Prejudice, Discrimination, and Their Implications for Successful Integration." *Women, Gender, and Families of Color* 4, no. 1 (2016): 57–85.

Arizmendi, Elba. "The Structure and Functioning of Ten Voluntary Puerto Rican Groups Concerned with Better Social Adjustment and Welfare of Puerto Ricans in NYC." Master's Thesis, Columbia University, 1952.

Armstrong, Michael F. *They Wished They Were Honest: The Knapp Commission and New York City Police Corruption*. New York: Columbia University Press, 2012.

Arnau, Ariel. "Put a Sticker on It: Civil Rights, Bilingual Voting and Puerto Ricans in Philadelphia in the 1970s." *Centro Journal* 27, no. 1 (spring 2015): 34–69.

Arnau, Ariel. "The Evolution of Leadership within the Puerto Rican Community of Philadelphia, 1950s–1970s." *The Pennsylvania Magazine of History and Biography* 136, no. 1 (2012): 53–81.

Ayala, César and Rafael Bernabe. *Puerto Rico in the American Century: A History since 1898.* Chapel Hill: University of North Carolina Press, 2007.

Ayala, César J. Bolívar José L. *Battleship Vieques: Puerto Rico from World War II to the Korean War.* Princeton, NJ: Markus Wiener Publishers, 2011.

Back, Adina. "Parent Power: Evelina López Antonetty, the Unite Bronx Parents, and the War on Poverty." In Annelise Orleck and Lisa Gayle Hazirjian, eds., *The War on Poverty: A New Grassroots History, 1964–1980.* Athens: University of Georgia Press, 2011.

Backstrand, Jeffrey R. and Stephen Schensul. "Co-Evolution in an Outlying Ethnic Community: The Puerto Ricans of Hartford, Connecticut." *Urban Anthropology* 11, no. 1 (1982): 9–37.

Badillo, Herman and Milton Haynes. *A Bill of No Rights: Attica and the American Prison System.* New York: Outerbridge and Lazard, 1972.

Baker, Susan S. *Understanding Mainland Puerto Rican Poverty.* Philadelphia: Temple University Press, 2002.

Barber, Llana. *Latino City: Immigration and Urban Crisis in Lawrence, Massachusetts, 1945–2000.* Chapel Hill: The University of North Carolina Press, 2017.

Benin, Leigh David. *The New Labor Radicalism and New York City's Garment Industry: Progressive Labor Insurgents in the 1960s.* New York: Garland, 2000.

Bergad, Laird W. and Klein Herbert S. *Hispanics in the United States: A Demographic, Social, and Economic History, 1980–2005.* New York: Cambridge University Press, 2010.

Block, Andrew. "Community in Action: The Central Harlem Experience in the War on Poverty, 1963–1968." Thesis, Vassar College, 2005.

Bonilla, Frank, and Ricardo Campos. "A Wealth of Poor: Puerto Ricans in the New Economic Order." *Daedalus* 110, no. 2 (1981): 133–76.

Bonilla, Frank. "Rethinking Latino/Latin American Interdependence" in F. Bonilla et al, eds., *Borderless Borders: U.S. Latinos, Latin Americans, and the Paradox of Interdependence.* Philadelphia: Temple University Press, 1998.

Bonilla-Santiago, Gloria. *Organizing Puerto Rican Migrant Farmworkers: The Experience of Puerto Ricans in New Jersey.* New York: P. Lang, 1988.

Briggs, Laura. "La Vida, Moynihan, and Other Libels: Migration, Social Science, and the Making of the Puerto Rican Welfare Queen." *Centro Journal* 14, no. 2 (spring 2002): 74–101.

Cabán, Pedro A. "Puerto Rican Studies and Political Economy." In M. Sánchez and A. Stevens-Arroyo, eds., *Toward a Renaissance of Puerto Rican Studies.* Highland Lakes, NJ: Atlantic Research and Publications, 1987, 73–78.

Cabán, Pedro A. "Moving from the Margins to Where? Three Decades of Latino/A Studies." *Latino Studies* 1 (2003): 5–35.

Cabán, Pedro A. "Puerto Rican Studies: Changing Islands of Knowledge." *Centro Journal* 21, no. 2 (fall 2009): 256–81.

Cabán, Pedro A. "From Challenge to Absorption: The Changing Face of Latina and Latino Studies." *Centro Journal* 15, no. 2 (fall 2003): 126–45.

Cardona, Luis. *The Coming of the Puerto Ricans.* Washington DC: Unidos Publications, 1976.

Cartagena, Juan. "Puerto Ricans and the 50th Anniversary of the Voting Rights Act of 1965." Available at https://centropr.hunter.cuny.edu/centrovoices/current-affairs/puerto-ricans-and-50th-anniversary-voting-rights-act.

Center for Puerto Rican Studies, "Demographic Transitions: Settlement and Distribution of the Puerto Rican Population in the United States." 2013.

Center for Puerto Rican Studies. "Post-Hurricane Maria Exodus from Puerto Rico and School Enrollment in Florida." 2017.

Center for Puerto Rican Studies, "Puerto Ricans in New Jersey, the United States, and Puerto Rico." 2015.

Chávez, Linda. *Out of the Barrio: Toward a New Politics of Hispanic Assimilation.* New York: Basic Books, 1991.

Colón, Alice Warren. "The Feminization of Poverty among Women in Puerto Rico and Puerto Rican Women in the Middle Atlantic Region of the United States." *The Brown Journal of World Affairs* 5, no. 2 (1998): 263–81.

Communist Party, Puerto Rican Affairs Committee. *Handbook on Puerto Rican Work.* New York, 1954.

Community Council of Greater New York. United States Bureau of the Census. *Population of Puerto Rican Birth or Parentage.* New York, 1952.

Contreras, Eduardo. *Latinos in the Liberal City: Politics and Protest in San Francisco.* Philadelphia: University of Pennsylvania Press, forthcoming.

Cordero-Guzmán, Hector R. "Puerto Rican Poverty: A Review of the Main Trends and Proposed Explanations with an Emphasis on the New York Experience." 1996. Manuscript.

Cruz, José E. "A Decade of Change: Puerto Rican Politics in Hartford, Connecticut, 1969–1979." *Journal of American Ethnic History* 16, no. 3 (1997): 45–80.

Cruz, José E. "Unfulfilled Promise: Puerto Rican Politics and Poverty." *Centro Journal* 15, no. 1 (spring 2003), 152–75.

Cruz, José E. *Identity and Power: Puerto Rican Politics and the Challenge of Ethnicity.* Philadelphia: Temple University Press, 1998.

Culliton-González, Katherine. "Time to Revive Puerto Rican Voting Rights." *Berkeley La Raza Law Journal* 19 (2008): 27–69.

Daponte, Beth Osborne. "Race and Ethnicity during an Economic Transition: The Withdrawal of Puerto Rican Women from New York City's Labour Force, 1960–1980." *Regional Studies* 30, no. 2 (1996): 151–66.

Darien, Andrew T. *Becoming New York's Finest: Race, Gender, and the Integration of the NYPD, 1935–1980.* New York: Palgrave Macmillan, 2013.

Dávila, Arlene M. *Barrio Dreams: Puerto Ricans, Latinos, and the Neoliberal City.* Berkeley: University of California Press, 2004.

De Genova, Nicholas, and Ana Yolanda Ramos-Zayas. *Latino Crossings: Mexicans, Puerto Ricans and the Politics of Race and Citizenship.* London: Routledge, 2004.

Delerme, Simone. "65th Infantry Veteran's Park: Contested Landscapes and Latinization in Greater Orlando." *Southern Cultures* 23, no. 4 (winter 2017): 116–25.

Delerme, Simone. "Reflections on Cultural Capital and Orlando's Puerto Rican and Latino "Elite." *Centro Journal* 29, no. 3 (fall 2017): 74–96.

De Jesús, Anthony and Pérez, Madeline. "From Community Control to Consent Decree: Puerto Ricans Organizing for Education and Language Rights in 1960s and '70s New York City." *Centro Journal* 21, no. 2 (fall 2009): 7–31.

Dietz, James. *Economic History of Puerto Rico: Institutional Change and Capitalist Development.* Princeton, NJ: Princeton University Press, 1986.

Doeringer, P. B. *Jobs and Training in the 1980s: Vocational Policy and the Labor Market.* Boston: Nijhoff, 1981.

Dossick, Jesse J. "Fifth Workshop--Field Study in Puerto Rican: Education and Culture." *The Journal of Educational Sociology* 26, no. 4 (1952): 177–86.

Duany, Jorge. "The Orlando Ricans: Overlapping Identity Discourses among Middle-Class Puerto Rican Immigrants." *Centro Journal* 22, no. 1 (spring 2010): 85–115.

Duany, Jorge. "El éxodo Boricua a la Florida antes y después del huracán María." Florida International University, 2018.

Enchautegui, Maria. "Education, Location, and Labor Market Outcomes of Puerto Rican Men during the 1980s." *Eastern Economic Journal* 19 (1993): 295–308.

Falcón, Angelo, and John Santiago. *The 'Puerto Rican Exception': Persistent Poverty and the Conservative Social Policy of Linda Chavez.* New York: The Institute, 1992.

Fernández, Delia. "Becoming Latino: Mexican and Puerto Rican Community Formation in Grand Rapids, Michigan, 1926–1964." *Michigan Historical Review* 39, no. 1 (2013): 71–100.

Fernández, Johanna. "The Young Lords and the Social and Structural Roots of Late Sixties Urban Radicalism." In *Civil Rights in New York City: From World War II to the Giuliani Era.* New York: Fordham University Press, 2011, 141–60.

Fernández, Lilia. *Brown in the Windy City: Mexicans and Puerto Ricans in Postwar Chicago.* Chicago: University of Chicago Press, 2012.

Findlay, Eileen. *We are Left without a Father Here: Masculinity, Domesticity, and Migration in Postwar Puerto Rico.* Durham, NC: Duke University Press, 2015.

Fink, Leon Greenberg Brian. *Upheaval in the Quiet Zone: A History of Hospital Workers' Union, Local 1199.* Champaign: University of Illinois Press, 1989.

Fink, Leon. "Bread and Roses, Crusts and Thorns: The Troubled Story of 1199." *Dissent* 33, no. 2 (1986): 179–88.

First National City Bank of New York. *Poverty and Economic Development in New York City.* New York: The Bank, 1968.

Fitch, Robert. *The Assassination of New York.* London; New York: Verso, 1993.

Fitzpatrick, Joseph P., *Puerto Rican Americans: The Meaning of Migration to the Mainland.* Englewood Cliffs, NJ: Prentice-Hall, 1971.

Fitzpatrick, Joseph Patrick. "Intermarriage of Puerto Ricans in New York City." *American Journal of Sociology* 71 (January 1966): 395–406.

Fitzpatrick, Joseph P., and Douglas T. Gurak. *Hispanic Intermarriage in New York City, 1975.* Monograph Series—Hispanic Research Center Monograph No 2. New York: Hispanic Research Center, Fordham University, 1979.

Flood, Joe. *The Fires: How a Computer Formula Burned Down New York City—and Determined the Future of American Cities.* New York: Riverhead Books, 2010.

Flores González, Nilda. "Paseo Boricua: Claiming a Puerto Rican Space in Chicago." *Centro Journal* 8, no. 3 (fall 2001): 6–23.

Flores, Juan. "Reclaiming Left Baggage: Some Early Sources for Minority Studies," *Cultural Critique* 59 (winter 2005): 187–207.

Franqui-Rivera, Harry. "Puerto Rican Veterans and Service Members' Wellbeing and Place within the Diaspora." In Edwin Meléndez and Carlos Vargas-Ramos, eds., *Puerto Ricans at the Dawn of the New Millennium.* New York: Centro Press, 2014.

Franqui-Rivera, Harry. "Military Service: Migration and a Path to Middle Class Status." In Edwin Meléndez and Carlos Vargas-Ramos, eds., *The State of Puerto Ricans.* New York: Centro Press, 2016.

Freeman, Joshua Benjamin. *American Empire: The Rise of a Global Power, the Democratic Revolution at Home, 1945–2000.* New York: Penguin Books, 2013.

Freeman, Joshua Benjamin. *In Transit: The Transport Workers Union in New York City, 1933–1966*. Philadelphia: Temple University Press, 2001.

Freeman, Joshua Benjamin. *Working-Class New York: Life and Labor since World War II*. New York: New Press, 2000.

García Colón, Ismael. "Claiming Equality: Puerto Rican Farmworkers in Western New York." *Latino Studies* 6, no. 3 (2008): 269–89.

Gerena Valentín, Gilberto. *Gilberto Gerena Velentín: My Life as a Community Organizer, Labor Activist, and Progressive Politician in New York City*. New York: Center for Puerto Rican Studies, Hunter College, 2013.

Gillete Jr., Howard. "The Wages of Disinvestment: How Money and Politics Aided the decline of Camden, New Jersey." In Jefferson Cowie and Joseph Heathcott, eds., *Beyond the Ruins: The Meanings of Deindustralization*. Ithaca, NY: Cornell University Press, 2003.

Glasser, Ruth. *Aquí Me Quedo: Puerto Ricans in Connecticut*. Middletown, NY: Connecticut Humanities Council, 1997.

Glazer, Nathan and Daniel Patrick Moynihan. *Beyond the Melting Pot: The Negroes, Puerto Ricans, Jews, Italians, and Irish of New York City*. Cambridge, MA: MIT Press, 1970.

Gold, Roberta. *When Tenants Claimed the City: The Struggle for Citizenship in New York Housing*. Champaign: University of Illinois Press, 2014.

Goldberg, Barry. "'The world of our children': Jews, Puerto Ricans, and the Politics of Place and Race on the Lower East Side, 1963–1993." Ph.D. Dissertation, City University of New York, 2017.

Goldsen, Rose K. "Puerto Rican Migration to New York City." Ph.D. Dissertation, Yale University, 1953.

Golland, David Hamilton. *Constructing Affirmative Action: The Struggle for Equal Employment Opportunity*. Lexington: University Press of Kentucky, 2011.

González, Evelyn. *The Bronx*. New York: Columbia University Press, 2006.

González, Juan. "The Turbulent Progress of Puerto Ricans in Philadelphia," *Centro Journal* 2, no. 2 (winter 1987–88): 358–41.

González, Juan. *Roll Down your Window: Stories of a Forgotten America*. New York: Verso, 1995.

Gordon, David M. "Poverty, Welfare, and Income Maintenance: I. Income and Welfare in New York City." *The Public Interest*, no. 16 (1969): 64–88.

Gottehrer, Barry, ed. *New York City in Crisis*. New York: D. McKay Co., 1965.

Hamilton, Konrad Mark. "From Equal Opportunity to Affirmative Action: A History of the Equal Employment Opportunity Commission, 1965–1980." Ph.D. Dissertation, Stanford University, 1998.

Handlin, Oscar. *The Newcomers: Negroes and Puerto Ricans in a Changing Metropolis*. Cambridge, MA: Harvard University Press, 1971, 111.

Haslip-Viera, Gabriel. Angelo Falcón, and Félix Matos-Rodríguez, eds., *Boricuas in Gotham: Puerto Ricans in the Making of Modern New York City*. Princeton, NJ: Markus Wiener, 2005.

Herbstein, Judith F. "Rituals and Politics of the Puerto Rican "Community" in New York City." Ph.D. Dissertation, City University of New York, 1978

Hickey, Neil, and Ed Edwin. *Adam Clayton Powell and the Politics of Race*. New York: Fleet Pub. Corp., 1965.

Hill, Herbert. "Race, Ethnicity and Organized Labor: The Opposition to Affirmative Action." *New Politics* 1, no. 2 (winter 1987): 31–82.

Hill, Herbert. "Race and Ethnicity in Organized Labor: The Historical Sources of Resistance to Affirmative Action." *Journal of Intergroup Relations*, 12, no. 4 (winter 1984), 5–50.

History Task Force, Centro de Estudios Puertorriqueños. *Labor Migration Under Capitalism.* New York: Monthly Review Press, 1980, 156.

Hodges, Graham Russell. *Taxi!: A Social History of the New York City Cabdriver.* Baltimore: Johns Hopkins University Press, 2007.

Hoffman, Lily M. *The Politics of Knowledge: Activist Movements in Medicine and Planning.* Albany: State University of New York Press, 1989.

Hubner, John. "Villa Victoria. Public Housing That Works," *Mother Jones,* Sept.-Oct. 1981, 14.

Human Rights Watch. *Shielded from Justice: Police Brutality and Accountability in the United States.* June 1998.

Instituto de Estadísticas de Puerto Rico. *Puerto Rican Diaspora Atlas.* 2013.

James, Winston. "Explaining Afro-Caribbean Social Mobility in the United States: Beyond the Sowell Thesis." *Comparative Studies in Society and History* 44, no. 2 (2002): 218–62.

Jeffries, Judson. "From Gang-Bangers to Urban Revolutionaries: The Young Lords of Chicago," *Journal of the Illinois State Historical Society* 96, no. 3 (2003): 288–304.

Jennings, James and Monte Rivera, eds., *Puerto Rican Politics in Urban America.* Westport, CT: Greenwood Press, 1984.

Jennings, James. "Missing Links in the Study of Puerto Rican Poverty in the United States." William Monroe Trotter Institute Publications, no. 12, 1995.

Jiménez de Wagenheim, Olga. "From Aguada to Dover: Puerto Ricans Rebuild Their World in Morris County, New Jersey, 1948 to 2000." In *The Puerto Rican Diaspora: Historical Perspectives.* Philadelphia: Temple University Press, 2005.

Johnson, Marilynn S. *Street Justice: A History of Police Violence in New York City.* Boston: Beacon Press, 2003.

Jonas, Gilbert. *Freedom's Sword: The NAACP and the Struggle against Racism in America, 1909–1969.* New York: Routledge, 2005.

Jonnes, Jill. *South Bronx Rising: The Rise, Fall, and Resurrection of an American City.* 2nd ed. New York: Fordham University Press, 2002.

Katz, Daniel. *All Together Different: Yiddish Socialists, Garment Workers, and the Labor Roots of Multiculturalism.* New York: New York University Press, 2011.

Katznelson, Ira. *City Trenches: Urban Politics and the Patterning of Class in the United States.* New York: Pantheon Books, 1981.

Knapp Commission. *The Knapp Commission Report on Police Corruption.* New York: G. Braziller, 1973.

Kornbluh, Felicia Ann. *The Battle for Welfare Rights: Politics and Poverty in Modern America.* Philadelphia: University of Pennsylvania Press, 2007.

Lahey, Laurie. "The Grassy Battleground": Race, Religion, and Activism in Camden's 'Wide' Civil Rights Movement." Ph.D. Dissertation, George Washington University, 2013.

Lahey, Laurie. "'Too Much Singing': Christianity and the Limitations of Nonviolence in the Ghetto." *New Jersey Studies: An Interdisciplinary Journal* 1:1 (2015), 152–79.

Lait, J., and L. Mortimer. *New York: Confidential!* Chicago: Ziff Davis Publishing Company, 1948.

Lapp, Michael. "Managing Migration: The Migration Division of Puerto Rico and Puerto Ricans in New York City." Ph.D. Dissertation, Johns Hopkins University, 1991.

Laurentz, Robert. "Racial/Ethnic Conflict in the New York City Garment Industry, 1933–1980." Ph.D. Dissertation, State University of New York at Binghamton, 1980.

Lauria Santiago, Aldo A. "A Chalk Line on Third Ave: Policing and Puerto Rican Riots." Manuscript.

Lauria Santiago, Aldo A. "A Better Life: Puerto Rican New York—A History of Class, Work, and Struggle, 1920–1970." Manuscript.

Lee, Sonia Song-Ha. *Building a Latino Civil Rights Movement: Puerto Ricans, African Americans, and the Pursuit of Racial Justice in New York City.* Chapel Hill: The University of North Carolina Press, 2014.

Lee, Sonia Song-Ha and Ande Díaz, "'I Was the One Percenter': Manny Díaz and the Beginnings of a Black-Puerto Rican Coalition." *Journal of American Ethnic History* 26, no. 3 (2007): 52–80.

López, Madeleine E. "Investigating the Investigators: An Analysis of 'The Puerto Rican Study'." *Centro Journal* 19, no. 2 (fall 2007): 60–85.

Lucas, Isidro, Council on Urban Education. *Puerto Rican Dropouts: Numbers and Motivation.* Washington D.C.: Office of Education, Bureau of Research, 1971.

Maffi, Mario. *Gateway to the Promised Land: Ethnic Cultures on New York's Lower East Side.* Amsterdam: Rodopi, 1995.

Maldonado, Adál Alberto. *Portraits of the Puerto Rican Experience.* Edited by Luis Reyes Rivera and Julio Rodríguez. Bronx, NY: IPRUS, 1984.

Mantler, Gordon Keith. *Power to the Poor: Black-Brown Coalition and the Fight for Economic Justice, 1960–1974.* Chapel Hill: University of North Carolina Press, 2015.

Martínez, Miranda J. *Power at the Roots: Gentrification, Community Gardens, and the Puerto Ricans of the Lower East Side.* Lanham, MD: Lexington Books, 2010.

Marzán, Gilbert. "Regional Variation in Socioeconomic Status Among Mainland Puerto Rican Males: A Comparative Analysis." Ph.D. Dissertation, State University of New York, 2001.

Marzán, Gilbert. "Still looking for that Else Where: Puerto Rican Poverty and Migration in the Northeast." *Centro Journal* 21, no. 1 (spring 2009): 101–17.

Massey, Douglas and Brooks Bitterman, "The Paradox of Puerto Rican Segregation," *Social Forces* 64, (Dec. 1985): 306–31.

Matos Rodríguez, Félix V. "Saving the Parcela: A Short History of Boston's Puerto Rican Community." in Carmen Teresa Whalen and Víctor Vázquez-Hernández, eds., *The Puerto Rican Diaspora: Historical Perspectives.* Philadelphia: Temple University Press, 2005.

McCaffrey, Katherine T. *Military Power and Popular Protest: the U.S. Navy in Vieques, Puerto Rico.* New Brunswick, NJ: Rutgers University Press, 2002.

McCauley, Margaret A. "A Study of Social Class and Assimilation in Relation to Puerto Rican Family Patterns." Ph.D. Dissertation, Fordham University, 1972.

Mele, Christopher. "Neighborhood 'Burn Out': Puerto Ricans at the End of the Queue." In Janet Abu-Lughod, ed., *From Urban Village to East Village.* Cambridge, MA: Blackwell, 1994.

Mele, Christopher. *Selling the Lower East Side: Culture, Real Estate, and Resistance in New York City.* Minneapolis: University of Minnesota Press, 2000.

Meléndez Vélez, Edgardo. "'The Puerto Rican Journey' Revisited: Politics and the Study of Puerto Rican Migration." *Centro Journal* 17, no. 2 (fall 2005): 192–221.

Meléndez, Edgardo. "Vito Marcantonio, Puerto Rican Migration, and the 1949 Mayoral Election in New York City." *Centro Journal* 22, no. 2 (fall 2010): 199–233.

Meléndez, Edwin and M. Anne Visser. "Low-Wage Labor, Markets and Skills Selectivity Among Puerto Rican Migrants. *Centro Journal* 23, no. 11 (fall 2011): 39–62.

Meléndez, Edwin. "The Economic Development of El Barrio." In Frank Bonilla et al., eds., *Borderless Borders: U.S. Latinos, Latin Americans and the paradox of Interdependence.* Philadelphia: Temple University Press, 1998.

Meléndez, Miguel. *We Took the Streets: Fighting for Latino Rights with the Young Lords.* New York: St. Martin's Press, 2003.

Meyer, Gerald. "Save Hostos: Politics and Community Mobilization to Save a College in the Bronx, 1973–78," *Centro Journal* 15, no. 1 (fall 2003): 73–97.

Meyer, Gerald. *Vito Marcantonio: Radical Politician, 1902–1954.* Albany: State University of New York Press, 1989.

Mills, C. Wright. *The Puerto Rican Journey; New York's Newest Migrants.* New York: Publications of the Bureau of Applied Social Research, Columbia University, 1950.

Mirengoff, William and Lester Rindler. *The Comprehensive Employment and Training Act, Impact on People, Places and Programs: An Interim Report: Staff Paper.* Washington, D.C.: National Academy of Sciences, 1976.

Mohr, Eugene. *The Nuyorican Experience.* Westport, CT: Greenwood Press, 1982.

Morales, Iris. *Through the Eyes of Rebel Women: The Young Lords 1969–76.* New York: Red Sugarcane Press, 2016.

Morris, Charles R. *The Cost of Good Intentions: New York City and the Liberal Experiment, 1960–1975.* New York: Norton, 1980.

Morrison, Cayce. "The Puerto Rican Study—What It Is—Where It Is Going." *Journal of Educational Sociology* 28, no. 4 (Dec. 1954): 167–73.

Morrison, Cayce. *The Puerto Rican Study, 1953–1957: A Report on the Education and Adjustment of Puerto Rican Pupils in the Public Schools of the City of New York.* New York: N.Y. Board of Education, 1958.

Mullan, Fitzhugh. *White Coat, Clenched Fist: The Political Education of an American Physician.* Ann Arbor: University of Michigan Press, 2006.

Muñiz-Velásquez, Josefina. "Background of Puerto Rican Migration." Master's Thesis, Columbia University, New York, 1949.

Muzio, Rose. "The Struggle against 'Urban Renewal' in Manhattan's Upper West Side and the Emergence of El Comité." *Centro Journal* 21, no. 2 (fall 2009): 109–41.

Muzio, Rose. *Radical Imagination, Radical Humanity Puerto Rican Political Activism in New York.* Albany: State University of New York Press, 2017.

New York State Division of Human Rights. *Puerto Ricans in New York State, 1960–1969.* New York, 1969.

Nuñez, Louis. "Reflections on Puerto Rican History: Aspira in the Sixties and the Coming of Age of the Stateside Puerto Rican Community." *Centro Journal* 21, no. 2 (fall 2009): 332–47.

Nuñez, Louis. *The Losers: A Report on Puerto Ricans and the Public Schools.* Washington, D.C: U.S. Department of Health, Education, and Welfare, Office of Education, 1968.

Olvera, Jaqueline. "Together but without Mixing: Mexican and Puerto Rican Relations in New Urban Destinations." Manuscript.

Ortiz Márquez, Maribel. "Beginnings: Puerto Rican Studies Revisited," *Centro Journal* 21, no. 2 (fall 2009): 177–96.

Ortiz, Altagracia. "'En la aguja y el pedal eche la hiel': Puerto Rican Women in the Garment Industry of New York City, 1920–1980." In Altagracia Ortiz, ed., *Puerto Rican Women and Work: Bridges in Transnational Labor.* Philadelphia: Temple University Press, 1996.

Ortiz, Altagracia. "Puerto Rican Workers in the Garment Industry of New York City, 1920–1960." In Robert Stephenson and Charles Asher, eds., *Labor Divided: Race and Ethnicity in United States Labor Struggles, 1835–1960*. Albany: State University of New York Press, 1990.

Otterstrom, Samuel M., and Benjamin F. Tillman. "Income Change and Circular Migration: The Curious Case of Mobile Puerto Ricans, 1995–2010." *Journal of Latin American Geography* 12, no. 3 (2013): 33–57.

Padilla, Félix M. *Puerto Rican Chicago*. Notre Dame, IN: University of Notre Dame Press, 1988.

Pantoja, Antonia. *Memoir of a Visionary, Antonia Pantoja*. Houston: Arte Publico Press, 2002.

Parmet, Robert D. *The Master of Seventh Avenue: David Dubinsky and the American Labor Movement*. New York: New York University Press, 2005.

Pérez, Gina M. "The Other 'Real World': Gentrification and the Social Construction of Place in Chicago." *Urban Anthropology and Studies of Cultural Systems and World Economic Development* 31, no. 1 (spring 2002): 37–68.

Pérez, Gina M. *The near Northwest Side Story: Migration, Displacement, and Puerto Rican Families*. Berkeley: University of California Press, 2004.

Pérez, Nélida. "Two Reading Rooms and the Librarian's Office: The Evolution of the Centro Library and Archives," *Centro Journal* 21, no. 2 (fall 2009): 199–220.

Phillips, Lisa Ann Wunderlich. *A Renegade Union Interracial Organizing and Labor Radicalism*. Champaign: University of Illinois Press, 2013.

Pimentel, Felipe. "The Decline of the Puerto Rican Fulltime Faculty at the City University of New York (CUNY) from 1981–2002." CENTRO Policy Brief 2: 3, fall 2005.

Portes, Alejandro and Cynthia Truelove, "Making Sense of Diversity: Recent Research on Hispanic Minorities in the United States," *Annual Review of Sociology* 13 (1987): 359–85.

Powers, Mary G., and John J. Macisco. *Puerto Ricans in New York City, 1970. Labor Force Characteristics and Migration Experience of the Puerto Ricans*. Rio Piedras, P.R.: Social Science Research Center, University of Puerto Rico, 1981.

Puente, Silvia and Victor Ortiz, "The Latino Institute." In Gilberto Cárdenas, ed., *La Causa: Civil Rights, Social Justice, and the Struggle for Equality in the Midwest*. Houston: Arte Público Press, 2004, 55–79.

Puerto Rican Forum. *A Study of Poverty Conditions in the New York Puerto Rican Community*. New York, 1970.

Puerto Rican Women in the United States: Organizing for Change, NACOPRW, Proceedings of Fourth Conference, Washington, D.C., 1977.

Purnell, Brian. *Fighting Jim Crow in the County of Kings the Congress of Racial Equality in Brooklyn*. Lexington: University Press of Kentucky, 2013.

Ramírez, Yasmin. "Nuyorican Visionary: Jorge Soto and the Evolution of an Afro-Taíno Esthetic at Taller Boricua," *Centro Journal* 17, no. 2 (fall 2005): 22–41.

Ricourt, Milagros. *Dominicans in New York City: Power from the Margins*. New York: Routledge, 2002.

Ristorucci, Michael Luis. "Some Observations on the Hispanic Labor Committee, the Labor Movement, and Post-World War II Latino Labor Activism in the Metropolitan New York Area." Research paper for Harry Van Arsdale Junior Memorial Foundation, 2002.

Rivera, Eugene, "La Colonia de Lorain." In Tavenner, Mary Hilaire. *Puerto Rico 2006: Memoirs of a Writer in Puerto Rico*. United States: Xlibris Corp., 2010.

Rivera, Melissa and Pedro Pedraza. "The Spirit of Transformation: An Education Reform Movement in a New York City Latino/a Community." In Sonia Nieto, ed. *Puerto Rican Students in U.S. schools*. Mahwah, NJ: Erlbaum, 2000.

Ruiz, Vicky and Virginia Sánchez-Korrol editors. *Latinas in the U.S.* Bloomington: Indiana University Press, 2006.

Sánchez-Korrol, Virginia. "In their Own Right: A History of Puerto Ricans in the U.S.A." In Jiménez Núñez, Alfredo, Nicolás Kanellos, and Claudio Esteva Fabregat, eds., *Handbook of Hispanic Cultures in the United States*. Houston: Arte Público Press, 1994.

Schepses, Erwin. "Puerto Rican Delinquent Boys in New York City," *The Social Science Review* 23 (March 1949): 51–61.

Schmitt, Edward R. *President of the Other America: Robert Kennedy and the Politics of Poverty*. Amherst: University of Massachusetts Press, 2010.

Schneider, Cathy Lisa. *Police Power and Race Riots: Urban Unrest in Paris and New York*. Philadelphia: University of Pennsylvania Press, 2014.

Schneider, Cathy. "Political Opportunities and Framing Puerto Rican Identity." In Hank Johnston and John Noakes, eds., *Frames of Protest: Social Movements and the Framing Perspective*. New York: Rowman and Littlefield, 2005.

Schwartz, Joel. "The New York City Rent Strikes of 1963–1964." *Social Service Review* 57, no. 4 (Dec. 1983): 545–64.

Sciorra, Joseph and Martha Cooper. "'I Feel like I'm in My Country': Puerto Rican Casitas in New York City." *The Drama Review* 34, no. 4 (winter 1990), 156–68.

Sevcenko, Liz. "Making Loisaida: Placing Puertorriqueñidad in Lower Manhattan." in Augustín Laó-Montes and Arlene Dávila, eds., *Mambo Montage*. New York: Columbia, 2001, 300–13.

Silén, Juan Angel. *Historia de la nación puertorriqueña*. Río Piedras, P.R.: Edil, 1973.

Silver, Patricia. "Latinization, Race, and Cultural Identification in Puerto Rican Orlando." *Southern Cultures* 19, no. 4 (2013): 55–75.

Silver, Patricia. "Puerto Ricans in Florida." In Edwin Meléndez and Carlos Vargas Ramos, eds., *Puerto Ricans at the Dawn of the New Millennium*. New York: Centro, 2014.

Silver, Patricia. "Sunshine Politics: Puerto Rican Memory and the Political in New Destinations." *Centro Journal* 29, no. 2 (summer 2017): 4–37.

Silver, Patricia and William Vélez, "'Let Me Go Check Out Florida': Rethinking Puerto Rican Diaspora." *Centro Journal* 29, no. 3 (fall 2017): 98–125.

Slavin, Sarah. *U.S. Women's Interest Groups: Institutional Profiles*. Westport, CT: Greenwood Press, 1995.

Small, Mario Luis. *Villa Victoria: The Transformation of Social Capital in a Boston Barrio*. Chicago: University of Chicago Press, 2004.

Snyder, Robert W. *Crossing Broadway: Washington Heights and the Promise of New York City*. Ithaca, NY: Cornell University Press, 2015.

Solis, Carmen Leonor. "The Impact of Community Policing in New York City's Puerto Rican Communities." Ph.D. Dissertation, City University of New York, 2004.

Sotomayor, Sonia. *My Beloved World*. New York: Knopf, 2013.

Staudenmaier, Michael J. "Between Two Flags: Cultural Nationalism and Racial Formation in Puerto Rican Chicago, 1946–1994." Ph.D. Dissertation, University of Illinois at Urbana-Champaign, 2016.

Subcommittee to Investigate the Administration of the Internal Security Act and Other Internal Security Laws of the Committee on the Judiciary, United States Senate. *The Puerto Rican Revolutionary Workers Organization: A Staff Study.* Washington, D.C.: U.S. Government Printing Office, 1976.

Sugrue, Thomas J. *The Origins of the Urban Crisis Race and Inequality in Postwar Detroit.* Princeton, NJ: Princeton University Press, 2014.

Taylor, Clarence, and Milton A. Galamison. *Knocking at Our Own Door: Milton A. Galamison and the Struggle to Integrate New York City Schools.* Lanham, MD: Lexington Books, 2001.

Thomas, Lorrin. *Puerto Rican Citizen: History and Political Identity in Twentieth-Century New York City.* Chicago: University of Chicago Press, 2010.

Thompson, Heather Ann. "Understanding Rioting in Postwar Urban America." *Journal of Urban History* 26, no. 3 (2000): 391–402.

Thompson, Heather Ann. *Blood in the Water: The Attica Prison Uprising of 1971 and Its Legacy.* New York: Knopf Doubleday Publishing Group, 2016.

Tienda, Marta. "Puerto Ricans and the Underclass Debate." *The ANNALS of the American Academy of Political and Social Science* 501, no. 1 (1989): 105–19.

Torres, Andrés and José E. Velázquez, eds., *The Puerto Rican Movement: Voices from the Diaspora.* Philadelphia: Temple University Press, 1998.

Torres, Andrés. "Labor Market Segmentation: African American and Puerto Rican Labor in New York City, 1960–1980." *Review of Black Political Economy* 20 (1991): 59–72.

Torres, Andrés. *Between Melting pot and Mosaic: African Americans and Puerto Ricans in the New York Political Economy.* Philadelphia: Temple University Press, 1995.

United States Bureau of Labor Statistics, and Horst Brand. *Characteristics of the Unemployed: Bedford-Stuyvesant, Central Harlem, East Harlem, South Bronx.* New York: U.S. Bureau of Labor Statistics, Middle Atlantic Regional Office, 1970.

United States Census Bureau. *Puerto Ricans in the United States: Social and Economic Data for Persons of Puerto Rican Birth and Parentage.* Washington, D.C.: U.S. Government Printing Office, 1960.

United States Commission on Civil Rights. *Puerto Ricans in the Continental United States: An Uncertain Future.* Washington, D.C.: U.S. Commission on Civil Rights, 1976.

United States. Census of Population. *Puerto Ricans in the Continental United States.* Washington, D.C.: U.S. Government Printing Office, 1953.

United States Congress, Committee on Education and Labor. *Investigation of the Garment Industry Hearings before the United States House Committee on Education and Labor, Ad Hoc Subcommittee on Investigation of the Garment Industry,* Eighty-Seventh Congress, Second Session, Sept. 21, 1962. Washington, D.C.: U.S. Government Printing Office, 1962.

Uriate-Gaston, Miren. "Organizing for Survival: The Emergence of a Puerto Rican Community." Ph.D. Dissertation, Boston University, 1988.

Vallon, Michael L. *Bias in the Building Industry: An Updated Report, 1963–1967.* New York: New York City Commission on Human Rights, 1967.

Vázquez-Hernández, Victor. "From Pan-Latino Enclaves to a Community: Puerto Ricans in Philadelphia, 1910–2000." In Carmen Teresa Whalen and Victor Vázquez-Hernández, eds., *The Puerto Rican Diaspora: Historical Perspectives.* Philadelphia: Temple University Press, 2005.

Vázquez, Hector. "Puerto Rican Americans," *Journal of Negro Education* 38 (summer 1969): 247–56.

Wakefield, Dan. *Island in the City.* Boston: Houghton Mifflin, 1959.

Wallace, Deborah, and Rodrick Wallace. *A Plague on Your Houses: How New York Was Burned Down and National Public Health Crumbled.* New York: Verso, 1998.

Whalen, Carmen Teresa. "'The Day the Dresses Stopped': Puerto Rican Women, the International Ladies' Garment Workers' Union, and the 1958 Dressmaker's Strike." In Vicki Ruíz and John R. Chávez, eds., *Memories and Migrations: Mapping Boricua and Chicana Histories.* Champaign: University of Illinois Press, 2008.

Whalen, Carmen Teresa. *From Puerto Rico to Philadelphia: Puerto Rican Workers and Postwar Economies.* Philadelphia: Temple University Press, 2001.

Wilson, William J. *The Truly Disadvantaged: The Inner City, the Underclass, and Public Policy.* Chicago: University of Chicago Press, 1987.

Wilson, William J. *When Work Disappears: The World of the New Urban Poor.* New York: Knopf, 1996.

INDEX

65th Infantry 26, 198

Abreu, Mario 65
Abu Lughod, Janet 131
Academy for Black and Latino Education (ABLE) 110
Acevedo, Roberto 147
Acosta, Flavia 26
Acosta, Ralph 167
advocacy organizations: postwar period 13, 16; 1955–1965 54; 1966–1973 97, 99; 1974–1980 126, 127, 128, 129, 154; 1980s onwards 180, 199; post-hurricane 199; unstudied 197
affirmative action 63, 126, 134, 135–36, 153, 168, 171
affordable housing 130, 131, 132, 172, 173–74
African Americans: antipoverty organizations 55–56; civil rights organizations 28, 48, 54, 60, 63, 77, 81, 92, 97, 99, 136, 152, 182; collaboration with 28, 33, 56, 60, 62–68, 75–76, 81, 84, 92, 98–99, 102–6, 134–36, 164, 167, 169, 174, 182, 184, 198 and political parties 46, 85–86; see also Black Panthers, Black Power, and NAACP
Afro-Latinx identity 199
Afro-Puerto Rican identity 111
agricultural laborers: postwar period 7, 8, 13, 19–20; 1955–1965 58, **59**; 1966–1973 89–90; 1974–1980 133, 135, 143

Agrón, Salvador 50
Agüeros, Jack 98, 102
Agujas de Oro 60
Aid for Mothers with Dependent Children (AFDC) 98
Albizu Campos, Pedro 110
Algarín, Miguel 140, 141
Alicea, Victor G. 138
Alinsky, Saul 17
Allentown, PA **125**, 163
Almeida, Salvador 45
Álvarez, Octavio 52
American Civil Liberties Union 90
American Federation of Labor–Congress of Industrial Organizations (AFL-CIO) 19, 59, 64, 89–90, 92, 135, 136, 180
American Federation of State, County, and Municipal Employees (AFSCME) 133
American Jewish Committee 54
American Jewish Congress 63
American Labor Party (ALP): postwar period 11, 12, 18, 23, 25, 30, 31, 32; 1955–1965 41, 42, 43, 48, 168
Amnesty International 185
anti-colonialism 31, 141–45
anti-communism 21, 23, 42
anti-discrimination policies 19, 57–58, 63, 65, 136, 168, 180
anti-gentrification campaigns 172–75
anti-imperialism 143
anti-poverty programs/funds: 1955–1965 40, 52–57, 62; 1966–1973 80, 89,

90–91, 93–94, 95, 97–98; 1974–1980 127, 146, 155; 1980s onwards 177, 178, 195; War on Poverty 53, 55, 57, 76, 79, 81, 87, 89, 93, 127, 128, 152
anti-war protests 3, 4, 110
Antonetty, Evelina López 99–100, 109, 127, 128, 129, 140
Antonini, Ramos 21
apprenticeships, construction industry 63
arson 95, 96, 114, 124, 130, 131, 173
arts 126, 137, 140, 142
Asian American communities 4
Aspira 28, 55, 100, 102, 103, 109, 151–52, 155, 168
Aspira Consent Decree 168
Assassin Lords 56
assimilation 22, 109, 196
"Associated Free State," Puerto Rico 25; *see also* commonwealth status
Association House 127
Association of Catholic Trade Unionists 19
attack on Congress 26–27, 31–32, 41, 143
Attica prison uprising 84–85, 112
austerity 124, 133, 169
autonomous self-rule, Puerto Rico 25

Back, Adina 100
Badillo, Herman 44, 45, 66, 84–86, 105, 128, 134, 145–46, 149, 156, 165–66, 167
Baez, Anthony 183–84
Baez, Luis 182
banking and finance sector 62–63, 176
Batista, Jorge 152, 156
Berrios, José 169
bilingual ballots 145
bilingual education 12, 15, 100, 102, 126, 149, 150–52, 155, 156, 168
Bilingual Education Act (1968) 102
bilingual teachers 12, 15
bilingual-bicultural programs 138
Black Americans 62; *see also* African Americans
Black Arts Movement 140
Black civil rights movement 17, 40, 64
Black Economic Survival (BES) 134
Black Lives Matter 198–99
Black Panther Party (BPP) 110–11
Black Panthers 94, 99, 109–10, 111, 173
Black Power 3, 4, 76, 91, 92–93, 140, 195
Black student activism 103–04
Black Studies 103, 104, 105, 106, 138, 139
Board of Education takeover 99, 100

bombings 25, 144
Bonilla, Frank 54, 178–79
Boricua College 138, 140
Borinqueña, La 26
Boston: 1955–1965 44; 1966–1973 93, 96–97; 1974–1980 **125**, 130, 131–32, 143, 144, 145; 1980s onwards 163, **164**, 174
boycotts 67, 98–99, 104, 135
Bridgeport 124, **125**, 163, **164**
brokered representation 149
Bronx: 1955–1965 42; 1966–1973 78, 81, 84, 86, 95, 99, 102, 113–14; 1974–1980 123–24, 128, 134, 138, 145–46, 156–57; 1980s onwards 166, 169, 173
Brooklyn demonstration (1964) 67, 68
Brotherhood of Hispanic Workers 58
"brown mafia" 165
budget cuts 169–70
Buffalo, NY 8, **125**
Buildings Services Union 179
Bundy, McGeorge 100
Bundy Commission 100
Bureau of Relocation 45

Cabo Rojenos Ausentes 60
Cabranes, Miguel 13
California 44, 163
Camacho, José 43
Camden: postwar period 4, 12, 22, 29; 1955–1965 44, 53; 1966–1973 83, 97, 108, 112; 1974–1980 124, **125**, 145, 147, 148, 157; 1980s-onward **164**
campus activism 103–08, 138–41, 153, 181
Canino, Maria 54
Capeman murder 50, 53
capitalism 40, 179
Carmichael, Stokely 99
Carrero, Jaime 140
Carro, John 54
Carter, President Jimmy 144, 155, 156
Casita Maria 128
casitas 175
Catholic church 96
Center for Puerto Rican Studies 105, 106, 107, 139, 140, 178
Central Labor Council (CLC) 91–92
Chávez, Cesar 90
Chávez, Linda 177
Chicago, IL: postwar period 4, 8, 11, 12, 14, 21, 22, 29; 1955–1965 39, 40, 50–51, 53, 57, 74n67; 1966–1973 76, 77, 78, 83, 86, 87, 93, 102–03, 105–06,

108, 109–10; 1974–1980 **125**, 127, 130, 131, 143, 145, 147, 151, 152, 195; 1980s onwards **164**, 167, 169, 174; bilingual education 151; college-level education 105–06; gang violence 50–51; Humboldt Park 103, 127, 131, 174; riots 75, 77, 93, 94, 108, 155; Young Lords 109–10
Chicago Commons Association 127–28
Chicago Defender 77
Chicano activism 3, 4, 8, 195
Chicano Studies 103, 105, 106, 139
Chinese Americans 152
Christadora House 172–73
church-based support 11, 90, 96, 146
Cintrón, Humberto 94
citizenship 2, 24, 194–95, 199
City College, New York 103–05
"city fathers" 29, 31
city populations **125**, **164**
City University of New York (CUNY) 103–05, 107, 111, 138, 152, 155, 181
Citywide Puerto Rican Action Committee 98, 102
Civil Rights Act (1964) 55, 135
civil rights activism: 1966–1973 76–82, 89, 92; 1974–1980 150–55; 1980s-onward 176
Civil Rights Bureau, New York 63
Civil Rights Commission 44, 134, 154, 155
Civil Rights Committee, Central Labor Council, New York 91
civil rights organizations: postwar period 22–28; 1955–1965 54, 60–62, 64–68, 195; 1974–1980 196; 1980s-onward 179, 182, 186; *see also specific organizations*
Civilian Review Board (CRB) 184
Clark, Dr. Kenneth 55, 56
class action suits 152
Clayton Powell, Adam 64
Clemente, Rosa 199
Cleveland, OH 4, 12, 44, 78, **125**, 168
Clinton, President Bill 179
Coalition for Human Housing 95
Coalition in Defense of Puerto Rican and Hispanic Rights 170
Cold War 25, 30, 33, 41
college-level education 54, 103–08, 138, 153, 181
Colón, Jesús 1, 16, 18, 32, 33, 40–41, 43, 48
Colón, Rafaela 112
colonialism 25, 26, 31, 108, 139, 199

Columbia University 139
Columbia University Bureau of Applied Social Research 24
Columbia University's Employment Project 136
Comanches gang 49
Commission on Civil Rights 177
Commission on Hispanic Concerns 170
Commission on Human Rights, New York 51–52, 79
Commission on Intergroup Relations (COIR) 12
Committee Against Exploitation of Workers 60
Committee of Twelve (Twelve Apostles), Camden 148, 157
Committee on Inter Group Relations, New York 54
Committee on Puerto Rican Affairs 48
Committee on Urban Opportunity, Chicago 93
commonwealth status, Puerto Rico 25, 26, 31
Communist party: postwar period 11, 18, 21, 25; 1955–1965 40, 43, 48, 51; 1966–1973 79
Community Action Program 78, 93, 94, 109
community building: postwar period 11–17; 1955–1965 52–57; 1966–1973 92–98; 1980s-onward 168–75
community colleges 105, 138
community control of schools 75, 92, 95, 98–103, 106
Community Development Agency, New York 98
Community Development Corporations 127, 174
Community Housing Education Corporation 131
community organizing: 1955–1965 47–52; 1966–1973 108–14; 1974–1980 127–33; 1980s-onward 165
Comprehensive Employment and Training Act (CETA) 156
Concilio de Acción, El (Council for Action) 96
Congreso de los Pueblos 17, 42, 52, 53, 62, 64, 67, 79
Congress, attack on, 1954 26–27, 31–32, 41, 143
Congress, Puerto Ricans elected to 44, 45, 84, 146, 147, 165, 167
Congress of Racial Equality (CORE) 63

Congressional Hispanic Caucus 149
Connecticut: postwar period 8, **9**;
    1955–1965 39, 44; 1966–1973 89, 90,
    96; 1974–1980 135, 143; 1980s-onward
    167, 179
Consejo de Organizaciones Hispano
    Americanas 16
Constitution, U.S. 25, 43
construction jobs 63–64, 92, 133, 134–35,
    136, 176
Contreras, Eduardo 19
Copiague, Long Island 51
Cordero Guzmán, Hector 178
corruption 82, 85, 128, 146, 166, 181, 184
Cosell, Howard 156
Cosme, Félix 80
Council against Poverty 55
Council of Hispanic Organizations 16
Council of Puerto Rican and Spanish
    American Organizations 16, 62
Council of Spanish Speaking
    Organizations (Philadelphia) 68
Cruz, Arcelis 77
Cruz, Eduardo "Pancho" 106
Cruz, José 83, 143, 145, 149
Cruz, Myriam 86
Cuban Americans 7, 86, 175, 177
cultural exchanges 16, 52
cultural nationalism 68–69
"culture of poverty" 186, 187
Cuomo, Governor 166, 178

Daley, Richard 77, 78, 86, 93, 131
Davila, Arlene 174
de Jesús, Eddie 180
de la Valle, Miguel 138
decolonization 31
deindustrialization 40, 76, 87, 88–89, 124,
    129–30, 133, 145, 163, 178, 195
Delerme, Simone 198
Democrats: postwar period 30, 31;
    1955–1965 41–42, 43, 44, 45–46,
    51, 195; 1966–1973 82, 84, 93, 105;
    1974–1980 149; 1980s-onward 165,
    166, 167, 169
deportation 24
desegregation schools 103, 168
despertar boricua "Puerto Rican awakening"
    3, 115, 126, 195
Detroit, MI 44, 78, 80
diaspora 9, 20, 171, 199
Díaz, Juan 78
Díaz, Manny 57, 91, 109

Dinkins, Mayor David 184
displacement housing 95, 110, 130,
    172–75
Division Street Urban Progress Center
    (DSUPC) 93
domestic labor 21, **59**
Dominican Americans 164, 175, 181
Dr. Pedro Albizu Campos High School
    103
drugs 40, 130, 145, 176, 181, 185
Dubinsky, David 60

East Harlem Tenants Council (EHTC) 56,
    94, 99, 109, 132
economic crisis 124, 128, 129–30, 132,
    149, 175–76, 199
economic growth 8, 39, 179
economic life *see* work and economic life
Economic Opportunity Act (1964) 55, 57
education: postwar period 10, 12, 15,
    28; 1955–1965 66–67; 1966–1973
    98–108; 1974–1980 129, 137–41,
    155, 196; 1980s-onward 168, 170,
    176, 178, 179, 180–81; access to
    education 153; bilingual education 12,
    15, 100, 102, 126, 149, 150–52, 155,
    156, 168; college-level education 54,
    103–08, 138, 153, 181; community
    control of schools 75, 92, 95, 98–103,
    106; decentralization 100–01;
    degree-granting programs 105, 138;
    desegregation 103; English literacy
    levels 43; focus of civil rights efforts
    66–67; graduation rates 104, 179, 180;
    Ocean Hill-Brownsville 103; open
    admissions policies 104, 138; school
    boycotts 67, 98–99; school segregation
    99; school takeovers 95, 99
El Barrio 173
El Barrio riot 103
El Comité 4, 95, 113, 129, 130, 142
El Comité-MINP (Movimiento de
    Izquierda Nacional Puertorriqueño, or
    Puerto Rican National Left Movement)
    130, 133, 135, 142, 143, 144, 168
El Diario 50
El Diario-La Prensa 185
El Puente 174
El Puertorriqueño 77
Electchester apartment complex 92
electoral politics: postwar period 28–32;
    1955–1965 40–47, 66; 1966–1973 79,
    82–87, 102–03; 1974–1980 143, 144,

145–50; 1980s-onward 163–67; voter
registration 43–44, 45, 145, 146, 148,
167, 170; voting rights 2, 152–53,
196, 197
employment: postwar period 9, 13–14,
17–22; 1955–1965 57–64; 1966–1973
87–92; 1974–1980 124–26; 1980s-
onward 175–78; agricultural laborers
19–20; discrimination 62, 63, 101,
125, 133, 176, 178; job training 65,
115, 127, 156, 176, 178; minimum
wage 60–62, 64, 115, 167, 176;
National Puerto Rican Forum 168;
training and employment programs
156, 197; *see also* work and
economic life
entrepreneurship and small businesses 197
Equal Employment Opportunity
Commission (EEOC) 135–36
Errichetti, Mayor Angelo 124, 148
Escobar, Elizam 142
Espada, Frank 81, 82, 83, 88, 97
Esteban Julia, Luis 46
exceptional, Puerto Ricans as 177

factory work *see* industrial jobs
fair housing 29, 66, 96, 130
Falcón, Angelo 141, 143, 170
farm workers *see* agricultural laborers
FBI 31–32, 113
Federal Comprehensive Employment and
Training Act (1973–82) 156, 178
feminism 154
Fernández, Lilia 14
Ferré, Maurice 86–87
Ferrer, Fernando 173
finance sector jobs 62–63, 176
Financial Oversight and Management
Board, Puerto Rico 199
Findlay, Eileen 20
fires 131, 156; *see also* arson
Flemming, Arthur 155
Florida 8, 86, 163, 198
Ford Foundation 56, 57, 100, 105, 139
Fort Apache, the Bronx 123
foster care placements 54
Franco, Hector 93
Frente Obrero Unido 135
Friends Neighborhood Guild 128
Fuentes, Louis 102
Fuerzas Armadas de Liberación Nacional/
Armed Forces of National Liberation
(FALN) 142, 144

Galamison, Rev. Milton 66–67, 99, 102
gangs 40, 49–50, 55, 56, 109, 110, 114,
123, 128, 129, 181
García, Carlos "Chino" 56, 141
García, Robert 45, 83, 85, 144, 146, 147,
165, 166, 167
García, Yolanda 173
García Colón, Ismael 89
García Rivera, Oscar 29, 42
Garden Acosta, Luis 174
garment workers 18, 60, 64, 88, 134
Garro, Guido 50
gender politics, equity 135, 147, 153
gentrification 96, 131, 132, 172–75
Gerena Valentín, Gilberto 17, 42, 45, 52,
53, 57, 65, 66–67, 78–79, 80, 81, 82,
85, 91, 97, 109, 154, 156
gerrymandering 85–86
Ghetto Brothers 114, 129
ghettoes 9, 15, 40, 66, 76, 96, 124, 126,
130, 137, 172, 176
Giboyeaux, José 32
Gigante, Fr. Louis 129, 146, 173
Glazer, Nathan 107, 108
globalization 133, 139
Gold, Roberta 94, 130
Goldwater, Barry 46
Gómez, Manuel 42
González, Agustín 54, 57
González, Juan 110, 182
government jobs 9, 58, 133
graduation rates 104, 179, 180
grape boycott, United Farm Workers 135
grassroots organizing: 1955–1965 40, 47,
53, 56, 57, 62; 1966–1973 92–93, 97,
114; 1974–1980 126, 127–33, 150, 153,
155, 195; 1980s onwards 166, 170, 176
Great Society 56
Guiliani, Mayor Rudolph 184–85
Gutiérrez, Juan 183
Gutiérrez, Luis 167
Guzmán, Pablo "Yoruba" 110, 111, 113

Hampton, Fred 109
Handlin, Oscar 107
Harriman, Averell 41
Harlem Council of Puerto Rican Affairs 30
Harlem Fightback 136
Hartford, CT: postwar period 4, 8, 22,
29; 1955–1965 53; 1966–1973 81, 83,
108, 112; 1974–1980 **125**, 126, 143,
144, 145, 147, 148–49; 1980s-onward
164, 167

HARYOU-ACT (Harlem Youth Opportunities Unlimited) 55, 56
Hasidic Jews 131, 174
Health Revolutionary Unity Movement 113
health sector employment 133–34
healthcare 111–12, 113, 132, 180
Hernández, Joseph 46
higher education 54, 103–08, 138–41, 153, 181
Hill, Herbert 60
Hilliard, Raymond 28
Hispanic Division, DNC 45–46
Hispanic Division, Republican party 46
Hispanic identities 22
Hispanic Labor Committee (HLC) 91
Hispanic Parade, New York 52–53
Hispanic Society, NYPD 183
"Hispanic strategy" 45–46
Hispanic Young Adult Association (HYAA) 27, 54, 155
History Task Force 139
homeless services 128
hometown associations 17, 60
hospital services 112
hospital workers 62
Hostos Community College 105, 138
housing: postwar period 9, 11, 14, 15; 1955–1965 40, 42; 1966–1973 92–98; 1974–1980 130–33; 1980s-onward 172–75; affordable housing 130, 131, 132, 172, 173–74; community control 131; fair housing 29, 66, 96, 130; public housing projects 15, 76, 94, 130–32, 172, 173; unions 92
Houston 179
Human Rights Commission 64, 81, 82
Human Rights Office 137, 147
Human Rights Watch 184
Humboldt Park, Chicago 103, 127, 131, 174
hunger strikes 82, 98, 102
Hunter College 105, 107, 139, 140
Hunts Point Multi-Service Center (HPMSC) 128, 146, 166
hurricanes (2017) 199

immigration 9, 43, 166
Impellitteri, Mayor Vincent 48
independence, Puerto Rican 30, 31, 75, 95, 130, 142–43, 171
industrial jobs: postwar period 18, 19–20, 21; 1955–1965 39–40, 58, **59**; 1966–1973 88, 91, 96; 1974–1980 124, 133, 134, 195; 1980s-onward 175, 177, 179

Inquilinos Boricuas en Acción 174
Inquilinos Puertorriqueños Unidos (United Puerto Rican Tenants) 131
Institute for Puerto Rican Policy 170, 171, 187
intellectuals see Puerto Rican Studies
inter-Latino cooperation 151, 164, 166, 169, 170, 171, 174, 180–82, 186, 187, 196–99
intermarriage 87, 197, 198
International Brotherhood of Electrical Workers (IBEW) 59, 90, 91, 92, 134, 179
International Ladies' Garment Workers' Union (ILGWU) 60, 64, 92, 133
Irish Americans 27, 52
Italian Americans 50, 52, 128–29

Jersey City, NJ 8, 68, **125**, **164**
Jewish Americans 24, 28, 49, 54, 59, 67, 84, 89, 131
Jiménez, José "Cha Cha" 109–10, 111
Jiménez, Olga 20
Jimenez, Ramón 170
job training 65, 115, 127, 156, 176, 178
Job Training Partnership Act (1982–98) 178
Johnson, Lyndon 46, 55, 79, 80
Jones-Shaforth Act (1917) 2, 7, 26
July 26 Movement 111
"juvenile delinquency" 50

Kennedy, President John 44
Kennedy, Senator Edward 156
Kerner Commission (National Advisory Commission on Civil Disorders) 80
King, Rodney 182
King Jr., Martin Luther 80, 97
Koch, Mayor Ed 134, 137, 146, 147, 156, 165, 166, 169–70, 172, 173, 182
Korean War 42, 51, 60, 198

La Borinqueña 26
La Fountain, Hernán 152
La Unidad Hispana 96
labor activism: postwar period 17–22; 1955–1965 57–64; 1974–1980 133–37; see also unions
labor schools 19
Lait, Jack 23
Last Poets 141–42
"Latin" identities 22, 197
Latino Institute 128, 151
Latino Rebels 199
Latino Studies 186–87, 196

LatinoJustice-PRLDEF 169, 180, 187; *see also* PRLDEF
Latinos United 174
Lebrón, José 182
leftist politics: interwar period 11; postwar period 12, 13, 18, 24, 29–30, 31, 33; 1955–1965 41, 43, 48, 53, 58; 1966–1973 85, 96, 108–14, 115, 195; 1974–1980 135, 142, 144, 153
legal advocacy for civil rights 5, 44, 63–64, 135–36, 150–55, 168–69, 180, 186, 196
Liberal Party 42
liberal politics: postwar period 24, 27; 1955–1965 40; 1966–1973 195; 1974–1980 126; 1980s-onward 177, 178
Liebowitz, Samuel 50
Lincoln Center 141
Lindsay, Mayor John 78, 79, 80, 82, 83, 98, 100, 101
literacy test (in English) 43–44, 65
literary salons and literature 140–41; *see also* Nuyorican arts movement
Livoti, Francis 183–84
Loisaida 141, 172
Loperana, Félix 47, 185
López, Toño 11
López Antonetty, Evelina 99–100, 109, 127, 128, 129, 140
López v. Dinkins 152
Lorain, Ohio 21
Los Angeles 44, 65, 97, **125**, 179
Los Desperados 173
Los Sures 130–31, 174
Luciano, Felipe 110, 141–42
Lumen Román, José 42

Madres por Welfare 97
Mailer, Norman 82, 105
Malcolm X 76, 109
Maoism 112
Marcantonio, Vito 23, 25, 30, 31, 32, 41, 95
March on Washington (1983) 182
March on Washington for Jobs and Freedom (1963) 64, 67, 81, 169
Margolis, Richard 102
Marrero, Victor 152
Martin, John 51, 53
Martínez, Ernesto 95
Massachusetts 44, 88, 89, 90, 96, 112, 143
Massive Economic Neighborhood Development (MEND) 56, 94, 99, 109

Mayor's Advisory Committee on Puerto Rican Affairs (MACPRA) 12
McCarren Park 49
Medgar Evers College 105
Medina, Manuel 30, 32
Meléndez, Benjy 114, 129
Meléndez, Mickey 108
Méndez, Olga 147, 166–67
Méndez, Tony 51
Méndez Mejía, Tomás 21
Mexican American Legal Defense and Education Fund (MALDEF) 169
Mexican Americans 14, 20, 21, 39, 106, 128, 147, 151, 164, 165, 167, 175, 177, 181
Meyner, Robert 58
Miami, FL 8, 44, 86, 97, **125**, 163, 168
Michigan 20
middle class status 87, 88, 126, 133, 134, 137, 153, 154, 163, 195, 198
migration: postwar period 2, 7–38; 1955–1965 39; 1966–1973 87; 1980s onwards 163, 171, 176, 177, 179; academic study of 139; ongoing out of U.S. 197–98; population by city (1970-1980) **125**; post-hurricane 199; reverse migration 87, 126; seasonal migration 20, 89, 90, 135; within U.S. 198
Migration Division: postwar period 12–14, 15–17, 18, 19, 20, 21, 24, 33; 1955–1965 41, 43, 44, 51, 52, 53, 54, 57, 58, 63, 64, 66–67, 68–69, 195; 1966–1973 82, 83; 1974–1980 128
Militancy, political 66, 82–87, 91–92, 106, 107, 129, 134, 136, 141–45, 195
military service 26, 42, 51, 60, 198; *see also* veterans
Mills, C. Wright 13, 24
Milwaukee, WI 44, **125**
minimum wage 60–62, 64, 115, 167, 176
Minority Group conference 81
Mobilization for Youth (New York City) 55, 97, 109, 152
Mobilization for Youth (MFY) 55
Model Cities program 94, 146, 148
Mohr, Nicholasa 141
Montserrat, Joseph 13, 43, 62, 67, 82, 83, 97, 102
Montalvo, Frida 60
Morales, Iris 110, 111
Morales, José 65, 109
Mortimer, Lee 23
"movement," definition of 3–4; *see also* Puerto Rican movement

Movement for National Liberation (Movimiento de Liberación Nacional, or MLN) 144

Movimiento Pro Independencia 142

Moynihan, Senator Daniel Patrick 107, 108

Muñoz, Julio 134

Muñoz Marín, Governor Luis 13, 20, 23, 25, 26, 31, 41, 48

Muñoz Rivera, Luis 2

music 114, 140–42

mutual aid societies 11, 17; *see also* hometown associations

Narváez, Alfonso 82

National Advisory Commission on Civil Disorders (Kerner Commission) 80

National Association for Puerto Rican Affairs 64

National Association for Puerto Rican Civil Rights (NAPRCR) 60, 65–66, 77, 82, 91

National Association for the Advancement of Colored People (NAACP) 28, 48, 54, 60, 63, 92, 136, 152, 182

National Coalition of Puerto Rican Civil Rights 168

National Committee on Pay Equity 154

National Conference of Puerto Rican Women (NACOPRW) 153–54

National Congress for Puerto Rican Rights (NCPRR) 170, 182, 184

National Council for Puerto Rican Rights 180, 186

National Endowment for the Humanities 105, 139

National Health Care Workers' Union 180

National Hispanic Caucus 166

National Hispanic Media Coalition 171

National Institute for Latino Policy 170, 171, 187; *see also* Institute for Puerto Rican Policy

National Organization of Welfare Rights (NOWR) 97

national Puerto Rican organizations 126, 150, 164–67, 168, 195–96

National Puerto Rican Coalition (NPRC) 155

National Puerto Rican Forum 168, 171

National Welfare Rights Organization (NWRO) 88, 97–98

Nationalism, Puerto Rican: postwar period 31; 1955–1965 58, 68–69; 1966–1973 85, 107, 108–14; 1974–1980 126, 133, 141–45, 146; 1980s onwards 171

Nationalist party 25–26, 27, 31, 41

nativist discrimination 22, 48, 89, 195

naval bases, Vieques Island 171

Negro American Labor Council (NALC) 63

"Negro-Puerto Rican Unity" 28

New Bedford, MA 112

New Deal 28

New Haven, CT 81, 124

New Jersey: postwar period 4, 8, **9**, 21; 1955–1965 39, 58; 1966–1973 77, 81, 88, 89, 90, 97; 1974–1980 135, 138, 143, 147, 148; 1980s-onward 179, 180, 197

New Left 110, 133

New Orleans, LA 179

New York City: postwar period 4, 7, 8, **9**, 10, 11, 12, 15–16, 17–19, 21, 22–26, 28, 29–32; 1955–1965 39, 40–57, 58, 60–63, 65; 1966–1973 76, 77, 78–79, 81, 83, 85–86, 87–88, 91, 92–95, 97, 98, 99, 102, 108–09, 110, 111–12, 113, 114; 1974–1980 123–24, **125**, 126, 128, 129–31, 132, 134, 136–37, 138, 144, 146–47, 152, 156–57, 195; 1980s-onward 163, **164**, 165, 168, 172, 177, 179, 180, 182–83; riots 77, 78; *see also* Bronx, El Barrio

New York Committee to Free the Nationalist Political Prisoners 144

New York Post 29, 48

New York State 89, 197

New York State Commission on Housing 14

New York Times 22–23, 26–27, 32, 41, 45, 52, 67, 82, 85, 95, 113, 123, 132, 156, 184, 186

New York Transit Workers Union 179

New York World Telegram 23–24

Newark, NJ: postwar period 4, 8, 29; 1966–1973 76, 81, 108, 112; 1974–1980 124, **125**, 126, 143, 145; 1980s-onward 163, **164**

Newton, Huey 99

Nieto Ortiz, Patria 137, 147

Nieves, Josephine 80

Nixon, President Richard 44, 45, 98, 165

Nos Quedamos 173

novels 141

Nuñez, Bernabe 51

Nuñez, Louis 102, 155

Nuyorican arts movement 140–42, 172
Nuyorican Poets Café 141

Obama administration 199
Ocean Hill-Brownsville 95, 101, 102
O'Dwyer, William 12, 30, 31
Office of Bilingual Education 152
Office of Economic Opportunity (OEO) 55–56, 80, 93, 94, 96, 99
Ogilvie, Richard 86
Ohio 4, 8, 21
open admissions policies, universities 104, 138
"Operation Friend" 52
Operation Move-In 95
Orlando, FL 163, 198
Ortiz, Altagracia 60
Ortiz, Ángel 167

Pabón, Julio 169–70
Padilla, Felix 57
Pan American Women's Association 28
Pantoja, Antonia 27–28, 54, 55, 57, 100, 109
Paseo Boricua 174
Pataki, Governor George 170
Patrolman's Benevolent Union (PBU) 183
patronage 57, 128, 145–46, 170
Pennsylvania 8, **9**, 21
People's Board of Education 99
People's Church 110, 112
Perales, César 152
Pereira, Federico 182–83
Pérez, Eddie 167
Pérez, Gina 174
Pérez, Richie 182
performing arts 140–41
Philadelphia, PA: postwar period 4, 7, 8, 11, 12, 14, 22, 27, 29; 1955–1965 44, 46, 51, 53, 68; 1966–1973 81, 83, 93, 97, 102–03, 108, 112; 1974–1980 124, **125**, 128, 140, 142–43, 144, 145, 147; 1980s-onward 163, **164**, 167, 174
Philadelphia Commission on Human Relations (PCHR) 27
Philadelphia Inquirer 142, 147
Pimentel, Felipe 181
Piñero, Miguel 141
plays 141
plumbers 63–64
poetry 126, 137, 140–41

police: postwar period 10; 1955–1965 40, 65–66, 68; 1966–1973 76, 79–80, 81–82, 89, 99, 112; 1980s-onward 173
police abuse: 1955–1965 40, 47–52; 1966–1973 76–77, 79–80, 96–97, 112; 1974–1980 148; 1980s onwards 181–86
Polish Americans 50
political prisoners 143–44
political redistricting 46, 85–86; *see also* gerrymandering
political representation,126 10, 28, 68, 82, 102–03, 164–67, 170
Poor People's Campaign (1968) 81, 97
Poor People's Coalition (PPC) 110
Popular Democratic Party (PPD) 31
poverty: postwar period 10–11; 1955–1965 40, 54, 55–56; 1966–1973 76, 87–88; 1974–1980 124, 125–26, 127, 130, 134, 154–55; 1980s-onward 163, 169, 175–79; academic study of 139; "culture of poverty" 186, 187; working poor 84, 87–88; *see also* anti-poverty programs/funds
Poverty Council, New York 93
Present, Harris 28
presidential elections 44–46, 156–57
prison uprising (Attica) 84–85, 112
professional employment 13, 33, 54, 88, 133, 136
PROPA v. Kusper 152
protests: postwar period 23–24; 1955–1965 51–52, 62, 67; 1966–1973 75, 89, 112; 1974–1980 135
public health campaigns 111–12, 131
public housing projects 15, 76, 94, 130–32, 172, 173
Public Law 600 25
public sector employment 9, 58, 124, 133, 177, 179
Puerto Rican Action Committee 98, 102, 167, 187
Puerto Rican Alliance 147–48
Puerto Rican Association of Community Affairs (PRACA) 54–55
Puerto Rican Community Development Project (PRCDP) 57, 99
Puerto Rican Congress of New Jersey 168
Puerto Rican Day Parade 53, 79
Puerto Rican Department of Labor 8, 12, 19, 20, 21, 41, 90
Puerto Rican Development Project 91

Puerto Rican Family Institute 54, 187
Puerto Rican flag 144
Puerto Rican Forum 54, 57, 80, 91, 100,
  106–07, 109, 168
Puerto Rican independence 30, 31, 75,
  95, 130, 142–43
Puerto Rican Legal Defense and
  Education Fund (PRLDEF) 90, 152,
  156, 168–69, 180, 182, 187
Puerto Rican March 97
Puerto Rican Merchants Association 58
Puerto Rican movement 2–4, 64, 67–68,
  75–78, 81, 108–15, 126–27, 137, 142,
  195–97
Puerto Rican National Merchants
  United 42
Puerto Rican Organization for Political
  Action (PROPA) 152
Puerto Rican Public Relations
  Committee 26
Puerto Rican Revolutionary Workers
  Organization (PRRWO) 113
Puerto Rican Socialist Party (PSP) 90, 97,
  130, 133, 135, 142–43, 144, 147, 149,
  168, 182
Puerto Rican Student Union 103
Puerto Rican Studies 103, 104, 105,
  106, 107, 138–40, 155, 176–77, 181,
  186–87, 196
Puerto Rican Week 77, 142–43,
  147, 153
Puerto Rican Welfare League 21
Puerto Ricans Employees Association 28
*Puerto Ricans in the Continental United
  States: An Uncertain Future* 154–55
Puerto Ricans Involved in Student
  Actions (PRISA) 104
Puerto Ricans Organized for Political
  Action 86

Quiles, Germán 147
quotas 63, 101, 105, 135

race: binary racial system 2, 9; migrant
  communities in U.S. 2, 9; mixed-
  race heritage 24; and redistricting 46;
  riots 80; and unions 91–92; "white"
  compared to "negro" Puerto Ricans 11
racial discrimination: postwar period 9, 10,
  14, 21–28; 1974–1980 126, 154–55;
  agricultural laborers 58; anti-poverty
  programs 89; constant theme 195;

differential pay gaps 135; education
  101, 103; high skill manual labor 63;
  hiring practices 62, 63, 101, 125, 133,
  176, 178; police 47–52, 182–83; and
  the professions 62–63; racial profiling
  186; and redistricting 46; rural farm
  workers 89; school segregation 66–67;
  and the union movement 92
racial justice 4, 5, 29, 105, 110
racketeer unions 19, 58, 62
radical politics: postwar period 25,
  31–32; 1974–1980 126, 130, 143;
  1980s-onward 164; unstudied 197
radicalization 76, 78, 82, 91, 109,
  110, 111
Ramírez, Diego 23
Ramírez, Gilberto 45
Ramos, Manuel 84, 85
Ramos López, José 42, 45
Randolph, A. Philip 62
Reagan, Ronald 132–33, 157, 164, 169,
  175, 176, 196
Real Great Society (RGS) 56–57,
  109, 141
redistricting 46, 85–86
rent strikes 94, 95
Republicans: postwar period 30; 1955-1965
  41, 42, 44, 45–46, 52; 1966–1973
  86; 1974–1980 132, 147, 149;
  1980s-onward 165, 167, 169
retail jobs 88
reverse migration 87, 126
Ricardo Varela, Julio 199
Rincón de Gautier, Felisa 25
Ríos, Carlos M. 45, 66
riots: 1955–1965 40, 52, 56, 65; 1966–1973
  75, 76–82, 93, 112; 1974–1980 124, 155
Rivera, Dennis 180
Rivera, Henry 48
Rivera, José 169
Rizzo, Mayor Frank 148, 167
Rochester, NY 4, 8, 125, 197
Rockefeller, Nelson 41, 45, 84, 112
Rockefeller Foundation 57
Rodríguez, Francisco 51–52
Rodríguez, Joseph 148
Rodríguez, René 149
Roosevelt, President Franklin Delano 31
Roosevelt Roads naval base 171
Rosaldo, Renato 196
Rosario, Anthony 185
Rosario, Margarita 185

Rosario, Oscar 148
Ruiz, Ruperto 16, 23, 45
rural areas 4, 8, 19–20, 58, 89–90; *see also* agricultural laborers
Rustin, Bayard 67, 102

Salguero, Joseph 65
San Francisco, CA 7, 11, 19, 22, 44, 97, 106, **125**, 130, 144
San Francisco State University (SFSU) 104, 111
Sánchez, Marta 148–49
Sánchez, Paul 65, 90, 91, 135
Sánchez, Yolanda 94
Santiago, George 59–60
Santiago Iglesias Society 91
school boycotts 67, 98–99
school takeovers 95, 99
Seale, Bobby 99
seasonal migration 20, 89, 90, 135
second-class citizenship 2, 33
second-generation Puerto Ricans 8, 14, 33, 87, 88, 142, 163, 175, 177, 195
second-wave feminism 3
sedition 32
self-determination 25, 111; *see also* Puerto Rican independence
Senior, Clarence 13, 19, 24, 139
Service Employees International Union (SEIU) 179
service sector employment 133–34, 175
settlement houses 11, 49, 53, 127, 128, 172–73
Shanker, Albert 101
Silver, Patricia 198
"sleeping giant" 150, 164–65
Smith Act (1940) 31, 32, 43
social mobility 18, 125, 177, 179
social services: postwar period 10, 12, 14, 17; 1955–1965 52–57; 1966–1973 75–76, 93; 1974–1980 126, 127; 1980s-onward 170
socialism 113, 141–45
Socialist party 18, 25, 30
Soto, Hector 184
Sotomayor, Sonia 139, 153, 169
South End Tenants Council 96
South East Bronx Community Organization (SEBCO) 173
Southern Christian Leadership Conference (SCLC) 81, 97
Spain, war with 2, 7

Spanish Action Committee of Chicago (SACC) 78, 93
Spanish American Party 42
Spanish Harlem 173
"Spanish" identities 22
Spanish language: electoral materials in 43, 86, 152–53; and the police 48–49; press 20, 49, 58, 62
Spanish-American Youth Bureau (SAYB) 15–16, 23, 24, 28, 45
Special Assistant for Hispanic Affairs, Chicago 86
Spivak, Jonathan 98
Springfield 90, **125**, 163, **164**
squatters 95, 130; *see also* tenant organizing
State Commission on Human Rights 63
State Investigating Committee 148
Statue of Liberty, Puerto Rican flag on 144
Steamfitters Union 136
street crime 124, 183, 186
strikes 59, 60, 62, 81, 101, 106, 107
student activism 103–08, 111–12, 114, 137–41, 152, 181
Student Nonviolent Coordinating Committee (SNCC) 99, 111
suburbanization 124, 126, 127
Surpless, Judge Abner 48

tabloid and right wing press 22–24, 26
Tactical Patrol Force 81–82
Taft-Hartley Act 28
Taíno Towers 94, 132–33
Taller Boricua 140
Taller Puertorriqueño 140
Tampa, FL 7, 22, 163, 179
taxi driving 118n44
teachers' strike 91–92
teen pregnancy 128, 178
Tejano labor migrants 20–21
Tenant Action Group (TAG) 174
tenant organizing 94, 130–31, 172, 174
Tenants Emergency Committee (TEC) 96, 131
Third World Liberation Front 111
Third World Studies 105, 106
third-generation Puerto Ricans 87
Thirteen Point Program 111; *see also* Young Lords
Tienda, Marta 177
Tolchin, Martin 123
"Tombs" jail 112
Torres, Andrés 177

Torres, Felipe 29, 42, 45
Torres, Frank 45
Torres, Mildred 149
Torres v. Sachs 152
Transit Worker Union (TWU) 92
transnational culture 139
Trenton, NJ 44, 97, 148
Truman, President 25, 26, 31, 143
Twelve Apostles (Committee of Twelve),
    Camden 148, 157

"underclass" status 176, 177, 187
unemployment 88–89, 124
Unidad Hispana, La 96
"unincorporated territory," Puerto Rico
    as 2, 7, 25, 171
Union of Needletrades, Industrial, and
    Textile Employees (UNITE) 179
unions: postwar period 10, 13, 18–19,
    21, 28, 30; 1955–1965 48, 57–64;
    1966–1973 88, 89–90, 91–92, 113;
    1974–1980 133–37; 1980s-onward
    179–80
United Bronx Parents (UBP) 99–100,
    114, 129, 140, 157
United Electrical, Radio and Machine
    Workers (UE) 179
United Farm Workers (UFW) 90, 135
United Federation of Teachers (UFT) 101
United Nations International Covenants
    on Rights 156
United Nations Universal Declaration of
    Human Rights 43
United Tremont Trades (UTT) 134–35
Unity conferences 85
University of Illinois Chicago Campus
    (UICC) 105–06, 138
University of Puerto Rico 13, 15
University of the Streets 56, 109
university students 103–08, 138–41,
    153, 181
urban renewal 95–96, 110, 131
U.S. Navy in Puerto Rico 171
Utah 21
Uviles, José 183

Valledares, Rafaela 60
Vargas. Edwin 149
Vega, Hilton 185
Velázquez, José 142
Vélez, Ramon 57, 85, 128–29, 145–46,
    165–66, 167

Vélez, Ted 55, 78, 81, 94
veterans 26, 51, 52, 95, 155, 198; *see also*
    military service
Vieques Island 171
Villa Victoria 131–32
Vineland, NJ 97
VISTA 96
visual arts 140–41, 142
Viva Kennedy campaign 44, 45
voter registration 43–44, 45, 145, 146,
    148, 167, 170
voting rights 2, 152–53, 196, 197
Voting Rights Act (1965) 44, 45, 85,
    152–53

WADO radio 14
wage equity 89
Wagner, Mayor Robert 12, 27, 42, 45,
    48–49, 50, 60, 62, 66, 80
Walker, Tom 123
Wall Street Journal 98
War Manpower Commission 8
War on Poverty 53, 55, 57, 76, 79, 81,
    87, 89, 93, 127, 128, 152
Washington, Benedetta 100
Washington, Mayor Harold 167, 174
Washington, D.C. 97
Waterbury, CT 112
Wedtech 166
welfare 23, 87–88, 97, 176–77, 178, 179;
    see also social services
Welfare Recipients League 97
welfare rights movement 97–98
West Side Committee on Civil Rights 63
West Side Story 50
West Side Urban Renewal Area 95
Whalen, Carmen 14, 60
white collar work 13, 88, 133, 175, 177
"whiteness" 11, 14, 22, 27
Wilkins, Roger 155–56
Williamsburg, Brooklyn 130–31, 174
Winn, Peter 139
Wise, Harold 123
women: access to education 153;
    employment 18, 21, **59**, 88; housing
    activism 95; National Conference of
    Puerto Rican Women (NACOPRW)
    153–54; political activism 153–54;
    political participation 147, 166–67;
    poverty 125; unemployment 89, 176,
    178; unions 60; welfare 176; women's
    rights 135–36

work and economic life: postwar period
17–22; 1955–1965 58–64; 1966–
1973 87–92; 1974–1980 133–37;
1980s-onward 175–81
working poor 84, 87–88
Worth, Robert 173

Young Lords 3–4, 94, 108, 109–13, 129,
135, 141, 142, 143, 152–3, 168, 180, 182
young people: postwar period 27–28;
activism 75–76, 107, 108–14, 126–27;

community organizing 54–55, 129;
employment 62; most vulnerable
groups 126; and the police 47, 49,
65–66; political power 83, 85; poverty
and unemployment 178; training and
employment programs 90–91; youth
exchanges 52
Youngstown, Ohio 21

zero-tolerance campaigns, policing
181–82, 185